THE REVELATION
OF JESUS CHRIST

THE REVELATION
OF JESUS CHRIST

A COMMENTARY BY
JOHN F. WALVOORD

MOODY PRESS
CHICAGO

Printed in the United States of America

CONTENTS

PREFACE

No OTHER BOOK of the New Testament evokes the same fascination as the book of Revelation. Attempts at its exposition are almost without number, yet there continues the widest divergence of interpretation. Because the book reveals truth relative to every important fundamental of Christian theology, it is inevitable that its interpretation be influenced by the contemporary confusion in biblical scholarship especially in the realm of eschatology. In some sense, the book is the conclusion to all previous biblical revelatiòn and logically reflects the interpretation of the rest of the Bible. The expositor is faced with innumerable hermeneutical decisions before beginning the task of understanding the peculiar contribution of the book of Revelation, an undertaking made more difficult by the fact that his decisions not only color the exposition of the book itself but also in a sense constitute an interpretation of all that precedes it in the Scriptures.

Even a casual reader of the book of Revelation is impressed with the tremendous scope of its prophecies. Here is obviously an important book, one intended by God to be a final word to man. The great truths treated are the termini for lines of revelation beginning in some cases in the book of Genesis and continuing throughout Scripture. Most important is the revelation concerning Jesus Christ, introduced as the major theme of the book in the first verse. If for no other reason, the book is important as the final chapter in scriptural self-disclosure of God through Jesus Christ. In earlier books of the Bible, Christ is introduced in the Messianic prophecies and the activities of the Angel of Jehovah in the Old Testament. The revelation of Jesus Christ is advanced in the Gospels and the Acts, which unfold the birth, life, ministry, death, resurrection, and ascension of the Son of God. The epistles add the theological interpretation of the person and work of Christ. To all of this dramatic and tremendously significant revelation, the last book of the Bible provides the capstone. It is indeed "the revelation of Jesus Christ" not only as the Lamb that was slain, a familiar portrayal in the book, but as King of kings and Lord of lords who is certain to return to the earth in power and glory to judge the wicked and reward the righteous. The book of Revelation is the counterpart of the Gospels, Christ in His glory in contrast to Christ in His humiliation and death.

It is implicit in any orthodox Protestant approach to the Scriptures to hold that the Bible was intended to be understood. What is true of other Scriptures is also true of the book of Revelation. However, it is too much to assume that the book, like the Old Testament apocalyptic books and prophecy generally, was intended to be comprehended fully by believers in the early church. As history unfolds and as prophecy is fulfilled in the future, much will be understood that could be only dimly comprehended by the first readers of the book. But even to early Christians, the main facts were clear.

The climax of human history was to involve a period of great suffering which would be worse than any of the trials which afflicted the church previously. The ultimate triumph of the saints and the final victory of our Lord Jesus Christ are plainly written in the book of Revelation for all to comprehend. Saints of all ages can be assured of the certainty of their hope which today shines brighter than ever in view of the approaching end of the age. The book of Revelation like all other unfulfilled prophecy provides particular instruction to the generation which will see its fulfillment, and it constitutes general exhortation and encouragement for those who await the coming day.

The expositor of the Revelation is inevitably forced to choose one of the systems of interpretation which have emerged in the history of the church as a proper approach to this last book of the Bible. The author has assumed that this book should be interpreted according to the normal rules of hermeneutics rather than as a special case. The prophetic utterance of the book has therefore been taken in its ordinary meaning unless the immediate context or the total revelation of the book indicates that terms are being used in a symbolic sense, as they frequently are in apocalyptic writings. Instead of assuming that the interpretation should be nonliteral unless there is proof to the contrary, the opposite approach has been taken, namely, that terms should be understood in their ordinary meaning unless contrary evidence is adduced. Hence stars are stars, earthquakes are earthquakes, et cetera, unless it is clear that something else is intended. The result has been a more literal interpretation of prophecy and revelation in general and a clearer picture of end-time events than is frequently held by expositors.

To avoid constant quotation of Scripture in the exposition, the Authorized Version of the Bible has been inserted before each section. Although the received text on which the Authorized Version is based has more textual problems than any other section of the New Testament, no other translation based on improved texts has achieved the stature of being used by the majority of Bible students. Therefore, it was considered adequate to introduce textual changes where these affect the meaning—

surprisingly few instances in comparison to the many variations in the text of Revelation. The Nestle Greek text was used with its critical apparatus unless otherwise indicated. In definition of words and in author's translations, though other lexicons were consulted, *A Greek-English Lexicon of the New Testament* by W. F. Arndt and F. W. Gingrich was generally followed. While many expositions of the book of Revelation and volumes providing collateral material were used, the Bibliography was limited to works actually cited. Acknowledgment is given for gracious permission of the publishers to quote copyrighted materials.

The author is indebted to Dr. S. Lewis Johnson for a careful critical reading of the manuscript and for many suggestions which have been incorporated in the text. The editors of Moody Press have also been most helpful.

In offering this new exposition of the book of Revelation, an attempt has been made to provide a norm for premillennial interpreters of the Bible. In many cases alternative views are offered even though they differ from the interpretation of the author. It is too much to hope that the interpretation will persuade all readers. But if added light is cast upon the Word of God, and the Christian hope is enriched thereby, the author's expectation will have been realized. Most of all may the Lord Jesus Christ, the subject of the revelation of the book, be glorified in this attempt to understand what John saw and heard on the Isle of Patmos.

INTRODUCTION

Authorship, Occasion, and Date

The opening verses of the book of the Revelation plainly claim the book was written by John, identified almost universally in the early church as the Apostle John. The apostolic authorship of the book has, nevertheless, been questioned ever since the time of Dionysius of Alexandria in the third century.

Dionysius challenged the traditional view that John the Apostle was the author on the ground that the book of Revelation had numerous cases of bad grammar. Dionysius said, "I perceive that the dialect and language is not very accurate Greek, but that he uses barbarous idioms, and in some places solecisms which it is now unnecessary to select."[1]

Beginning with Dionysius those who object to Johannine authorship or to inclusion of the Apocalypse in the canon have tended to magnify the problems of grammar and alleged inaccuracies. Impartial scholarship has admitted that there are expressions in the book of Revelation which do not correspond to accepted Greek usage, but this problem is not entirely confined to this book of the Bible. Conservative scholarship has insisted that infallibility in divine revelation does not necessarily exclude expressions which are not normal in other Greek literature and that such instances do not mar the perfection of the truth that is transmitted. Swete, after acknowledging "that the Apocalypse of John stands alone among Greek literary writings in its disregard of the ordinary rules of syntax," goes on to say that it does so "without loss of perspicuity or even of literary power. The book seems openly and deliberately to defy the grammarian, and yet even as literature it is in its own field unsurpassed."[2] It is important to note, however, that some of the supposedly bad grammar in Revelation was used in contemporary Koine literature, as is revealed by discoveries in the Papyri.

When due allowance is made for the character of the book, as H. B. Swete has noted, there are remarkable similarities in some respects between the Fourth Gospel and the book of Revelation and that fact "creates a strong presumption of affinity between the Fourth Gospel and the

[1]Cited by Paton J. Gloag, *Introduction to the Johannine Writings*, p. 301.
[2]Henry B. Swete, *The Apocalypse of Saint John*, p. cxx.

Apocalypse, notwithstanding their great diversity both in language and in thought."[3]

The arguments for rejecting the apostolic authorship stem largely from the theological climate of the third century. At that time the Alexandrian School of Theology, including Dionysius, opposed the doctrine of the millennial kingdom which is plainly taught in chapter 20 with its reference to the thousand years. An attack by them on the authorship of John tended to weaken the force of this prophecy. Another early objection to the view that John the Apostle was the author of this book was occasioned by the fact that he never describes himself as an apostle, but rather as a "servant." Many scholars, motivated by other reasons, have advanced the theory that the John of the book of Revelation is another person known as John the Presbyter or John the Elder, mentioned by Papias in a statement preserved in the writing of Eusebius. Another author considered but rejected by Dionysius of Alexandria was John Mark.

The substantiating evidence for any other author than John the Apostle, however, is almost entirely lacking. While notable scholars can be cited in support of divergent views, the proof dissipates upon examination. It seems clear that the early church attributed the book to John the Apostle. Justin Martyr quotes John's view that Christ would dwell a thousand years in Jerusalem.[4] Irenaeus quotes every chapter of the book of the Revelation.[5] In like manner, Tertullian cites the author as "the Apostle John" and quotes from almost every chapter of the book.[6] Hippolytus quotes extensively from chapters 17 and 18, attributing them to John the Apostle.[7] Many other early fathers can be cited in similar fashion, such as Clement of Alexandria and Origen. The latter not only quotes from the book but confirms that John the Apostle was on the Isle of Patmos.[8]

The first commentary on the book of Revelation to be preserved, written by Victorinus, regards John the Apostle as the author. Though the book of Revelation was not commonly received by the church as canonical until the middle of the second century, it is most significant that the Johannine authorship was not questioned until the strong antichiliastic influence arose in the Alexandrian School of Theology at the end of the second century.

The evidence for the Johannine authorship is based first on the fact that four times the writer calls himself by the name John (1:1, 4, 9; 22:8). Describing himself as a "servant" (1:1) and "your brother, and com-

---

[3] *Ibid.*, p. cxxv; cf. pp. cxxi–xxv.
[4] Justin Martyr, "Dialogue with Trypho," chap. 80, *Ante-Nicene Fathers*, I, 239.
[5] Henry C. Thiessen, *Introduction to the New Testament*, p. 317.
[6] *Ibid.*
[7] Hippolytus, "Treatise on Christ and Antichrist," sect. 36–42, *Ante-Nicene Fathers*, V, 251–53.
[8] Cf. Thiessen, pp. 317–18.

panion in tribulation, and in the kingdom and patience of Jesus Christ" (1:9), John never states that he is an apostle. Taking into consideration, however, that in the Fourth Gospel there is a similar anonymity, this does not seem to be strange. Most conservative expositors regard the name John as genuine rather than a pseudonym as is common in nonscriptural apocalyptic books. There is really no solid evidence against accepting John the Apostle as the author, and there is much that confirms it. In fact, it may be argued that the reference to John without further identification would presume a familiarity on the part of the readers which would make naming him unnecessary.

The evidence for John the Apostle hangs largely on the question whether the Apostle John actually was exiled on the Isle of Patmos, as the author of this book claims (1:9). There is good historical evidence in support of this claim. Clement of Alexandria refers to the Apostle John as returning from the Isle of Patmos.[9] Eusebius not only affirms John's return from the isle but dates it immediately following the death of Domitian, which occurred in A.D. 96.[10]

Irenaeus adds his confirming word when he states that John lived in Ephesus after returning from Patmos until the reign of Trajan.[11] Though the Scriptures do not dogmatically confirm that John the Apostle is the author, the existing evidence is heavily in favor of this conclusion.

Related to the total problem is the question of date of the book. Though the tendency among conservative scholars has been to regard the date as A.D. 95 or 96, some have contended for an earlier date, such as 68 or 69, a conclusion supported by such worthies as Westcott, Lightfoot, Hort, Salmon, and others.[12] The early date is supposedly supported by a statement attributed to Papias to the effect that John the Apostle was martyred before the destruction of Jerusalem in A.D. 70. Swete in his thorough discussion of this point feels that if the statement of Papias is to be considered genuine, "it disposes of the apostolic authorship of the Apocalypse."[13] Accordingly, Swete concludes that if the evidence of Papias be acknowledged, the probability is that John the Elder is the John referred to in the book of Revelation.

The evidence for the early date, before A.D. 70, which depends both upon the genuineness of the quotation from Papias and the question whether Papias knew what he was talking about, has been challenged by many conservative scholars. The majority opinion seems to be that the traditional date of 95 or 96 has better support. The historical evidence previously cited ·from Clement of Alexandria, Eusebius, and Ire-

[9]Clement, "Who Is the Rich Man?" XLII, *Ante-Nicene Fathers*, II, 603.

[10]Eusebius, "Ecclesiastical History," III, xx, *The Fathers of the Church*, I, 168.
[11]Irenaeus, "Against Heresies," III, iii, 4, *Ante-Nicene Fathers*, I, 416.
[12]Swete, *op. cit.*, pp. cii–vi.
[13]*Ibid.*, p. clxxx.

naeus would be left without any explanation if John the Apostle actually suffered martyrdom before the destruction of Jerusalem in A.D. 70. As previously noted, Irenaeus placed the writing of the book in the reign of Domitian, which ended A.D. 96.

The weight of evidence is against accepting the testimony of Papias as valid and is for setting the date as 95 or 96. In any case, there is little tendency among scholars who accept the inspiration of the Apocalypse to place the date later as some liberal scholars have attempted to do. It is most significant that in many cases the theological bias against the chiliastic teaching of the book of Revelation seems to be the actual motive in rejecting the apostolic authorship. Based on the historical evidence, the date, therefore, must be before the death of Domitian, who was assassinated in A.D. 96, as the apostle was apparently released from his exile shortly after this. Interpretive problems, such as those raised by the identification of the seven kings of Revelation 17:10, are not of sufficient weight to challenge the historical evidence for the traditional date. The contents of the book fit this time.

In contrast to other apocalyptic books, the revelation recorded by John the Apostle is presented as having a solid historical basis in his exile on the Isle of Patmos. It was there these visions were given to him and in obedience to the command to write them and send them to the seven churches, John recorded the prophecies of the book. It would seem entirely reasonable that in the midst of persecution the church should be given a book of such assurance as that embodied in the content of the Revelation, which holds before them not only a realistic explanation as to why persecution is permitted but also a promise of ultimate triumph and reward.

INSPIRATION AND CANONICITY

Because the book of Revelation was addressed to seven different churches, it would be only natural that each of these churches would want its own copy, and thus the circulation of the entire book would be given a good start. Some believe that Ignatius (110-17) and the early *Epistle of Barnabas* contained allusions to the book though Swete considers it uncertain.[14] In the literature of the second half of the second century, evidence begins to reveal wide circulation of the Apocalypse. Andreas quotes Papias about Revelation 12:7 ff.[15] Irenaeus refers to old copies of the book and to people who knew John.[16] Other early authors who mention the book are Justin, Eusebius, Apollonius, and Theophilus

[14]*Ibid.*, pp. cvii–viii.
[15]*Ibid.*, p. cviii.
[16]*Ibid.*

the Bishop of Antioch.[17] It is referred to a number of times in the
Epistle of the Churches of Vienne.[18] Other references to the book abound.
Tertullian, according to Swete, quotes from eighteen out of the twenty-
two chapters of the book, and cites it as Scripture.[19] Some literature from
the period seems to refer to the book using similar phraseology, e.g.,
the *Shepherd of Hermas,* which refers to the great tribulation, and the
Acts of Perpetua and Felicitas, which according to Swete abounds in
imagery similar to the book of Revelation.[20] The circulation and wide
use of the book as Scripture are evident by the beginning of the third
century.

It is true, nevertheless, that Revelation was slow in gaining universal
recognition as Scripture. Important in the reasons for this is opposition
to the chiliasm which is expressly taught in Revelation 20. Other theological objections arose from various sects which for the most part were
heretical. The more orthodox churches seem to have had less difficulty in
accepting it as Scripture. The reasons for a slower reception arose princi-
pally from the unusual character of this book, the only apocalyptic book
in the New Testament. As previously noted, critics also were quick to
point to grammatical difficulties and to cite apparent discrepancies.
Swete in his thorough discussion of the vocabulary, grammar, and style
demonstrates that most of these objections have a suitable explanation
and do not have real weight against acceptance of the book as inspired
Scripture.[21]

As Thiessen has shown, most of the objections and difficulties dissolve
upon study and do not militate against either apostolic authorship or the
inspiration of the book itself.[22] The fact is that the early church, in spite
of certain objections, generally accepted the book of Revelation by the
end of the second century and the eastern church soon followed suit.
Among conservative scholars, there is little disposition to exclude the book
of Revelation from the canon, even though Luther, Zwingli, and Erasmus
considered it nonapostolic.[23] For the purpose of the present study, the
inspiration of the book is assumed.

INTERPRETATION

Blunt, in his preface, like a number of others, comments on the fact
that Joseph Scaliger, a sixteenth century French critic, complimented
John Calvin thus: ". . . he has shown his sense as much by not commenting on the Book of Revelation as he had by the manner in which

[17]*Ibid.,* pp. cviii–ix.
[18]*Ibid.,* p. cix.
[19]*Ibid.,* p. cx.
[20]*Ibid.*
[21]*Ibid.,* pp. cxx–xxx.
[22]Thiessen, pp. 319–20.
[23]*Ibid.,* p. 319.

he had commented on the other Books of the Bible."[24] Most of the difficulty in the interpretation of this last book in the Scriptures has come
from treating it as an ordinary piece of literature produced by a variety
of human authors. With such presuppositions, the book becomes a
literary monstrosity devoid of any real revelation from God. Simcox
points out, "Many orthodox readers are content to leave at least the bulk
of the book absolutely uninterpreted."[25]

When approached as divinely inspired and to be interpreted by the
phraseology and symbolism of other portions of the Bible, the depth and
breadth of Revelation become immediately apparent. The book offers
knowledge far beyond the investigating power of man and claims revelation not only in relation to spiritual and moral truths, as in the letters
to the seven churches, but revelation extending to visions of heaven and
earth and prophetic revelation of the future including the eternal state.
If a human invention, the book is of little value; if divinely inspired, it is
an open door into precious eternal truth.

If the inspiration of the book and its apostolic authorship be accepted,
there still remain, however, serious exegetical problems illustrated in the
variety of approaches found in conservative scholarship. These have often
been divided into four categories.

1. *The nonliteral or allegorical approach.* This point of view, originating in the Alexandrian School of Theology represented in Clement of
Alexandria and Origen, regarded the book of Revelation as one great
allegory going far beyond the natural symbolism which is found in the
book. They understood in a nonliteral sense much of what other expositors interpreted literally. They were motivated by their antichiliastic
premises which led them to take in other than literal sense anything which
would teach a millennial reign of Christ on earth. They claimed that
their view was the true "spiritual" interpretation as opposed to the literal-
ism of their opponents.

Though the Alexandrian School in the early church is generally regarded as heretical, its leaders undoubtedly influenced such men as
Jerome and Augustine and were responsible for turning the early church
from its previous chiliastic position. The interpretative method of the
Alexandrian school in its entirety has found little favor with modern interpreters, but there is a persistent tendency to return to some use of this
method to avoid the premillennial implications of the book of Revelation,
if understood more literally. Cady H. Allen, like many others, regards the
book only as a form of spiritual encouragement and assurance of the ulti-

[24]Henry Blunt, A *Practical Exposition of the Epistles to the Seven Churches of
Asia*, p. v.
[25]William H. Simcox, *The Revelation of S. John the Divine*, p. lii.

mate triumph of Christianity to those of the first century; but he feels the book is not intended to predict the future.[26]

The more moderate form of allegorical interpretation, following Augustine, has achieved respectability and regards the book of Revelation as presenting in a symbolic way the total conflict between Christianity and evil or, as Augustine put it, the City of God versus the City of Satan.

The modern liberal point of view expressed by Niles emphasizes a contemporary meaning of the book, averring that even the final consummation of the triumph of righteousness has already begun. Niles states

> But there is a distinction between prophecy and apocalypse, for whereas prophecy is a thrust of the Word of God into the present, apocalypse is also an unveiling of the meaning of the present in the light of the final end. Christian apocalypse is written from the standpoint of the contemporaneousness of the Church to the Christ who is risen and who will come again.[27]

Though the book is still regarded as somewhat prophetic, its specific character as prophesying definite future events is thus dissipated.

Lenski in the introduction to his exposition of the Revelation denies that any chronology is intended in the book.

> As far as the writer is able to see, the visions, from the first to the last, present lines or vistas. These start at various points, but like radii or rays all focus upon the final judgment and the eternal triumph. The final visions (chapters 21 and 22) present the triumph at length. All history is covered, but not as we read history, only as God sees it. The veiling clouds open now and again, allowing us to see vision after vision, till at last our eyes behold in vision the Holy City itself. Times and seasons are not for us (Acts 1:7) but the sure triumph, glorious over and amid them all, is.[28]

2. *The preterist approach.* In general, adherents of this point of view hold that the book of Revelation is a record of the conflicts of the early church with Judaism and paganism, with the closing chapters (20–22) constituting a picture of the contemporary triumph of the church. Though similar in some ways to the allegorical method, it considers Revelation as a symbolic history, rather than prophetic. Though some in the early church may have had similar views, credit is usually given to the Jesuit Alcasar (d. 1613) as originating this view, which was held also by Grotius, famous theologian of the Netherlands. A variation of this is the idea that Revelation is descriptive rather than predictive. David Brown writes concerning the design of the Apocalypse, "There are but two possible theories of what the Apocalypse is written for. It is either essentially *predictive* or purely *descriptive.*" In keeping with his post-

[26]*The Message of the Book of Revelation*, pp. 13–15.
[27]D. T. Niles, *As Seeing the Invisible*, p. 27.
[28]R. C. H. Lenski, *Interpretation of St. John's Revelation*, p. 25.

millennial viewpoint, he follows almost completely the descriptive interpretation.[29]

Hendriksen dismisses both the historical and the futurist interpretations
of the book of Revelation on the assumption that the book was intended
for the use of first century Christians to whom a detailed prophecy of the
entire church age would have been meaningless. Hendriksen instead
seems to follow the view that the book is a symbolic word of encouragement to early Christians suffering persecution and a general assurance of
ultimate triumph in Christ;[30] hence he is only partially a preterist.

The preterist view, in general, tends to destroy any future significance
of the book, which becomes a literary curiosity with little prophetic
meaning. Contemporary liberal works usually follow a combination of
the preterist and symbolical methods of interpretation, disregarding the
strictly historical interpretation as well as the futurist. Illustrative of
this tendency is Laymon's work, *The Book of Revelation*, which significantly does not include a single premillennial work in its bibliography.[31]
Even universalists have attempted commentaries on the book of Revelation in which they explain away all judgment upon sin and make all
future judgment contemporary, as in the work of Whittemore written
over a century ago.[32] Milligan regards the Apocalypse as a statement of
principles with no time periods or specific events in view: "While the
Apocalypse thus embraces the whole period of the Christian dispensation, it sets before us within this period the action of great principles
and not special incidents."[33]

3. *The historical approach.* Adherents to this theory consider Revelation as a symbolic presentation of the total of church history culminating
in the second advent. Though it had earlier disciples, Joachim, a Roman
Catholic scholar, is largely responsible for this as he was also the origina-
tor of the first forms of postmillennialism. This method of interpreting the
book of Revelation achieved considerable stature in the Reformation because of its identification of the pope and the papacy with the beasts
of Revelation 13. Thiessen cites Wycliffe, Luther, Joseph Mede, Sir
Isaac Newton, William Whiston, Elliott, Vitringa, Bengel, and Barnes
as adherents of this approach. It has undoubtedly influenced a large
number of subsequent expositors, especially those of the postmillennial
point of view.[34]

The historical method of interpretation has achieved the status of
respectability and in some ways is superior to the other two methods in

[29]*The Apocalypse: Its Structure and Primary Prediction*, p. 26.
[30]W. Hendriksen, *More Than Conquerors*, pp. 11–15.
[31]Charles M. Laymon, *The Book of Revelation*, pp. 165–66.
[32]Thomas Whittemore, *A Commentary on the Revelation of St. John*.
[33]William Milligan, *Lectures on the Apocalypse*, p. 153.
[34]Thiessen, p. 325.

that it provides a profound philosophy of history as well as a guide to the general principles of divine providence. Its major difficulty is that its adherents have succumbed to the tendency to interpret the book as in some sense climaxing in their generation. As many as fifty different interpretations of the book of Revelation therefore evolve, depending on the time and circumstances of the expositor.

Moses Stuart wrote more than one hundred years ago of the distress engendered in his day by the historical interpretation of the book of Revelation with its many conflicting theories resulting in the opinion that the book is impossible of plain exposition. Stuart raised the question:

> Must this state of things always continue? This is a question of great interest to those who believe that the Apocalypse rightfully belongs to the Canon of Scripture. Hitherto, scarcely any two original and independent expositors have been agreed, in respect to some points very important in their bearing upon the interpretation of the book. So long as the Apocalypse is regarded principally as an epitome of civil and ecclesiastic history, this must continue to be the case. Different minds will make the application of apocalyptic prophecies to different series of events, because there is something in each to which more or less of these prophecies is seemingly applicable. Such has always been the case, in past times, whenever this method of interpretation has been followed; and why should anything different from this be expected for the future?[35]

The very multiplicity of such interpretations and identifications of the personnel of Revelation with a variety of historical characters is its own refutation. If the historical method is the correct one, it is clear until now that no one has found the key. As Gehman has pointed out, in the historical interpretation of Revelation,

> variations exist in an almost endless stream . . . touch every aspect of the book [and] even on major themes there is little agreement: . . . the inescapable conclusion is that historical interpreters are on the wrong highway of interpretation.[36]

Abraham Kuyper in his last work, written after he was seventy-six years of age, interprets the book of Revelation in a devotional and spiritual sense. The translator, John Hendrik de Vries, in his introduction has this interesting criticism of the historical method of interpretation of Augustine that both he and Kuyper reject:

> He who has made a serious study of the marginal notes of Revelation has been impressed of necessity with the uncertainty into which Augustine's method brings him. He is told again and again that this one finds this and the other one that in it. As the several figures present themselves the expositor can not make up his mind whether one king is meant or another, this pope or another, or whether the

---
[35]A Commentary on the Apocalypse, p. v.
[36]W. T. Gehman, "A Critique of the Historical Interpretation of Revelation," p. 47.

writer refers to a persecution of the past or to one that is still to come. Moreover it breaks the thread of devotional reading when the mind is continually diverted by historical and numerical calculations of dates, which as pawns on a chessboard are moved back and forth, and in any case lie outside the horizon of the devout among God's people. Again, this method of interpretation leads to results which reflect the time in which the expositor lives. S. Augustine, who knew nothing of the papal hierarchy, is reminded of the early persecutors of the church and of the great heresies of those early days, while the writers of the marginal notes, who were reared in the heat of the struggle with Rome, had in mind almost exclusively what had gone out from Rome's seat against God's counsel. All this breeds uncertainty and confusion. It turns exegesis into an artful play of ingenuity. And when men of such eminent piety as Bengel devote years of their life to the calculation that the final period was to begin in 1836; or locate the end of the world in a year that is long past; we realize that such exegesis can not meet what God's church expects from this particular part of Scripture.[37]

Kuyper attempts to combine the historical and the idealistic, and in his spiritual interpretation, the book of Revelation is considered primarily a message of comfort to a suffering church.

Typical of contemporary amillennialism is the viewpoint of McDowell equating the millennium with the present age and more particularly to the intermediate state to which martyrs go after death. McDowell writes:

The binding of Satan (20:1–3) for a thousand years represents the cosmic result of the defeat of Satan in history. The defeat of the beast and his allies is a defeat for Satan and signalizes the limitation of his power for a long, indeterminate period of time (1,000 years). The reign of the martyrs and saints begins in this period of struggle. Those who are faithful to Christ in this struggle go from this earth at their death to reign with Christ for a long, indeterminate period of time (1,000 years): "This is the first resurrection" (20:4–6).[38]

McDowell's point of view is a combination of the historical and the spiritual interpretation of the book of Revelation, characteristic of contemporary amillennialism.

4. *The futuristic approach.* Limited to conservative expositors who are usually premillennial, this point of view regards Revelation as futuristic beginning with chapter 4 and therefore subject to future fulfillment. Some have attempted to make even chapters 1, 2, and 3 futuristic and the seven churches as future assemblies, but the great majority of futurists begin with chapter 4. Under this system of interpretation, the events of chapters 4 through 19 relate to the period just preceding the second coming of Christ. This is generally regarded as a period of seven years with emphasis on the last three and one-half years, labeled the

[37]Foreword, *The Revelation of St. John.*
[38]Edward A. McDowell, *The Meaning and Message of the Book of Revelation,* p. 18.

"great tribulation." Chapter 19, therefore, refers to the second coming of Christ to the earth, chapter 20 to the future millennial kingdom which will follow, and chapters 21 and 22 to events either contemporary or subsequent to the millennium.

In contrast to the other approaches to the book of Revelation, the futuristic position allows a more literal interpretation of the specific prophecies of the book. Though recognizing the frequent symbolism in various prophecies, the events foreshadowed by these symbols and their interpretation are regarded as being fulfilled in a normal way. Hence, the various judgments of God are actually poured out on the earth as contained in the seals, trumpets, and vials. Chapter 13 is considered a prophecy of the future world empire with its political and religious heads represented by the two beasts of this chapter. The harlot of chapter 17 is the final form of the church in apostasy. In a similar way all other events of Revelation relate to the climax of history contained in the second coming of Christ.

Objections to the futuristic view often stem from the claim that it would rob the early church of practical comfort. Summers expresses a common point of view when he states,

> I do not believe that any interpretation of Revelation can be correct if it is meaningless and if it fails to bring practical help and comfort to those who first received the book. To start from any other viewpoint is to follow the road which leads away from the truth of the book rather than the road which reveals the marvelous message of truth here given to troubled hearts.[39]

It is questionable whether any view, even the most extreme futuristic view, denies that there is a present value to the study of the book of Revelation. Summers is adroitly begging the question. The point is that portions of the book of Revelation can be appreciated and understood now. Other portions will not be understood until they are fulfilled. The general tenor of the book, even in unfulfilled sections, however, is the assurance that God will ultimately triumph, the saints will be blessed, and sin will be judged. To use the argument that the book must be understood by the first generation of Christians completely as a refutation of the futuristic position is not reasonable nor backed by the study of prophecy in Scripture in general. Summers himself adopts the combination of the preterist and historical views which obviously gives the interpreter a great deal of freedom but leaves his results mostly subjective.[40]

Milligan makes a similar objection to the futuristic system, that, if the main body of the book deals with the period immediately preceding the second coming of Christ, it robs the reader of immediate blessing.[41] It is

[39]Ray Summers, *Worthy Is the Lamb*, p. vii.
[40]*Ibid.*, pp. 45–51.
[41]Milligan, pp. 135–39.

strange that such an objection should be considered weighty. Much of the prophecy of the Bible deals with the distant future, including the Old Testament promises of the coming Messiah, the prophecies of Daniel concerning the future world empires, the body of truth relating to the coming kingdom on earth as well as countless other prophecies. If the events of chapters 4 through 19 are future, even from our viewpoint today, they teach the blessed truth of the ultimate supremacy of God and the triumph of righteousness. The immediate application of distant events is familiar in Scripture, as for instance II Peter 3:10-12, which speaks of the ultimate dissolution of the earth; nevertheless the succeeding passage makes an immediate application: "Wherefore, beloved, seeing that ye look for such things, be diligent . . ." (II Peter 3:14). Milligan's substitution of the spiritual interpretation of the book of Revelation in effect robs it of its prophetic character.

Though the premillennial conclusions of the futuristic view seem to have been held by the early church, the early fathers did not in any clear or consistent way interpret the book of Revelation as a whole in a futuristic sense. In fact, it can be demonstrated that the principal error of the fathers was that they attempted to interpret the book of Revelation as being fulfilled contemporaneously in the trials and difficulties of the church. Subsequent history has shown that the events which would have naturally followed did not come to pass, and the assumption of contemporaneous fulfillment was thereby discredited. The futuristic school has gained a hold upon a large segment of interpreters of prophecy in conservative evangelicalism largely because the other methods have led to such confusion of interpretation and have tended to make Revelation a hopeless exegetical problem. The futurist approach is rejected by most amillenarian and postmillenarian scholars, but is normally held by contemporary premillenarians who tend to follow the futuristic form of interpretation. Though many difficulties and obscurities remain, the futuristic school has the advantage of offering a relatively clear understanding of the principal events of future fulfillment, and tends to treat Revelation as a more normative piece of literature than the other interpretative principles.

One of the common assumptions of those who reject the futurist position is that the Apocalypse is the creation of John's thinking and was understandable by him in his generation. Moses Stuart expresses this:

> The original and intelligent readers of this book, beyond all reasonable doubt, could understand the meaning of the writer; else why should he address his work to them? Their acquaintance with the circle of things in which he moved, and their familiarity with the objects to which he refers, superseded the use of all the critical apparatus which we must now employ.[42]

42Stuart, p. v.

The difficulty with this point of view is twofold: (1) Prophecy, as given in the Scripture, was not necessarily understandable by the writer or his generation, as illustrated in the case of Daniel (Dan. 12:4, 9). It is questionable whether the great prophets of the Old Testament always understood what they were writing (cf. I Peter 1:10–12). (2) It is of the nature of prophecy that often it cannot be understood until the time of the generation which achieves fulfillment. The assumption, therefore, that the book of Revelation was understandable in the first generation or that it was intended to be understood by that generation is without real basis.

The second and third chapters of the book, however, are primarily a message to the seven historic churches of Asia. Inasmuch as these exhortations are set in the prophetic context of the chapters which follow, the book of Revelation is therefore seen to be designed for the church at large. If it were not for the book of Revelation, the New Testament canon would have ended with an obviously unfinished character.

The book of Revelation is in many respects the capstone of futuristic prophecy of the entire Bible and gathers in its prophetic scheme the major themes of prophecy which thread their way through the whole volume of Scripture. The scope and plan of the book as contained in the opening phrase "to show unto his servants things which must shortly come to pass" (1:1) indicate that the primary intent of the book was to prepare the way for the second coming of Christ. The book, therefore, has a special relevance for the generation which will be living on earth at that time. Because that event is undated, it constitutes a challenge to each succeeding generation of believers.

APOCALYPTIC CHARACTER

The book of Revelation, beginning as it does with the Greek word *apokalypsis,* by its very title is apocalyptic in character, that is, a book which claims to unfold the future, the unveiling of that which would otherwise be concealed. The nature of such a revelation requires a supernatural understanding of future events. Although the book of Revelation is the only apocalyptic book of the New Testament, many other apocalyptic works preceded its appearance; and there were others which followed.

A sharp distinction should be observed between apocalyptic works outside the Bible and apocalyptic works which are Scripture, whose writing was guided by the inspiration of the Holy Spirit. Apocalyptic literature outside the Bible can be classified as pseudepigrapha. They were works pretending to emanate from characters of the Bible who are cast in the role of predicting the future. The actual authors, however, often lived long after the character to whom the work is ascribed. Among the most important pseudepigrapha are *Ascension of Isaiah, Assumption of Moses, Book of Enoch, Book of Jubilees, The Greek Apocalypse of Baruch, Letters of Aristeas, III and IV Maccabees, Psalms of Solomon, Secrets of Enoch, Sibylline Oracles, The Syriac Apocalypse of Baruch,* and *Testament of the Twelve Patriarchs.* These works are usually dated as beginning about 250 B.C. and as continuing into the period following the apostolic church. A great many other apocalyptic works are sometimes cited as of lesser importance, such as: *The Apocalypses of Adam, Elijah,* and *Zephaniah;* and *Testament of Abram, Isaac, and Jacob.*

It is characteristic of apocalyptic literature outside the Bible to have a pessimistic view of the contemporary situation and to paint the future in glowing terms of blessing for the saints and doom for the wicked. The real author's name is never divulged in apocalyptic works outside the Bible.

Apocalyptic portions of the Scriptures are in sharp contrast to these pseudepigrapha. The more important apocalyptic works of the Old Testament are Isaiah, Ezekiel, Daniel, Joel, and Zechariah. Liberal scholars have sometimes drawn unfair comparisons between the apocalyptic writers outside the Bible and those within the canon. For instance, a common assumption is that the book of Daniel was not actually written by Daniel, as the book purports to be, in the sixth century B.C., but rather in the period of the second century when much of the book of Daniel would have been history. This, however, has been refuted by adequate conservative scholarship, and the apocalyptic character of scriptural books is not a just ground for denying the historical content or the authorship indicated. It is an unwarranted assumption to conclude from the pseudoauthorship of apocalyptic writings outside the Bible that the same principle also applies to Scripture.

H. B. Swete although making unwarranted concessions,[43] such as the late date of Daniel, points out that the Apocalypse of John is a new departure from former apocalyptic writings in the following particulars:

> (1) The Jewish apocalypses are without exception pseudepigraphic; the Christian apocalypse bears the author's name. This abandonment of a long-established tradition is significant; by it John claims for himself the position of a prophet who, conscious that he draws his inspiration from Christ or His angel and not at second hand, has no need to seek shelter under the name of a Biblical saint.

(2) In contrast to the pseudepigrapha whose actual dates are often impossible to determine, Swete states:

> The Apocalypse of John, on the contrary, makes no secret of its origin and destination; it is the work of a Christian undergoing exile in one

---

[43]Swete, p. xxiv.

of the islands of the Aegean; and it is addressed to Christian congregations in seven of the chief cities of the adjacent continent, under circumstances which practically determine its date.

(3) The Apocalyptist differs from his Jewish predecessors in that

he has produced a book which, taken as a whole, is profoundly Christian, and widely removed from the field in which Jewish apocalyptic occupied itself. The narrow sphere of Jewish national hopes has been exchanged for the life and aims of the society whose field is the world and whose goal is the conquest of the human race. . . . In the Apocalypse of John the presence of the Spirit of Revelation is unmistakably felt, and the Christian student may be pardoned if he recognizes in this book a fulfillment of the promise of a Paraclete who *shall declare . . . the things that are to come.*[44]

The Apocalypse of John stands in sharp contrast not only to apocalyptic writings outside the Bible which preceded it but also to the Christian apocalypses which followed, such as *Anabaticon and Pauli,* the *Revelations of St. Steven and Thomas,* the *Decree of Gelasius, The Apocalypse of Peter* (which for a brief time in the early church seems to have been considered genuine), *The Apocalypse of Paul, A Spurious Apocalypse of John, The Apocalypse of Sedrach,* and *The Apocalypse of the Virgin.* The reverent student, however, has little difficulty distinguishing the superlative and inspired character of the genuine Apocalypse of John from these apocalyptic writings which followed.

SYMBOLISM

Symbolisms occur throughout Scripture as a vehicle for divine revelation, but it is undoubtedly true that the final book of the New Testament because of its apocalyptic character contains more symbols than any other book in the New Testament.[45] In this particular it is similar to the book of Daniel to which, in many respects, it is a counterpart, and also to Ezekiel and Zechariah in the Old Testament. Many apocalyptic books appeared prior to as well as contemporary with the book of Revelation. The fact that Revelation was included in the canon and all other contemporary apocalyptic books were excluded is in itself a testimony to the unusual character of Revelation. Among the apocalyptic books produced in the early church were the *Apocalypse of Paul,* the *Apocalypse of Peter,* the *Apocalypse of Zechariah,* and others like them, which though similar in style are not inspired and are far inferior as vehicles of conveying truth. These writings should not be confused with the genuine Paul-

---

[44]*Ibid.,* pp. xxviii–xxx.

[45]Among the excellent treatments of the symbolism of the book of Revelation, the work of Swete, *The Apocalypse of John,* pp. cxxxi–xxxix, may be mentioned along with Merrill Tenney's *Interpreting Revelation,* pp. 186–93. Difference of opinion often exists whether an expression is a symbol, a figure of speech other than a symbol, or a literal reference.

ine and Petrine epistles and the book of Zechariah in the Old Testament. Apocalyptic books in general are so designated because they reveal truth expressed in symbolic and guarded language.

The symbolism of the book of Revelation has been explained on many principles. One of the most probable and popular, however, is that it was necessary to state opposition to the Roman Empire during the persecutions of Domitian by expressing the revelation from God in symbolic terms which would not be easily apprehended by the Roman authorities. Ethelbert Stauffer explains the need for symbolism in the Apocalypse in this way:

> We may read the Book of Revelation with new understanding when we see it as the apostolic reply to the declaration of war [on Christianity] by the divine emperor in Rome. And when we realize the perilous political situation in which the book was both written and "published" (22:10), we understand the reason for its mysterious and veiled pictorial language and its preference for words and pseudonyms from the Old Testament.[46]

The exposition of this point of view is expressed by Stauffer in his account of the developments during the reign of Domitian (A.D. 81–96). As Stauffer notes, Domitian gradually applied to himself all the attributes of God and established a form of religion which was anti-Christian. As Stauffer states,

> Domitian was also the first emperor to wage a proper campaign against Christ; and the Church answered the attack under the leadership of Christ's last apostle, John of the Apocalypse. Nero had Paul and Peter destroyed, but he looked upon them as seditious Jews. Domitian was the first emperor to understand that behind the Christian "movement" there stood an enigmatic figure who threatened the glory of the emperors. He was the first to declare war on this figure, and the first also to lose the war—a foretaste of things to come.[47]

Stauffer traces the development of Domitian's opposition to Christianity and his claim of divine attributes on the coins which were issued during the reign of Domitian and which were used as an important propaganda vehicle to communicate to the people Domitian's assumption of divinity.

Almost every aspect of nature is used as well as grotesque nonnatural forms as a vehicle of the symbolism of the book of Revelation. Hence, from the animal world, frequent symbols appear, such as the horses of Revelation 6, the living creatures seen in heaven, Christ as the Lamb, and the calf, the locust, the scorpion, the lion, the leopard, the bear, the frog, the eagle, the vulture, birds, fish, as well as unnatural beasts, such as those in Revelation 13. There is also allusion to the botanical world, and trees and grass are mentioned in a context of reference to earth, sky,

[46]*Christ and the Caesars*, p. 176.
[47]*Ibid.*, p. 150.

and sea. The sun, moon, and stars in the heavens; the thunder, lightning, and hail of the atmospheric heavens, as well as rivers and seas on earth often form a vehicle of divine revelation. Various forms of humanity are also mentioned, such as the mother and child of Revelation 12, the harlot of Revelation 17, and the wife of Revelation 19. Weapons of war such as swords are named as well as reapers with their sickles. Trumpeters with their trumpets are introduced as well as the flute and lyre. In many cases John had to use unusual expressions to describe scenes in heaven and in earth which transcend normal human experience.

Some items allude either to biblical background or to the geography of the Bible, but much of the imagery found in the book of Revelation is familiar also to students of Daniel, Ezekiel, and Zechariah. The golden lampstand of the churches of Asia has some correspondence to the lampstand of the Tabernacle and Temple. Allusions to the heavenly Tabernacle and Temple, to the altar, ark, and censer, all have Old Testament background. Geographic descriptions refer also to Old Testament names and places such as the River Euphrates, Sodom, Armageddon—the hill of Megiddo—Jerusalem, Babylon, Egypt, and to Old Testament characters such as Balaam and Jezebel. In many cases there are indirect allusions to Old Testament ideas and situations.

A fair analysis of this compilation of symbols furnishes proof of frequent allusion to the Old Testament. In the center is Christ as the Lamb and Lion of the tribe of Judah and the Root of David. The twelve tribes of Israel are mentioned. As Snell states,

> In the Revelation, THE LAMB is the centre around which all else is clustered, the foundation on which everything lasting is built, the nail on which all hangs, the object to which all points, and the spring from which all blessing proceeds. THE LAMB is the light, the glory, the life, the Lord of Heaven and earth, from whose face all defilement must flee away, and in whose presence fulness of joy is known. Hence, we cannot go far in the study of the Revelation, without seeing THE LAMB, like direction-posts along the road, to remind us that He who did by Himself purge our sins is now highly exalted, and that to Him every knee must bow, and every tongue confess.[48]

It is nevertheless true that much of the imagery of the book of Revelation is new; that is, it is created as a vehicle for the divine revelation which John was to record. To attempt, as many writers have done, to consider this symbolism as allusion to extrabiblical apocalyptic literature, is to press the matter beyond its proper bounds. It is also true that some items, while partially symbolic, may also be intended to be understood literally, as in numerous instances where reference is made to stars, the moon, the sun, rivers, and seas. While there will never be complete

---

[48]H. H. Snell, *Notes on the Revelation*, p. xvi.

agreement on the line between imagery and the literal, the patient exegete must resolve each occurrence in some form of consistent interpretation.

Very prominent in the book of Revelation is the use of numbers, namely, 2, 3, 3½, 4, 5, 6, 7, 10, 12, 24, 42, 144, 666, 1,000, 1,260, 1,600, 7,000, 12,000, 144,000, 100,000,000, and 200,000,000. These numbers may be understood literally, but even when understood in this way, they often carry with them also a symbolic meaning. Hence the number seven, used fifty-four times, more than any other number in the book, refers to seven literal churches in the opening chapter. Yet by the very use of this number (which speaks of completion or perfection) the concept is conveyed that these were representative churches which in some sense were complete in their description of the normal needs of the church. There were not only seven churches but seven lampstands, seven stars, seven spirits of God, seven seals on the scroll, seven angels with seven trumpets, seven vials or bowls containing the seven last plagues, seven thunders, 7,000 killed in the earthquake of chapter 12, a dragon with seven heads and seven crowns, the beast of chapter 13 with seven heads, seven mountains of chapter 17, and the seven kings. Next in importance to the number seven and in the order of their frequency are the numbers twelve, ten, and four. Some of this stems from the fact that there are twelve tribes of Israel. Twelve thousand were sealed from each of the twelve tribes. The elders of chapter 4 are twice twelve or twenty-four. The new Jerusalem is declared to be 12,000 furlongs wide and long, and its wall twelve times twelve, or 144 cubits in height.

From these indications it is clear that the use of these numbers is not accidental. Though the symbolism is not always obvious, the general rule should be followed to interpret numbers literally unless there is clear evidence to the contrary. The numbers nevertheless convey more than their bare numerical significance.

Of special importance is the reference to forty-two months or 1,260 days, describing the precise length of the great tribulation. This is in keeping with the anticipation of Daniel 9:27 that the last half of the seven-year period would be a time of unprecedented trouble. Endless speculation has also risen over the number 666, describing the beast out of the sea in Revelation 13:18.[49] The most natural and simple explanation of this number, however, is that the beast is characterized by the number six, just falling short of the number seven and signifying that he is only a man after all. Possibly the threefold occurrence of the number six is in vague imitation of the trinity formed by his association with the devil and the false prophet.

[49]For further discussion, see exposition of 13:18; cf. also J. B. Smith, *A Revelation of Jesus Christ*, pp. 206-7; Swete, p. cxxxviii.

The wide use of symbols is attended, however, by frequent interpretations in the book of Revelation itself either by direct reference or by implication. Symbols can often be explained also by usage elsewhere in Scripture. The following list may be helpful:

The seven stars (1:16) represent seven angels (1:20).

The seven lampstands (1:13) represent seven churches (1:20).

The hidden manna (2:17) speaks of Christ in glory (cf. Exodus 16:33–34; Heb. 9:4).

The morning star (2:28) refers to Christ returning before the dawn, suggesting the rapture of the church before the establishment of the Kingdom (cf. Rev. 22:16; II Peter 1:19).

The key of David (3:7) represents the power to open and close doors (Isa. 22:22).

The seven lamps of fire represent the sevenfold Spirit of God (4:5).

The living creatures (4:7) portray the attributes of God.

The seven eyes represent the sevenfold Spirit of God (5:6).

The odors of the golden vials symbolize the prayers of the saints (5:8).

The four horses and their riders (6:1 ff.) represent successive events in the developing tribulation.

The fallen star (9:1) is the angel of the abyss, probably Satan (9:11).

Many references are made to Jerusalem: the great city (11:8), Sodom and Egypt (11:8), which stand in contrast to the new Jerusalem, the heavenly city.

The stars of heaven (12:4) refer to fallen angels (12:9).

The woman and the child (12:1–2) seem to represent Israel and Christ (12:5–6).

Satan is variously described as the great dragon, the old serpent, and the devil (12:9; 20:2).

The time, times, and half a time (12:14) are the same as 1,260 days (12:6).

The beast out of the sea (13:1–10) is the future world ruler and his empire.

The beast out of the earth (13:11–17) is the false prophet (19:20).

The harlot (17:1) variously described as the great city (17:18), as Babylon the great (17:5), as the one who sits on seven hills (17:9), is usually interpreted as apostate Christendom.

The waters (17:1) on which the woman sits represent the peoples of the world (17:15).

The ten horns (17:12) are ten kings associated with the beast (13:1; 17:3, 7, 8, 11–13, 16–17).

The Lamb is Lord of lords and King of kings (17:14).

Fine linen is symbolic of the righteous deeds of the saints (19:8).

The rider of the white horse (19:11–16, 19) is clearly identified as
  Christ, the King of kings.
The lake of fire is described as the second death (20:14).
Jesus Christ is the Root and Offspring of David (22:16).

In many instances, where symbols are explained in the book of Revelation, they establish a pattern of interpretation which casts a great deal of
light upon the meaning of the book as a whole. This introduces a presumption that, where expressions are not explained, they can normally
be interpreted according to their natural meaning unless the context
clearly indicates otherwise. The attempt to interpret all of the book of
Revelation symbolically ends in nullifying practically all that entails the
book and leaving it unexplained, as in the work by Lilje, written during
the early days of World War II and completed while the author was in
prison in Germany.[50]

The problems of interpretation of Revelation have often been made far
greater than they really are. They frequently yield to patient study and
comparison with other portions of Scripture. The linguistic study of
Revelation is an endless task but offers rich rewards to the patient student.

THEOLOGY

Few books of the Bible provide a more complete theology than that
afforded by the book of Revelation. Because of its apocalyptic character,
the emphasis of the book is eschatological in the strict sense of dealing
with last things (note "the word of this prophecy," Rev. 1:3). More
specifically, however, it is Christological, as the material of the book
relates to the "revelation of Jesus Christ." The objective is to reveal
Jesus Christ as the glorified One in contrast to the Christ of the Gospels,
who was seen in humiliation and suffering. The climax of the book is
the second coming of Jesus Christ. Events preceding the second coming
constitute an introduction, and all events which follow constitute an
epilogue. The wide range of revelation, however, deals with many subjects not specifically eschatological or Christological. In all important
fields of theology, there are major contributions and, though written with
the imagery and Hebraisms of the Old Testament, the revelation is definitely New Testament.

Bibliology. The doctrine of Scripture of the Apocalypse is deduced
mostly by implication in that there are frequent allusions to other books
of the Bible. One does not proceed more than a few verses, however,
before a special blessing is pronounced upon the reader and hearer in a
context which refers to the book as "the Word of God, and of the testimony of Jesus Christ" (Rev. 1:3). John claims divine authority and

[50]Hanns Lilje, *The Last Book of the Bible.*

inspiration both for the book itself and for the revelation it contains. The book of Revelation, however, is not only Scripture itself but is saturated with Old Testament references. Swete cites Westcott and Hort to the effect "that of the 404 verses of the Apocalypse, there are 278 which contain references to the Jewish Scriptures."[51]

Swete submits a table demonstrating the richness of Old Testament reference which proves that most of the books of the Old Testament including all of its three major divisions are referred to, with emphasis on the Psalms, Isaiah, Ezekiel, and Daniel, with Daniel having the greatest number of references.[52] The fact that the Apocalypse is saturated with Old Testament references in itself tends to tie the book to the rest of Scripture and makes it a fitting climactic volume, a terminal for major lines of Scripture revelation.

Theology Proper. Apart from its eschatology, the Apocalypse contributes more to the doctrine of God than to any other field. The study of its contribution to the doctrine of the Father, the Son, and the Holy Spirit would in itself merit a volume of considerable proportions. God is presented in all the majesty of the Jehovah of the Old Testament, who is holy, true, omnipotent, omniscient, and eternal. There is emphasis on the righteousness of God and His divine judgment upon sin, with comparatively little mention made of His love and mercy. The character of God is in keeping with the role in which He is presented as the divine Judge of men.

Though there is reference to both the Father and the Son, the central revelation concerns Christ, in keeping with the title of the book. Many allusions are made to His human origin as coming from the tribe of Judah and the house of David and to His humiliation while on earth as represented in the symbol of a slain lamb. Always, however, Christ is depicted as triumphant over death, the eternal One of infinite power and majesty who is worthy of all honor and adoration. Before His glorified humanity the apostle falls as one dead.

The supreme revelation is continued in chapter 19 where He is described as descending from heaven as King of kings and Lord of lords to slay the wicked, to deliver the righteous, and to accomplish His righteous purpose in the earth. Though the Apocalypse contains no defense of the deity of Christ, no book of the Bible is more plain in its implications, for here indeed is the eternal God who became man. This is, of course, confirmed by His relationship to God the Father described in 4:2-3 and 5:1, 7. Complementing the revelation of Christ is that of the Spirit through whom John received the revelation (1:10) and who appears frequently in various symbols, as in the seven horns and seven eyes

[51]Swete, p. cxl.
[52]*Ibid.*, p. cliii.

of 5:6, and the seven spirits of 1:4 and 4:5, and who is seen in the special relationship to Christ in 3:1 and 5:6. It is fitting that the book of Revelation should close with another reference to the Spirit in 22:17 climaxing other indirect references to the Spirit throughout the book.

Anthropology and Hamartiology. The emphasis on the doctrines of man and of sin in the book of Revelation is apparent. Man is revealed in his utter need of the grace of God as righteously deserving the judgment of God for sin, in partaking, even in his best form, of the limitations of the creature. Few books of the Bible describe man in greater depravity and as the object of more severe divine judgment. The acme of human blasphemy and wickedness is portrayed in the beast and the false prophet who are the supreme demonstration of Satan's handiwork in the human race.

Angelology. No other book in the New Testament speaks more often of angels than the book of Revelation. They are the principal vehicle of communication to John of the truth which he is recording. The holy angels are seen in power and majesty in sharp contrast to the wicked or fallen angels also described in the book. Angels are prominent in the scenes of heaven in chapters 4 and 5, and they reappear to sound the seven trumpets in chapters 8 through 11. The truth of chapter 11 concerning the two witnesses is transmitted to John through an angel, and the warfare against the wicked angels is described dramatically in chapter 12. The seven vials of the wrath of God are also administered by the angels in chapters 15 and 16, and the judgment upon Babylon is related to angelic ministry. Angels apparently accompany the Lord in His second coming in chapter 19. The final message of the book recorded in chapter 22 comes to John through the ministry of angels.

Soteriology. The redemptive purpose of God is constantly in view in the Apocalypse, beginning with the reference in 1:5 to Christ as the One who "loved us, and washed us from our sins in his own blood." His crucifixion is mentioned in 1:7, and constant allusions follow as Christ is presented as the slain Lamb, as the One who redeemed mankind by His blood out of every kindred, tongue, and nation in 5:9, and the One whose blood can make white the robes of the martyrs in 7:14. It is because of His finished work in sacrifice that the invitation of the Spirit and bride of 22:17 can be made to anyone who chooses to partake of the water of life without cost. Salvation is ascribed to God three times (7:10; 12:10; 19:1). Emphasis is on the doctrine of redemption, and the saints are declared to be a redeemed people.

Ecclesiology. A major section and contribution to ecclesiology is found in the opening chapters of Revelation with the incisive letters to the seven churches. Here the emphasis is on practical truth and holy living, in keeping with their relationship to the head of the church, Jesus Christ. Reference to the New Testament church as the *ekklesia* is not to be found in chapters 4 through 18, but the church as the wife of the Lamb reappears in 19:7–8 and is included in the mention of the apostles in the description of the new Jerusalem, which the church shares with saints of other ages. As in other books of the New Testament, *ekklesia*, when used in a religious sense referring to saints in the Body of Christ, is nowhere found in Revelation from 3:14 to 22:16; rather, the general word *hagios* ("saint") is used to include the saved of all ages. This tends to support the concept that the church as the Body of Christ is raptured before events pictured in the book of Revelation beginning in chapter 4. The true church is in contrast to the harlot of chapter 17, and it is to be distinguished from the saints described as Jews or Gentiles. The peculiar hope of the church, in contrast to that of other saints, is alluded to only obliquely and is not the main substance of the revelations in chapters 4 through 19.

Eschatology. Undoubtedly, the principal contribution of the book of Revelation is in the realm of eschatology. Here is presented not only the eschatology of the church in a few scattered references to the doctrine of the rapture of the church (2:25; 3:10–11) but the majestic completion of the prophetic program of the times of Gentiles and Daniel's program for Israel, both culminating in the second coming of Christ. Nowhere else in Scripture is there more detailed description of the period just before the second coming with special reference to the great tribulation. The events immediately preceding and following the second coming are also spelled out in detail.

Here alone the millennial kingdom is declared to be one thousand years in length, and a clear distinction is made between the millennium and the eternal state which follows. Emphasis in the book is on the second coming of Christ itself, which stands in sharp relief against the sphere of humiliation depicted in the Gospels. Prominent also are the doctrine of divine judgment upon sin, the doctrine of resurrection, and the doctrine of reward. No book of Scripture more specifically sets before the believer in Christ his eternal hope in the new heaven and earth and gives greater assurance of God's triumph over wickedness, rebellion, and unbelief. In a word, the book of Revelation is the eschatological section of the New Testament. Every major theme of prophecy is treated to some extent in this book, with special attention to completion or fulfillment of the prophetic program of God. For this reason the book of Revelation cannot be understood apart from the sixty-five books which precede it, although it is in itself a Bible in miniature.

1

INTRODUCTION: THE THINGS WHICH THOU HAST SEEN

PROLOGUE (1:1–3)

1:1 The Revelation of Jesus Christ, which God gave unto him, to shew unto his servants things which must shortly come to pass; and he sent and signified it by his angel unto his servant John.

THE OPENING VERSE of the first chapter introduces immediately the central theme of the book of Revelation, namely, Jesus Christ in His present and future glory. The futuristic and prophetic character of the book is indicated in the words "a revelation of Jesus Christ" in which God will declare to John "things which must shortly come to pass." The word *revelation* is the translation of *apokalypsis* without the article, meaning a "revelation, disclosure, or unveiling." It is a revelation of truth *about* Christ Himself, a disclosure of future events, that is, His second coming when Christ will be revealed. It is as well a revelation which comes *from* Christ.

The common title of the book, "The Revelation of John," merely identifies the human author. The subject actually is a revelation of Jesus Christ, described as given by God the Father to Christ the Son and then revealed "unto his servant." The revelation of the Father to the Son is previously mentioned in John 3:34–35; 5:20–24; 7:16; 8:28; 12:49; 14:10, 24; 16:15; 17:8. The substance of the revelation is described as "things which must shortly come to pass" (cf. a similar expression in Dan. 2:28–29, 45 and Rev. 4:1; 22:6).

That which Daniel declared would occur "in the latter days" is here described as "shortly" (Gr., *en tachei*), that is, "quickly or suddenly coming to pass," indicating rapidity of execution after the beginning takes place. The idea is not that the event may occur soon, but that when it does, it will be sudden (cf. Luke 18:8; Acts 12:7; 22:18; 25:4; Rom. 16:20). A similar word, *tachys*, is translated "quickly" seven times in Revelation (2:5, 16; 3:11; 11:14; 22:7, 12, 20).

The channel through which the revelation comes from Christ is "by his angel unto his servant John." The communication spoken of as "signified," while often meaning revelation *through symbols*, as in this

35

book, includes also revelation through words which communicate the meaning. The name of the angel is not given, though Gabriel has been suggested (cf. Dan. 8:16; 9:2, 21–22; Luke 1:26–31). John is declared to be the recipient of the revelation, his name occurring four other times in this book (1:4, 9; 21:2; 22:8). The best explanation is that the writer is the Apostle John (see Introduction). That John should be called a servant (Gr., *doulos*) rather than an apostle is not strange in view of common usage of the term in reference to the apostles in the New Testament (cf. Rom. 1:1; Phil. 1:1; Titus 1:1; James 1:1; II Peter 1:1; Jude 1). The opening verse of this chapter therefore sets forth the basic scheme of the entire book, its subject matter, purpose, angelic channel, as well as its human writer.

1:2 Who bare record of the word of God, and of the testimony of Jesus Christ, and of all things that he saw.

The expression "bare record" in verse 2 (Gr., *emartyrēsen*), occurring three times in this chapter, means "to bear witness" or "to testify." The book of Revelation is not only "the Word of God," that is, originating in God, but John bears witness of his reception of it. It has the added weight of being "the testimony of Jesus Christ" (Gr., *martyria*), and the record of John is a complete recital "of all things that he saw." John is an eyewitness.

1:3 Blessed is he that readeth, and they that hear the words of this prophecy, and keep those things which are written therein: for the time is at hand.

An unusual feature of the opening verses is the special threefold blessing which is invoked in verse 3: (1) "blessed is he [singular] that readeth"; (2) "blessed are they [plural] that hear the words of this prophecy"; (3) "blessed are they that keep those things which are written therein." As all would not have a copy of the book, a special blessing attends the one who reads. Those who hear, however, are also blessed, but for both reader and hearer it is most important that they keep, that is, fulfill (observe or pay attention to) what is written. All three participles are in the present tense, implying continued reading, hearing, and observing. The book of Revelation is the only book of Scripture containing such a direct promise of blessing. The blessing here pronounced is the first of seven beatitudes in the book (1:3; 14:13; 16:15; 19:9; 20:6; 22:7, 14). It seems to anticipate that many would neglect this book or ignore its prophetic revelation. It is singular that the one book in the New Testament which invokes a special blessing on the reader should be often left unread.

The book of Revelation is described by the phrase "the words of this prophecy," implying that the book as a whole is prophetic. The importance of the prophecy is emphasized by the phrase "for the time is at hand," "the time" (Gr., *kairos*) referring to a period of time. Daniel mentions the "time of the end" five times (Dan. 8:17; 11:35, 40; 12:4, 9). "The time" is also declared to be at hand in Revelation 22:10, and there are five other references to time, using *kairos* (11:18; 12:12, 14—three occurrences in v. 14). A season of time indicated by *kairos* is to be contrasted to "hour" (Gr., *hōra*) and time in general (Gr., *chronos*). The expression "at hand" indicates nearness from the standpoint of prophetic revelation, not necessarily that the event will immediately occur.

SALUTATION (1:4–8)

1:4 John to the seven churches which are in Asia: Grace be unto you, and peace, from him which is, and which was, and which is to come; and from the seven Spirits which are before his throne.

Having introduced the content and general character of the book which follows, John addresses what he writes to the seven churches which are in Asia, that is, the province of Asia in Asia Minor described as Proconsular Asia, including at this time Phrygia, Mysia, Caria, and Lydia. All the seven churches were located in the western half of Asia Minor.

The customary invocation of grace and peace common to Paul's letters is used by John here and in his second epistle. These two words capture the richness of the Christian faith, grace embodying God's attitude toward the believer coupled with His loving gifts, and peace speaking of relationship, here especially the peace of God. Grace represents standing; peace represents experience.

The eternal God, the source of all grace and peace, is introduced as the One "which is, and which was, and which is to come." Because of subsequent references to Christ and the Holy Spirit, this is considered as relating to God the Father. The truth is presented in an unusual grammatical construction which occurs with variations four other times (1:8; 4:8; 11:17; 16:5). The concept of past, present, and future corresponds to the threefold chronological division of the book itself (1:19). Joining the Father in salutation are "the seven Spirits which are before his throne." Some have considered the term an allusion to the Holy Spirit (cf. Isa. 11:2–3). Others believe these were seven angels in places of high privilege before the throne of God (cf. 3:1; 4:5; 5:6). The word *spirit* (Gr., *pneuma*) is commonly used of evil spirits, that is, demons or fallen angels; of the human spirit (cf. Mark 8:12); and occasionally of holy angels (cf. Heb. 1:7, 14). Angels are contrasted to spirits in Acts 23:8–9. Those who favor the seven spirits as referring to the Holy Spirit find justification in Isaiah 11. The message originates in God the Father and the Spirit.

1:5-6 And from Jesus Christ, who is the faithful witness, and the first begotten of the dead, and the prince of the kings of the earth. Unto him that loved us, and washed us from our sins in his own blood, and hath made us kings and priests unto God and his Father; to him be glory and dominion for ever and ever. Amen.

The salutation, according to verse 5, also climactically comes from Christ in His character as the faithful Witness (cf. 3:14), the first Begotten or, better, the Firstborn of the dead, referring to His resurrection, and as the Prince or Ruler of the kings of the earth. As the faithful Witness He fulfilled the role of a prophet (John 18:37). In contrast to those who were previously restored to life only to die again, Christ is the Firstborn, the first to receive a resurrection body, which is immortal (cf. Acts 26:23). As Christ is "the firstborn of every creature" (Col. 1:15), indicating that He was before all creation in time, so Christ was first also in resurrection. His resurrection is *out of* the mass of men who died. Some manuscripts use *ek*, "out of." Compare a similar selective resurrection for the church (Phil. 3:11). As Christ is first (cf. "firstfruits," I Cor. 15:20) so others are to follow Christ in His resurrection. Christ and all the righteous dead are included in "the first resurrection" (Rev. 20:5–6). The wicked dead are raised last, after the millennium (20:12–13).

His witness and His resurrection are now past. His fulfillment of the role of "ruler of the kings of the earth" is future, to be achieved after his victory over the beast and the false prophet (Rev. 19), fulfilling Isaiah 9:6–7 and many other verses such as Psalm 72:11 and Zechariah 14:9.

Special emphasis, however, is given to what has already been accomplished for believers, mentioned in the form of ascription of praise. Christ is the One who keeps on loving us (present tense) and who "loosed us" (aorist tense) once for all, in or by His own blood.[1]

Just as Christ has the right to rule, though He is not exercising this right over the kings of the earth now, so believers are made "kings[2] and priests" or, better, "a kingdom, priests unto God and his Father." Believers form both a priesthood and a kingdom (cf. I Peter 2:9; Rev. 5:10). The full manifestation and exercise of prerogatives of this royal priest-

---

[1]This rendering follows Westcott and Hort rather than the text used in the Authorized Version, where "loved" is past tense and *louō* (washed) is substituted for *luō* (loosed). Either rendering makes sense. On the basis that it is easier for copyists to drop out a letter than to add a letter some prefer "washed" to "loosed." As there are many variations of texts in the book of Revelation, the tendency of modern scholars is to overdo the correction of the text used in the Authorized Version. In either case there is a heartwarming testimony to the love of Christ and His effective redemption through sacrificial blood.

[2]"Kings" (lit., "kingdom"; Gr., *basileia*); for the concept of the kingdom in the Revelation, see John Peter Lange, *Commentary on the Holy Scripture*, Excursus on the *Basileia*, by E. R. Craven, pp. 93–100.

hood are subject to future manifestations. To such a Saviour and Lord the right to everlasting glory and dominion is attributed (cf. Dan. 7:14) in John's benediction of worship and praise. To this the apostle adds, "Amen" ("So be it").

> **1:7** Behold, he cometh with clouds; and every eye shall see him, and they also which pierced him: and all kindreds of the earth shall wail because of him. Even so, Amen.

Introduced by the first of many instances of "behold" or "see," announcement is made in verse 7 of the glorious second coming of Christ, one of the central revelations of the book. The present tense of "he cometh" has been interpreted by some as the prophetic foreview out of place chronologically, but it can be simply understood as the futuristic use of the present in which a future action is stated as already coming to pass. It is an emphatic form of declaration (cf. "I will come again," lit., "I come again," John 14:3). As Christ was received by a cloud in His ascension (Acts 1:9), so He will come in the clouds of heaven (Matt. 24:30; 26:64; Mark 13:26; 14:62; Luke 21:27). Clouds are also mentioned in Daniel 7:13, but this seems to be a scene in heaven rather than on earth. In Revelation 14:14, 16 the Son of Man is pictured sitting on a cloud. In contrast to the event of the ascension, when clouds removed Christ from sight, at His second coming "every eye shall see him" (cf. Matt. 24:30; Mark 13:26; Luke 21:27).

There is no indication that the world as a whole will see Christ at the time of the rapture of the church. At His coming to establish His kingdom, however, all will see Him. Especially mentioned is the fact that they who pierced Him will behold His coming. This creates a problem in that those who crucified Christ are now dead. The difficulty is solved by reference to Zechariah 12:10 where Jehovah declares, "And I will pour upon the house of David, and upon the inhabitants of Jerusalem, the spirit of grace and of supplications: and they shall look upon me whom they have pierced, and they shall mourn for him, as one mourneth for his only son, and shall be in bitterness for him, as one that is in bitterness for his firstborn." Not only Israel as a nation shall behold Him, but also "all kindreds of the earth shall wail because of him." This expression is almost identical to that found in Matthew 24:30, where it states, "Then shall all the tribes of the earth mourn."

To this John adds, "Even so, Amen." The Greek word *amēn* is a transliteration of a Hebrew word of similar sound meaning "truth" or "faithfulness," hence the meaning "be it true" or "so be it." An Old Testament illustration of its use is found in Isaiah 65:16 in the twice repeated phrase "the God of truth." Christ is called "the Amen" in Revelation 3:14, with the added ascription "the faithful and true witness." In John 14:6 Christ said, "I am the way, the truth, and the life."

> 1:8 I am Alpha and Omega, the beginning and the ending, saith the Lord, which is, and which was, and which is to come, the Almighty.

In concluding the salutation in verse 8, Christ is quoted as declaring Himself to be the Alpha and the Omega, the first and last letters of the Greek alphabet, and "the beginning and the ending," that is, the eternal One. The eternity, present power, and future glory of Christ are in view. The description of the Father given in verse 4 is then repeated concluding with the title "the Almighty" (Gr., *pantocratōr*), a word which occurs ten times in the New Testament, nine instances being in Revelation. It is probable that verse 8 applies to Christ and the ascription of eternity of verse 4 to the Father. There is no reason, however, why eternity should not be ascribed to Christ as well as to the Father (cf. Rev. 1:10–18; 22:12–13).

Jesus Christ is the central figure of the opening eight verses of Revelation. As the Source of revelation He is presented in verse 1. As the Channel of the word and testimony of God He is cited in verse 2. His blessings through His revealed word are promised in verse 3. In verse 5 He is the faithful Witness, the Firstborn of the dead, and the Ruler of the kings of the earth. He is revealed to be the source of all grace who loves us and cleanses us from our sins through His shed blood. He is the source of our royal priesthood who has the right to gather in Himself all glory and dominion forever. He is promised to come with clouds, attended with great display of power and glory, and every eye shall see the One who died for men. He is the Almighty One of eternity past and eternity future. If no more had been written than that contained in this introductory portion of chapter 1, it would have constituted a tremendous restatement of the person and work of Christ such as found in no comparable section of Scripture.

THE VISION OF CHRIST GLORIFIED (1:9–18)

> 1:9 I John, who also am your brother, and companion in tribulation, and in the kingdom and patience of Jesus Christ, was in the isle that is called Patmos, for the word of God, and for the testimony of Jesus Christ.

The important facts which form the background for the revelation are introduced at this point. Though John mentions his name twice before, this is the first of three instances of the expression "I John" (cf. 21:2; 22:8). In the Gospel of John he refers to himself as "the disciple which testifieth of these things" (John 21:24). In his epistles John describes himself as an elder (II John 1; III John 1). Here John describes himself only as "brother, and companion" of the seven churches in their trouble. He was of course well known to the churches to whom the book is addressed. He was bound by ties of spiritual life and kinship and therefore was a companion (partaker or sharer) with them in their time of tribulation. He shared not only trouble, however, but their place "in the kingdom and patience" in Jesus. In the Greek text the expression is more compact by omission of prepositions, hence reading, "brother and companion in tribulation, kingdom, and patience in Jesus."[3] The word *patience* (Gr., *hypomonē*) connotes the hope of faith which issues in endurance. The best texts omit the word *Christ*. John himself is in trial, being in exile on the Isle of Patmos because of his active preaching of the Word of God and his testimony concerning Jesus Christ (cf. I Peter 4:12–19).

The exile of John to the Isle of Patmos is in itself a moving story of devotion to Christ crowned with suffering. This small island, rocky and forbidding in its terrain, about ten miles long and six miles wide, is located in the Aegean Sea southwest of Ephesus just beyond the Island of Samos. Early church fathers such as Irenaeus, Clement of Alexandria, and Eusebius state that John was sent to this island as an exile under the ruler Domitian. (See Introduction.) According to Victorinus, John, though aged, was forced to labor in the mines located at Patmos. Early sources also indicate that about A.D. 96, at Domitian's death, John was allowed to return to Ephesus when the Emperor Nerva was in power.

It was in these bleak circumstances, shut off from friends and human fellowship, that John was given the most extensive revelation of future things shown to any writer of the New Testament. Though men could circumscribe his human activities, they could not bind the Spirit of God nor the testimony of Jesus Christ. John's experiences paralleled those of the Old Testament prophets. Moses wrote the Pentateuch in the wilderness. David wrote many psalms while being pursued by Saul. Isaiah lived in difficult days and died a martyr's death. Ezekiel wrote in exile. Jeremiah's life was one of trial and persecution. Peter wrote his two letters shortly before martyrdom. Thus in the will of God the final written revelation was given to John while suffering for Christ and the gospel.

> **1:10-11** I was in the Spirit on the Lord's day, and heard behind me a great voice, as of a trumpet, Saying, I am Alpha and Omega, the first and the last: and, What thou seest, write in a book, and send it unto the seven churches which are in Asia; unto Ephesus, and unto

[3] Henry Alford comments at length on the order of the words *tribulation, kingdom,* and *patience.* He states that the probable significance is that "the tribulation brings in the kingdom (Acts 14:22), and then as a corrective to the idea that the kingdom in its blessed fulness was yet present, the *hypomonē* is subjoined" (*The Greek New Testament,* IV, 553).

Smyrna, and unto Pergamos, and unto Thyatira, and unto Sardis, and unto Philadelphia, and unto Laodicea.

John's statement in verse 10 that he was in the Spirit refers to his experience of being carried beyond normal sense into a state where God could reveal supernaturally the contents of this book. Such was the experience of Ezekiel (Ezek. 2:2; 3:12, 14; etc.), Peter (Acts 10:10–11; 11:5), and Paul (Acts 22:17–18).

The expression "on the Lord's day" has been taken by some to refer to the first day of the week, by others to the day of the Lord. The word *Lord* in this passage is actually an adjective, used in the sense of "lordian." Though today the expression is used commonly of the first day of the week, it is nowhere so used in the Bible. The day of Christ's resurrection is consistently referred to as "the first day of the week" and never as the Lord's day (Matt. 28:1; Mark 16:2, 9; Luke 24:1; John 20:1, 19; Acts 20:7; I Cor. 16:2). It is true that the same adjective (Gr., *kyriakos*) is found in I Corinthians 11:20 referring to the Lord's Supper characteristically observed by the early church on the first day of the week. Moulton and Milligan also call attention to the fact that the word is frequently used outside the Bible in the sense of "imperial" and cite Deissmann: "that the distinctive title 'Lord's Day' may have been connected with the conscious feelings of protest against the cult of the Emperor with its 'Emperor's Day.' "[4]

There is no solid evidence, however, that the expression used by John was ever intended to refer to the first day of the week. It is rather a reference to the day of the Lord of the Old Testament, an extended period of time in which God deals in judgment and sovereign rule over the earth.[5] The adjectival form can be explained on the ground that in the Old Testament there was no adjectival form for "Lord," and therefore the noun had to be used. The New Testament term is therefore the equivalent to the Old Testament expression "the day of the Lord."

On the basis of the evidence, the interpretation is therefore preferred that John was projected forward to the future day of the Lord. It is questionable in any case whether the amazing revelation given in the entire book could have been conveyed to John in one twenty-four-hour day, and it is more probable that it consisted of a series of revelations. Although John was far removed from fellow Christians and the possibility of spiritual fellowship, he was given instead the transcending experience of seeing the Lord in glory and the unique revelations contained in the book he wrote.[6]

[4]James Moulton and George Milligan, *Vocabulary of the Greek New Testament*, p. 364, citing Deissmann, *Light from the Ancient East*, cf. pp. 362–64.
[5]E. W. Bullinger, *The Apocalypse*, pp. 9–15.
[6]William Hoste, who considers the Lord's day here as the first day of the week, holds that the expression "the Lordian day" is distinct from "the day of the Lord"

While in the Spirit, John heard a great voice as of a trumpet. The speaker is identified in verse 11 as the "Alpha and Omega, the first and the last." This is undoubtedly a reference to Christ (cf. 1:8, 17). Some texts omit this description of Christ and begin immediately with "what thou seest." John is given the command to write what he sees in keeping with 1:2. The command to write, found twelve times in the book, indicates that John was to write after seeing each vision, in contrast to 10:4, where he is told not to write. The message of the entire book is to be sent to each of the seven churches along with the particular message to the individual church. The seven churches are mentioned in the order of the letters of chapters 2 and 3, based on their location geographically. There seems to have been no superintending organization over these seven churches at this time, and Christ deals directly with the local church. For the location and characteristics of each of these seven churches, see chapters 2 and 3.

> **1:12** And I turned to see the voice that spake with me. And being turned, I saw seven golden candlesticks.

The unusual expression, "I turned to see the voice that spake with me," in verse 12 is obviously a figure of speech meaning that he turned to see the one who spoke. Having turned, he sees the seven candlesticks. John then records the vision, "I saw seven golden candlesticks," more accurately translated "seven golden lampstands." In the Tabernacle and in the Temple one of the items of equipment was a seven-branched lampstand, a single stand with three lamps on each side and one lamp in the center forming the central shaft. It would seem from the description here that instead of one lampstand with seven lamps there are seven separate lampstands each made of gold and arranged in a circle.

The symbolism of the lampstands is explained in verse 20. The seven lampstands represent the seven churches and are significant symbols of the churches in their principal function of giving forth light. The golden metal, as in the Tabernacle and Solomon's Temple, represents the deity and glory of Christ, and the implied olive oil is symbolic of the power of the Spirit issuing in witness.

> **1:13-16** And in the midst of the seven candlesticks one like unto the Son of man, clothed with a garment down to the foot, and girt about the paps with a golden girdle. His head and his hairs were white like wool, as white as snow; and his eyes were as a flame of fire; And his feet like unto fine brass, as if they burned in a furnace; and his voice as the sound of many waters. And he had in his right hand

because of the fact of the differing expression in the Greek New Testament where the day of the Lord is *he hemera tou kyriou* (cf. I Thess. 5:2; II Thess. 2:2; II Peter 3:10). However, he does not offer any factual evidence that the expression used by John is indeed the first day of the week (*The Visions of John the Divine*, p. 13).

seven stars: and out of his mouth went a sharp twoedged sword: and
his countenance was as the sun shineth in his strength.

Christ is portrayed in verse 13 as in the midst of the lampstands, that is,
in the midst of the seven churches. The title assigned to Him is that of
"the Son of man," a frequent title in the Gospels, but infrequent in Revelation, being found only once more (14:14). The title emphasizes His
humanity and Messianic character.

The description which follows is a symbolic representation of the attributes of Christ in special relationship to the events which are portrayed in the book of Revelation. His being clothed with a garment to
His feet is best explained by the clothing of a priest and judge, like
Aaron's robe being designed "for glory and beauty" (Exodus 28:2). The
golden girdle corresponds to that used by the high priest to bind his
garments higher on the body than at the loins. Josephus explains this as
being in keeping with the dignity and majesty of the high priest and as
being designed to allow greater freedom in movement. The golden girdle
corresponds to the girdle of the high priest which has golden thread in it,
but here it is made entirely of gold. The somber presence of Christ in
His role as judge and priest in the midst of the churches is a significant
introduction to chapters 2 and 3.

The graphic description of Christ given in verse 14 and following
verses portrays various aspects of His deity. The fact that His head and
His hair are as white as snow corresponds to the vision of God described
in Daniel 7:9, where "the ancient of days did sit, whose garment was
white as snow, and the hair of his head like the pure wool." The reference to the fact that "his eyes were as a flame of fire; and his feet unto
fine brass, as if they burned in a furnace" corresponds to Daniel's description: "his throne was like the fiery flames, and his wheels as burning
fire." The Ancient of Days in Daniel's vision (Dan. 7:13–14) is represented to be the Father or the First Person of the Trinity to whom the
Son of Man, that is, Christ, comes to receive power and authority over
the entire world. The attributes of the Father, however, are also attributes of the Son to whom power and authority have been given and
who with the Father possesses all the attributes of God.

The fact that His head and His hair are white like snow seems to have
the primary significance of complete purity rather than age, but may
imply also the eternity of the Son of Man in His divine nature. His eyes
as a flame of fire speak of the searching righteousness and divine judgment upon all that is impure. This is further emphasized in verse 15
where His feet are described like unto fine brass burning in a furnace.
The metal described as brass or, more properly, bronze (a copper alloy),
symbolizes divine judgment as embodied in the Old Testament types of

the brazen altar and other items of brass used in connection with sacrifice for sin (cf. Exodus 38:30). The burning brass, which may be taken as highly refined brass, represents Christ standing in the midst of the churches on the basis of divine and righteous judgment portrayed both in the fire and in the metal mentioned. Representation of His attributes is completed by the declaration that "his voice" boomed "as the sound of many waters." The scene which John saw is accompanied by the tremendous sound of many waters used to describe the thundering voice of the Son of God revealing the majesty and power before which human authority must bow.

Three additional aspects of the revelation are mentioned in verse 16. John records that in the right hand of the Son of God were seven stars. Stauffer relates the seven stars to a gold coin minted in A.D. 83 by Domitian, picturing the dead child of Domitian

> sitting on the globe of heaven, playing with the stars. The legend runs DIVUS CAESAR IMP DOMITIANI F—the divine Caesar, son of the Emperor Domitian. The seven stars indicate the seven planets, a symbol of heavenly dominion over the world.[7]

The symbolism of the seven planets originated in Crete where the mythical god Zeus was born. On Cretan coins he is shown playing on a heavenly globe, symbolizing a rule over the world from heaven. Stauffer further observes,

> In the context of Domitian's whole coinage this means that the imperial Zeus child, who has been exalted to be lord of the stars, ushers in the age of universal salvation which is to come.[8]

The mystery of the seven stars is defined in the Scriptures, however, in verse 20: "The seven stars are the angels of the seven churches." The heavenly messengers ordinarily indicated by the word *angel* seem here to refer to messengers from the seven churches, rather than to the seven stars on Domitian's coins. It is possible that these messengers had come actually to the Isle of Patmos, but it is more probable that they refer to the leaders in these churches to whom the messages primarily are addressed. The spiritual significance is that these angels are messengers who are responsible for the spiritual welfare of these seven churches and are in the right hand of the Son of Man, indicating possession, protection, and sovereign control. As the churches were to emit light as a lampstand, the leaders of the churches were to project light as stars.

Christ is described as having a sharp two-edged sword proceeding out of His mouth, representing divine judgment corresponding to that given

[7]Ethelbert Stauffer, *Christ and the Caesars*, p. 152.
[8]*Ibid.*

in Revelation 19:15 where it is recorded, "And out of his mouth goeth a sharp sword, that with it he should smite the nations." As Vegetius stated, the Romans were accustomed to using the sword as a principal weapon of offense. They were instructed to use it in such a way as not to expose themselves to a thrust from their enemy. They were to employ the sword in a stabbing action, as a stroking movement with its edge would seldom kill an enemy. The objective was to kill, not merely to wound. Hence, as used here in Revelation, it implies slaying the wicked.[9] The particular word used for *sword* (Gr., *romphaia*) here refers to a long and heavy sword mentioned five other times in the book of Revelation. By contrast, a different word for sword is used in Hebrews 4:12 where it speaks of the Word of God as "quick, and powerful, and sharper than any twoedged sword." The sword mentioned in Revelation has the character of a sword of devastating judgment rather than a sword uncovering unbelief as in Hebrews 4:12, and indicates the omnipotence and sovereignty of the Son of Man.

The concluding reference in verse 16 is to the brilliant glory of His countenance represented by the sun shining in his strength. The bright light which seems to attend the glory of God was that which blinded Paul on the road to Damascus and that which is the terror of the sinner as well as the assurance of the saint. In their glorified body, saints will be able to see the glory of God. The assurance is given in I John 3:2: "We know that, when he shall appear, we shall be like him; for we shall see him as he is." In this revelation of the Son of Man are seen the attributes of omnipotence, righteousness, sovereignty, majesty, truth, and love.

> **1:17-18** And when I saw him, I fell at his feet as dead. And he laid his right hand upon me, saying unto me, Fear not; I am the first and the last: I am he that liveth, and was dead; and, behold I am alive for evermore, Amen; and have the keys of hell and of death.

The majesty and the glory of the vision as seen by John were such that he records in verse 17, "And when I saw him, I fell at his feet as dead." In contrast to those periods of intimate fellowship which characterized John's relationship with Christ in His earthly life when frequently John laid his head upon the bosom of the Saviour and had intimate fellowship with Him, John is now in the presence of the glorified Son of God whose power and majesty are no longer veiled and whose righteousness is revealed to be a consuming fire.

The revelation of God and His glory on other occasions in the Bible had a similar stunning effect, as illustrated in the case of Abraham (Gen. 17:3), Manoah (Judges 13:20), Ezekiel (Ezek. 3:23; 43:3; 44:4), Daniel

[9]Flavius Vegetius Renatus, *The Military Institutions of the Romans,* pp. 19-21.

(Dan. 8:17; 10:8–9, 15–17), and the disciples on the mount of transfiguration (Matt. 17:6). Those who do not fall down before God at the revelation of His glory and majesty are brought to immediate self-judgment and reverent fear as illustrated in the case of Gideon (Judges 6:22–23), Job (Job 42:5–6), Isaiah (Isa. 6:5), Zacharias (Luke 1:12), and Peter (Luke 5:8). In compassion toward the disciple whom He loved, Christ "laid his right hand" upon John and assured him, "Fear not; I am the first and the last" (Rev. 1:17). The very sovereignty of God revealed in the earlier verses, though the terror of the wicked, is the comfort of the saint.

In verses 17 and 18 the eternity of Christ is described in the expression "the first and the last" found in some texts in verse 11. As the eternal One, He is the One who lives (present tense, i.e., "lives continually"), who in time died, and in resurrection is "alive for evermore." As the One who conquered death, He has "the keys of hell and of death."

The expression "was dead" is literally "became dead," the state of death, in contrast to His being alive from eternity past and living on into eternal future.

The statement that He has the keys of hell and of death implies that He is sovereign over physical death which terminates life in this world as well as over hell (Gr., *hades*), the life after death. The Greek word *hades* commonly translated "hell" refers to the intermediate state and is to be distinguished from the lake of fire or Gehenna, which refers to the eternal state. To avoid confusion it is better to transliterate the word *hades* and to use the word *hell* as referring to the eternal state only. The confusion is in the translation, not the original.

In His death and resurrection, Christ wrested from Satan any authority the devil may have had over death (cf. Heb. 2:14–15). In some texts the order is reversed to read, "and have the keys of death and hell." As Christ possesses the key or authority over death, no man can die apart from divine permission even though afflicted by Satan and in trial and trouble. As the One who is in authority over Hades, Christ is sovereign over the life to come.

John Commissioned to Write (1:19-20)

1:19-20 Write the things which thou hast seen, and the things which are, and the things which shall be hereafter; The mystery of the seven stars which thou sawest in my right hand, and the seven golden candlesticks. The seven stars are the angels of the seven churches: and the seven candlesticks which thou sawest are the seven churches.

John, restored to normal activity, is commanded in verse 19, "Write the things which thou hast seen, and the things which are, and the things which shall be hereafter." Though many outlines have been suggested for the book of Revelation, none seems to be more practical or illuminating than the threefold outline given here.[10] The things referred to as having already been seen are those contained in chapter 1 where John had his preliminary vision. This vision, of course, introduces the main subject of the entire book, Jesus Christ the glorious coming King. The second division, "the things which are," most naturally includes chapters 2 and 3 with the seven messages Christ delivered to the churches. This contemporary situation gives the historical context for the revelation which follows. The third division, "the things which shall be hereafter," would naturally include the bulk of the book which was to be prophetic as anticipated in 1:3 in the expression "the words of this prophecy."

The advantage of this outline is that it deals in a natural way with the material rather than seizing on incidentals as some expositors have done or avoiding any outline at all, as is true of other expositors. It is not too much to claim that this outline is the only one which allows the book to speak for itself without artificial manipulation and which lays guidelines of sufficient importance so that expositors who follow this approach have been able to establish a system of interpretation of the book of Revelation, namely, the futurist school. It is significant that practically all other approaches to the book of Revelation yield widely differing interpretations in which there is little uniformity when one interpreter is compared to the next. The futurist school at least agrees on some of its main lines of interpretation.

The decision to follow this outline is a major one and can only be supported by the self-consistency of the interpretation of the book as a whole to which it gives rise. Further support will also be found in the exposition of chapter 4 with its evidence for prophecy of future events.

Criswell, commenting on the threefold outline here, states,

> Is there a key to this book from God? Does God have an analysis of it? Does God have an interpretation? Is there something from heaven by which we can study the meaning of these visions? Yes, there is. When I was a student in school, I remember some lecturers saying that there was a key to the interpretation and the meaning of the Revelation, possessed in ancient times, but that key has been lost and we do not possess it today. Therefore, those lecturers concluded, the book is an enigma to us. I have learned just the opposite of that as I have studied the book. The same key that those first and primitive Christians had in the Roman province of Asia to whom the letters were addressed, we have today; because the key is written here in the first chapter of the book itself. This is the grand foundation. This is the great starting point. This is the key to the meaning of this vast outline of God's future.[11]

[10]See Lewis S. Chafer, *Systematic Theology*, IV, 297.
[11]W. A. Criswell, *Expository Sermons on Revelation*, p. 177.

Baines, while accepting the threefold division of Revelation based on verse 19, notes that the "things which thou hast seen" is by nature of introduction; "the things which are" is properly the first division. The second division relates to judgments falling on the earth before the second advent, followed by the third division dealing with the reign of Christ, the millennium, and the eternal state.[12]

The concluding verse in chapter 1 gives the key to the symbolism of the preceding revelation. The mystery of the seven stars is revealed to be a representation of the messengers to the churches, and the seven golden lampstands are the churches themselves. It is significant as indicated in this verse that the revelation embodied in this book, though often in symbols, is designed to reveal truth, not to hide it. Though all the symbols are not explained, in the great majority of cases the symbols are interpreted in one way or another in the Word of God.

The first chapter, emphasizing as it does the glory of Christ, is in essence the theme of the entire book moving progressively to the climax, the second coming of Christ in power and glory to the earth, in chapter 19. The spiritual significance of the person of Christ and His coming to judge the world is applied in chapters 2 and 3 to the spiritual problems of the contemporary church, and forms the second major division of the entire book.

[12]T. B. Baines, *The Revelation of Jesus Christ*, p. 2.

2

THE LETTERS TO EPHESUS, SMYRNA, PERGAMOS, AND THYATIRA

INTRODUCTION

IN THE SECOND CHAPTER of the book of Revelation the second major division of the book begins. As previously mentioned, chapter 1 seems to fulfill the command of 1:19, "Write the things which thou hast seen." Beginning in chapter 4, the material deals with "the things which shall be hereafter" (1:19). In chapters 2 and 3 the messages to the seven churches are referred to as "the things which are" (cf. 1:19). These messages, therefore, contain divine revelation and exhortation pertaining to the present age; and, having special pertinence in the present situation in the church, they constitute one of the most incisive and penetrating exhortations in the entire New Testament in relation to church doctrine and Christian living.

It is remarkable that so little attention has been paid to the importance of these two chapters. Archbishop Trench is cited by Seiss as lamenting that the Church of England omits reference to any of the material in these two chapters in portions selected for use in public services. Trench writes,

> It is . . . to be regretted that while every chapter of every other book of the New Testament is set forth to be read in the Church, and, wherever there is daily service, is read in the Church, three times in the year, and some, or portions of some, oftener, while even of the Apocalypse itself two chapters and portions of others have been admitted into the service, under no circumstances whatever can the second and third chapters ever be heard in the congregation.[1]

In the revival of interest in eschatology in the twentieth century there has been a partial remedy of the previous neglect of the book of Revelation including special attention to the messages to the seven churches. Recent studies such as *The Postman of Patmos* by C. A. Hadjiantoniou have helped to dramatize the living character of these letters in the modern church, and the attention to their contribution has been duly

[1]Richard Chenevix Trench, *Epistles to the Seven Churches*, p. 10, cited by J. A. Seiss, *The Apocalypse*, p. 67.

given by competent New Testament scholars. It remains true, however, that many casual worshipers in Christian churches today who are quite familiar with the Sermon on the Mount are not aware of the existence of these seven messages of Christ. Their incisive character and pointed denunciation of departure from biblical morality and theology have tended to keep them out of the mainstream of contemporary theological thought. Many of the evils and shortcomings which exist in the church today are a direct outgrowth of neglect of the solemn instruction given to these seven churches.

There has been some debate concerning the theological significance of these seven churches. It is obvious, as there were many churches located in the area where these churches were found, that God divinely selected seven and seven only, and did not send messages to other churches that conceivably might have been more important. Swete states that there were from five hundred to one thousand townships in the province of Asia in the first century, some of them far larger than the cities of Thyatira and Philadelphia, and undoubtedly a number of them had Christian churches.[2] He suggests that the answer to the problem of selection is found in the geographical location of the seven churches in the form of a gentle arch and located on a circular road connecting the most populous part of the province. The messages directed to these seven churches should therefore be considered as sent to the rest of the province and other churches as well.

The geographical order of presentation is followed, beginning at Ephesus, moving north to Smyrna, then farther north to Pergamos, then east to Thyatira, south to Sardis, east to Philadelphia, and southeast to Laodicea. However, other churches in the area were ignored, such as the church at Colossae and the churches at Magnesia (Manisa) and Tralles. It is understandable that the number of churches should be limited to seven as this is the number of completeness or universality in the Scripture, but there undoubtedly were other principles which determined the selection.

First of all, each church needed a particular message, and the spiritual state of each church corresponded precisely to the exhortation which was given. The selection of the churches was also governed by the fact that each church was in some way normative and illustrated conditions common in local churches at that time as well as throughout later history. The messages to the seven churches therefore embody admonition suitable for churches in many types of spiritual need. Along with the messages to the churches were exhortations which are personal in character constituting instruction and warning to the individual Christian. Each of

[2]Henry B. Swete, *The Apocalypse of St. John*, pp. lvii–lviii.

the messages as given to the churches therefore ends in a personal exhortation beginning with the phrase "He that hath an ear, let him hear."

Many expositors believe that in addition to the obvious implication of these messages the seven churches represent the chronological development of church history viewed spiritually. They note that Ephesus seems to be characteristic of the Apostolic Period in general and that the progression of evil climaxing in Laodicea seems to indicate the final state of apostasy of the church. This point of view is postulated upon a providential arrangement of these churches not only in a geographical order but by divine purpose, presenting also a progress of Christian experience corresponding to church history. As in all scriptural illustrations, however, it is obvious that every detail of the messages addressed to these particular churches is not necessarily fulfilled in succeeding periods of church history. What is claimed is that there does seem to be a remarkable progression in the messages. It would seem almost incredible that such a progression should be a pure accident, and the order of the messages to the churches seems to be divinely selected to give prophetically the main movement of church history.

Milligan is quite opposed to the idea that the seven churches represent chronological periods:

> If we examine the tables of such a period drawn up by different inquirers, we shall find them so utterly divergent as to prove fatal to the principle upon which they are constructed. No one has been able to prepare a chronological scheme making even an approach to general acceptance. The history of the Church can not be portioned off into seven successive periods marked by characteristics to which those noted in the seven epistles correspond. Besides this, the whole idea rests upon that historical interpretation of the Apocalypse which is simply destructive both of the meaning and influence of the book.[3]

The prophetic interpretation of the messages to the seven churches, to be sure, should not be pressed beyond bounds, as it is a deduction from the content, not from the explicit statement of the passage. It is fully in keeping with the futurist point of view rather than the historic, as Milligan claims. It is not necessary to hold, as some have, that without the second and third chapters of the book of Revelation the church would be left without instruction regarding its progress in the present age. Other passages such as I Timothy 4 and II Peter 2–3 give information on this subject.

Much additional light, however, is given by a study of the messages to the seven churches, and the general trend indicated confirms other Scripture that, instead of progressive improvement and a trend toward righteousness and peace in the church age, it may be expected that the

[3]William Milligan, *Discussions on the Apocalypse,* p. 269.

age will end in failure as symbolized in the church of Laodicea. This is taught expressly in passages describing the growing apostasy in the professing church culminating in the apostate Christendom of the time of the great tribulation. Simultaneous with this development in the church as a whole there will be fulfillment of the divine plan of God in calling out a true church designed to be a holy bride for the Son of God and a promised translation from the earth before the final tragic scenes of the tribulation are enacted.

Each message addressed to the seven churches of Asia has its own distinctive characteristics, but there are also many similarities. Each message begins with the expression "I know thy works." Each offers a promise, "to him that overcometh." Although there is variation in the order, each has the same concluding sentence, "He that hath an ear, let him hear what the Spirit saith unto the churches." Each of the messages begins with an introduction in which the Lord Jesus is described, but in each message the description differs in keeping with the message addressed to the church. Most of the letters to the churches contain words of warning as well as promise to those who hear and respond. In general, these messages are letters of reproof, rebuke, and reassurance.

The Letter to Ephesus: The Church Without Love (2:1–7)

2:1 Unto the angel of the church of Ephesus write; These things saith he that holdeth the seven stars in his right hand, who walketh in the midst of the seven golden candlesticks;

Christ the Sovereign Judge. The first letter is addressed to the angel or messenger of the church of Ephesus. The Greek word *aggelos,* which has been transliterated in the English word *angel,* is frequently used in the Bible of angels, and this seems to be its principal use as noted by Arndt and Gingrich.[4] However, it is often used also of men in Greek literature as a whole, and in several instances this word referred to human messengers in the Bible (Matt. 11:10; Mark 1:2; Luke 7:24, 27; 9:52). It is properly understood here as referring to human messengers to these seven churches. These messengers were probably the pastors of these churches or prophets through whom the message was to be delivered to the congregation.

The messenger of the church at Ephesus, which at that time was a large metropolitan city, was undoubtedly an important person and a leader in Christian testimony at that time. When the book of Revelation was written, Ephesus, the most prominent city in the Roman province of Asia, had already had a long history of Christian witness. Paul had ministered there for three years as recorded in Acts 19. The effectiveness of his

[4]William F. Arndt and Wilbur F. Gingrich, *A Greek-English Lexicon of the New Testament,* s.v. *aggelos,* pp. 7–8.

THE REVELATION OF JESUS CHRIST

ministry is stated in Acts 19:10: "All they which dwelt in Asia heard the word of the Lord Jesus, both Jews and Greeks." The preaching of the gospel had affected the worship of Diana, in whose honor the temple of Diana had been built in Ephesus, a structure considered one of the seven wonders of the world. The reduction in the sale of idols of Diana and the Christian teaching that these idols were not worthy of worship resulted in the riot recorded in Acts 19:23–41.

Demetrius, a leader among the silversmiths in Ephesus, called a meeting of his fellow craftsmen and addressed them in these words: "Sirs, ye know that by this craft we have our wealth. Moreover ye see and hear, that not alone at Ephesus, but almost throughout all Asia, this Paul hath persuaded and turned away much people, saying that they be no gods, which are made with hands: So that not only this our craft is in danger to be set at nought; but also that the temple of the great goddess Diana should be despised, and her magnificence should be destroyed, whom all Asia and the world worshippeth" (Acts 19:25–27). The resulting riot forced Paul's departure from Ephesus, but the incident is a remarkable testimony to the power and effectiveness of early Christian witness in this important city.

After Paul's ministry at Ephesus came to a close, evidence indicates that Timothy for many years led the work as superintendent of the churches in the area. There is reason to believe that the Apostle John himself, now exiled on Patmos, had succeeded Timothy as the pastor at large in Ephesus. It was to this church and to Christians living in Ephesus at the close of the first century, some thirty years after Paul, that the first of the seven messages is addressed.

Christ is introduced in the message to Ephesus as the One who "holdeth the seven stars in his right hand, who walketh in the midst of the seven golden candlesticks." This portrayal of Christ corresponding to that given early in the first chapter of Revelation is a symbolic presentation of the fact that Christ holds the messengers of these churches in His right hand, a place of sovereign protection as well as divine authority over them. The word for "hold" (Gr., *kratōn*) means "to hold authoritatively." The messengers, therefore, are held in divine protection and under divine control. Earlier, John had written of the security of the believer in the hands of an Almighty God in John 10:28–29: "And I give unto them eternal life; and they shall never perish, neither shall any man pluck them out of my hand. My Father, which gave them me, is greater than all; and no man is able to pluck them out of my Father's hand." The same truth is presented symbolically in this vision of Christ.

> **2:2-3** I know thy works, and thy labour, and thy patience, and how thou canst not bear them which are evil: and thou hast tried them

which say they are apostles, and are not, and hast found them liars:
And hast borne, and hast patience, and for my name's sake hast la-
boured, and hast not fainted.

Commendation of doctrine and diligence. The second important fact
in this vision, Christ walking in the midst of the seven golden candlesticks or lampstands (Gr., *lychniōn*), symbolizes His presence and observation of the testimony of the churches of Asia. His message to the
church is based on His knowledge of their notable and commendable
works. He mentions their labor or toil, their patience or steadfastness,
their abhorrence of those who were evil, and their ready detection of false
teachers who claimed to be apostles but who were not. These remarkable characteristics are sorely needed in the church today where too
often there is failure to serve the Lord patiently, and the tendency is to
compromise both with moral and theological evil. The Ephesian church
is therefore commended for abhorring that which is morally bad as well
as that which is theologically in error.

In contrast to the fact that they could not bear those who were evil,
he commends them for continuing to bear their proper burdens, repeating
again the fact that they have patience, literally, that they "keep on having
patience," which is an advance on the statement in verse 2. Likewise it
is noted that their labor is motivated as work "for my name's sake" and
that they have not fainted or grown weary. These remarkable characteristics establish the fact that the church had served the Lord well, and
few modern churches could qualify for such commendation.

2:4-5 Nevertheless I have something against thee, because thou
hast left thy first love. Remember therefore from whence thou art
fallen, and repent, and do the first works; or else I will come unto
thee quickly, and will remove thy candlestick out of his place, except
thou repent.

Indictment for lack of devotion. In spite of these most desirable traits
Christ declared that the church at Ephesus had failed in one important
matter, namely, "thou hast left thy first love." In the Greek the order
of the words is especially emphatic in that the object of the verb is before
the verb—"thy first love thou hast left." The word for love (Gr., *agapēn*)
is the deepest and most meaningful word for love found in the Greek
language. Though they had not departed completely from love for God,
their love no longer had the fervency, depth, or meaning it once had had
in the church.

The spiritual problem of the church at Ephesus can best be seen in
the perspective of the threefold nature of man's spiritual poverty. Some
spiritual needs stem from lack of faith in God so that the individual
either falls short of salvation itself, or, if saved, he lacks an abiding

dependence on God and the promises of His Word. This constitutes a defect in the area of the intellect or in theology. The second problem of spiritual experience is in the exercise of human will. Many who have trusted in God have never yielded themselves completely to God, and as a result have not been filled with the Spirit. There is no indication that the church had seriously fallen short in either of these two spiritual areas. Their defect was a matter of heart rather than of head or will. The ardor which they once had had grown cold.

In the letter to the Ephesians, written some thirty years before in the early days of the history of this church, Paul commended them for their love for all saints. He wrote at that time, "Wherefore I also, after I heard of your faith in the Lord Jesus, and love unto all the saints, Cease not to give thanks for you, making mention of you in my prayers" (Eph. 1:15–16). The church seems to have fulfilled the same commendable qualities found in the apostolic church in Jerusalem. The period following Pentecost, described in Acts 2, was characterized by love and devotion for Christ Himself, a love for the Word of God, a love manifested in fellowship with the saints and in their prayer to God, and a love expressed in commendation to Timothy of "all them also that love his appearing" (II Tim. 4:8).

The church at Ephesus was now in its second generation of Christians, those who had come into the church in the thirty years since Paul had ministered in their midst. Though they continued to labor faithfully as those who had preceded them, the love of God which characterized the first generation was missing. This cooling of heart which had overtaken them in relationship to God was a dangerous forerunner of spiritual apathy which later was to erase all Christian testimony in this important center of Christian influence. Thus it has ever been in the history of the church: first a cooling of spiritual love, then the love of God replaced by a love for the things of the world, with resulting compromise and spiritual corruption. This is followed by departure from the faith and loss of effective spiritual testimony.

In other portions of Scripture the danger of fading love for God is described. In Paul's first letter to Timothy he wrote, "For the love of money is the root of all evil: which while some coveted after, they have erred from the faith, and pierced themselves through with many sorrows" (I Tim. 6:10). In similar vein the Apostle John wrote in one epistle, "Love not the world, neither the things that are in the world. If any man love the world, the love of the Father is not in him" (I John 2:15). The danger of substituting love for idols for love for God is stated in the closing verse of the same epistle: "Little children, keep yourselves from idols" (I John 5:21). Even loved ones can stand between the child of God and his love for his heavenly Father. Christ Himself said, "He that loveth father or mother more than me is not worthy of me: and he that loveth son or daughter more than me is not worthy of me" (Matt. 10:37). Even the God-given institution of marriage can stand in the way of a true love for God. As Paul wrote to the Corinthians, "The unmarried woman careth for the things of the Lord, that she may be holy both in body and in spirit: but she that is married careth for the things of the world, how she may please her husband" (I Cor. 7:34). Whatever the object of love, anything which hinders a true love for God may cause a Christian to lose his first love even as was true of Ephesus so long ago.

To correct the spiritual declension into which they had fallen, the Lord directs three urgent exhortations. First He commands, "Remember therefore from whence thou art fallen." To correct any departure from God the first step is to go back to the place of departure. Ephesian Christians were therefore exhorted to remember the ardor which once gripped their hearts, the causes for it, the wonder of their newfound salvation, and the joy and satisfaction that were theirs in Christ. So often spiritual defection, whether of mind or heart, comes from forgetting that which once was known. The second aspect of his exhortation is embodied in the word *repent* (Gr., *metanoēson*, meaning "to change the mind"). They were to have a different attitude toward Christ and should resume that fervent love which once they had. In keeping with these first two exhortations the final one is embodied in the words "do the first works." A true love for God is always manifested in the works which it produces. Though the Ephesian church had been faithful in many appointed tasks, these did not in themselves reflect a true love for God. They were not merely bondslaves of Jesus Christ bound by legal obligation, but they were those whose hearts had been given to the Saviour.

The Ephesian Christians were also sharply warned that if they did not heed the exhortation, they could expect sudden judgment and removal of the candlestick. As Alford comments, this is "not Christ's final coming, but His coming in special judgment is here indicated."[5] The meaning seems to be that He would remove the church as a testimony for Christ. This, of course, was tragically fulfilled ultimately. The church retained its vigor for several centuries and was not only the seat of Eastern bishops but also the meeting place of the third General Council which took place in A.D. 431 and was held in the Church of Saint Mary, whose ruins are still extant today. Ephesus declined as a city, however, after the fifth century, and the Turks deported its remaining inhabitants in the fourteenth century. The city, now uninhabited, is one of the important ruins in that area, located seven miles from the sea due to accumula-

[5]Henry Alford, *The Greek New Testament*, IV, 563.

tion of silt which has stopped up the harbor of this once important seaport.

2:6 But this thou hast, that thou hatest the deeds of the Nicolaitanes, which I also hate.

Commendation of hating the enemies of truth. Coupled with the exhortation to repent is the final word of approbation in verse 6 in which the Ephesian church is commended for hating the deeds of the Nicolaitans. Much scholarly speculation has arisen concerning the precise nature of this group's error.[6] The Nicolaitans apparently were a sect, and some have interpreted their name as meaning "conquering of the people" from *nikaō*, meaning "to conquer" and *laos*, meaning "the people." This view considers the Nicolaitans as the forerunners of the clerical hierarchy superimposed upon the laity and robbing them of spiritual freedom. Others have considered them as a licentious sect advocating complete freedom in Christian conduct including participation in heathen feasts and free love. Alford states, "The prevailing opinion among the fathers was, that they were a sect founded by Nicolaus the proselyte of Antioch, one of the seven deacons."[7] Alford believes that this is substantially correct, and that it is supported by the statement "which I also hate" (v. 6) concerning which Alford states, "This strong expression in the mouth of our Lord unquestionably points at deeds of abomination and impurity: cf. Isa. 61:8; Jer. 44:4; Amos 5:21; Zech. 8:17."[8] That which was hated by the Ephesians was embraced by the church at Pergamos according to Revelation 2:15. Whatever the precise nature of this sect, it is noteworthy that a true love for God involves a fervent hate of that which counterfeits and distorts the purity of biblical truth. David raised the same question when he wrote, "Do not I hate them, O LORD, that hate thee? and am not I grieved with those that rise up against thee? I hate them with perfect hatred: I count them mine enemies" (Ps. 139:21–22). Though the Christian, like God, should love the world in the sense of desiring to extend to it the benefits of salvation, like David he should hate those who are the enemies of God.

2:7 He that hath an ear, let him hear what the Spirit saith unto the churches; To him that overcometh will I give to eat of the tree of life, which is in the midst of the paradise of God.

The invitation and promise. The letter to the Ephesians, like the other six letters, closes with an invitation and a promise: "He that hath an ear, let him hear what the Spirit saith unto the churches." Though the message is directed to the church as such through its pastor, the individual

[6]Cf. Scofield Reference Bible, note 1, p. 1332.
[7]Alford, IV, 563.
[8]*Ibid.*, IV, 564–65.

is urged to respond to the exhortation and warning. So it is ever that God speaks to the ones who will hear.

Similarly to the closing messages to other churches, the message to the church at Ephesus contains a promise given to those who overcome: "To him that overcometh will I give to eat of the tree of life, which is in the midst of the paradise of God." The promise here mentioned for overcomers is not a message to a special group of Christians distinguished by their spirituality and power in contrast to genuine Christians who lack these qualities; it is rather a general description of that which is normal, to be expected among those who are true followers of the Lord. The Apostle John in his first epistle asks, "Who is he that overcometh the world?" (I John 5:5). He answers the question, "He that believeth that Jesus is the Son of God." In other words, those in the Ephesian church who were genuine Christians and by this token had overcome the unbelief and sin of the world are promised the right to the tree of life which is in the midst of the paradise of God.

This tree, first mentioned in the Garden of Eden in Genesis 3:22, is later found in the midst of the street of the new Jerusalem, where it bears its fruit for the abundant health and life of the nation (Rev. 22:2). It is especially appropriate that those who hate the evil deeds of the world and the idolatrous wicked worship are given that spiritual recompense of abiding in the abundant life which is in Christ in the eternity to come. The gracious nature of the promise is designed to restore and rekindle that love of Christ known in the early fervent days of the church and to be realized without diminishing in the eternity to come.

THE LETTER TO SMYRNA: THE CHURCH IN SUFFERING (2:8–11)

The church of Smyrna was singled out by our Lord for the second of the seven letters. If one traveled from Ephesus to Smyrna, he would cover a distance of about thirty-five miles to the north, entering Smyrna by what was called the "Ephesian Gate." Smyrna was a wealthy city, second only to Ephesus in the entire area and, like Ephesus, a seaport. Unlike Ephesus, which today is uninhabited, Smyrna is still a large city and contains a Christian church. Unger states,

> Anciently it was one of the finest cities of Asia, and was called "The lovely—the crown of Ionia—the ornament of Asia." It is now the chief city of Anatolia, with a mixed population of 200,000 people, one-third of whom are Christians.[9]

In this large and flourishing commercial center was the little church to which this message was sent. Smyrna is mentioned only here in Scripture, but from other literature it is evident that this city was noted for its wickedness and opposition to the Christian gospel in the first century.

[9]Merrill F. Unger, *Unger's Bible Dictionary*, p. 1033.

2:8 And unto the angel of the church in Smyrna write; These things saith the first and the last, which was dead, and is alive;

Christ the Eternal One. To this church our Lord is introduced as the One who is "the first and the last, which was dead, and is alive." In describing Himself as "the first and the last" Christ is relating Himself to time and eternity. He is the eternal God who has always existed in the past and who will always exist in the future. In keeping with this attribute He is also portrayed as the One who was dead, literally, the One "who became dead," referring to His death on the cross. He is also the One who is alive, literally, "who lives," referring to His resurrection as the eternal and resurrected One. He is not only the eternal One in relation to time but the resurrected One in relation to life. In His person He therefore is presented as the eternal One, a description which is prominent in the first chapter in the Revelation as given to John on the Isle of Patmos. The church at Smyrna is told that the One who was eternal became incarnate and died, a reminder that even the eternal Son of God willingly became subject to the rejection and persecution of man. Like Christ, the church at Smyrna should anticipate ultimate victory. Even as the grave could not hold Christ, and He is now described as the One who "lives," symbolizing His triumph over death, rejection, and mistrial, so they too could anticipate their ultimate victory.

These features of the person and work of Christ are especially adapted to constitute words of encouragement to the church at Smyrna which was undergoing great trial and affliction. The word *Smyrna* itself means "myrrh," a sweet perfume used in embalming dead bodies, and included in the holy anointing oil used in the Tabernacle worship in the Old Testament (Exodus 30:23). It was also a common perfume and is mentioned as used by the bridegroom in the Song of Solomon 3:6 where the question is asked, "Who is this that cometh out of the wilderness like pillars of smoke, perfumed with myrrh and frankincense, with all powders of the merchants?" Likewise in Psalm 45:8, the heavenly Bridegroom is described as using myrrh as perfume: "All thy garments smell of myrrh, and aloes, and cassia, out of the ivory palaces, whereby they have made thee glad." The fragrance of Christ as the bridegroom is thus represented typically by the myrrh.

2:9 I know thy works, and tribulation, and poverty, (but thou art rich) and I know the blasphemy of them which say they are Jews, and are not, but are the synagogue of Satan.

Commendation of faithfulness in trial. In the best manuscripts the expression "thy works" is omitted, making the statement much more direct: "I know thy tribulation, and poverty." In referring to their tribulation He assures them that He knows of their oppression by their enemies and its resulting affliction. The word used for "poverty" (Gr., *ptōcheian*) is the word for abject poverty. They were not just poor (Gr., *penia*). It may be that they were drawn from a poor class of people, but it is more probable that their extreme poverty is explained by the fact that they had been robbed of their goods in the process of their persecution and affliction. He quickly reminds them, however, "But thou art rich." In the same spirit James refers to "the poor of this world rich in faith" (James 2:5) using the same Greek words for poverty and riches. Paul used the verb forms of the same words in his statement "as poor, yet making many rich" (II Cor. 6:10).

It would seem that their persecutors were not only pagans, who naturally would be offended by the peculiarities of the Christian faith, but also hostile Jews and Satan himself. Recognition of the opposition of Jews is made in verse 9 where Christ said, "I know the blasphemy of them which say they are Jews, and are not, but are the synagogue of Satan." As Alford observes,

> These slanderers were in all probability actually Jews by birth, but not (see Rom. 2:28; Matt. 3:9; John 8:33; II Cor. 11:22; Phil. 3:4 ff.) in spiritual reality; the same who everywhere, in St. Paul's time and afterwards, were the most active enemies of the Christians.[10]

Alford confirms this interpretation by the account of the martyrdom of Polycarp in which the Jews were active.[11] Thus it has always been in the church; false religion has been most zealous in opposing that which is true. The Smyrna Christians found few friends in the hostile world around them.

> **2:10-11** Fear none of those things which thou shalt suffer: behold, the devil shall cast some of you into prison, that ye may be tried; and ye shall have tribulation ten days: be thou faithful unto death, and I will give thee a crown of life. He that hath an ear, let him hear what the Spirit saith unto the churches; He that overcometh shall not be hurt of the second death.

The exhortation and promise. Their present persecution, however, was only the forerunner of that which was to come. Christ predicted that the devil would cast some of them into prison, doing all in his power to stamp out this testimony in the midst of his domain. Christ indicated that they would be cast into prison and would be tried and would have tribulation ten days. He exhorted them, nevertheless, "Fear none of those things which thou shalt suffer . . . be thou faithful unto death, and I will give thee a crown of life."

Scholars have pondered the allusion to the ten days. If the church at Smyrna is taken as representative of the church in persecution in the

[10]Alford, IV, 566.
[11]*Ibid.*

second or third century, ten days may be representative of this period. W. A. Spurgeon, assuming that the seven churches correspond to church history as a whole, states,

> Is it not obvious that the "ten days" of persecution during which Satan would cast some of this Church into prison, refers to one of the seven church *epochs* to which the seven churches correspond? Then the "ten days" of persecution must refer to the ten persecutions of secular history during which great numbers of Christians were imprisoned and slain. Over these martyrs the *second death* will have no power[12]

Some have found ten specific periods of persecution in these centuries. Walter Scott, who does not hold this view, quotes White in itemizing ten pagan persecutions as follows:

> The *first* under Nero, A.D. 54; the *second* under Domitian, A.D. 81; the *third* under Trajan A.D. 98; the *fourth* under Adrian [Hadrian], A.D. 117; the *fifth* under Septimius Severus, A.D. 193; the *sixth* under Maximin, A.D. 235; the *seventh* under Decius, A.D. 249; the *eighth* under Valerian, A.D. 254; the *ninth* under Aurelian, A.D. 270; the *tenth* under Diocletian, A.D. 284.[13]

The date mentioned is the beginning of the reign of each emperor, not necessarily the beginning of the persecution. Some have applied the "ten days" to the ten years of persecution under Diocletian.

Most commentators such as Swete and Walter Scott take the reference to ten days as a symbolic representation of a specific period of time. Walter Scott writes for instance,

> The expression "ten days" signifies a *limited period,* a brief time inconsistent with the length and period of pagan persecutions covering 250 years. The following reference to "ten days" will confirm the meaning of the term as implying a brief and limited time: Genesis 24:55; Nehemiah 5:18; Daniel 1:12; Acts 25:6; Jeremiah 42:7, etc.[14]

Likewise Alford states, "The expression is probably used to signify a short and limited time."[15] Alford cites scriptural support in the following references: Genesis 24:55; Numbers 11:19; Daniel 1:12; see also Numbers 14:22; I Samuel 1:8; Job 19:3; Acts 25:6.[16] It is clear in any case that the church at Smyrna could expect further persecution including imprisonment for some of their number.

The problem of human suffering raised in the message to the church at Smyrna has occupied the minds of men through the centuries. For those of the Christian faith it is not difficult to understand why the un-

---

[12]*The Conquering Christ,* p. 28.
[13]*Exposition of the Revelation of Jesus Christ,* p. 72, note.
[14]*Ibid.,* p. 69.
[15]Alford, IV, 567.
[16]*Ibid.*

godly should suffer. The question remaining, however, is why the godly should suffer as in the case of the Smyrna church. The answer to this question is largely bound up in the doctrine of the sovereignty of God. The will of God, however, is holy, just, and good. An explanation is given in Scripture for varied aspects of Christian suffering. In some cases, suffering in the life of a child of God may be disciplinary as indicated in God's dealings with the church at Corinth (I Cor. 11:30–32; cf. Heb. 12:3–13). In other cases it may be preventative as illustrated in Paul's thorn in the flesh (II Cor. 12:7). Paul was kept from exulting above measure in the divine revelation given to him through the humiliation of his thorn in the flesh.

Suffering is also represented in Scripture as teaching the child of God what could otherwise remain unlearned. Even Christ is said to have "learned . . . obedience by the things which he suffered" (Heb. 5:8), and for Christians in general the experience of suffering is educative. Paul writes in Romans 5:3-5, "And not only so, but we glory in tribulations also: knowing that tribulation worketh patience; And patience, experience; and experience, hope: And hope maketh not ashamed; because the love of God is shed abroad in our hearts by the Holy Ghost which is given unto us."

Still a further reason for suffering is found in the fact that Christians through suffering can often bear a better testimony for Christ. This was true of Paul of whom it was said in Acts 9:16, "For I will shew him how great things he must suffer for my name's sake." The experience of the church at Smyrna, therefore, though undesired by them, was undoubtedly designed by an infinitely wise and loving God for their good as well as for the better testimony of the gospel.

To this suffering church Christ addresses two exhortations which are His watchword to all in similar circumstances. First, in 2:10 He writes them, "Fear none of those things," which literally translated is "Stop being afraid." They had nothing really to fear in this persecution because it could not rob them of their priceless eternal blessings in Christ. In any case they were in the hands of God. Whatever was permitted was by His wise design. Second, Christ exhorts them, "Be thou faithful unto death," which translated literally is "Become faithful even unto death." Up to this time apparently none of their number had died. They were exhorted to be faithful to the Lord when the test came even if it resulted in their death. Though their own lives might be sacrificed, their real riches were as far removed from this world as the heavens are above the earth. Being faithful unto death, they would be all the more sure that they would receive the crown of life. This is not to be understood as a crown or a reward attending eternal life, but rather that their crown

THE REVELATION OF JESUS CHRIST

would be life eternal itself. These words of encouragement and exhortation no doubt strengthened John himself as he was enduring the rigors of exile on a bleak island in his aged condition.

The persecutions and trials of the church at Smyrna were to be continued, as witnessed not only by the prophecy recorded here but by secular history. According to Ignatius, not long after the book of Revelation was written, Polycarp, the famous early church father, assumed the office of bishop in the church in Smyrna. It may be that he was already pastor of this church.[17] Here he was a minister for many years, finally climaxing his testimony by dying a martyr's death. When asked by his heathen judges to recant his Christian faith, he replied, "Four score and six years have I served the Lord, and He never wronged me: How then can I blaspheme my King and Savior?"[18] The faithfulness of Polycarp to the end seems to have characterized this church in Smyrna in its entire testimony and resulted in this church's continuous faithful witness for God after many others of the early churches had long lost their testimony.

The crown of life is apparently the crown of eternal life. The glories of life eternal stand in contrast to the trials of martyrdom and erase the dark shadows of persecution and death. The crown of life may be contrasted to the other crowns promised the child of God: the crown of righteousness for a godly life (II Tim. 4:8), the crown of glory for faithful shepherds (I Peter 5:4), the crown of gold, the evidence of our redemption (Rev. 4:4), the crown of rejoicing (I Thess. 2:19), believers in heaven won by Paul, and the incorruptible crown (I Cor. 9:25) for self-control in the race of life. The crown follows the cross. Some would limit the crown of life to martyrs, however, as a crown of abundant blessing—a crown of "royal environment," a "symbol of victory," and a "crown of joy."[19]

In concluding the message to the church at Smyrna, the promise is given, "He that overcometh shall not be hurt of the second death." The world in its rejection of the Christian message can inflict martyrdom and terminate life in this world, but those who are faithful in their opportunity to receive Christ in this life are promised that they will not be overcome with the second death, the sad lot of those who depart this life without faith in Jesus Christ as Saviour and Lord. The rich reward of those who are faithful unto death was also the expectation of the Apostle Paul who wrote as he was facing imminent martyrdom, "For I am now ready to be offered, and the time of my departure is at hand. I have fought a good fight, I have finished my course, I have kept the

[17]G. A. Hadjiantoniou, The Postman of Patmos, pp. 34–35.
[18]Jamieson, Fausset, and Brown, A Commentary Critical, Experimental, and Practical on the Old and New Testaments, VI, 662.
[19]Hadjiantoniou, pp. 47–49.

faith: henceforth there is laid up for me a crown of righteousness, which the Lord, the righteous judge, shall give me at that day: and not to me only, but unto all them also that love his appearing" (II Tim. 4:6–8).

Just as the church at Ephesus in large measure is representative of the spiritual state of the church of Jesus Christ in the world at the close of the first century, the fruit of apostolic ministry and faithful labor, so the trials of the church in Smyrna symbolize the persecution and trials the early church endured until the time of Constantine in the beginning of the fourth century. Though beset by many foes and without the power of wealth which characterized the later church, these years witnessed to the purity and fidelity of those who represented Christ.

It is noteworthy that the word of Christ to the church of Smyrna contains no word of rebuke. The very trials that afflicted them assured, them of deliverance from any lack of fervency for the Lord and kept them from any impurity or compromise with evil. Such is the recompense for those who endure trial for Christ in this age. The purifying fires of affliction caused the lamp of testimony to burn all the more brilliantly. The length of their trial, described here as being ten days, whether interpreted literally or not, is short in comparison with the eternal blessings which would be theirs when their days of trial were over. They could be comforted by the fact that the sufferings of this present time do not continue forever, and the blessings that are ours in Christ through His salvation and precious promises will go on through eternity. The second death with its reference to the judgment at the great white throne (Rev. 20:11–15) was not to be their lot, but they were assured eternal blessings in the presence of the Lord.

THE LETTER TO PERGAMOS: THE CHURCH IN COMPROMISE (2:12–17)

2:12 And to the angel of the church in Pergamos write; These saith he which hath the sharp sword with two edges;

Christ the judge of compromise. To the church at Pergamos, or Pergamum, one of the most prominent cities of Asia, the third message of Christ was directed. Located in the western part of Asia Minor north of Smyrna and about twenty miles from the Mediterranean Sea, it was a wealthy city with many temples devoted to idol worship and full of statues, altars, and sacred groves. It was an important religious center where the pagan cults of Athena, Asclepius, Dionysus, and Zeus were prominent. This city was the official residence of the Attalic princes. A university was also located there. Among its famous treasures was a large library of two hundred thousand volumes, later sent to Egypt as a gift from Anthony to Cleopatra. One of the products for which this city was famous was paper or parchment, which seems to have originated here, the paper itself being called *pergamenu*. One of the prominent buildings was the magnificent temple of Esculapius (also spelled *Asklepios*), a pagan god whose idol was in the form of a serpent. Alford observes that some, such as Grotius and Wetstein, interpret the expression "Satan's seat" (v. 13) as referring to this temple.[20] As Alford points out, however, the expression is "Satan's throne" not "the serpent's throne."[21] Alford prefers to leave the expression an undefined allusion to satanic power. Others identify it with the great altar of Zeus that once stood in the city and now may be seen in East Berlin. Although the glory of the ancient city has long since vanished, a small village named Bergama is located below the ruins of the old city. A nominal Christian testimony has continued in the town to modern times.

In this atmosphere completely adverse to Christian testimony was situated the little church to which Christ addressed this letter. As in the messages to the other churches, Christ is introduced in special character: here as the One who "hath the sharp sword with two edges," a description given to Him earlier, in 1:16. Here there is added emphasis by the repeated use of the article before the word *sword* and before each adjective. Christ is described as having the sword, the two-edged one, the sharp one. The sword mentioned is a long spearlike sword, apparently referring to the double-edged character of the Word of God. Reference is made to this spearlike sword seven times in the Bible (Luke 2:35; Rev. 1:16; 2:12, 16; 6:8; 19:15, 21). The last two references in Revelation 19, where it speaks of the sword proceeding from the mouth of Christ in keeping with the introductory description in 1:16, seem to make plain that the sword here refers to the Word of God. Its representation as a double-edged sword indicates on the one hand the sword as the Word of God which separates the ones who are the vessels of grace from condemnation with the world, and which by its promises and message of salvation cuts loose the chains of sin and condemnation which bind the helpless sinner. On the other hand, the same Word of God is the means of condemnation and rejection for those who refuse the message of grace. The Word of God is at once the instrument of salvation and the instrument of death. This twofold character is especially pertinent to the church at Pergamos, which needed to be reminded of the distinct position of those who are true Christians as opposed to those who reject the gospel.

> **2:13** I know thy works, and where thou dwellest, even where Satan's seat is: and thou holdest fast my name, and hast not denied my faith, even in those days wherein Antipas was my faithful martyr, who was slain among you, where Satan dwelleth.

[20]Alford, IV, 568. The pagan mystery cults at Babylon had transferred to Pergamos after the death of Belshazzar, and later moved to Rome (cf. Alexander Hislop, *The Two Babylons*, p. 240).
[21]*Ibid.*

Commendation for holding fast. In verse 13 Christ extends a word of commendation to the church in Pergamos. He first notes the fact that they were dwelling "where Satan's seat is." In the best manuscripts the expression "thy works" is omitted, which gives added emphasis to the fact that "Satan's seat" is the place of their dwelling. The mention of Satan's seat or throne, referred to again at the end of the verse in the expression "where Satan dwelleth," is a reference to satanic power in the evil religious character of the city of Pergamos manifested in persecution of Christians and perhaps epitomized in the worship of Esculapius, the serpent god.

Christ notes that in spite of their evil environment the Pergamos Christians have held fast to His name and have not denied the faith. The reference to "my name" seems to embody a personal loyalty and faith in the Lord Jesus Christ with all that this represented; in addition to this they have not denied the body of Christian truth which accompanies faith in Christ, to which He refers in the expression "my faith." Divine judgment takes into consideration the forces of evil arrayed against the Christian. To those who are found faithful in such circumstances commendation is all the more generous. The faithfulness of the church at Pergamos is a challenge to Christians today to stand true when engulfed by the evil of this present world, the apostasy within the ranks of religion, and the temptation to compromise their stand for the truth.

As a symbol of the faithfulness of these saints in Pergamos, one of the early martyrs is here named as "Antipas," who is declared to be "my faithful martyr, who was slain among you, where Satan dwelleth." There has been speculation as to the character of this person, but there is no certain word concerning the nature of his martyrdom. His name means "against all" which perhaps symbolizes the fact that he may have stood alone against the forces of evil and was faithful even unto death. The church at Pergamos as a whole was commended for standing unwaveringly for Christ even though one of their members had paid the supreme price.

> **2:14-15** But I have a few things against thee, because thou hast there them that hold the doctrine of Balaam, who taught Balac to cast a stumblingblock before the children of Israel, to eat things sacrificed unto idols, and to commit fornication. So hast thou also them that hold the doctrine of the Nicolaitanes, which thing I hate.

Rebuke for compromise. In spite of these many tokens of faithfulness in a time of temptation and trial, the Lord indicated that all was not well with the church at Pergamos. Two blots on their record labeled them as the compromising church. According to verses 14 and 15 they held the doctrine of Balaam and the doctrine of the Nicolaitans.

The reference to Balaam is an allusion to the experience of Balaam recorded in Numbers 22–25 when he was hired by the kings of the Midianites and the Moabites to curse the children of Israel. The sad record of the prophet, who went along with this plan as far as he was able but without being successful in cursing Israel, is given a large place in the book of Numbers. According to Numbers 31, Moses was angry with the children of Israel for not exterminating the women of the Midianites. Here we learn for the first time that the prophet Balaam had advised King Balak to corrupt Israel by tempting them to sin through intermarriage with their women and the resulting inducement to worship idols.

Numbers 31:15–16 records that Moses said to the children of Israel, "Have ye saved all the women alive? Behold, these caused the children of Israel, through the counsel of Balaam, to commit trespass against the LORD in the matter of Peor, and there was a plague among the congregation of the LORD." The doctrine of Balaam therefore was the teaching that the people of God should intermarry with the heathen and compromise in the matter of idolatrous worship. This is in contrast to "the way of Balaam," that is, selling his prophetic gift for money (II Peter 2:15), and "the error of Balaam," his assumption that God would curse Israel (Jude 11).

Undoubtedly intermarriage with the heathen and spiritual compromise were real issues in Pergamos where civic life and religious life were so entwined. It would be most difficult for Christians in this city to have any kind of social contact with the outside world without becoming involved with the worship of idols or in the matter of intermarriage with non-Christians. Practically all meat was offered to idols before it was consumed, and it was difficult for Christians to accept a social engagement or even to buy meat in the market place without in some sense compromising in respect to the meat offered to idols.

Intermarriage with the heathen was also a real problem. Social relations with the heathen world would lead in some instances to partaking of the heathen feasts which in turn led to heathen immorality which was a part of the idolatrous worship. Apparently there were some in the Pergamos church who held that Christians had liberty in this matter. Christ's absolute condemnation of the doctrine of Balaam as it related to the church at Pergamos is a clear testimony to the fact that Christians must at all costs remain pure and separate from defilement with the world and its religion and moral standards. In a similar way they were rebuked for holding the doctrine of the Nicolaitans. That for which the Ephesian church was commended as hating now becomes embraced by some in the church of Pergamos. Nicolaitanism seems to represent moral departure (see discussion at 2:6).

The expression "which things I hate" is not found in the best manuscripts in verse 15, but it does occur in the original reference to this doctrine (2:6). What God hates the Christian ought to hate as well. The modern tendency to blur distinctions of moral and theological character and to manifest unconcern in those areas had its counterpart in the early church of Pergamos. The word of Christ to this church on this point constitutes a stern warning to modern Christians to examine their morality and faith and to demand freedom to follow the Word of God with the guidance of the Holy Spirit where this conflicts with the standards of men.

The parallel in the history of the church to the temptation and failure foreshadowed at Pergamos is all too evident to students of church history. With the so-called conversion of Constantine the Emperor, the time of persecution which the church had previously endured was replaced by a period in which the church was favored by the government. The edicts of persecution which had characterized the previous administration were repealed and Christians were allowed to worship according to the dictates of their conscience. Near the end of the fourth century, Theodosius actually proscribed paganism.

Under these circumstances it soon became popular to be a Christian, and the conscience of the church was quickly blurred. It became increasingly difficult to maintain a clear distinction between the church and the world and to preserve the purity of biblical doctrine. Though some benefit was secured by the successful defense of biblical truth by the Council of Nicea in A.D. 325 as opposed to the defection from the faith by Arius and his followers, the history of the three centuries which followed is a record of increasing corruption of the church, departure from biblical doctrine, and an attempt to combine Christian theology with pagan philosophy.

As a result the church soon lost its hope of the early return of Christ, and biblical simplicity was replaced by a complicated church organization which substituted human creeds and worship of Mary, the mother of our Lord, for true biblical doctrine. The church committed the same sin of which Israel was guilty in the Old Testament, namely, the worship of idols and union with the heathen world. The solemn warning of Christ given to the church at Ephesus was forgotten.

> **2:16** Repent; or else I will come unto thee quickly, and will fight against them with the sword of my mouth.

Warning to repent. In this abrupt command, Christ issued a sharp word to the church at Pergamos and their modern counterparts: "Repent;

or else I will come unto thee quickly, and will fight against them with the sword of my mouth." Even though many in the church at Pergamos had been faithful and one of their number had died as a martyr to the faith, it was nevertheless true that the evil character of those things which were invading the church was so serious in the mind of Christ that it involved fighting against them with the sword of His mouth. There is no alternative to continued impurity and compromise with the truth except that of divine judgment. The apostasy which is seen in its early stage in the church at Pergamos has its culmination in the future apostate church in Revelation 17 which is ultimately brought into divine judgment by Christ the Head of the church.

> **2:17** He that hath an ear, let him hear what the Spirit saith unto the churches; To him that overcometh will I give to eat of the hidden manna, and will give him a white stone, and in the stone a new name written, which no man knoweth saving he that receiveth it.

Invitation and promise. As in His messages to the other churches, Christ gives a promise and an invitation to individuals. "He that hath an ear" is invited to listen. To him is given the threefold promise of verse 17, contained in this revelation. First of all, the believer is assured that he will have the benefit of eating of the hidden manna. Just as Israel received manna from heaven as its food in the wilderness replacing the onions and garlic of Egypt, so for the true believer in the Lord Jesus there is the hidden Manna, that bread from heaven which the world does not know or see which is the present spiritual food of the saints as well as a part of their future heritage. This seems to refer to the benefits of fellowship with Christ and the spiritual strength that is afforded by that experience.

In addition to the hidden manna, those who overcome by faith are promised a white stone, possibly a brilliant diamond. In courts of law being given a white stone is thought to represent acquittal in contrast to a black stone which would indicate condemnation. Hadjiantoniou suggests several other representations such as happiness, or a symbol of friendship, or a passport to important social events.[22] Alford in an extended discussion, after listing many divergent views, supports the position of Bengel along with Hengstenberg and Duesterdieck "that the figure is derived from the practice of using small stones inscribed with writing, for various purposes, and that, further than this, the imagery belongs to the occasion itself only."[23] Alford believes that the real value of the stone is the inscription on it rather than the stone's intrinsic worth.

[22]Hadjiantoniou, pp. 63–68.
[23]Alford, IV, 572.

The stone's value rests in the new name of the recipient which is his title to eternal glory.[24]

The giving of the white stone to the believer here, then, is the indication that he has been accepted or favored by Christ, a wonderful assurance especially for those who have been rejected by the wicked world and are the objects of its persecution. In addition to receiving the stone, a new name written on the stone is promised them, the name described as one "which no man knoweth saving he that receiveth it."

In the Old Testament the high priest had the names of the twelve tribes of Israel inscribed upon the stones carried upon his breast, symbolic of the fact that whenever he appeared before God he was a mediator representing the entire twelve tribes of Israel. Here is a name that belongs to the individual. Some consider it to be that of Jehovah, the unspoken name of God in the Old Testament. Others have regarded it as a personal name indicating their own enrollment in heaven. Whatever its character, the name symbolizes the personal heritage of the glories that are beyond this world and the assurance of eternal salvation. Christians in this modern day as well as Christians in the church at Pergamos are reminded by this Scripture that it is God's purpose to separate them from all evil and compromise and to have them as His peculiar inheritance throughout eternity. However difficult their lot in this life, they are assured infinite blessing in the life to come.

The Letter to Thyatira: The Church Tolerating Apostasy (2:18–29)

2:18 And unto the angel of the church in Thyatira write; These things saith the Son of God, who hath his eyes like unto a flame of fire, and his feet are like fine brass.

Christ the Holy One. The fourth message of Christ was addressed to the angel of the church in Thyatira, a small thriving town located about forty miles southeast of Pergamos. The city had been established as a Macedonian colony by Alexander the Great after the destruction of the Persian empire. Located in a rich agricultural area, Thyatira was famous for the manufacture of purple dye, and numerous references are found in secular literature of the period to the trade guilds which manufactured cloth.[25] It is remarkable that Christ should single out a very small church in a relatively obscure city for such an important letter. However, the message reaches far beyond the immediate circumstances in the church at Thyatira. One other mention of Thyatira is found in Acts 16:14–15 where the conversion of Lydia is recorded in these words: "And a certain woman named Lydia, a seller of purple, of the city of Thyatira, which

[24]*Ibid.*
[25]Swete, p. 41.

71

worshipped God, heard us: whose heart the Lord opened, that she attended unto the things which were spoken of Paul."

As there is no record in Scripture of any evangelistic effort in the city of Thyatira, it may be that the gospel was first brought to Thyatira through the instrumentality of Lydia. Her role of a seller of purple indicates that she was a representative of the thriving trade in purple cloth originating in Thyatira. Though Lydia was probably already deceased, Christ directed the longest of the seven letters to this small Christian assembly which may have been the fruit of her witness. All was not well in Thyatira, and to this little church is addressed one of the most severe of the seven epistles.

Christ is introduced in verse 18 as "the Son of God, who hath his eyes like unto a flame of fire, and his feet are like fine brass." In 1:14–15 a similar description is given where Christ is pictured as the righteous Judge who, knowing all things, can ferret out every evil. His sovereign judgment deals with all who fail to measure up to His perfect righteousness. The chief point of distinction in this description of Christ is that He is named the Son of God in contrast to the designation in chapter 1 where He is called the Son of Man. His title here is in keeping with the character of the judgment pronounced upon the church. Their diversion from the true worship of Jesus Christ the Son of God was so serious that it called for a reiteration of His deity. The description of His eyes as a flame of fire speaks of burning indignation and purifying judgment. In a similar way His feet are declared to be like fine brass (Gr., *chalkolibanō*). This word, found only here in the Bible, has puzzled scholars. It seems to represent an alloy of precious metal such as gold, silver, brass, or copper. Its exact character is not known, but there is general agreement with the conclusion of Swete that it is "the name of a mixed metal of great brilliance."[26] The point in mentioning it here is in reference not to its quality as metal, but to its brilliant appearance enhancing the revelation of Christ as a glorious judge.

> **2:19** I know thy works, and charity, and service, and faith, and thy patience, and thy works; and the last to be more than the first.

Commendation of works, faith, and love. In verse 19 Christ commends the church at Thyatira in a remarkable way, considering the severe condemnation, which may be translated freely as follows: "I know your works and the love and the faith and the service and your patience and your last works being more than the first." In the commendations of the church at Smyrna and at Pergamos the expression "thy works" is not in the best manuscripts, which emphasizes the fact that the principal point of commendation in Smyrna was their faithful suffering and in Pergamos

[26]*Ibid.*, p. 17.

the place in which they were giving their testimony. In Thyatira, however, works are mentioned, because their works were prominent, and of these the omniscient Christ was fully aware.

It is remarkable that the church was commended first for its charity, or love, especially when none of the three preceding churches was commended for this quality. In addition, mention is made of their service, their faith, and their patience, and of the fact that their last works were greater than the former works, in contrast, for instance, to the case of the Ephesian church. In spite of these most commendable features, the church at Thyatira was guilty of terrible sin; and with this fact Christ deals beginning in verse 20.

> **2:20-23** Notwithstanding I have a few things against thee, because thou sufferest that woman Jezebel, which calleth herself a prophetess, to teach and to seduce my servants to commit fornication, and to eat things sacrificed unto idols. And I gave her space to repent of her fornication; and she repented not. Behold, I will cast her into a bed, and them that commit adultery with her into great tribulation, except they repent of their deeds. And I will kill her children with death; and all the churches shall know that I am he which searcheth the reins and hearts: and I will give unto every one of you according to your works.

Indictment for spiritual wickedness. Here is a sweeping indictment of the church's toleration of the woman named Jezebel and her teaching and influence which led the church to commit fornication and to eat things sacrificed to idols. The expression "a few things" found in the Authorized Version is omitted in the best manuscripts, the point being that there is one principal objection to the church at Thyatira, namely, the evil works of the woman called Jezebel. Some manuscripts add *sou* to the word *woman*, hence meaning "thy woman," or "thy wife." Alford favors the interpretation that Jezebel was actually the wife of the pastor at Thyatira on the ground that "on the whole, the evidence for *sou* being inserted in the text seems to me to be preponderant."[27] Alford is not sure, however, that the phrase should be taken literally, perhaps only symbolically.[28]

In any case, it is possible that there was actually a woman leader in the church at Thyatira and that her dominant position may have been derived from the fact that Lydia, another woman, had brought them the message in the first place. This woman, Jezebel, is not a true messenger of divine truth. Though she claimed the right and office of a prophetess, she had urged the Christians in Thyatira to continue their pagan worship of idols which characterized the unbelievers in the city. They were therefore not

[27]Alford, IV, 573.
[28]*Ibid.*

only permitted to participate in the idolatrous feasts by eating things sacrificed to idols but they were also instructed to take part in the immorality which characterized the worship of idols.

In promoting these wrongs, the woman prophetess, whose real name was probably not Jezebel, was fulfilling the role of the historic Jezebel in the Old Testament. According to I Kings, Jezebel was the wife of Ahab, the king of Israel, and she was the daughter of Ethbaal, king of the Sidonians. She was one of the most evil characters of the Old Testament, who attempted to combine the worship of Israel with the worship of the idol Baal. She did what she could to stamp out all true worship of the Lord and influenced her weak husband to the extent that it is recorded in I Kings 16:33, "And Ahab made a grove; and Ahab did more to provoke the LORD God of Israel to anger than all the kings of Israel that were before him."

Jezebel herself had a most unenviable record of evil. She was responsible for the killing of Naboth and possession of his vineyard for her husband (I Kings 21:1–16). She had also killed practically all the prophets of the Lord and did what she could to kill the Prophet Elijah (I Kings 19:2). So evil was Jezebel's character that she is singled out by Elijah for a special prophecy that she would come to a sudden end and that her body would be eaten by dogs—a prophecy fulfilled in II Kings 9:33–35. She is therefore the epitome of subtle corruption and a symbol of immorality and idolatry.

The Jezebel in Thyatira had a similar influence upon the church and broke down all boundaries of moral separation from the wicked world. According to verse 21 she was given "space" or "time" (Gr., *chronon*) to repent, and she had not done so. A terrible judgment is therefore pronounced upon her that she herself will be cast into the bed of affliction and that those who shared her evil deeds will be cast into tribulation. As Swete expresses it, "In this case there is a sharp contrast between the luxurious couch where the sin was committed and the bed of pain."[29] In the expression "I will cast" (Gr., *ballō*) the present tense is used for an emphatic future as if Christ were already in the process of executing His judgment. He describes those who will share her judgment as committing adultery with her.

Though fornication referring to sexual immorality in general is frequently mentioned in the book of Revelation, this is the only place where adultery is indicated, with more particular reference to violation of the marriage vow. Those in Thyatira who had sinned in this way had not only violated the moral law of God but had sinned against their covenant relationship with the Lord which bound them to inward purity as well as outward piety.

[29]Swete, p. 44.

74

Christ also predicts that Jezebel's children will be killed "with death," an emphatic judgment of such character that "all the churches shall know that I am he which searcheth the reins and the hearts: and I will give unto every one of you according to your works." The word translated "reins" in the Authorized Version (Gr., *nephrous*), literally "kidneys," was a reference to the fact that Christ searches the innermost being of the individual. In modern terminology the term would be "minds and hearts." There can be no hiding from Christ of any iniquity whether overt or covert act. These solemn words addressed to the church at Thyatira are applicable to anyone who dares to corrupt the purity of the truth of God and spoil the worship of the Lord with idolatrous and heathen practices.

The message to the assembly in Thyatira seems to foreshadow that period of church history known as the Middle Ages preceding the Protestant Reformation. In that period the church became corrupt as it sought to combine Christianity with pagan philosophy and heathen religious rites so that much of the ritual of the church of that period is directly traceable to comparable ceremonies in heathen religion. During this period also there began that exaltation of Mary the mother of our Lord which has tended to exalt her to the plane of a female deity through whom intercession to God should be made, and apart from whose favor there can be no salvation. The prominence of a woman prophetess in the church at Thyatira anticipates the prominence of this unscriptural exaltation of Mary. Along with this, the church experienced spiritual depravity, and idols in the form of religious statues were introduced. Not only gross immorality but spiritual fornication resulted, much as was true in the church of Thyatira.

Like the church in Thyatira, however, many noble qualities can be found in the church in the Middle Ages. Individuals, in spite of the ecclesiastical system of which they were a part, were often characterized by a true love for God and selfless service and faith. Of such God is the rewarder, and due recognition is made of their faithfulness without glossing over the evil that is inherent in the system as a whole.

The participation in idol worship and eating of things offered to idols also foreshadows the departure from the scriptural doctrine of the finished sacrifice of Christ. In the Middle Ages the false teaching of the continual sacrifice of Christ was advocated, transforming the observance of the elements of the Lord's Supper into another sacrifice of Christ. This fundamental error of the church in the Middle Ages has been corrected in modern Protestantism by the recognition of the bread and the cup as symbols, but not the sacrifice itself, which Christ performed once and for all upon the cross of Calvary. In contrast to the false doctrine exalting the Virgin Mary to the role of deity and coredeemer, Christ introduces Himself in this message to the church of Thyatira as the Son of God, the One to whom alone we owe our redemption and in whose hands alone our final judgment rests.

> 2:24-25 But unto you I say, and unto the rest in Thyatira, as many as have not this doctrine, and which have not known the depths of Satan, as they speak; I will put upon you none other burden. But that which ye have already hold fast till I come.

Exhortation to the godly remnant. It is significant that having brought into judgment those who were evil in the church of Thyatira a special word is given to the godly remnant in this church. Here for the first time in the messages to the seven churches a group is singled out within a local church as being the continuing true testimony of the Lord. The godly remnant is described as not having or holding the doctrine of Jezebel and as not knowing "the depths" or the deep things of Satan. Here reference is made to the satanic system often seen in great detail in false cults which compete with the true Christian faith. Just as there are the deep things of God (I Cor. 2:10) which are taught by the Spirit, so there are the deep things of Satan which result from his work.

The meaning of the expression "as they speak" is debatable. Alford believes that the subject of the verb "speak" is a reference to apostolic teaching embraced in the command which immediately follows: "I will put upon you none other burden." A parallel is found in Acts 15:28 where the council of Jerusalem determined, "It seemed good to the Holy Ghost, and to us, to lay upon you no greater burden than these necessary things." The clause is therefore an introduction to the material which follows rather than a conclusion of the material which preceded. As Alford summarizes it, "This act of simple obedience, and no deep matters beyond their reach, was what the Lord required of them."[30]

To the godly remnant, then, Christ gives a limited responsibility. The evil character of the followers of Jezebel is such that they are beyond reclaim, but the true Christians are urged to hold fast to what they already have and await the coming of the Lord. It is remarkable that here first in the seven churches there is reference to the coming of Christ for His church as the hope of those who are engulfed by an apostate system.

> 2:26-29 And he that overcometh, and keepeth my works unto the end, to him will I give power over the nations: And he shall rule them with a rod of iron; as the vessels of a potter shall they be broken to shivers: even as I received of my Father. And I will give him the morning star. He that hath an ear, let him hear what the Spirit saith unto the churches.

[30]Alford, IV, 577.

The invitation and promise. As in the letters to the other churches, Christ closes His message to the church at Thyatira with a challenge to those who are overcomers. He promises that those who keep His works unto the end will be given a responsible position of judgment over the nations. Closely following the prediction of a second coming is this first reference in Revelation to the millennial reign of Christ (cf., however, 1:6-7). The overcoming Christians are promised places of authority. They will share the rule of Christ over the nations of the world.

The word for "rule" (Gr., *poimanei*) means literally "to shepherd." Their rule will not be simply that of executing judgment, but also that of administering mercy and direction to those who are the sheep as contrasted to the goats (Matt. 25:31-46). The power to rule in this way was given to Christ by His heavenly Father (John 5:22).

To the overcomers also is given the promise of "the morning star." While various explanations of this expression have been given,[31] it seems to refer to Christ Himself in His role as the returning One who will rapture the church before the dark hours preceding the dawn of the millennial kingdom.

The letter to the church at Thyatira closes with the familiar invitation to individuals who have ears to hear. Beginning with this letter this exhortation comes last in contrast to its position before the promise to overcomers in preceding letters. The word of Christ to the church of Thyatira is therefore addressed to any who will hear, who find themselves in similar need of this searching exhortation.

[31]*Ibid.*, IV, 578.

3

THE LETTERS TO SARDIS, PHILADELPHIA, AND LAODICEA

INTRODUCTION

THE THIRD CHAPTER of the book of Revelation contains the final three messages of the churches of Asia: those addressed to Sardis, Philadelphia, and Laodicea respectively. The city of Sardis mentioned first in this chapter was located in West Asia Minor about fifty miles east of Smyrna and thirty miles southeast of Thyatira. It was an important and wealthy city located on the commercial trade route running east and west through Lydia. An ancient city with a long history, Sardis had come back into prominence under Roman rule. At one time it was the capital of the Kingdom of Lydia. Much of its wealth came from its textile manufacturing and dye industry and its jewelry trade. Most of the city practiced pagan worship, and there were many mystery cults or secret religious societies. The magnificent Temple of Artemis dating from the fourth century B.C. was one of its points of interest and still exists as an important ruin. The remains of a Christian church building, which have been discovered immediately adjacent to the temple, testify of postapostolic Christian witness to this wicked and pagan city noted for its loose living. The church to which the letter was addressed continued its existence until the fourteenth century, but it never was prominent. Today only a small village known as Sart exists amid the ancient ruins.

THE LETTER TO SARDIS: THE CHURCH THAT WAS DEAD (3:1-6)

3:1 And unto the angel of the church in Sardis write; These things saith he that hath the seven Spirits of God, and the seven stars; I know thy works, that thou hast a name that thou livest, and art dead.

Christ the Possessor of the Spirit. The message addressed to the angel of the church of Sardis is notable for several reasons. Like the letter to Laodicea it is an unmixed message of rebuke and censor. It is almost devoid of any word of commendation such as characterized the word of Christ to the other churches. The reason for the sad condition in Sardis was that the people were surrounded by the grossest form of idolatry. As Andrew Tait states,

The people of Sardis were idolaters—they worshipped the mother goddess, Cybele. The fragments of the temple that was erected to her honour still remain, and there are two stately columns, with Ionic capitals, which are fully 60 feet high and about 6⅓ feet in diameter, whose bases are deeply imbedded in the rubbish that has fallen down from the citadel. Her worship was of the most debasing character, and orgies like those of Dionysos were practiced at the festivals held in her honour. Sins of the foulest and darkest impurity were committed on those occasions; and when we think of a small community of Christians rescued from such abominable idolatry, living in the midst of scenes of the grossest depravity, with early associations, and companionships, and connections, all exerting a force in the direction of heathenism, it may be wondered that the few members of the church in Sardis were not drawn away altogether, and swallowed up in the great vortex.[1]

G. Campbell Morgan observes that there is a change in approach beginning with this letter:

There is a marked change in our Lord's method of address to the church at Sardis. Hitherto He has commenced with words of commendation. Here, He commenced with words of condemnation. In the other churches, evil had not been the habit, but rather the exception, and therefore it was possible first to commend. Here the case is reversed, and no word of commendation is addressed to the church as a church.[2]

In relation to Sardis Christ is introduced in verse 1 as the One that "hath the seven Spirits of God, and the seven stars." This reference to the fact that Christ has the seven Spirits of God is similar to the description given in 1:4. Alford notes that in 1:4 the seven spirits are declared merely to be before the throne. In both cases, however, the Holy Spirit is in view.[3] Here there is an apparent allusion to the sevenfold character of the Holy Spirit as resting upon Christ according to the prophecy of Isaiah 11:2-5. There the Holy Spirit is described thus: "the spirit of the LORD . . . the spirit of wisdom and understanding, the spirit of counsel and might, the spirit of knowledge and of the fear of the LORD." There also He is described as coming from God and resting upon Christ. A similar description is found later in Revelation 5:6. This portrait of Christ points out the qualities which insure the righteous judgment of the wicked, and it is in this character that Christ is introduced to the church of Sardis.

In addition to having the sevenfold Spirit of God, Christ is revealed as the One who has the seven stars, interpreted in 1:20 as the angels or messengers of the seven churches. The fact that the leaders of the church represented by these messengers belong to Christ makes their leadership and transmission of the message all the more authoritative and responsi-

[1]*The Messages to the Seven Churches of Asia Minor*, p. 299.
[2]*The Letters of Our Lord*, p. 68.
[3]Henry Alford, *The Greek New Testament*, IV, 579.

ble. The same description of Christ as holding the seven stars in His right hand was given in relation to the letter to the church at Ephesus in 2:1 to make clear that the leaders of the church are responsible to no human representative of Christ and must give account directly to the Lord Himself.

Of the church at Sardis He declares, "I know thy works." As in the case of the other churches, the actions and testimony of the church at Sardis are an open book to the omniscient Lord, and nothing is hid from His searching gaze. That which is not visible to man is perfectly apparent to Him, and He defines that which He sees in the closing part of verse 1 in a word of sharp condemnation: "Thou hast a name that thou livest, and art dead."

The church at Sardis evidently had a reputation among the churches in the area and was considered a spiritual church and one that had an effective ministry and testimony for God. From the divine standpoint, however, it is considered as a church that had only a name of being alive and actually was dead as far as spiritual life and power were concerned. This searching judgment of Christ as it relates to the church of Sardis is one to be pondered by the modern church, which often is full of activity even though there is little that speaks of Christ and spiritual life and power. Barclay observes that a church

> is in danger of death when it begins to worship its own past . . . when it is more concerned with forms than with life . . . when it loves systems more than it loves Jesus Christ . . . when it is more concerned with material than spiritual things.[4]

> **3:2-3** Be watchful, and strengthen the things which remain, that are ready to die: for I have not found thy works perfect before God. Remember therefore how thou hast received and heard, and hold fast, and repent. If therefore thou shalt not watch, I will come on thee as a thief, and thou shalt not know what hour I will come upon thee.

Indictment and warning. Though the church at Sardis was classified as being dead in the sight of God, it is obvious from verse 2 that there were some in the church who still had true life and spirituality. Otherwise it would not have been possible to "strengthen the things which remain." On the other hand a full restoration of the will of God was also impossible. In the best manuscripts the article is omitted before "works," hence, literally, "not any of your works have I found perfect before God." They are therefore exhorted to be watchful lest a further invasion of spiritual deadness come upon them.

The previous history of Sardis should have warned them concerning the possibility of sudden and unexpected judgment. Although the situation of the city was ideal for defense, as it stood high above the valley

---

[4]William Barclay, *Letters to the Seven Churches,* pp. 87–88.

of Hermus and was surrounded by deep cliffs almost impossible to scale, Sardis had twice before fallen because of overconfidence and failure to watch. In 549 b.c. the Persian King Cyrus had ended the rule of Croesus by scaling the cliffs under the cover of darkness. In 214 b.c. the armies of Antiochus the Great (III) captured the city by the same method. The city of Sardis at the time it received this letter was in fact in a period of decline as compared to its former glory, having been reduced by these invasions.. The spiritual history of the church was to correspond to the political history of the city.[5] Their works are also declared to be not perfect, literally, "not fulfilled," that is, not achieving the full extent of the will of God. Their works were short either in motive or in execution, and they are exhorted to fill to the full the opportunity for service and testimony.[6]

Not only are they exhorted to be watchful and strengthen the things which remain, but they are also warned to remember the truth that they have received and heard, and to hold it fast and to turn away from any defection from it. If they refuse to heed the exhortation, Christ promises that He will come upon them as a thief, meaning that He will come upon them unexpectedly with devastating suddenness and bring judgment upon them, as He explains: "Thou shalt not know what hour I will come upon thee." The same symbolism is used at the second coming of the Lord, but here the figure is not related to that event. The judgment upon the church at Sardis, however, is going to be just as unexpected, sudden, and irrevocable as that which is related to the second coming.

> 3:4-6 Thou hast a few names even in Sardis which have not defiled their garments; and they shall walk with me in white: for they are worthy. He that overcometh, the same shall be clothed in white raiment; and I will not blot out his name out of the book of life, but I will confess his name before my Father, and before his angels. He that hath an ear, let him hear what the Spirit saith unto the churches.

Invitation and promise to godly remnant. To those individuals in the Sardis church who overcome, the promise is given that they shall be clothed in white raiment. In reference to the white robes, Morgan observes,

> In Scripture the robing of the saint is ever an expression of the saint's own service and character. In the description of the white-robed multitude in Revelation, it is said that their white robes are the righteousness of the saints—not the righteousness of God, but the righteousness of the saints. This is to say, that fidelity of character and of service shall presently have its outward manifestation.[7]

[5]Cf. J. D. Douglas, *The New Bible Dictionary,* p. 1144.
[6]Cf. G. A. Hadjiantoniou, *The Postman of Patmos,* pp. 91–92.
[7]Morgan, p. 75.

Swete suggests that white apparel in Scripture denotes (1) festivity; (2) victory; (3) purity; (4) the heavenly state.[8] The thought seems to be that the righteousness of the saints bestowed in the form of a garment is a token of their acceptability to God and the divine recognition of their office and ministry as the priests of God. They have not defiled their garments as others have done in Sardis, and now they are promised that in the future they will have the heavenly white garment and will walk with Christ because they are judged as "worthy."

Further it is promised, "I will not blot out his name out of the book of life, but I will confess his name before my Father, and before his angels." This verse has troubled expositors in view of other promises of the Scripture which seem to indicate that a person who has once received Jesus Christ as Saviour is forever secure in his salvation. How then can his name be blotted out of the book of life? Seiss interprets the expression "I will not blot out his name out of the book of life" as referring to the name of a believer as written in heaven. He writes,

> There is a celestial roll-book of all those who name the name of Jesus.
> But it depends on the persevering fidelity of the individual whether
> his name is to continue on that roll or to be blotted out.[9]

To make the continuance of our salvation depend upon works, however, is gross failure to comprehend that salvation is by grace alone. If it depended upon the believer's perseverance, the name would not have been written there in the first place. Other explanations of the meaning of the book of life have been given which are more satisfactory. Some have indicated that there is no explicit statement here that anybody will have his name blotted out, but rather the promise that his name will not be blotted out because of his faith in Christ. The implication, however, is that such is a possibility. On the basis of this some have considered the book of life not as the roll of those who are saved but rather a list of those for whom Christ died, that is, all humanity who have possessed physical life. As they come to maturity and are faced with the responsibility of accepting or rejecting Christ, their names are blotted out if they fail to receive Jesus Christ as Saviour; whereas those who do accept Christ as Saviour are confirmed in their position in the book of life, and their names are confessed before the Father and the heavenly angels. In either interpretation the implication of the passage is that those who put their trust in Christ and thus overcome by faith have the privilege of being recognized as the saints of God throughout eternity even though they come from such a church as Sardis where the spiritual testimony was at a low ebb and much was offensive to their holy Lord.

[8]Henry B. Swete, *The Apocalypse of St. John*, pp. 51–52.
[9]J. A. Seiss, *Letters to the Seven Churches*, p. 201.

In keeping with the prophetic foreshadowing of the church age as seen in the other churches, some have held that the church at Sardis is a picture of the church in the time of the Protestant Reformation when a great mass of Christendom was dead even though it had a name that it lived. During those years only a small believing portion took their stand for true biblical revelation and trusted in Christ as Saviour. The characteristics of the church in Sardis remarkably parallel those of the church in the period of the Protestant Reformation. This fact seems to confirm the judgment that the message delivered to this first century church was prophetic of the future of the church at large during this period.

The message is therefore a series of exhortations not only to the church of the first century but to those who need the same exhortations in every century. To such the commands are given to be watchful, to strengthen the things which remain which are ready to die, to remember the truth and experience of the past, to hold fast that which remains, and to repent in mind and heart. The message also includes the warning of the alternative of divine judgment. The promise of the benefits of eternal life is given to those who heed the invitation, who are represented here as a godly remnant within the church at Sardis. As in the other churches the message closes with the individual invitation "He that hath an ear, let him hear what the Spirit saith unto the churches."

THE LETTER TO PHILADELPHIA: THE CHURCH FAITHFUL TO CHRIST
(3:7–13)

The message to the church at Philadelphia is in some respects one of the most interesting of all the messages to the churches. Here is a church which was faithful to Christ and the Word of God. The city of Philadelphia itself, known in modern times as Alasehir, is located in Lydia some twenty-eight miles southeast of Sardis and was named after a king of Pergamos, Attalus Philadelphus, who built the city. The word *Philadelphia,* meaning "brotherly love," is found six other times in the New Testament (Rom. 12:10; I Thess. 4:9; Heb. 13:1; I Peter 1:22; II Peter 1:7*a,b*). Here the word occurs for the seventh and final time, but only here is it used of the city bearing this name.

The city of Philadelphia had a long history and several times was almost completely destroyed by earthquakes. The most recent rebuilding was in A.D. 17. The land area around Philadelphia was rich in agricultural value, but had noticeable tokens of previous volcanic action. Grapes were one of the principal crops, and, in keeping with this, Dionysus was one of the chief objects of pagan worship. Through the centuries, a nominal Christian testimony continued in this city of Philadelphia and prospered even under Turkish rule. But all nominal Christians left the city for Greece after World War I.

The message addressed to the church at Philadelphia has the unusual characteristic of being almost entirely a word of praise, similar to that received by the church at Smyrna, but in sharp contrast to the messages to Sardis and Laodicea.

> **3:7** And to the angel of the church in Philadelphia write; These things saith he that is holy, he that is true, he that hath the key of David, he that openeth, and no man shutteth; and shutteth, and no man openeth.

Christ the holy and sovereign God. The letter addressed to the angel of the church of Philadelphia is introduced in verse 7 by the description of Christ as preeminently the holy One and the One who is always true. Such a one is qualified to call the Christians of Philadelphia to a life of faith in Him and a corresponding life of holiness, even as Peter wrote, "But as he which hath called you is holy, so be ye holy in all manner of conversation" (I Peter 1:15). As the One who is true, Christ is the Author of truth in contrast to all error or false doctrine. In the midst of so much that is false and perverted, Jesus Christ stands alone as the One who is completely true. This aspect of the person of Christ, linked with His holiness earlier in the verse, brings out the great truth that right doctrine and right living go together. There can be no holiness without truth.

Christ is also presented as the One who has the key of David, the One that opens in such a way that no man can shut, and the One who shuts so that no man can open. The description of Christ as He is introduced to the Philadelphian church is less similar to the vision of Christ in chapter 1 than any of the other presentations to the seven churches. He is declared in 1:18 to "have the keys of hell and of death." Here the allusion seems to be to Isaiah 22:22 where, speaking of Eliakim the son of Hilkiah, it is recorded that "the key of the house of David will I lay upon his shoulder; so he shall open, and none shall shut; and he shall shut, and none shall open." Eliakim had the key to all the treasures of the king, and when he opened the door it was opened, and when he closed the door it was closed. Christ, the great antitype of Eliakim, has the key to truth and holiness as well as to opportunity, service, and testimony. To the church at Philadelphia surrounded by heathendom and wickedness, Christ gives assurance that He has power to open and close according to His sovereign will.

> **3:8-9** I know thy works: behold, I have set before thee an open door, and no man can shut it: for thou hast a little strength, and hast kept my word, and hast not denied my name. Behold, I will make them of the synagogue of Satan, which say they are Jews, and are not,

but do lie; behold, I will make them to come and worship before thy feet, and to know that I have loved thee.

Commendation and promised victory. Christ says to the church at Philadelphia as to the other churches, "I know thy works." The entire panorama of testimony and witness in Philadelphia was before Him as He wrote words of commendation for their faithfulness to the Lord. In keeping with the description of His person in verse 7, He declares to them, "Behold, I have set before thee an open door, and no man can shut it." Ramsay explains the reference to the door as arising from the geographical situation of the city of Philadelphia. He states,

> The situation of the city fully explains this saying. Philadelphia lay at the upper extremity of a long valley, which opens back from the sea. After passing Philadelphia the road along this valley ascends to the Phrygian land and the great Central Plateau, the main mass of Asia Minor. This road was the one which led from the harbour of Smyrna to the north-eastern parts of Asia Minor and the East in general, the one rival to the great route connecting Ephesus with the East, and the greatest Asian trade-route of Mediaeval times. . . . Philadelphia, therefore, was the keeper of the gateway to the plateau.[10]

The testimony of the Philadelphian church was divinely ordained by God and assured by His power and sovereignty. It is significant that the testimony of this church continued through the centuries in evident fulfillment of His promise that they should have an open door.

The church at Philadelphia is commended by Christ with the words, "For thou hast a little strength, and hast kept my word, and hast not denied my name." Some have interpreted the expression "little strength" as a word of rebuke rather than commendation. It is obviously short of a full commendation, but it is evident that the thrust of the passage is that Christ recognizes in the Philadelphian church at least a significant degree of spiritual power which comes from God, and this assured them a continuance of their testimony through the open door which He had set before them. Also they are commended for having kept His Word; that is, they had guarded and kept the truth of God as it was committed to them and had not departed from the faith, that system of doctrine which was held by the apostolic church.

Added to their other commendable qualities, the church at Philadelphia manifested a loyalty to the name of Christ Himself and had made a public confession of their trust in Him. In recognition of this fact He says to them, "Thou hast not denied my name." As the result of their faithfulness in witness He promises that their adversaries, described in verse 9 as "synagogue of Satan," will be forced to acknowledge that the Philadelphian church were true servants of God. The reference to the

---

[10]W. M. Ramsay, *The Letters to the Seven Churches of Asia*, pp. 404-5.

synagogue of Satan and to those who say they are Jews is to unbelieving Jews who were opposing the witness of the gospel in Philadelphia and making it difficult for the Christians to bear a good testimony before the pagan world.

Tait observes,

> The most inveterate enemy of the Church of Christ were the Jews. We read of them in Thessalonica, in Smyrna, and here in Philadelphia; and in every case most hostile and embittered against Christians. In Palestine, they were the sole persecutors of the Church; and, elsewhere, if they did not directly oppose the gospel, they instigated others to do so. In Smyrna, the same term, "Synagogue of Satan," is applied to them as here.[11]

Tait goes on to note, however, that their very opposition to Christ sometimes led them to faith.

> We have seen in the history of the Church, many who were its greatest enemies—who were infuriated against it—led to the feet of Jesus. Nothing is too hard for the Lord.[12]

There does not seem to be any evidence that there was satanic opposition in all the churches, though it was found in Pergamos and Smyrna. The Philadelphian church overcomes this opposition and has ultimate victory over it. McCarrell observes:

> The Philadelphia letter reminds that any true church at any time, and especially during the last days, meets Satanic opposition . . . through imitation, religious ritualism, and hypocrisy—opposition strengthened by mixture of worldliness and religiousness—Church and State.[13]

Those in the church today who are experiencing such affliction and persecution may be assured that however violent the opposition and however direct the efforts to thwart and hinder the work of God, in the end there will be victory for the cause of Christ.

> **3:10-11** Because thou hast kept the word of my patience, I also will keep thee from the hour of temptation, which shall come upon all the world, to try them that dwell upon the earth. Behold, I come quickly: hold that fast which thou hast, that no man take thy crown.

Promise of deliverance from hour of trial. One of the outstanding compliments given to the Philadelphian church is contained in verse 10. Because of their faithfulness the Christians in Philadelphia are promised that they will be kept from the hour of trial which will come upon the earth as a divine judgment. It should be noted that this deliverance is not only from trial but from a period of time in which the trial exists, "the hour of temptation." If the expression had been simply deliverance

---

[11]Tait, p. 352.
[12]*Ibid.*, p. 354.
[13]William McCarrell, *Christ's Seven Letters to His Church*, p. 57.

from trial, conceivably it could have meant only partial deliverance. The expression seems to have been made as strong as possible that the Philadelphian church would be delivered from this period.

Many have observed also that the preposition "from" (Gr., *ek*) is best understood as "out of" rather than simply "from." Other instances of the use of the same verb and preposition together, such as John 17:15 and James 1:27, would indicate that it is perhaps too much to press it to mean an absolute deliverance. In view of the context of the book of Revelation, however, as it subsequently unfolds the horrors of this very tribulation period, it is evident that the promise here to the church at Philadelphia is one of deliverance from this time of trouble.

This conclusion has, of course, been resisted by all posttribulationists as an unwarranted interpretation of this passage. If this promise has any bearing on the question of pretribulationism, however, what is said emphasizes deliverance *from* rather than deliverance *through*. As far as the Philadelphian church was concerned, the rapture of the church was presented to them as an imminent hope. If the rapture had occurred in the first century preceding the tribulation which the book of Revelation describes, they were assured of deliverance. By contrast, those sealed out of the twelve tribes of Israel in 7:4 clearly go through the time of trouble. This implies the rapture of the church before the time of trouble referred to as the great tribulation. Such a promise of deliverance to them would seemingly have been impossible if the rapture of the church were delayed until the end of the tribulation prior to the second coming of Christ and the establishment of the kingdom.

This passage therefore provides some support for the hope that Christ will come for His church before the time of trial and trouble described in Revelation 6 to 19. This time of tribulation will overtake the entire world, as God inflicts His wrath upon unbelieving Gentiles as well as upon Christ-rejecting Jews. The Philadelphian church is therefore promised deliverance from the time of trouble which will overtake the world but will not overtake them. By so much they are encouraged to bear their present suffering and to continue their faithfulness and patience as they bear witness for the Lord Jesus.

The Lord's coming for them is compared to an imminent event, one which will come suddenly without announcement. In view of this expectation they are to hold fast to their testimony for Christ in order to receive their reward at His coming. The expression "quickly" is to be understood as something which is sudden and unexpected, not necessarily immediate.

In this passage the rapture of the church is in view. The coming of Christ to establish a kingdom on earth is a later event following the predicted time of tribulation which is unfolded in the book of Revelation

itself. By contrast, the coming of Christ for His church is portrayed here
as elsewhere in the book as an event which is not separated from us by
any series of events, but is one of constant expectation in the daily walk
of the believer in this age. This promise was historically true as directed
to the church at Philadelphia. If the church at Philadelphia foreshadows
a future period of church history just as other churches seem to do, the
promises given to this church can be taken as given to all churches bearing a true witness for Christ even down to the present day.

Many churches may fulfill the characteristics of the other churches
mentioned in these chapters of Revelation and share the condemnation
that is involved. It is also true that some churches like the church in
Philadelphia are worthy of commendation and bear a true testimony for
the Lord Jesus. Individual Christians living in expectation of coming
deliverance from this present world can therefore anticipate the coming
of Christ for them. In regard to the hope of Christ's return, J. N. Darby
writes:

> That which characterizes the church of Philadelphia is its immediate
> connection with Himself; It is Christ Himself who is coming. It is
> neither knowledge nor prophecy that can satisfy the heart; but the
> thought that Jesus is coming to take me to Himself is the blessed hope
> of one who is attached to Him by grace.[14]

> 3:12-13 Him that overcometh will I make a pillar in the temple of
> my God, and he shall go no more out: and I will write upon him the
> name of my God, and the name of the city of my God, which is new
> Jerusalem, which cometh down out of heaven from my God: and I
> will write upon him my new name. He that hath an ear, let him hear
> what the Spirit saith unto the churches.

Invitation and promised reward. To the Christians of Philadelphia
promise is also given as it is in the earlier letters that salvation and blessing and eternity to come will be their portion. They are not only promised the implication of verse 11 that they will have a crown of reward
if they are faithful but they are promised in verse 12, "Him that overcometh will I make a pillar in the temple of my God." This is of course
a figure of speech. The entire heavenly city is considered a temple. In
keeping with the symbolism, the Philadelphian Christians will be permanent like a pillar in the temple and, speaking figuratively, they will stand
when all else has fallen. This perhaps had peculiar significance to those
who were in Philadelphia because of their historic experiences with
earthquakes which frequently had ruined their buildings and left only
the pillars standing. They are assured of continuance throughout eternity because of their faith in Christ as the One who enables them to
overcome the world.

[14]*Seven Lectures on the Prophetical Addresses to the Seven Churches,* pp. 158–59.

Further, the promise is given, "He shall go no more out." This seems to mean that they will no longer be exposed to the temptations and trials of this present life and will have their permanent residence in the very presence of God. In addition to this promise Christ gives them a threefold assurance that they will be identified with God, because (1) they will have the name of God, (2) they will have the name of the city of God, the new Jerusalem, and (3) they will have a new name belonging to Christ. The expression "new Jerusalem" is a reference to the future eternal city described in Revelation 21 and 22. Some like Trench spiritualize the city and deplore the concept that the city will actually come down from heaven. The new Jerusalem, however, will probably be just as literal as the new heaven and the new earth.[15] Those who, like the Philadelphia Christians, are faithful in their testimony and sure in their salvation are promised these eternal realities attending those who receive Christ as Saviour and Lord. As they have been faithful in receiving grace in the present age, so they will be rewarded by God with full tokens of their salvation in eternity to come.

As in the messages to the other churches, the church of Philadelphia is given the invitation to hear "what the spirit saith unto the churches." The challenge to all who hear today is to receive Jesus Christ as Saviour and, having received Him, to bear a faithful witness for the Lord. This will confirm their salvation and their possession of eternal life with God. Like those in Philadelphia, they can contemplate not only present but future deliverance from this world and the enjoyment of all the privileges of eternity because of the Lord's provision.

THE LETTER TO LAODICEA: THE CHURCH WITH UNCONSCIOUS NEED (3:14–22)

The seventh and concluding message to the seven churches of Asia is addressed to the angel of the church in Laodicea. This city founded by Antiochus II in the middle of the third century before Christ and named after his wife Laodice was situated about forty miles southeast of Philadelphia on the road to Colossae. Under Roman rule Laodicea had become wealthy and had a profitable business arising from the production of wool cloth. When destroyed by an earthquake about A.D. 60, it was able to rebuild without any outside help. Its economic sufficiency tended to lull the church to sleep spiritually; and though there is mention of the church as late as the fourteenth century, the city as well as the church now is in complete ruins.

There is no evidence that Paul ever visited the church in Laodicea, but it is evident that he knew some of the Christians there from his refer-

[15]Richard Chenevix Trench, *Commentary on the Epistles to the Seven Churches in Asia*, p. 246.

ence in Colossians 2:1 where he speaks of his "great conflict" for the Christians both at Colossae and at Laodicea and for others whom he had not seen. Salutations are also sent to the church at Laodicea in Colossians 4:15. Some believe that the epistle to the Ephesians was also sent to the Laodiceans. In any event the church had had a long history, and at the time this letter was addressed to it by Christ it was a well-established church.

> 3:14 And unto the angel of the church of the Laodiceans write; These things saith the Amen, the faithful and true witness, the beginning of the creation of God;

Christ the eternal and faithful Witness. As in His introduction to other churches of Asia, Christ describes Himself in an unusual way as "the Amen" in addressing the angel of the church "in" Laodicea, as the best texts read, instead of "the church of the Laodiceans." The frequent use of *Amen,* meaning "so be it," is a feature of the declarations of Christ and is usually translated "verily," or used as an ending to a prayer. As a title of Christ it indicates His sovereignty and the certainty of the fulfillment of His promises. As Paul wrote the Corinthians, "For all the promises of God in him are yea, and in him Amen, unto the glory of God by us" (II Cor. 1:20). When Christ speaks, it is the final word, and His will is always effected.

Christ is called the faithful and true Witness in contrast to the church in Laodicea which was neither faithful nor true. Christ had been earlier introduced as "the faithful witness" in 1:5 and as "he that is true" in 3:7. The fact that Christ is both a faithful and a true witness gives special solemnity to the words which follow.

Finally, He is described as "the beginning of the creation of God." As "the beginning" (Gr., *archē*), He is not the first of creation but He is before all creation.

As Alford observes, *archē* out of this context could possibly mean "that Christ is the first created being: see Gen. 49:3; Deut. 21:17; and Prov. 8:22."[16] While Arians took it this way, the whole context of Revelation indicates that Christ is God the Creator rather than a created being. As Alford states, "In Him the whole creation of God is begun and conditioned: He is its source and primary fountain-head."[17]

No doubt the Laodiceans were familiar with the letter to Colossae which must have been in their possession for at least a generation. There Christ is described as "the image of the invisible God, the firstborn of every creature" (Col. 1:15), and as the One "who is the beginning, the firstborn from the dead" (Col. 1:18). In a similar way Christ declares

[16]Alford, IV, 588.
[17]*Ibid.*

in Revelation 21:6, "I am Alpha and Omega, the beginning and the end."
As the Laodiceans had reveled in material riches, Christ reminds them
that all of these things come from Him who is the Creator.

> **3:15-16** I know thy works, that thou art neither cold nor hot: I
> would thou wert cold or hot. So then because thou art lukewarm, and
> neither cold nor hot, I will spue thee out of my mouth.

The indictment: neither cold nor hot. With this introduction of Himself, Christ addresses His message to the angel of the church in Laodicea
without a word of commendation and with the most scathing rebuke to
be found in any of the seven letters. The letter is first of all addressed
to the angel or minister of the church. Because of the mention of Archippus in Colossians 4:17, some have suggested that Archippus may have
been the angel or minister of the church in Laodicea. Paul had strictly
charged Archippus, "Take heed to the ministry which thou hast received
of the Lord, that thou fulfil it" (Col. 4:17). In verse 15 he had sent
greetings to the church in Laodicea and stated in the following verse
that the Colossians should also read a letter they would receive from the
Laodiceans. Though it cannot be determined whether this is a letter
now lost or a reference to the epistle to the Ephesians, there seems to be
concern on the part of the Apostle Paul even at that time for the spiritual
state of the church at Laodicea. It is improbable that Archippus was
still pastor of the church, however, as thirty years or more had elapsed
since the epistle to the Colossians was written. The state of the church,
however, may well have stemmed from faulty ministry and leadership on
the part of Archippus whether or not he was still pastor.

The difficulty seems to be that the church was lukewarm rather than
cold or hot. The word translated "lukewarm" (Gr., *chliaros*) is used
only here in the New Testament and refers to tepid water. It is obvious
that in this portion of Scripture Christ is referring to three different
spiritual states which may be enumerated respectively as a state of
coldness, a state of warmth or fervor, and a state of lukewarmness. Christ
had reference to the fact that many in the world are cold to the things of
Christ, that is, the gospel leaves them totally unmoved and arouses no
interest or spiritual fervor. Such were many who were later won to the
gospel, but in their prior cold state they had no evidence of grace or of
salvation. By contrast those who are described as hot are those who show
genuine spiritual fervor and leave no question as to the presence of eternal life, the sanctifying power and presence of the Holy Spirit, and a
fervent testimony manifesting to all that they are believers in the Lord
Jesus Christ.

The normal transition is from a state of coldness to a state of spiritual
warmth and is manifested in the experience of many prominent servants

of God. The Apostle Paul himself at one time was cold toward Christ and bitter in his persecution of Christians; but once he met Christ on the Damascus Road, the opposition and lack of interest were immediately dissolved and replaced by the fervent heat of a flaming testimony for the Lord. The One whom he formerly persecuted then became an object of such affection that he would cheerfully die for Christ's name. Similarly Moses in the Old Testament, though not always identified with his people Israel, when faced with a choice of either going the way of the Egyptians or the way of the people of God, according to the Scriptures chose to suffer affliction with his people rather than to enjoy the pleasures of Egypt for a brief season. It is obvious that he also manifested fervency in a real work for God. Such has been the pattern also of countless souls who have been won from spiritual deadness and coldness to fervency of Christian testimony.

The third state, that of lukewarmness, is what characterized the church in Laodicea. This state refers to those who have manifested some interest in the things of God. They may be professing Christians who attend church but have fallen far short of a true testimony for Christ and whose attitude and actions raise questions concerning the reality of their spiritual life. They have been touched by the gospel, but it is not clear whether they really belong to Christ. Such was the case of the messenger of the church at Laodicea as well as his congregation.

Trench comments that Jeremy Taylor, in his sermon "Of Lukewarmness and Zeal," "urges well that it is the 'lukewarm,' not as a transitional, but as a *final* state, which is thus the object of the Lord's abhorrence." Trench cites Taylor as saying, "In feasts or sacrifices the ancients did use *apponere frigidam* or *calidam;* sometimes they drank hot drink, sometimes they poured cold upon their gravies or their wines, but no services of tables or altars were ever lukewarm."[18]

To the angel of the church in Laodicea Christ therefore addresses this sharp word of rebuke. Both the messenger and the church are neither cold nor hot. They can hardly be classified with the worldly who are totally unconcerned about the things of Christ nor with those who unmistakably bear a true testimony for the Lord. This intermediate state of lukewarmness is the occasion for the extreme statement which Christ makes that He will spue them out of His mouth.

Ramsay comments on the state of the church at Laodicea as follows:

> The ordinary historian would probably not condemn the spirit of Laodicea so strenuously as St. John did. In the tendency of the Laodiceans toward a policy of compromise, he would probably see a tendency toward toleration and allowance, which indicated a certain

[18]Trench, pp. 261–62.

sound practical sense and showed that the various constituents of the
population of Laodicea were well mixed and evenly balanced.[19]

It is apparent that there is something about the intermediate state of
being lukewarm that is utterly obnoxious to God. Far more hopeful is
the state of one who has been untouched by the gospel and makes no
pretense of putting his trust in Christ than the one who makes some
profession but by his life illustrates that he has not really honored the
Christ whose gospel he has heard and professed. There is no one farther
from the truth in Christ than the one who makes an idle profession without real faith. The church at Laodicea constitutes a sad picture of much
of the professing church in the world throughout the history of the Christian era and serves as an illustration of those who participate in the
outer religious worship without the inner reality. How many have outwardly conformed to requirements of the church without a true state of
being born again into the family of God? How many church members
are far from God yet by their membership in the professing church have
satisfied their own hearts and have been lulled into a sense of false
security?

In the history of the human race no one has been harder to reach for
Christ than the religionist, the one who is quite satisfied with the measure
of his devotion to God and with the items which to him represent religion. Far easier to win are the harlots and publicans than the Pharisees
and the Sadducees. Especially sad is the fact that in the church at
Laodicea the minister or angel of the church is here described as lukewarm.

The indifference embodied in the term "lukewarm" in this passage
seems to extend to their conviction respecting the central doctrines of the
Christian faith, such as the necessity of the new birth and the need for
a dramatic change in life and perspective required of a true Christian.
If those who are shepherds of the flock never make clear the necessity of
the new birth and do not proclaim accurately the depravity and sin of
the human heart and the divine remedy provided alone in the salvation
offered by the crucified Christ, one can hardly expect the church itself
to be better than those who lead it. The result is churchianity, membership in an organization without biblical Christianity and without membership in the Body of Christ accompanied by the miracle of the new
birth.

It is remarkable, however, that in the indictment of the church in
Laodicea none of the sins mentioned in the preceding churches are itemized. On the one hand there are no works which are commended, but on
the other hand there is no citation of departure in doctrine or morals.

[19]Ramsay, p. 425.

Perhaps such defection did not occur, or it may have stemmed from the sin of being lukewarm. In either case the quality of being lukewarm assumes the dimension of being utterly intolerable by God.

> 3:17-18 Because thou sayest, I am rich, and increased with goods, and have need of nothing; and knowest not that thou art wretched, and miserable, and poor, and blind, and naked: I counsel thee to buy of me gold tried in the fire, that thou mayest be rich; and white raiment, that thou mayest be clothed, and that the shame of thy nakedness do not appear; and anoint thine eyes with eyesalve, that thou mayest see.

Their poverty in riches. The lack of spiritual perception, devotion, and faith in God manifested in the lukewarm state is revealed in the exaltation of material wealth in contrast to spiritual riches. The Laodiceans were well provided for as far as material goods were concerned, and Christ quotes the pastor representing the church as boasting, "I have need of nothing." Their lack of economic need seems to have blinded their eyes to their dire need of spiritual riches. Christ points this out by saying that they do not know that they are "wretched, and miserable, and poor, and blind, and naked." As in the other churches, the state of the pastor is the state of the congregation. They are "wretched," a term Paul uses in reference to himself in Romans 7:24. They are "miserable" (pitiable), an expression Paul also uses in I Corinthians 15:19 of one who does not believe in resurrection. In describing the Laodiceans as "poor" Christ indicates that they are extremely poor, that is, reduced to begging. In addition to those indications of their need, they are described as "blind" (unable to perceive spiritual things), and "naked" (stripped of clothes, or without proper clothes). Their spiritual condition was the exact opposite of their supposed sufficiency in temporal matters.

The church at Laodicea with their unconscious need were lulled into false contentment by their temporal sufficiency. Spiritually they were in a wretched state but did not realize it. Without the real joy of the Lord, they were miserable in spite of their temporal wealth. They were poor because they were without real and eternal possessions and were lacking the eye of faith that could ascertain the true riches which endure forever. They were blind to things which could be seen only by spiritual sight, and they were naked of spiritual clothing, the righteousness which comes from God, even though they were clothed with rich garments of silk and wool. The Laodiceans are typical of the modern world, which revels in that which the natural eye can see but is untouched by the gospel and does not see beyond the veil of the material to the unseen and real eternal spiritual riches.

To these who were in such unconscious need, Christ addresses a word of admonition. He could command but instead, with a touch of irony, He offers His advice: "I counsel thee to buy of me gold tried in the fire, that thou mayest be rich; and white raiment, that thou mayest be clothed, and that the shame of thy nakedness do not appear; and anoint thine eyes with eyesalve, that thou mayest see." Barclay observes that the city of Laodicea was famous for two kinds of medicine, namely, an ointment for sore ears and an eye powder for sore eyes. He states,

> The *tephra Phrygia*, the eye-powder of Laodicea, was world-famous. It was exported in tablet form; and the tablets were ground down and applied to the eye. This Phrygian powder was held to be a sovereign remedy for weak and ailing eyes.[20]

There is gentle irony in the exhortation for them to buy these needed spiritual things. The fact was that though they were well endowed with the riches of this earth, what they needed they could not buy. The gold of which Christ spoke was not obtainable at their bankers. There may be an allusion here to Isaiah 55:1 where the invitation is given, "Ho, every one that thirsteth, come ye to the waters, and he that hath no money; come ye, buy, and eat; yea, come, buy wine and milk without money and without price."

It is obvious that Christ is referring not to the physical items which are mentioned but to their spiritual counterparts. They were to obtain gold from Christ, that is, the true riches and, more specifically, that which corresponds to the glory of God Himself. They were to have white raiment speaking of righteousness which God provides. The merchants of Laodicea were famous for their manufacture of a certain black garment which was widely sold. They grew their own glossy black wool used in making this garment. There may be a reference to the contrast between that which the merchants could provide, a black garment, and a white garment which God alone could supply. In any case the white garment alone would be a satisfactory covering of their nakedness before God.

Christ also advises them to anoint their eyes with eyesalve. In this exhortation He states that they lacked spiritual insight. In the temple of Asklepios in Laodicea there was a famous medical school. Here again there may be relevance to what the Laodiceans were accustomed to doing, that is, using medicine for eyesalve, in contrast to their real need of having their spiritual eyes opened. Both pastor and people seem to have been blind to the things of God. There are few passages in Scripture more searching, more condemning, more pointed than the message to this church, and few messages are more needed by the church today, which in many respects sadly parallels the spiritual state of the church at Laodicea.

[20]Barclay, p. 113.

3:19 As many as I love, I rebuke and chasten: be zealous therefore, and repent.

Warning to repent. To such in the Laodicean church as would listen, Christ says, "As many as I love, I rebuke and chasten: be zealous therefore, and repent." Obviously this verse is not addressed to those who are still cold, those who are still out of Christ, those who make no pretense of putting their trust in Him. It is directed rather to those who profess to follow Christ and who in some sense may be classified as belonging to Him. These are the objects of the love of God. If they are in a lukewarm state, short of what they should be spiritually, they are the objects of the rebuke and chastening judgments of God. God is not seeking to discipline those who make no pretense of following Him but rather deals with those who claim to be His children. If by faith they have entered into the fold, even though they still fall short of a true testimony for God, they become the objects of God's divine chastening just as children are corrected by a faithful father.

The exhortation is addressed to "as many as I love." The word used for love is not *agapaō* as in 2:4 but rather *phileō*, a term for affection with less depth. Those who are the objects of His affection are also the objects of His rebuke and chastening. The word translated "rebuke" (Gr., *elegchō*) could also be translated "expose, convict, or punish." It is not simply a verbal rebuke but is effective in dealing adequately with the person who is rebuked. Such are also chastened (Gr., *paideuō*), which means to train, discipline, or educate a child. It is evident that Christ has in mind here those few in the Laodicean church who are actually born again but whose lives have taken on the same lukewarm characteristics as those about them who are merely professing Christians. The fact that they are rebuked and chastened is evidence that they are true children of God, as such a program is not addressed to those who are unsaved (cf. Heb. 12:3–15).

Though the state of lukewarmness should never exist in those who have believed in Christ, Christians are often indistinguishable from those who are merely making an idle profession. God, however, knows the difference. Those who are truly His are the objects of His chastening judgment. The Scriptures faithfully warn us as in the words of Paul to the Corinthians in I Corinthians 11:31–32: "For if we would judge ourselves, we should not be judged. But when we are judged, we are chastened of the Lord, that we should not be condemned with the world." In other words the true believer has an alternative. If he will judge himself and put away his sin, God will not be required in that case to bring chastening judgment upon him. If he will not judge himself, however, it is clear that God will undertake to deal with him. As Darby observes,

The immediate occasion, object, inner spring of all the terrible judgment which is coming, is the professing Church itself. It ought to have been God's witness on the earth, Christ's epistle known and read of all men; but, having become corrupt, it is this professing Church that primarily and definitely brings down the wrath of God.[21]

3:20-22 Behold, I stand at the door, and knock: if any man hear my voice, and open the door, I will come in to him, and will sup with him, and he with me. To him that overcometh will I grant to sit with me in my throne, even as I also overcame, and am set down with my Father in his throne. He that hath an ear, let him hear what the Spirit saith unto the churches.

Invitation and promise. Having concluded the messages to the seven churches culminating in the message to the church at Laodicea, the invitation becomes a personal one to all who will hear the words of warning. The prophetic foreshadowing provided in the seven churches as representative of churches found throughout the entire history of the church has special application in connection with the church at Laodicea. Under this point of view the state of this church is typical of the church of the last days and is therefore an exhortation to self-judgment and dedication to the will of God especially appropriate for consideration in modern days.

To all who will hear, Christ gives the invitation contained in verse 20. Christ is represented in relation to the church as well as to the individual as standing outside the door and awaiting an invitation to come in. This is, of course, true of any local professing church. Christ must be invited to come in and become the center of worship, adoration, and love, but it is also true of the heart of man. In this present age God does not force Himself upon anyone. No one is saved against his will. No one is compelled to obedience who wants to be rebellious. The gracious invitation is extended, however, that if one opens the door—the door of faith, the door of worship, the door of love—Christ will come in and, having come in, will sup or dine with the one who thus permits Him to enter. Morgan observes,

> The only cure for lukewarmness is the re-admission of the excluded Christ. Apostasy must be confronted with His fidelity, looseness with conviction born of His authority, poverty with the fact of His wealth, frost with the mighty fire of His enthusiasm, and death with the life divine that is in His gift. There is no other cure for the loneliness of heaven, for the malady of the world, for the lukewarmness of the Church than the re-admitted Christ.[22]

Some like Swete consider the picture here to be eschatological. To them the opening of the door represents the joyful response of the church

[21]Darby, p. 181.
[22]Morgan, p. 108.

to Christ's last call, that is, His second coming. Contrast to this is afforded in Matthew 25:10.[23] It is hardly true, however, that at His second coming Christ will knock at the door and invite men to let Him in. The picture here seems more applicable to the present, when Christ remains on the outside unless He is welcomed.

Some have found in this imagery a parallel to the scene in the Song of Solomon chapter 5 where the bridegroom stands outside the door and knocks in the middle of the night attempting to awaken the bride within to open the door and permit him to enter. A similar idea is found in Luke 12:35-36 in connection with the second coming of Christ: "Let your loins be girded about, and your lights burning; And ye yourselves like unto men that wait for their lord, when he will return from the wedding; that when he cometh and knocketh, they may open unto him immediately." The point in all these illustrations is that Christ does not force Himself upon any but awaits the human decision relative to the recognition of His person and the blessings that will come if He be admitted.

What blessed condescension is revealed here in the attitude of God, the infinite Creator and Sovereign, who awaits the decision of His creature who is so unworthy of the least of divine blessing. The attitude of Christ throughout the present age is one of knocking at the door, waiting for men to decide to receive Him. The day will come when this attitude will be changed. He will come in power and glory, leading the armies of heaven, no longer awaiting the decision of men; but then by His own power and majesty, He will take control, judging those who did not invite Him to come in and rewarding those who opened the door and received Him unto themselves.

The Scriptures do not enlarge upon what constitutes the fellowship except that the word used for "sup" indicates that it is the main meal of the day, the one to which an honored guest would be invited. The significant thing is that the one who invites Him in will sit down at the same table with Him and partake of the same food. This undoubtedly represents things that are of mutual interest: the things of God, the things of salvation, the things of our hope, the present sustaining grace of God, and the blessings of God provided through salvation in Christ. Christ is to become the center of our fellowship and that upon which we feed. How rich is this feast, how representative of that fellowship which will be ours throughout all eternity to come.

In keeping with the promises given to the overcomers in the other churches, the promise is made to the Laodicean church to "sit with me in my throne." This promise like the others is not granted to those who are especially spiritual within the church but rather to all who are

[23]Swete, pp. 63-64.

genuine Christians who overcome by faith and are victorious over the world (I John 5:4). To such is the promise granted that they will sit with Christ in His throne. What amazing condescension! To those who previously came under the condemnation of being lukewarm to such an extent that they were in danger of being spued out of the mouth of Christ the promise is now given that they will share His glory. It is obvious that this hinges upon their separation from the lukewarm state and their manifestation of true devotion to Christ.

In this portion of Scripture as elsewhere in the New Testament, the present position of Christ is contrasted to His future millennial reign. Now Christ is sharing the Father's throne and glory, and this forms the basis of His promise to the overcomer. The day will come, however, when He will establish His own throne on the earth (Matt. 25:31) which will be the fulfillment of the predicted throne of David, subject of Old Testament prophecy. Then He will rule with power and glory not only over the nation Israel but over all nations. In that future time when His sovereignty will be manifested to the entire world, those who put their trust in Him will reign with him as His bride and consort, as the ones who have identified themselves with Christ in this present age of grace.

In the church at Laodicea there was so much that was obnoxious to God and so little that was commendable. Yet Christ extended His personal invitation to them even as He extends to all who will receive it today. This invitation involves recognizing Him as Saviour and Lord and entering fully into the blessings of the Christian life. As in the messages to the other churches, the message to the church at Laodicea concludes with "He that hath an ear, let him hear what the Spirit saith unto the churches."

Taken as a whole the messages to the seven churches of Asia constitute a comprehensive warning from Christ Himself as embodied in the exhortations to each of the churches. There is warning to the churches of today to "hear what the Spirit saith unto the churches." The church at Ephesus represents *the danger of losing our first love* (2:4), that fresh ardor and devotion to Christ which characterized the early church. The church at Smyrna representing *the danger of fear of suffering* was exhorted, "Fear none of those things which thou shalt suffer" (2:10). In a modern day when persecution of the saints has been revived, the church may well heed the exhortation "Fear not." The church at Pergamos illustrates *the constant danger of doctrinal compromise* (2:14–15), often the first step toward complete defection. Would that the modern church which has forsaken so many fundamentals of biblical faith would heed the warning! The church at Thyatira is a monument to *the danger of moral compromise* (2:20). The church today may well take heed to the departure

99

from moral standards which has invaded the church itself. The church at Sardis is a warning against *the danger of spiritual deadness* (3:1-2), of orthodoxy without life, of mere outward appearance, of being, like the Pharisees, whited sepulchers. The church at Philadelphia commended by our Lord is nevertheless warned against the *danger of not holding fast* (3:11), and exhorted to keep "the word of my patience," to maintain the "little strength" that they did have and to wait for their coming Lord. The final message to the church at Laodicea is the crowning indictment, a warning against *the danger of lukewarmness* (3:15-16), of self-sufficiency, of being unconscious of desperate spiritual need. To contemporary churches each of these messages is amazingly relevant and pointed in its searching analysis of what our Lord sees as He stands in the midst of the lampstands.

The present age is an age of grace, an age in which God is testifying concerning Christ and His work, an age in which those who wish to hear may receive Christ and be saved. The invitation given long ago to the seven churches of Asia to hear what the Spirit says is extended to men today. A loving God would have men hear and believe, turn from their idols of sin and self, and look in faith to the Son of God, who loved them and gave Himself for them.

4

THE CHURCH IN HEAVEN

THE INVITATION FROM HEAVEN (4:1)

4:1 After this I looked, and, behold, a door was opened in heaven: and the first voice which I heard was as it were of a trumpet talking with me; which said, Come up hither, and I will shew thee things which must be hereafter.

BEGINNING WITH CHAPTER 4, the third major section of the book of Revelation is introduced following the divinely inspired outline of 1:19 and fulfilling the promise of revelation of "the things which shall be hereafter." Bleek, almost a century ago, stated the futurist view of Revelation beginning in 4:1 much in the fashion of contemporary futurists.[1] This section is in contrast to what John saw in chapter 1, his vision of the glorified Christ described in the clause, "the things which thou hast seen," and in contrast to the revelation of chapters 2 and 3, messages to the seven churches designated as "the things which are." Beginning in chapter 4, things to come are unfolded which have to do with the consummation of the age.

The concept that the book of Revelation beginning with 4:1 is future, from the standpoint of the twentieth century, is a broad conclusion growing out of the lack of correspondence of these prophecies to anything that has been fulfilled. A normal interpretation of this section which understands these prophecies as literal events would require that they be viewed as future. The futuristic concept is supported by the similarity of the expression in 1:19, "the things which shall be hereafter" (Gr., *ha mellei genesthai meta tauta*) to the clause in 4:1, "things which must be hereafter" (Gr., *ha dei genesthai meta tauta*).

Chapters 4 and 5 are the introduction and background of the tremendous sweep of prophetic events predicted in the rest of the book. If chapter 4 and succeeding chapters relate to the future, they provide an important clue concerning the interpretation of the vision and the prophetic events which unfold in those chapters. One of the principal reasons for confusion in the study of the book of Revelation has been the failure to grasp this point. If Revelation has no chronological structure and is merely a symbolic presentation of moral truth, its prophetic sig-

[1]Friedrich Bleek, *Lectures on the Apocalypse*, pp. 6 ff.

101

nificance is reduced to a minimum. If, as others hold, the predictions of this section of Revelation are already fulfilled in the early persecution of the church, it also robs the book of any prophecy of the future.[2] (For discussion of the various systems of interpretation of the book of Revelation, see the Introduction.)

A literal interpretation of the prophecies beginning in chapter 4 is not fulfilled in any historic event and must therefore be regarded from the futuristic viewpoint if it is indeed valid prophecy. The events anticipated in the angel's promise to "shew thee things which must be hereafter" (4:1), should be regarded as a prediction of events which shall occur at the end of the age.

C. A. Blanchard summarized the futuristic position in these words:

> What will follow the church age? Evidently in some form or other the time of the tribulation. Why must the time of tribulation follow the church age? Because when the church has been withdrawn, while Satan, godless governments and Christless religions remain in the world there *must be* tribulation, and such a time of tribulation as the world has never known in the mixed state which has been from the beginning until now. From the fourth chapter through the nineteenth, speaking generally, there seems to be an account of this time of trouble.[3]

The expression "after this" (Gr., *meta tauta*), with which verse one begins, identifies the revelation as subsequent to that of chapters 2 and 3. John, having been the channel of revelation to the seven churches existing in the first century, now is being introduced to a new field of prophecy. As he beheld, he saw a door opened into the very presence of God in heaven. The reference to heaven is not to the atmospheric heavens nor to the starry heavens but to that which is beyond the natural eye which the best of telescopes cannot reveal. This is the third heaven, the immediate presence of God.

John also hears a voice described as "the first voice which I heard," that is, a reference to the same voice he heard in Revelation 1:10 and following. It is described as the voice of a trumpet (cf. 1:10), and he understands it to say, "Come up hither, and I will shew thee things which must be hereafter." The command does not anticipate any self-effort on the part of John to enter heaven but is rather an announcement of the purpose of God to show him that which will "be hereafter" or, better

[2]Edward H. Horne, for instance, although a premillenarian, interprets Revelation 4:1–16:17 as belonging to the present age, with the millennial age a literal period beginning with Revelation 19:11, and the eternal age introduced at Revelation 21:2. Though a follower of the historical school, Horne recognizes dispensations, namely the Mosaic in the Old Testament, the dispensation of the Spirit in the present age, the future millennial kingdom, and the eternal age (*The Meaning of the Apocalypse*, p. 23).

[3]*Light on the Last Days*, pp. 25–26.

translated, that which will "be after these things." The implication is that the prophecies now to be unfolded will occur after the events of the present age.

The invitation to John to "come up hither" is so similar to that which the church anticipates at the rapture that many have connected the two expressions. It is clear from the context that this is not an explicit reference to the rapture of the church, as John was not actually translated; in fact he was still in his natural body on the island of Patmos. He was translated into scenes of heaven only temporarily. Though there is no authority for connecting the rapture with this expression, there does seem to be a typical representation of the order of events, namely, the church age first, then the rapture, then the church in heaven. Though the rapture is mentioned in letters to two of the churches (cf. 2:25; 3:11), the rapture as a doctrine is not a part of the prophetic foreview of the book of Revelation. This is in keeping with the fact that the book as a whole is not occupied primarily with God's program for the church. Instead the primary objective is to portray the events leading up to and climaxing in the second coming of Christ and the prophetic kingdom and the eternal state which ultimately will follow.

From a practical standpoint, however, the rapture may be viewed as having already occurred in the scheme of God before the events of chapter 4 and following chapters of Revelation unfold. The word *church*, so prominent in chapters 2 and 3, does not occur again until 22:16, though the church is undoubtedly in view as the wife of the Lamb in Revelation 19:7. She is not a participant in the scenes of the tribulation which form the major content of the book of Revelation. The familiar phrase "what the Spirit saith unto the churches" found in 2:7, 11, 17, 29; 3:6, 13, 22 is significantly absent in 13:9.

It seems that the church as the Body of Christ is out of the picture, and saints who come to know the Lord in this period are described as saved Israelites or saved Gentiles, never by terms which are characteristic of the church, the Body of Christ. Saints mentioned from this point on do not lose their racial background as is commonly done in referring to the church where Jew and Gentile are one in Christ. At the beginning of chapter 4, then, the church may be considered as in heaven and not related to events which will take place on the earth in preparation for Christ's return in power and glory.

THE VIEWING OF GOD'S THRONE (4:2-3)

4:2-3 And immediately I was in the spirit: and, behold, a throne was set in heaven, and one sat on the throne. And he that sat was to lock upon like a jasper and a sardine stone: and there was a rainbow round about the throne, in sight like unto an emerald.

From the beginning of verse 2 John finds himself in heaven "in the spirit" in much the same way as he indicated in 1:10, only this time his location is changed. Though actually on the Isle of Patmos, he is experiencing being in the presence of God and seeing these glorious visions. The first object which appears to his startled eyes is a throne in heaven with one sitting upon it. The primary impression received by John is that of color, and he describes the presence of the One on the throne as "like a jasper and a sardine stone." The sight of a rainbow around the throne like an emerald further enriches the color scheme.

Without reference to other portions of Scripture, this verse would be more or less meaningless except as a general expression of the glory of God. The details furnished, however, though not explained by John, undoubtedly have a deep significance. It is first of all important to note that this is a throne in heaven, a reminder of the sovereignty of God who is far removed from the petty struggles of earthly government. Here is the true picture of the universe as being subject to the dominion of an omnipotent God.

The precious stones mentioned also seem to have meaning. The jasper stone is described in chapter 21 as a precious stone which is clear like crystal, which would seem to indicate that it may be what we would today call a diamond. The sardine stone, or the sardius, is a familiar stone in color like a ruby, a beautiful red.

The significance, however, goes far beyond the color. Though the clear jasper might refer to the purity of God and the sardine stone to His redemptive purpose, according to the Old Testament these stones had a relationship to the tribes of Israel. Each tribe of Israel had a representative stone, and the high priest had stones representing each of the twelve tribes of Israel on his breast when he functioned in his priestly office before the altar. This symbolized the fact that he as the high priest was representing all twelve tribes before the throne of God.

Significantly, the jasper and the sardine stone are the first and last of these twelve stones (cf. Exodus 28:17–21). The jasper represented Reuben, the first of the tribes, since Reuben was the firstborn of Jacob. The sardine stone represented Benjamin, the youngest of the twelve sons of Jacob. In other words the two stones represented the first and the last and therefore may be regarded as including all the other stones in between, that is, the whole of the covenanted people.

Furthermore, the names Reuben and Benjamin have significance. The word *Reuben* means "behold, a son." The word *Benjamin* means "son of my right hand." In both cases these terms seem to have a double meaning: first, the fact that though Christ is the representative of Israel, He is also the Son of God. Like Reuben, Christ is the first begotten son.

104

Second, like Benjamin, Christ is also the "son of my right hand" in relation to God the Father. The person whom John sees on the throne looking like a jasper and sardine stone is, therefore, God in relation to the nation Israel.

It is of interest that these same stones are used to describe the majesty of the king of Tyrus (Ezek. 28:13) where, in a list of nine precious stones, the sardius (sardine) is mentioned first and the jasper is sixth in the list. In the description of the foundation of the new Jerusalem in Revelation 21:19–20, the jasper is first and the sardius is sixth. The emerald is listed as eighth in Ezekiel and fourth in Revelation 21:19. It is evident that these stones have a peculiar significance of glory and majesty which are characteristic of God on His throne. Coupled with the brilliant reflections of the jasper and the deep red of the sardine stone, the rainbow described as all of green like an emerald forms a rich background for the glorious scene which John beheld.

The question has been raised as to the identity of the One who was on the throne. In chapter 4 it appears that He is to be identified as God the Father because Christ is represented separately as the Lamb. Alford states that the One seated is "The Eternal Father . . . for He that sitteth on the throne is distinguished in ch. 6:16; 7:10 from the Son, and in [ch. 4] ver. 5 from the Holy Spirit."[4]

The difficult problem of identification has been solved in various ways. Actually both the Father and the Son are properly on the throne as Christ Himself mentioned in Revelation 3:21. One explanation would have Christ on the throne in chapter 4 and the Father on the throne in chapter 5. Another point of view is that both chapters picture God the Father on the throne in the special character of the God of Israel. The seeming contradiction may also be resolved in the doctrine of the Trinity as Christ expressed it in John 14:9: "He that hath seen me hath seen the Father." It is significant that God is not given an anthropomorphic figure in this revelation and does not appear as a man. Apart from the fact that He is said to sit on the throne, no description is given except the colors which impressed John. It is evident that the glory of God was the intent of the vision rather than an anthropomorphic representation.

THE TWENTY-FOUR ELDERS (4:4)

4:4 And round about the throne were four and twenty seats: and upon the seats I saw four and twenty elders sitting, clothed in white raiment; and they had on their heads crowns of gold.

In addition to the glory of the throne and the One who sat upon it John's attention is next directed to twenty-four thrones upon which the twenty-four elders are seated. The term "seats" is properly "thrones."

[4]Henry Alford, *The Greek New Testament,* IV, 594.

The elders are represented as in a situation of repose, sitting on their thrones, clothed in white raiment and having on their heads crowns of gold. Considerable discussion has arisen concerning the identity of these twenty-four elders, and three principal views have been advanced. Some regard them as a representative body of all the saints of all ages. Others regard them as representative only of the church, the Body of Christ. Still a third view is that they represent an order of angels.

The fact that they are a representative group, however, seems to be clear from the parallel of the Old Testament where the priesthood was represented by twenty-four orders of priests. There were actually thousands of priests in Israel's day of ascendancy under David and Solomon, but they all could not minister at the same time. Accordingly, they were divided into twenty-four orders, each of which was represented by a priest. When these priests met together, even though there were only twenty-four, they represented the whole priesthood and at the same time the whole of the nation of Israel. In a similar way the twenty-four elders mentioned in the book of Revelation may be regarded as a representative body.

The text itself does not give a specific statement concerning the identity of these elders. In chapter 5 additional information is given, and our later study of this chapter will throw further light on the problem. Some help, however, is afforded in the description given here.

The elders are described as being clothed in white raiment and having on their heads crowns of gold. There are two kinds of crowns in the book of Revelation, involving two different Greek words. One is the crown of a ruler or a sovereign (Gr., *diadem*), which is a crown of governmental authority. The other is the crown of a victor (Gr., *stephanos*), such as was awarded in the Greek games when a person won a race or some contest. This crown was usually made of leaves.

The word here is the crown of a victor rather than that of a sovereign. It was made of gold, indicating that the elders had been rewarded for victory accomplished. It is significant that the passage states the twenty-four elders already have their crowns of gold as victors. If this passage is regarded as chronologically before the time of the tribulation which succeeding chapters unfold, it would seem to eliminate the angels, as at this point they have not been judged and rewarded since their judgment seems to come later. For the same reason the elders do not seem to be a proper representation of Israel, for Israel's judgment also seems to come at the end of the tribulation, not before. Only the church which is raptured before chapter 4 is properly complete in heaven and eligible for reward at the judgment seat of Christ. In that case, the crowns of gold on the heads of the twenty-four elders would be fitting at this point and would seem to confirm the idea that these may be representative of the church in glory.

Alford states,

> These 24 elders are not *angels*, as maintained by Rinck and Hofmann (Weiss u. Erfull. p. 325 f.), as is shown (not by ch. 5:9, as generally argued,—even by Elliott, vol. I, p. 81 f.: see text there: but) by their white robes and crowns, the rewards of *endurance*, ch. 3:5; 2:10,— but *representatives of the Church*, as generally understood.[5]

Alford continues with a long discussion designed to prove that the church includes the saints of the Old Testament.[6] This, of course, is not taught here but rests on other grounds.

Recent New Testament scholarship has tended to abandon the traditional interpretation in favor of identification of the twenty-four elders as angels. Typical is the discussion of N. B. Stonehouse who dedicates a whole chapter to this in his work *Paul Before the Areopagus*. He offers several important arguments in favor of interpreting the elders as angels. Stonehouse holds that the revised text is definitely to be preferred and that the tendency to cling to the interpretation that the elders are redeemed and translated saints is largely because this view has been considered the traditional orthodox interpretation. Stonehouse concludes,

> The late expositors do not appear to do justice to the implications of the current critical text which records a song celebrating the redemption of a diverse multitude, *but which evidently ascribes the song to beings who are distinguished from the redeemed.*[7]

Stonehouse supports his conclusion by endeavoring to prove that Revelation 5:11 does not necessarily distinguish "many angels" from the elders, which would imply that they are not elders, and holds that unless it is clearly otherwise stated celestial spirits should be classified as some kind of angel. While Stonehouse does as well as anyone could to support the identification of the elders as angels, it is evident that he does not have any final or conclusive proof, and the controversy cannot be resolved. Identification of the twenty-four elders should not be dogmatically held, but such evidence as there is seems to point to the conclusion that they may represent the church as the Body of Christ. See chapter 5 for further discussion.

THE SEVEN SPIRITS OF GOD (4:5)

4:5 And out of the throne proceeded lightnings and thunderings and voices: and there were seven lamps of fire burning before the throne, which are the seven Spirits of God.

[5]Alford, IV, 596.
[6]*Ibid.*, 596-97.
[7]*Paul Before the Areopagus*, p. 92.

The all-inspiring scene described by John in this verse is in keeping with the majesty of the throne and the dignity of the twenty-four elders. The lightnings, thunderings, and voices which proceed from the throne are prophetic of the righteous judgment of God upon a sinful world. They are similar to the thunders, lightnings, and voice of the trumpet which mark the giving of the law in Exodus 19:16 and are a fitting preliminary to the awful judgments which are to follow in the great tribulation as God deals with the earth in righteousness.

John's attention is also directed to seven lamps of fire which are seen burning before the throne. These are identified as "the seven Spirits of God" mentioned earlier in 1:4 and 3:1. These are best understood as a representation of the Holy Spirit in a sevenfold way rather than seven individual spirits which would require that they be understood as seven angels. Ordinarily the Holy Spirit is not humanly visible unless embodied in some way. When the Holy Spirit descended on Christ on the occasion of His baptism, the people saw a dove descending. If it had not been for the dove, they could not have seen the Holy Spirit. In a similar way on the day of Pentecost, the coming of the Spirit would not have been visible if it had not been for the "cloven tongues like as of fire" (Acts 2:3). The seven lamps of fire therefore are the means by which John is informed of the presence of the Holy Spirit. The number seven is characteristic of the perfection of the Spirit and is in keeping with the revelation of Isaiah 11:2–3. In the heavenly scene it may be concluded on the basis of both chapters 4 and 5 that all three Persons of the Trinity are in evidence, each in His particular form of revelation.

THE FOUR LIVING CREATURES (4:6–8)

4:6-8 And before the throne there was a sea of glass like unto crystal: and in the midst of the throne, and round about the throne, were four beasts full of eyes before and behind. And the first beast was like a lion, and the second beast like a calf, and the third beast had a face as a man, and the fourth beast was like a flying eagle. And the four beasts had each of them six wings about him; and they were full of eyes within: and they rest not day and night, saying, Holy, holy, holy, Lord God Almighty, which was, and is, and is to come.

Occupying an important part of the scene before John is a sea of glass described as "like unto crystal," and in the background are four living creatures. Apart from indicating that the sea of glass is like crystal, John gives us no explanation of the meaning of this sea. As in other portions of the book of Revelation, however, John expects the reader to draw conclusions from similar scenes elsewhere in the Bible. There seems here to be an analogy or comparison to the sea of brass in the Tabernacle in the Old Testament or the molten sea in the Temple. Both were lavers, or washstands, designed for the cleansing of the priests, and contained water used for various ceremonial rites. This may represent typically the sanctifying power of the Word of God.

No sure interpretation of the sea of glass may be advanced. As Alford states, "All kinds of symbolic interpretations, more or less fanciful, have been given."[8] Alford supports this by citing a long number of complicated and conflicting interpretations. He prefers the following view:

> The primary reference will be to the clear ether in which the throne of God is upborne and the intent of setting this space in front of the throne will be, to betoken its separation and insulation from the place where the Seer stood, and indeed from all else about it.[9]

The fact is that no explanation is given in the text.

John, however, is not occupied at this point with the sea of glass, but rather with the four living creatures described as in the midst of the throne and round about the throne. He records that they are full of eyes, before and behind, and each of them has six wings. Further, each of the four beasts is to be distinguished according to verse 7. They are described respectively as like a lion, a calf, a man, and a flying eagle. Their ministry before the throne of God is that of ceaselessly ascribing holiness to the Lord.

The translation "beasts" is quite inaccurate and should be changed to "living ones." In the Greek the word used is *zōon*, which means "living ones." An entirely different word, *thērion*, meaning "a beast," such as a wild animal, is used in Revelation 13 to speak of the beast coming out of the sea. The emphasis here is on the quality of life and the attributes that relate to it.

There has been much speculation concerning the identity of these living ones and the significance of their presence and ministry in this heavenly scene. As Alford states, "In enquiring after their symbolic import, we are met by the most remarkable diversity of interpretation."[10] Four important explanations are among the possibilities. Some interpret the four living creatures as representative of the attributes or qualities of God presented to John here as living entities. This is probably the best interpretation. Just as the Holy Spirit is represented by seven lamps, so the attributes of God in general are represented by the four living ones. The fact that the creatures are full of eyes is taken as significant of the omniscience and omnipresence of God who sees all and knows all.

In a similar way the four beasts as respectively a lion, a calf, a man, and an eagle are considered different aspects of divine majesty. All of these are supreme in their respective categories. The lion is the king of

[8]Alford, IV, 598.
[9]*Ibid.*
[10]*Ibid.*, IV, 599.

beasts and represents majesty and omnipotence. The calf or ox, representing the most important of domestic animals, signifies patience and continuous labor. Man is the greatest of all God's creatures, especially in intelligence and rational power; whereas the eagle is greatest among birds and is symbolic of sovereignty and supremacy.

Comparison has also been made of the four living creatures to the four Gospels which present Christ in four major aspects of His person. As the lion, He is the Lion of the tribe of Judah, represented as the king of Matthew. As the calf or ox, He is the Servant of Jehovah, the faithful one of Mark. As man, He is the human Jesus, presented in the Gospel of Luke, and as the eagle, He is the divine Son of God presented in the Gospel of John. Alford thinks that this has the least to commend itself of all of the many diverse interpretations. He states, after quoting at length Victorinus who championed this view,

> I have cited this comment at length, to show on what fanciful and untenable ground it rests. For with perhaps the one exception of the last of the four, not one of the Evangelists has any inner or substantial accordance with the character thus assigned.[11]

In support of his objection he points out how many commentators disagree as to what Gospel is represented by each of the living ones.

Scott observes that ancient rabbinical writers declared that the tribes of Israel pitched their tents and standards on the four sides of the Tabernacle in this same order; namely, the tribe of Judah, a lion; the tribe of Ephraim, an ox; the tribe of Reuben, a man; the tribe of Dan, an eagle[12] (cf. Num. 2:2). The fact that there are four living creatures is also noteworthy. It seems to be indicative of the relationship of God to the material universe or the world in general.[13] Taken in general, the four living creatures are representative of God; they are, as in the case of the seven lamps, a physical embodiment of that which would be otherwise invisible to the natural eye.[14] To John the scene was unmistakably one of majestic revelation.

An alternative explanation is that the four living creatures are angels whose function it is to bring honor and glory to God. Angels as seen in the Scriptures vary widely in their appearance, and this explanation is a plausible one. Angels are frequently seen in the Bible especially in

---

[11]*Ibid.*, IV, 600.

[12]Walter Scott, *Exposition of the Revelation of Jesus Christ*, p. 126, note, quoting F. Brodie, *Notes on the Revelation.*

[13]*Ibid.*

[14]J. L. Martin offers the somewhat fantastic explanation that the four beasts represent the four quarters of the earth; the first, Asia; the second, Africa; the third, Europe; the fourth, America. He bases this on the fact that John is invited by these four beasts to come and see but not invited to behold the contents of the fifth, sixth, and seventh seals. This is another product of the historical interpretation (*The Voice of the Seven Thunders*, pp. 81–82).

apocalyptic books of the Bible such as Ezekiel and Revelation. The fact that the living creatures have six wings as do the seraphim of Isaiah 6:2–3 adds weight to the interpretation that they are angels. The living creatures in Revelation 4 and the seraphim of Isaiah 6 have a similar function in that both ascribe holiness to the Lord of hosts (cf. Isa. 6:3). The ministry of the living creatures is designed to emphasize the holiness of God and His eternity, in that according to the Scripture, "they rest not day and night, saying, Holy, holy, holy, Lord God Almighty, which was, and is, and is to come." Their presence in the heavenly scene contributed much to the overall impression of the majesty, holiness, sovereignty, and eternity of God.

THE WORSHIP OF THE LIVING CREATURES AND THE ELDERS (4:9–11)

4:9-11 And when those beasts give glory and honour and thanks to him that sat on the throne, who liveth for ever and ever, The four and twenty elders fall down before him that sat on the throne, and worship him that liveth for ever and ever, and cast their crowns before the throne saying, Thou art worthy, O Lord, to receive glory and honour and power: for thou hast created all things, and for thy pleasure they are and were created.

Though it is stated earlier that the living creatures do not rest in their ascription of holiness to God, according to verse 9, periodically they give special glory and honor and praise to God sitting on His throne. On such occasions, according to verse 10, the twenty-four elders join with them in worship and fall down before God on His throne. In their worship, they cast their victors' crowns before the throne declaring that God is worthy of glory and honor and power because all things have been created by Him and for His pleasure.

The closing scene of chapter 4 brings out several important truths. It is evident that the living ones are designed to give glory, honor, and thanks to God sitting upon His throne. The emphasis of their praise is on the divine attributes and worthiness of God.

The worship of the twenty-four elders has a more particular note. They not only worship and recognize these attributes of God but support their worship by recognition of the fact that God is the sovereign Creator of the universe and, as such, is sovereign over it. In other words they recognize not only the attributes but the works of God which reveal the attributes. Further, in casting their crowns before the throne they testify that if it had not been for God's grace, salvation, and goodness, they could not have had victory over sin and death. Here the creature honors His Maker and accepts the dictum that man necessarily must be subject to his Creator.

The world today does not give such honor to the Lord God. Though

111

men benefit from His goodness and live in a universe of His creation, they tend to neglect the worship of God. One of the important aims of the book of Revelation is to trace the divine movement of history toward the goal of universal recognition of God. This purpose of God, especially as related to the Son of God, is also spelled out in Philippians 2:9–11:

> Wherefore God also hath highly exalted him, and given him a name which is above every name: That at the name of Jesus every knee should bow, of things in heaven, and things in earth, and things under the earth: And that every tongue should confess that Jesus Christ is Lord, to the glory of God the Father.

As if anticipating the ultimate consummation where all will recognize the exalted name of Jesus whether in heaven or hell, Revelation 4 reveals this intimate glimpse of heaven where all created beings join in a symphony of praise and give their honor and worship to the Almighty God. The worthiness of God to receive such praise is related to His sovereign right to rule as the One who sits upon the throne. The twenty-four elders bear witness to His majesty and glory, His holiness and power, and the eternity of the One "which was, and is, and is to come." All creatures owe their very existence to Him as their Creator, "for thou hast created all things, and for thy pleasure they are and were created." Chapter 4 is a fitting introduction to that which follows in the next chapter, where the glory of Christ as Redeemer, as the "Lamb that was slain," is an added reason for praise. Wise is the soul who finds in the Scriptures the revelation of such a God and who bows now in this day of grace in faith and worship before the God whom he will serve in eternity.

5

THE LAMB AND THE SEVEN-SEALED BOOK

THE SEVEN-SEALED BOOK IN THE RIGHT HAND OF GOD (5:1-4)

5:1-4 And I saw in the right hand of him that sat on the throne a book written within and on the backside, sealed with seven seals. And I saw a strong angel proclaiming with a loud voice, Who is worthy to open the book, and to loose the seals thereof? And no man in heaven, nor in earth, neither under the earth, was able to open the book, neither to look thereon. And I wept much, because no man was found worthy to open and to read the book, neither to look thereon.

CHAPTER 5 of the book of Revelation continues the vision of the throne of heaven given in the preceding chapter. John is now introduced to an item of central importance, namely, a book which contains the prophecy of impending events to be unfolded in the book of Revelation. The book is actually a scroll (Gr., *biblion*), which is given prominence in the scene by the fact that it is in the right hand of God who is on the throne. The importance and comprehensive character of the revelation contained is indicated by the fact that the book is written on both sides of the parchment. Further, the document is made impressive by seven seals, apparently fixed on the edges of the scroll in such a way that the seals must be successively broken if the scroll is to be unrolled and read. Stauffer observes that the Roman law required a will to be sealed seven times as illustrated in the wills left by Augustus and Vespasian for their successors.[1]

John's attention is especially directed to this book by the pronouncement of a strong angel. The adjective "strong" (Gr., *ischyros*) means "mighty or powerful," and hence indicates that an important angel is selected for this pronouncement. J. B. Smith comments on the "strong angel" as follows:

> The vision opens with three notes of emphasis: a strong angel—only twice more is reference made to a strong angel in the book, viz., 10:1 and 18:21 (Greek). The angel proclaims—not merely says. The word signifies to announce as a herald. *With a loud voice* denotes

[1]Ethelbert Stauffer, *Christ and the Caesars*, pp. 182–83.

urgency and great concern. . . . Who is the strong angel making the
challenge? The answer is, doubtless, Gabriel, the one who ordered
the closing and sealing of the book to Daniel.[2]

The proclamation itself is given with a loud voice, literally, a loud
sound (Gr., *phonē*). The angel raises the question "Who is worthy to
open the book, and to loose the seals thereof?" John then records in
verse 3 that no one in heaven, in earth, or under the earth was able (Gr.,
edynato, meaning "have the power or authority") to open the book. It
is evident that the contents of the book are impressive in character and
require the power of God for their revelation as well as for the execution
of their program. John records that he wept much because no one was
found worthy either to open and read or even to look upon the book.
The purpose of this dramatic presentation of the seven-sealed book was
to impress upon John the importance of its contents and of the revelation contained therein.

THE LAMB DECLARED WORTHY TO RECEIVE THE BOOK (5:5-7)

5:5-7 And one of the elders saith unto me, Weep not: behold, the
Lion of the tribe of Juda, the Root of David, hath prevailed to open
the book, and to loose the seven seals thereof. And I beheld, and lo,
in the midst of the throne and of the four beasts, and in the midst of
the elders, stood a Lamb as it had been slain, having seven horns and
seven eyes, which are the seven Spirits of God sent forth into all the
earth. And he came and took the book out of the right hand of him
that sat upon the throne.

As John weeps because in all creation no one is found worthy to open
the book, one of the elders is recorded in verse 5 as telling him that he
shall not keep on weeping, for one is worthy to open the book, namely,
"the Lion of the tribe of Juda, the Root of David." The allusion to "the
Lion" is a reference to Genesis 49:9-10, where it is predicted that the
future ruler of the earth shall come from the tribe of Judah, the lion tribe.

Reference to Christ as the Root of David stems from the prophecy of
Isaiah 11:1: "And there shall come forth a rod out of the stem of Jesse,
and a Branch shall grow out of his roots" (cf. Isa. 11:10). It is declared
that He "hath prevailed" (Gr., *enikēsen*, meaning "to conquer"). In the
Greek the verb comes first in the sentence for emphasis. Hence, translated literally it is "Behold, he has conquered, the Lion of the tribe of
Judah, the Root of David."

His victory is such that He has the right not only to take the book but
to open it and loose the seven seals thereof. The Scriptures seem to
distinguish between opening the book (which would involve beginning
the process of unrolling the scroll) and the complete authority to break

[2]*A Revelation of Jesus Christ*, p. 112.

all the seven seals successively. It implies that Christ is completely worthy and has full authority and sovereignty in respect to the contents of the seven-sealed book.

With this introduction John fixes his gaze upon one portrayed as a Lamb standing in the midst of the throne and of the four living creatures. The Lamb is described as having been slain and then raised from the dead and as possessing seven horns and seven eyes. As J. Vernon McGee contrasts the lion and the lamb characteristics of Christ, he states that the lion character refers to His second coming, since the lion speaks of His majesty. As lion He is sovereign; as lion He is Judge. The lion speaks of the government of God. The lamb character refers to His first coming, for the lamb speaks of His meekness. As lamb He is Saviour; as lamb He is judged. The lamb speaks of the grace of God.[3] As far as the book of Revelation is concerned, however, Christ is referred to as the Lion only once, here in 5:5, in contrast to the many times He is identified as the Lamb. The purpose of the use of the term "lamb" seems to be to identify the glorified Christ of Revelation with Christ the Lamb of sacrifice in His first coming.

The horns seem to speak of the prerogative of a king (cf. Dan. 7:24; Rev. 13:1). The seven eyes are identified as "the seven Spirits of God" sent forth into all the earth (cf. Zech. 3:9; 4:10). Though this may be a reference to seven angels, the preferable view is that it is another reference to the sevenfold Spirit of God. The Holy Spirit was sent by Christ into the world (cf. John 16:7).

Taking the contents of these verses together, the Lamb is represented as one sovereign in His own authority, omnipotent in power, and worthy as the Redeemer who died. Merrill C. Tenney says that the title *Lamb*

> stresses particularly His redemptive aspects since it is modified by the phrase "as though it had been slain" (5:6, 9, 12; 13:8). Never is the exact word "Lamb" used of Christ outside of Revelation, although a similar word meaning "sacrificial lamb" occurs in four passages elsewhere (John 1:29, 36; Acts 8:32; I Peter 1:19).[4]

Walter Scott observes,

> The term *lamb* occurs in the Apocalypse twenty-eight times; the word employed signifies a diminutive animal *Arnion*, not *Amnos*, as in the Gospel (chap. 1:29, etc.). The word *lion* is only once applied to Christ in this book.[5]

Consummating the revelation of His person and authority is the declaration of verse 7, that He takes the book out of the right hand of the One sitting upon the throne, who is clearly God the Father.

[3]*Reveling Through Revelation*, I, 47.
[4]*Interpreting Revelation*, p. 174.
[5]*The Book of Revelation*, p. 135.

In the act of receiving the book from God the Father, it is made evident that judgment and power over the earth are committed to Christ the Son of God. Daniel 7:13–14 is a parallel passage. There Daniel reveals the ultimate triumph of Christ when the kingdoms of the world are given to Christ. Daniel declares,

> I saw in the night visions, and, behold, one like the Son of man came with the clouds of heaven, and came to the Ancient of days, and they brought him near before him. And there was given him dominion, and glory, and a kingdom, that all people, nations, and languages, should serve him: his dominion is an everlasting dominion, which shall not pass away, and his kingdom that which shall not be destroyed.

In that future day complete authority over the world will be realized by Christ, an authority which He will exercise both in the judgments which precede His second coming and in His reign for one thousand years which will follow His second advent. Once again in the book of Revelation the focus is upon Christ, the central character of the book and the One whose glory is supremely revealed in the unfolding pages of its prophecies.

THE LIVING CREATURES AND THE ELDERS WORSHIPING THE LAMB (5:8–10)

> **5:8-10** And when he had taken the book, the four beasts and four and twenty elders fell down before the Lamb, having every one of them harps, and golden vials full of odours, which are the prayers of saints. And they sung a new song, saying, Thou art worthy to take the book, and to open the seals thereof: for thou wast slain, and hast redeemed us to God by thy blood out of every kindred, and tongue, and people, and nation; And hast made us unto our God kings and priests: and we shall reign on the earth.

The importance and significance of the scene which John saw in heaven are recognized on the part of the four living creatures and the twenty-four elders. By their obeisance and worship of the Lamb as recorded in verse 8 it should be clear that the Lamb is not merely a prophet or an exalted angel but none other than the Lord Jesus Christ in all the majesty of deity, even though portrayed in His sacrificial role as the Lamb who died on the cross.

In connection with their worship of the Lamb, it is mentioned that the creatures and the elders have harps which are symbols and instruments of divine worship, and that they possess and pour out golden vials full of odors which are declared to be the prayers of the saints. The same Lamb of God who suffered the abuse of the soldiers and the scoffing of the crowd as well as the agony on the cross is here being given His rightful worship. Apart from the trumpet, the harp (lyre) is the only

116

instrument mentioned in heavenly worship and was employed commonly in the worship of the Old Testament. There is no direct statement that they are played on this occasion, but this is the implication.

The golden vials or bowls filled with sacred perfume or incense represent the prayers of the saints according to the text. Here in heaven the importance of prayer in the earthly scene is inferred. Later in the book testimony is made to the continued witness on earth of those who trust in Christ during the time of dreadful tribulation. Their prayers are said to be as sweet incense before the throne of God. The role of the elders seems to be one of sympathetic presentation, not that of a mediator of earthly prayers. The symbolism of bowls of incense representing the prayers of the saints is reflected in Psalm 141:2 where David cried to the Lord, "Let my prayer be set forth before thee as incense; and the lifting up of my hands as the evening sacrifice."

Along with their worship and the use of the harps and the incense, they sing a new song in which Christ is declared to be worthy because of His work of redemption and His transformation of men into kings and priests. Bloomfield expresses the wonder "that someone has not written a great oratorio on Revelation. The references to songs, trumpets, and chants provide an important aspect of the moving scene of the book of Revelation."[6] Swete believes that the reference to "kings and priests" which occurs two other times in Revelation (1:6; 20:6) may have been part of an early hymn which had the line "Thou hast made us a kingdom, priests to God and our father, and we shall reign on the earth."[7]

In the comment on Revelation 4:4 it was observed that there is difference of opinion as to the identity of the twenty-four elders. In 5:9–10 additional light is cast upon their character. If the text of the Authorized Version is correct, the twenty-four elders in their new song declare that God has redeemed them by His blood out of every kindred, tongue, people, and nation and has made them kings and priests. If the twenty-four elders are actually redeemed by the blood of Christ, it is clear that they could not be angels but must be redeemed men.

Some ancient versions of Scripture give a different rendering. In keeping with this variation in text, the song herein recorded is translated in the American Standard Version of 1901 as follows:

> Worthy art thou to take the book, and to open the seals thereof: for thou wast slain, and didst purchase unto God with thy blood *men* of every tribe, and tongue, and people, and nation, and madest them *to be* unto our God a kingdom and priests; and they reign upon the earth.

[6]Arthur E. Bloomfield, *All Things New*, p. 17.
[7]Henry B. Swete, *The Apocalypse of St. John*, p. 82.

If this latter rendering is the proper one, it leaves undetermined whether the twenty-four elders are men or angels. It records only that they pay tribute to the Lamb, as the One who was slain and who purchased men from every tribe, tongue, people, and nation. Such a song would be worthy of angels as well as redeemed men.

The fact that there is a variation in texts in this passage, however, by no means determines beyond question that the text used by the Authorized Version is incorrect. This is still debatable, although most textual scholars of the twentieth century prefer the revised text.[8] Even if the revised text is accepted, however, though it removes absolute proof of the human origin of the twenty-four elders, it does not constitute specific proof that they are angels. It merely leaves the matter open. In view of the fact that the twenty-four elders are pictured as having crowns of gold and clothed in white raiment, as if they are already a complete people judged and rewarded, the weight of evidence still is in favor of considering them as representatives of the church, the Body of Christ. The alternative suggestion that they are angels, however, is possible. Adherents of this view point out that the "crowns" could be representative of government of the universe in which angels participate (cf. Col. 1:16). Probably most New Testament scholars today interpret the elders as angels.

The controversy over the text should not obscure the marvelous symphony of praise that is here ascribed to the Lamb. It is declared to be a new song, that is, a song which could not have been sung prior to His redemptive act, a song over and beyond an ascription of praise to His person or a recognition of His attributes. Here He is declared to have the right to rule, not simply in virtue of His deity but in His victory over sin and death in His act of supreme redemption. The right to the book has been secured by conquering death and providing a complete sacrifice for sin. The act of redemption is declared to be worldwide in that every kindred, tongue, and nation has been redeemed and has transformed sinners, who once were under the wrath of God, into kings and priests who will reign with Christ on the earth.

The song of redemption recorded in this chapter would be entirely normal for saints but would be rather unusual if the angels were involved. Nowhere else in the Bible are angels pictured as singing since sin entered the world. In the early joy of creation before it was spoiled by sin, Job refers to the time "when the morning stars sang together, and all the sons of God shouted for joy" (Job 38:7). The morning stars here are commonly identified with the angels. Since Adam's sin, however, there

---

[8]Cf. the excellent discussion in support of the revised text of Revelation 5:9-10 by N. B. Stonehouse, *Paul Before the Areopagus*, pp. 95-101.

is no further record of angels singing. On the occasion of the birth of Christ, the angels praised God, but this seems to have been a recital of words of praise, not given in the form of a song. The fact of the wonderful redemption that is in Christ Jesus by which sinners of all kindreds, tribes, and nations can be redeemed and enter into the blessing of saints is the occasion for the new song of redemption; and whether sung by men or angels it is a worthy ascription of praise and worship addressed to the Lamb of God.

The peculiar purpose of God for His church is intimated in verse 10 of the Authorized Version in that the twenty-four elders are declared to be kings and priests who shall reign on earth. Here again it is more natural to refer this to men than to angels. The peculiar privileges of the church are clearly indicated. The church is a priesthood rather than having a priesthood, and is a royal family rather than merely being ruled by a king. The members will not be so much subjects of the kingdom as they will be reigning with Christ on the earth. Here again is intimated the purpose of God to consummate and fulfill the prophecies of an earthly kingdom in which Christ will reign as King of kings and Lord of lords. The phrase "on the earth" is significant as referring to the earthly millennial reign of Christ in which the church will participate. The Greek preposition *epi* is properly translated "on" or "upon." In this glorious earthly scene to follow the dark hour of the tribulation, the church will share the glory of Christ as joint heirs with Christ and sharers of His sovereign rule.

THE WORSHIP OF THE ANGELS (5:11–12)

5:11-12 And I beheld, and I heard the voice of many angels round about the throne and the beasts and the elders: and the number of them was ten thousand times ten thousand, and thousands of thousands; Saying with a loud voice, Worthy is the Lamb that was slain to receive power, and riches, and wisdom, and strength, and honour, and glory, and blessing.

John introduces the exaltation of the Lamb in verse 11 with the familiar words "And I beheld, and I heard." Forty-four times in the book he declares that he beheld or saw something and twenty-seven times he declares, "I heard." The tremendous scene left a lasting impression upon John. In concentric circles with the Lamb in the center surrounded by the living creatures and the twenty-four elders, the angelic hosts are seen on every side numbering ten thousand times ten thousand, an innumerable throng in one mighty symphony of praise. They joined in saying with a loud voice, "Worthy is the Lamb that was slain to receive power, and riches, and wisdom, and strength, and honour, and glory, and blessing." The sevenfold attributes ascribed to the Lamb sum up their wor-

119

ship and adoration. This great chorus of praise is a prelude to the mighty scenes which will unfold, when in succeeding chapters, the seven-sealed book is unrolled. The twenty-four elders sing, and the angels chant their praise in this impressive scene.

THE WORSHIP OF ALL CREATION (5:13–14)

5:13-14 And every creature which is in heaven, and on the earth, and under the earth, and such as are in the sea, and all that are in them, heard I saying, Blessing, and honour, and glory, and power, be unto him that sitteth upon the throne, and unto the Lamb for ever and ever. And the four beasts said, Amen. And the four and twenty elders fell down and worshipped him that liveth for ever and ever.

To this mighty chorus in heaven is added the praise of every creature on earth and under the earth and in the sea. John hears them all joining in blessing and praise to the One on the throne and to the Lamb. Climaxing the scene of worship, the four living creatures pronounce their amen, and the twenty-four elders once again fall down and worship. The closing expression of verse 14, "that liveth for ever and ever," is omitted in some manuscripts, but the reference is clear in any case. With this tremendous awesome introduction, the ground is laid for the unfolding revelation beginning in chapter 6, when the scene shifts once again from heaven to the earth.

The beauty and wonder of the scene in chapter 5 are in startling contrast to the dark clouds of divine judgment portrayed as falling upon the earth in the tribulation as revealed in the chapters which follow. The scenes of earth are always dark in comparison to the glory of heaven. The Christian engulfed by temptation, persecution, and trial can take heart in the fact that our Lord also suffered and was tried, and that He in triumph ascended on high having completed His earthly work. Those who follow in His steps while in the world may endure many afflictions, but they are assured that they will share with the Lord His glory and His grace throughout all eternity.

The scene of chapter 5 can be considered as prophetic of future events in which the church of Jesus Christ bearing witness in the world today will be in the presence of the Lord in heaven. Those who have received Jesus Christ as Saviour and who have entered into the blessings of His redemptive work will be numbered among the tens of thousands pictured in chapter 5 as giving their worship and praise to the Saviour. That which John contemplated in prophetic vision will be an actual part of the future experience of the saints of God as they wait with Christ for the consummating events of the age and the establishment of His kingdom.

With the introduction provided in chapters 4 and 5 which give us the heavenly side of the picture, the narrative in John's vision now turns to the earth in chapter 6. The same Lord and Redeemer who is the object of worship and praise on the part of the saints is also the righteous Judge of the wicked earth and the One by whose authority the terrible events of the tribulation unfold. In the light of these future events, how important is the decision that faces every human soul. Today is the day of grace as the Scriptures make plain. Those who hear and respond to the divine invitation have the promise of blessing throughout eternity and deliverance from the time of judgment which will fall upon those who neglect to enter into the safety of salvation in their day of opportunity.

For many Christians heaven is an unreal place. Even Christians tend to be occupied too much with the things of this present world, which can be seen and touched and felt. Too often goals in life have little to do with eternity's values. Though to the ordinary Christian the privilege of a vision of heaven such as was given the Apostle John and the Apostle Paul is seldom granted, what they saw has been plainly written in the Word of God, and we can see through their eyes the glorious picture of the majesty which surrounds the Lord in heaven. By comparison to the heavenly scene, earth is revealed to be temporary and transitory, and its glory and glitter are tarnished. As far as the heavens are above the earth, so far the glory of heaven transcends what the natural eye can see in this world.

Revelation puts earth and heaven in proper perspective, the scenes of earth ending in the tragic denouement of the great tribulation, and the scenes of heaven fulfilled both in the millennial glory and in the eternal state. The true occupation of the child of God should be one of praise and worship of the God of glory while awaiting the fulfillment of His prophetic Word.

6

THE BEGINNING OF THE GREAT DAY
OF GOD'S WRATH

INTRODUCTION

THE OPENING OF CHAPTER 6 of the book of Revelation marks an important milestone in the progressive revelation of the end of the age. In chapter 5 John is introduced to the seven-sealed book in the hand of Christ. In chapter 6 the first six seals are opened with the resultant tremendous events occurring in the earth. The interpretation of these events depends upon the understanding of other portions of the prophetic Word. If the events portrayed are taken in any literal sense, it should be clear that they describe an event yet future, in the words of Christ "the things which shall be hereafter" (1:19). Van Ryn expresses the common pretribulational position:

> The opening of the seals ushers in the terrible judgments to fall upon this earth after the Church has been caught up to glory, as we saw in chap. 4:1.[1]

The events here revealed also depend for their interpretation on the question of whether a translation of the church has already taken place. Though the book of Revelation itself does not determine this important question with finality, it is significant that the church so prominent in chapters 2 and 3 is not mentioned again until 22:16 except as the wife of the Lamb at the close of the tribulation. Nowhere in scenes of earth which describe the end time (chaps. 6–19) is the church pictured as involved in the earthly struggle. Further, the hope of the rapture mentioned to the church of Thyatira and the church at Philadelphia does not appear in the detailed prophetic program which unfolds in the book of Revelation. This lends credence to the conclusion that the rapture of the church has occurred before the events pictured beginning with chapter 4.

Expositors of the book of Revelation usually agree that there is some relation between the events at the end of the age and Daniel's seventieth week, to be understood as the last seven years of Israel's program proph-

[1]August Van Ryn, *Notes on the Book of Revelation*, p. 87.

esied in Daniel 9:27. Many have assumed that the events of earth in chapters 6 through 19 coincide with the seven years of Israel's program culminating in the second coming of Christ. Expositors of this point of view have usually taken for granted that the book gives a panoramic view of the entire seven years even though there is no explicit proof of this in the book itself. There is some evidence, however, that the events pictured in the seals, trumpets, and vials are instead a concentrated prophecy of the latter half of this week, i.e., a period of three and one-half years, designated as a time of wrath and the great tribulation, and constituting the introduction to the second coming of Christ. Evidence for this is presented as the exposition unfolds.

There is a remarkable similarity between the progress of chapter 6 as a whole and the description given by our Lord of the end of the age in Matthew 24:4-31. In both passages the order is (1) war (Matt. 24:6-7; Rev. 6:3-4), (2) famine (Matt. 24:7; Rev. 6:5-6), (3) death (Matt. 24:7-9; Rev. 6:7-8), (4) martyrdom (Matt. 24:9-10, 16-22; Rev. 6:9-11), (5) the sun darkened, the moon darkened, and the stars falling (Matt. 24:29; Rev. 6:12-14), (6) a time of divine judgment (Matt. 24:32-25:26; Rev. 6:15-17). The general features of Matthew 24 are obviously quite parallel to the events of the book of Revelation beginning in chapter 6.[2]

It is inevitable therefore that any exposition of Revelation must have presuppositions based upon a study of the entire Word of God and involving the question as to whether prophecy should be interpreted with the same degree of literalness as other portions of Scripture. Though Revelation abounds in signs and symbols, it was intended to be interpreted with far greater literalness than has been commonly exercised. Such an approach yields a remarkable revelation of the end of the age which coincides with other prophetic revelation.

The picture before us, in a word, is God's revelation of the dramatic and terrible judgment which will climax the present age. This constitutes a warning to those who are living carelessly in unbelief to beware lest this age engulf them. The prophecy of the end of the age is a spur to Christians to snatch souls as brands from the burning and thus prepare them for the coming of the Lord.

THE FIRST SEAL (6:1-2)

6:1-2 And I saw when the Lamb opened one of the seals, and I heard, as it were the noise of thunder, one of the four beasts saying, Come and see. And I saw, and behold, a white horse: and he that sat on him had a bow; and a crown was given unto him: and he went forth conquering, and to conquer.

[2]Cf. J. Dwight Pentecost, *Things to Come*, pp. 280-82.

As the first seal is opened, John in his vision hears the noise of thunder, a symbolic token of a coming storm. On a warm summer day one can hear thunder in the distance even though the sun is still shining where he is. The approaching dark clouds and the roar of the thunder presage the beginning of the storm.

It is important to note that the revelation here given indicates a succession of events, though not all expositors have agreed on this conclusion. Lange, for instance, holds that the seals, trumpets, and vials are a symbolic presentation of the whole of human history.[3] The six seals seem to unfold successively in a chronological pattern. Out of the seventh seal will come another series of seven trumpets and out of the seventh trumpet will come another series of seven vials or bowls of the wrath of God.[4] Different actors are prominent, namely, the Lamb opening the seal, the angels sounding the trumpets, and God Himself pouring out the vials. Actually, however, the seven seals comprehend the whole, as all the trumpets and all the vials are comprehended in the seventh seal. The seven-sealed book therefore is the comprehensive program of God culminating in the second coming of Christ.

John Cumming presents a typical historical interpretation of the seals, trumpets, and vials in these words:

> The first six seals contain the history of the temporal glory and decline of Rome Pagan, the most illustrious empire of the ancient earth. This is my strong, and I think demonstrable conviction. The first six trumpets, which are comprehended in the seventh seal, contain the desolation of Rome Christian by the Goths, the Saracens, and the Turks. The first six vials, which are comprehended in the seventh trumpet, embody the events that occurred subsequent to the breaking forth of the great European revolution in 1793. Thus the twenty-one apocalyptic symbols, the seven seals, the seven trumpets, and the seven vials, represent in succession the progress of the church along the obstructions of time, her vicissitudes of experience, her trials, her cruel mockings, her perils, and her final triumph and permanent prosperity, contemporaneously with overwhelming judgments on the nations, and on the apostasy.[5]

[3]John Peter Lange, *Commentary on the Holy Scriptures: Revelation*, pp. 147 ff.; cf. note on symbolism by the American author, E. R. Craven, pp. 145–47; 178–79.

[4]Roadhouse in his chart of the book of Revelation offers a novel interpretation of the book in which the first three and one-half years of the seven-year period preceding Christ's coming to earth are divided into four periods corresponding to the first four messages to the churches, the first four seals, the first four trumpets, all of which are viewed as simultaneous, that is, the first church, the first seal, and the first trumpet coincide. The saints are raptured after the first three and one-half years, and the last three and one-half years which follow fulfill that which is anticipated in the last three messages to the churches, the last three seals, and the last three trumpets. The vials operating independently are fulfilled toward the close of the second three and one-half years. Roadhouse also suggests that the four riders of Revelation 6 correspond to the four kings and empires of Daniel 7. The novelty of these suggestions is their own refutation (W. F. Roadhouse, *Seeing the "Revelation,"* Appendix).

[5]John Cumming, *Lectures on the Apocalypse*, pp. 44–45.

Cumming, though following the historical school, believes in the pre-millennial return of Christ and the futuristic character of the latter portion of the book of Revelation. Of special interest is his chapter "Signs of the Second Advent" among which signs he names satanic unbelief. He states, "I believe that one-half of the professors of the gospel are nothing better than practical infidels."[6] He also names as signs the selfishness and increment of sin manifested in the present world, the increase and spread of popery, the continued hope of the Jews for a national home and their hope for their Messiah (even in the mid-nineteenth century), the efforts on the part of men at self-regeneration, the increase in knowledge, increase in the activity of Satan, the increase of systems of error, great judgments upon the earth, the growth in apathy and unbelief concerning the second coming.[7]

The decision to reject the historical school of interpretation (of which Cumming is a member), in favor of the futuristic approach is most important in understanding the subsequent chapters of the book of Revelation. While many arguments can be cited pro and con, the final choice must be based upon the judgment as to which provides the most sensible and self-consistent interpretation of the book of Revelation. The historical school as well as any which tends to spiritualize much of the book does not meet the test of providing such a self-consistent interpretation. At least fifty different systems of interpretation have arisen from the historical view alone. While even in the futurist school minor variations will be found in various expositors, the general conclusion that these chapters picture future definite events is the important coherent factor. The subsequent exposition of Revelation must be its own proof that the futuristic school provides a sensible explanation of the major events prophesied in the book. Many of the historical interpretations have already been proved false by historical developments. The ultimate proof of the futuristic interpretation will be in future events.

At the noise of thunder, John is invited by one of the four living creatures to come and see. Some texts omit the "and see." In verse 2 John repeats the expression "And I saw" of verse 1, as if to emphasize the sight he beholds. He further adds the word *behold*, indicating the startling character of the vision. What he sees is described as a white horse on which a man is sitting carrying a bow. The rider, to whom a crown is given, is pictured as going forth conquering and to conquer.

Stauffer traces the symbolism of the four horses to the custom of having four teams of horses in the races which were a part of the elaborate celebrations which characterized the reign of Domitian.[8] The idea, though

[6]*Ibid.*
[7]*Ibid.*, pp. 453–74.

interesting, does not do much to explain the eschatological significance of the four horsemen of the Apocalypse.

No explanation is given of this vision. In many cases the reader of Revelation is not left to his own ingenuity but is given the meaning of what is beheld. Here as in many other instances, however, the appeal is to a general knowledge of Scripture. In this instance, because there is no specific interpretation of the vision, more diverse explanations have been given of verse two than probably any other portion of the entire book.

Of the many possibilities two stand out as worthy of mention. Some believe the rider of the white horse is none other than Christ Himself.[9] This is characteristic of the historical school of interpretation which regards the Revelation as history rather than prophecy. However, some of this school regard this scene as future and as picturing Christ as the ultimate Victor of the ages. A more plausible explanation is that the rider of the white horse is none other than the "prince that shall come" of Daniel 9:26, who is to head up the revived Roman Empire and ultimately become the world ruler. Ainslie believes the rider of the white horse will appear at the beginning of the seventieth week of Daniel and that the rider himself "is the Roman prince of an empire that must rise again to fulfill the great prophecies of the book of Daniel."[10] He is Satan's masterpiece and the counterfeit of all that Christ is or claims to be. He is therefore cast in the role of a conqueror, which seems to be the significance of the white horse.

Jennings states,

> The whole context and character of these seals absolutely forbid our thinking of this rider being the Lord Jesus, as so many affirm. *His* reign shall not bring war, famine, and strife in its train.[11]

Jennings believes that the riders are personifications, not individuals, and that the first rider "may be the personification of government or rule in the last days in the hands of Gentiles."[12]

In biblical times it was customary for a conqueror to ride in triumph on a white horse. In the symbolization of Revelation 19 Christ Himself is pictured as riding on a white horse leading the armies of heaven to the earth. To hold that the rider in 6:2 is Christ Himself, however, is

[8]Ethelbert Stauffer, *Christ and the Caesars*, p. 170.
[9]William Milligan, while sure that the rider of the first horse must represent Christ, in recognition of the difficulty of linking the four riders together, comes to the conclusion that each rider "is rather a cause, a manifestation of certain truths connected with the kingdom of Christ when that kingdom is seen to be, in its own nature, the judgment of the world" (*The Book of Revelation*, p. 89). His supporting arguments, however, are not convincing.
[10]Edgar Ainslie, *The Dawn of the Scarlet Age*, p. 74.
[11]F. A. Jennings, *Studies in Revelation*, p. 201.
[12]*Ibid.*

out of order chronologically, for Christ comes on a white horse not at the beginning but at the end of the tribulation.

Beckwith states that although

> the first rider unquestionably symbolizes the *victorious warrior*, . . . it is hardly conceivable that Christ should be represented here as the Lamb in the court of heaven breaking the seal and at the same time by that act revealing himself as a figure coming into view from another quarter and in another form in response to a summons from an archangel. . . . The first rider, like the three others, is a personification of a judgment to be sent upon the earth.[13]

While the dispute as to the identity of the rider cannot be finally settled, especially in the brief compass of this discussion, the conclusion identifying him as the world ruler of the tribulation, the same individual described as the beast out of the sea in Revelation 13, is preferred.

Tatford, after a survey of possible interpretations, concludes:

> The brilliant career of this imperial rider on the white horse has been interpreted by the historicists as applying to the golden age of prosperity and good government that elapsed from the death of Domitian to the accession of Commodus. It is far more probable, however, that the reference is to the rise and career of a mighty imperial ruler after the rapture of the Church, who brings under his sway a vast territory in an endeavour to maintain peace, order, and prosperity.[14]

Commentators have noted the description of the rider. He is pictured as having a bow, symbol of distant victory, but no mention is made of the arrows. This has been construed as indicating a bloodless victory, but this interpretation cannot be dogmatically held. He is, however, given a crown, that is, the crown of a victor (Gr., *stephanos*), not the crown of a sovereign. The emphasis is not so much on his authority as on his victory, as confirmed by the latter part of verse 2, where he is said to go forth conquering and to conquer. Though he is in fact destined to be a world ruler, the emphasis is on the temporary victory which is his.

Stevens notes that at this point in Revelation the scene refers to the tribulation period preceding the coming of Christ:

> From what has already been plainly found, the time here is that of the earliest stage of Anti-Christ's times. It has been learned from II Thess. 2:7–8 that his open revelation succeeds the removal from the earth of the restraining agency of the overcoming saints. And from Dan. 7:8, 20; 8:9; and 11:40-43, it is made plain that Anti-Christ first conducts in the earth a period of sweeping, victorious warfare. The field of conflict will be the territories of the restored northern (Syrian), southern (Egyptian), and eastern (Mesopotamian) kingdoms of the old Grecian Empire. The figure of a white horse,

[13]Isbon T. Beckwith, *The Apocalypse of John*, pp. 517–19.
[14]F. A. Tatford, *Prophecy's Last Word*, p. 86.

and of his rider seated erect with drawn bow and with victor's wreath upon his brow, is the favorite oriental symbol of the military conqueror.[15]

Peake, who finds the second, third, and fourth riders respectively meaning war, famine, and pestilence, says of the first rider:

> The problem of the first rider remains. Since in xix. II, when heaven is opened, Christ comes forth to make war, seated on a white horse, many interpreters have identified the first rider with Him. It is not impossible that Christ, who opens the seal which is the signal for the rider to appear, should Himself be the rider who obeys the summons. It is, however, most improbable in itself. Moreover it brings Him on the scene much too early; for it is not till a very late point in the development that He enters on His victorious career. This identification should therefore be set aside without hesitation.

Peake goes on to identify the first rider with the Parthians, which is most unlikely, though not an uncommon interpretation.[16]

THE SECOND SEAL: WAR (6:3-4)

6:3-4 And when he had opened the second seal, I heard the second beast say, Come and see. And there went out another horse that was red: and power was given to him that sat thereon to take peace from the earth, and that they should kill one another: and there was given unto him a great sword.

As the Lamb opens the second seal of the seven-sealed book, the second living creature invites John to come and see. Some texts leave off the expression "and see" in this instance, as well as in verse 1. John in this case observes another horse described as red and bearing a rider to whom power is given to take peace from the earth and to cause men to kill one another. As a symbol of this, he is given a great sword. Clyde C. Cox suggests not only that the rider on the white horse is the world's political ruler but that the rider on the red horse is his associate, the false prophet. He finds support in that red is "typical of the beast kingdom,"[17] and cites the red dragon of Revelation 12:3, the scarlet beast, and the woman in scarlet of Revelation 17:3-4. The difficulty with this interpretation is that it does not properly account for the riders on the third and fourth horses.

If the first seal is a period of peace, as some have held, though this seems to be contradicted by the fact that the rider of the first horse conquers, in any case when the second seal is broken, military warfare breaks out and peace is taken from the world. The constant tension among nations and the ambitions of men have their climax in this period before

---

[15]W. C. Stevens, *Revelation, The Crown-Jewel of Biblical Prophecy*, II, 129.
[16]Arthur S. Peake, *The Revelation of John*, pp. 270–71, 273.
[17]*Apocalyptic Commentary*, p. 73.

Christ comes. Though "wars and rumours of wars" (Matt. 24:6) are characteristic of the age, it is evident that warfare occupies a large place in the consummation of the age with a resultant great loss of life. There apparently is a series of wars, the greatest of which is under way at the time of the second coming. The hope of permanent peace by means of the United Nations and other human efforts is doomed to failure.

THE THIRD SEAL: FAMINE (6:5-6)

6:5-6 And when he had opened the third seal, I heard the third beast say, Come and see. And I beheld, and lo a black horse; and he that sat on him had a pair of balances in his hand. And I heard a voice in the midst of the four beasts say, A measure of wheat for a penny, and three measures of barley for a penny; and see thou hurt not the oil and the wine.

In verses 5 and 6 the aftermath of war is seen and a great famine is revealed. In his vision John hears the third living creature invite him to come and see. John records that he sees a black horse and one sitting on the horse with a pair of balances in his hand used to weigh different commodities. A voice is heard from the midst of the four living creatures saying, "A measure of wheat for a penny, and three measures of barley for a penny; and see thou hurt not the oil and the wine."

In order to determine the meaning of this vision it must be understood that the silver coin designated as a penny is actually the Roman denarius, worth about fifteen cents. In the wage scale of that time it was common for a person to receive one denarius for an entire day's work. For such a coin, one measure of wheat or three measures of barley could be purchased in the vision here.

The explanation seems to be this: A measure of wheat is approximately what a laboring man would eat in one meal. If he used his penny to buy barley, a cheaper grain, he would have enough from an entire day's wages to buy three good meals of barley. If he bought wheat, a more precious grain, he would be able to buy enough for only one meal. There would be no money left to buy other things, such as oil or wine, which were considered essential in biblical times. To put it in ordinary language, the situation would be such that one would have to spend a day's wages for a loaf of bread with no money left to buy anything else. The symbolism therefore indicates a time of famine when life will be reduced to the barest necessities; for famine is almost always the aftermath of war. The somber picture is emphasized by the color of the horse, black being the symbol of suffering (cf. Lam. 5:10).

THE FOURTH SEAL: DEATH (6:7-8)

6:7-8 And when he had opened the fourth seal, I heard the voice

129

of the fourth beast say, Come and see. And I looked, and behold a pale horse: and his name that sat on him was Death, and Hell followed with him. And power was given unto them over the fourth part of the earth, to kill with sword, and with hunger, and with death, and with the beasts of the earth.

With the opening of the fourth seal a dramatic picture of divine judgment upon the world is unfolded. In some manuscripts the invitation is simply "come" with the omission of "and see." However, John is obviously invited to witness the scene. He introduces the vision with the same dramatic expression he uses in verse 2, "I looked, and behold," indicating that what he sees again startles him. He describes a horse on which Death is the rider and which Hell, or Hades, follows. The horse is an unearthly color described as "pale," literally a pale green, like young vegetation, the same word being used to describe the color of the grass in Mark 6:39 and Revelation 8:7; 9:4. In the context it is a ghastly color. The rider is pictured as Death and the aftermath of his ride, or that which follows, as Hades, the abode of the dead. In keeping with this startling picture, it is revealed to John that this rider has power over one-fourth part of the earth, to kill with the sword, hunger, and the beasts of the earth. The area covered by this judgment, described as the earth (Gr., *gē*), though sometimes used only of the promised land given Israel, is a general word referring to the inhabited world and in this context apparently extends to the entire earth.

Following the historical school of interpretation, David N. Lord suggests that the rider on the first horse represents the true minister of the gospel. The rider on the second horse, who takes peace from the earth, represents the succession of Roman rulers in early Christian centuries, many of whom were usurpers. The rider of the third seal represents the excessive taxation of the Roman Empire. The fourth seal represents Roman rulers who destroyed by execution and famine those who opposed them. The strained nature of such interpretation is apparent, and there is no real support in the text for it.[18]

McIlvaine makes the penetrating observation that the authority given to the riders of the four horses to kill with sword, famine, death, and wild beasts extends to all four equally or as a group. This would make impossible identifying the first rider as Christ and the succeeding riders as forces of evil, but would tie them together. McIlvaine says,

> It is in these words that we find our Seer's interpretation of the first seal . . . it would be very surprising that no one seems ever to have thought of reading this closing statement as a paragraph by itself, and consequently as referring, not exclusively to the last, but to all of these four seals . . . . Here, then, according to the Seer's own inter-

[18]*An Exposition of the Apocalypse,* pp. 65–153.

pretation, this rider upon a white horse, with a crown and bow, and called forth by the lion-like living creature, is the symbol of the plague of wild beasts . . . all the members of a class must be of the same sort, so that they can be obtained by one principle of analysis; and this principle in three of these, war, pestilence, and famine, is that of a judgment or scourge; consequently, in the remaining one, that of the first seal, it must be a judgment or scourge; otherwise the laws of thought are violated in the classification.[19]

Though McIlvaine's historical interpretation of this passage as having been fulfilled in the early centuries of the Christian era should be considered inadequate, his observation that these four seals form a unit has a good deal of merit and would seem to forbid making Christ the rider on the white horse.

By any standard of comparison this is an awesome judgment. If one-fourth of the world population is destroyed in the fourth seal, it would represent the greatest destruction of human life ever recorded in history. The population of the human race in Noah's day undoubtedly was far less than the figure here cited as dying. If such a judgment would fall upon a world population of approximately three billion people, it would mean that seven hundred and fifty million would die. Treated geographically it would be equivalent to the destruction of more than the entire population of Europe and South America. It should be clear from this description that the divine judgments being meted out to the earth are not trivial in character but describe a period of world history awful beyond any words, a period without precedent in its character and extent.

The fact that this devastating judgment comes at this stage in the revelation casts light on the important problem of determining when in the sequence of Revelation the great tribulation predicted by our Lord and Saviour (Matt. 24:15–26) begins in relationship to the seal judgments.

If the revelation of the final stage of Israel's predicted program be considered future, as recorded in Daniel 9:27, the last seven years or the seventieth week of Daniel's prophecy will immediately precede the second coming of Christ. According to Daniel 9:27 it is divided into two halves: the first three and one-half years are a period in which Israel is apparently protected under a covenant with the Gentile world ruler, the prince mentioned in Daniel 9:26. By contrast, however, Daniel indicates that the last three and one-half years cover an entirely different situation, one in which there is unprecedented trouble. In this period Israel becomes the object of persecution instead of being protected from her enemies.

The Prophet Daniel speaks of this period again when he predicts in Daniel 12:1:

[19]J. H. McIlvaine, *The Wisdom of the Apocalypse*, pp. 133–35.

> And at that time shall Michael stand up, the great prince which stand-
> eth for the children of thy people: and there shall be a time of trouble,
> such as never was since there was a nation even to that same time:
> and at that time thy people shall be delivered, every one that shall be
> found written in the book.

Jeremiah the prophet refers to the same event in Jeremiah 30:7 when
he declares, "Alas! for that day is great, so that none is like it; it is even
the time of Jacob's trouble, but he shall be saved out of it."

Other Old Testament passages bear witness to the awful character of
this future time of trouble (cf. Joel 2:1–3). Inasmuch as the judgment
described in the fourth seal is unparalleled, it seems to correspond with
greater accuracy to the latter half of Daniel's seventieth week than to
the earlier half and for that reason must be the time of great tribulation
which Christ declared would exceed by far anything the world had
previously known.

So great will be the trial of that period that Christ exhorted those
living in Palestine at that time to flee to the mountains to escape their
persecutors:

> For then shall be great tribulation, such as was not since the begin-
> ning of the world to this time, no, nor ever shall be. And except those
> days should be shortened, there should no flesh be saved: but for the
> elect's sake those days shall be shortened (Matt. 24:21–22).

If the supreme mark of this great tribulation is unprecedented trouble,
the fourth seal certainly qualifies as describing this period. Though some
expositors believe the great tribulation does not begin until chapter 11,
on the basis of this evidence, some have come to the conclusion that the
great tribulation must begin much earlier, possibly as early as the first
seal of Revelation 6. Though the book of Revelation itself does not state
specifically what event begins the great tribulation, the characteristics
unfolded in the fourth seal would indicate the great tribulation is under-
way at the time. The wars and famines predicted in the second and
third seals are not unfamiliar events in the history of the world, but
never before since the time of Noah has a judgment so devastating been
consummated as to destroy one-fourth of the earth's population at one
stroke.

Though it is impossible to settle this question conclusively, some believe
that the rider on the white horse in the first seal is a picture of the
prince (Dan. 9:26) at that stage in his career where he assumes control
over the entire world (Dan. 7:23; Rev. 13:7), which seems to coincide
with the beginning of the great tribulation. Though he comes as a
pseudo prince of peace who will bring order to a troubled world, the
peace is short-lived and is followed by war, famine, and death, as well

as the devastating judgments of God recorded later in the book of Revelation. The fifth and sixth seals advance the narrative and describe the period specifically as "the great day of his wrath" (6:17), which almost certainly is a reference to the great tribulation.

From this introduction to the judgments portrayed in the book of Revelation, it should be evident that the world is facing a time of trouble such as man has never known before. The dream of the optimist for a world becoming increasingly better scientifically, intellectually, morally, and religiously does not fit the pattern of God's prophetic Word. The ultimate triumph of God is assured; and as the book of Revelation makes plain, Christ will reign over the earth and bring in a kingdom of peace and righteousness after the time of trouble has run its course. First, however, there must be the awful time of the great tribulation.

There is much in the modern world which seems to portend just such a period. The introduction of modern means of warfare with new capacity to destroy life and property, the shrinking of the world by rapid transportation, and the invention of modern weapons of war make all the earth vulnerable to such scenes of devastation and destruction of human life in the event of a world conflict. The darkness of the human hour is in sharp contrast to the bright hope of the imminent return of Christ for His church as an event preceding the time of trouble.

THE FIFTH SEAL: THE MARTYRED SOULS IN HEAVEN (6:9-11)

6:9-11 And when he had opened the fifth seal, I saw under the altar the souls of them that were slain for the word of God, and for the testimony which they held: And when they cried with a loud voice, saying, How long, O Lord, holy and true, dost thou not judge and avenge our blood on them that dwell on the earth? And white robes were given unto every one of them, that they should rest yet for a little season, until their fellowservants also and their brethren, that should be killed as they were, should be fulfilled.

In the fifth seal the scene shifts from earth to heaven and John sees a vision of those who will be martyred for their faith in Christ. They are described as being under the altar, in keeping with the fact that the blood of the sacrifices of the Old Testament was poured out under the altar (Exodus 29:12; Lev. 4:7). In this case it is the "souls of them that were slain for the Word of God" which are seen under the altar. John hears them crying with a loud voice asking why God has not judged their persecutors.

The introduction of these martyred dead in heaven at this point immediately after the fourth seal seems to imply that these martyrs have come from the tribulation scene on the earth. There have been many martyrs in every generation, and even in the twentieth century tens of thousands have died for Christ in Asia, Africa, Central America, and South America. There are several reasons, however, for believing that a greater period of martyrdom is yet ahead. If the church has already been raptured, the dead in Christ have been raised from the dead before the time pictured here, and those pictured do not include the martyrs of the present dispensation.

In the fact that the martyrs ask for judgment upon those that dwell on the earth it is apparent that their persecutors are still living. Their cry for righteous judgment is in the same spirit as the Psalmist's call to God to vindicate His holiness and righteousness in dealing with the injustice and oppression which characterize the human race. In answer to their question as to how long it will be, the reply is given in verse 11 that there is still a little time required for the fulfillment of God's program, that other events must take place, that still additional martyrs must be added to their number. In a word, they are to wait until the time of Christ's return in power and glory when God will deal in summary judgment with the earth.

The revelation of the fifth seal makes clear that in the future time of tribulation it will be most difficult to declare one's faith in the Lord Jesus. It may very well be that the majority of those who trust Christ as Saviour in that day will be put to death. This is confirmed in chapter 7 where another picture of the martyred dead of the tribulation is given, and in chapter 13 where death is inflicted on all who will not worship the beast. Martyrdom in those days will be as common as it is uncommon today. Thousands will be martyred, sealing their testimony with their own blood. Those who trust in Christ in that day will be forced to stand the acid test of being faithful even unto death.

In verse 11 it is revealed that the white robes given unto every one of the martyrs are symbolic of righteousness. This introduces another question often debated by theologians, namely, what kind of a body will saints have in heaven before their own bodies are raised from the dead? If the martyred dead here pictured are those who have come from the tribulation, it is clear that they will not receive their resurrection bodies until the end of the tribulation, according to Revelation 20:4. Scholars have been divided as to whether saints who die receive temporary bodies in heaven prior to the resurrection body, or whether only their spiritual beings are in heaven before the resurrection.

In this verse there is a contribution to an answer to this question. The martyred dead here pictured have not been raised from the dead and have not received their resurrection bodies. Yet it is declared that they are given robes. The fact that they are given robes would almost demand that they have a body of some kind. A robe could not hang upon an immaterial soul or spirit. It is not the kind of body that Christians now have, that is, the body of earth; nor is it the resurrection body of flesh and bones of which Christ spoke after His own resurrection. It is a temporary body suited for their presence in heaven but replaced in turn by their everlasting resurrection body given at the time of Christ's return.

The introduction of these martyred saints in heaven also has bearing upon the chronology of chapter 6. In support of the common interpretation that the seals cover the entire seven years of Daniel's seventieth week (Dan. 9:27), it is sometimes pointed out that two classes of martyrs are here mentioned, namely, those already slain, and those who are yet to be slain. It has been inferred, accordingly, that those previously slain were killed in the first half of Daniel's seventieth week whereas those who are yet to be slain will perish in the great tribulation or the last half of the week, as A. C. Gaebelein suggests.[20] Confirmation is found in the expression "for a little season" in verse 11 (Gr., *eti chronon mikron*).

There is no reason, however, why the last three and a half years could not have the same distinction, namely, certain martyrs at the beginning as contrasted to martyrs at the end. The ultimate decision depends on more weighty matters, namely, whether there is unprecedented tribulation prior to the fifth seal as seems to be clearly indicated in this context, and the fact that the book of Revelation never speaks of a seven-year period, only of a period of three and a half years, forty-two months, or a similar designation. The ultimate decision depends upon what evidence is considered decisive.

THE SIXTH SEAL: THE DAY OF DIVINE WRATH (6:12-17)

6:12-17 And I beheld when he had opened the sixth seal, and lo, there was a great earthquake; and the sun became black as sackcloth of hair, and the moon became as blood; And the stars of heaven fell unto the earth, even as a fig tree casteth her untimely figs, when she is shaken of a mighty wind. And the heaven departed as a scroll when it is rolled together; and every mountain and island were moved out of their places. And the kings of the earth, and the great men, and the rich men, and the chief captains, and the mighty men, and every bondman, and every free man, hid themselves in the dens and in the rocks of the mountains; And said to the mountains and rocks, Fall on us, and hide us from the face of him that sitteth on the throne, and from the wrath of the Lamb: For the great day of his wrath is come; and who shall be able to stand?

It would be difficult to paint any scene more moving or more terrible than that described at the opening of the sixth seal. All the elements of a great catastrophic judgment of God are here present, namely, a great earthquake, the sun becoming black, the moon becoming as blood, the stars of heaven falling like ripe figs, the heaven departing as a scroll, and every mountain and island moving. This is an awe-inspiring scene, but what does it mean prophetically?

[20]*The Revelation*, p. 55.

Students of Revelation have had difficulty interpreting this passage, and the tendency has been to regard these judgments as symbolic rather than real. The motive behind this interpretation has been a reluctance to accept a literal interpretation of these judgments falling on the earth at this time; hence, the disturbances of the heavens have been taken to refer to changes in human government, and disturbances in the earth as referring to the upsetting of tradition and commonly fixed ideas.

H. A. Ironside, for instance, comments:

> It is therefore not a world-wide, literal earthquake that the sixth seal introduces, but rather the destruction of the present order—political, social, and ecclesiastical—reduced to chaos; the breaking down of all authority, and the breaking up of all established and apparently permanent institutions.[21]

On the other side, Peake urges interpretation of Revelation in its plain sense unless good reasons indicate otherwise:

> The Apocalypse is no doubt often obscure and its language is often allegorical. But it has to be interpreted in its plain sense far more frequently than many expositors are willing to admit. Much is written in simple characters which expositors have insisted on treating as hieroglyphics. In particular natural phenomena have been interpreted of historical events and the author has been credited with describing a political movement when he has been really speaking of God's judgments through nature. And the temptation has been especially great to find allegories where the author describes things in a matter-of-fact way, when the descriptions are bizarre and uncongenial to modern taste.[22]

There are a number of reasons for preferring to take this passage in its literal meaning. While this is not the final breakup of the world as described later in Revelation, when a further period of terrible judgments will be poured on the world, it does seem to indicate that beginning with the sixth seal God is undertaking a direct intervention into human affairs. The judgments of war, famine, and death, and the martyrdom of the saints have largely originated in human decision and in the evil heart of man. The judgment described here, however, originates in God as a divine punishment inflicted upon a blasphemous world.

In view of the catastrophic and climactic character of the period, there is no good reason why there should not be precisely the elements mentioned here, namely, disturbances in the heavens and earthquakes on the earth. This is borne out by the effect upon the kings of the earth, the great men, the rich men, the chief captains, the mighty men, bondmen, and freemen mentioned in verse 15, who hide themselves in dens and in the rocks of the mountains. The events are of such character that all are

[21]*Lectures on the Revelation,* p. 114.
[22]Peake, pp. 178–79.

impressed with the fact that the day of the wrath of the Lord has come and their judgment is now about to take place. In support of this, E. W. Bullinger writes, "It is impossible for us to take this as symbolical; or as other than what it literally says. The difficulties of the symbolical interpretation are insuperable, while no difficulties whatever attend the literal interpretation."[23]

It is questionable whether changes in government and in human affairs would have brought such a striking transformation in the hearts of these wicked people. As is often the case with desperate men, instead of availing themselves of the grace of God, they attempt to hide from the wrath of the Lamb by seeking escape in death. However their hope is futile, for death is not an escape but merely a change from one state to another. Those who escape through death from the immediate judgment of God are destined for eternal judgment at the judgment of the great white throne. The earth today so indifferent to the claims of God, so bent upon pleasure, luxury, and fame, will face in that day its terrible need.

All levels of society are here. Some are great men, some are slaves. In relation to judgment of the Lord Jesus Christ, however, everyone is exactly in the same predicament. Success in the world does not help; no one escapes.

The elements of divine judgment pictured here are common in the prophecies pertaining to the end of the age. Christ Himself predicted earthquakes (Matt. 24:7). Both earthquakes and the sun becoming black are intimated by Joel (Joel 2:2, 10, 30–31). The heavens departing as a scroll are mentioned in Isaiah 34:4 (cf. also Isa. 13:6–13). The resulting impression upon the unbelieving world is that the time of the judgment of God has come. They themselves say to the mountains and rocks, "Fall on us, and hide us from the face of him that sitteth on the throne, and from the wrath of the Lamb: For the great day of his wrath is come; and who shall be able to stand?" It is apparent that creatures of earth have had some foreboding that their blasphemous unbelief and worship of the beast pictured in Revelation 13 are in defiance of the true God. They therefore seek refuge from the One sitting on the throne and apparently realize that the day of divine wrath has come.

In describing the period of judgment as a day of wrath, reference is not to a twenty-four-hour day but to a time period longer or shorter. The day of wrath in one sense is the whole period of the great tribulation, when God will deal in direct judgment with the world, climaxing with the return of Christ in power and glory and divine judgment upon all who oppose His coming. E. W. Bullinger describes the first six seals as

a summary of the judgments distributed over the whole book; a brief

[23]*The Apocalypse*, p. 274.

137

summary of what will occur in "the day of the Lord," up to the time
of His actual Apocalypse or Unveiling in chap. xix.[24]

The day of wrath is at the beginning of the day of the Lord, that extended period when God is going to deal directly in governing the entire world. It is significant that early in the book of Revelation the day of wrath is declared as having already come. It is another evidence that the great tribulation is already under way.

The day of wrath is in contrast to the day of grace. Though God in every dispensation deals with believers and saves them by grace, the present age is supremely designed to manifest grace not only as the way of salvation but as the way of life. Today God is not attempting to bring divine judgment to bear upon sin. Though there may be some forms of immediate retribution, for the most part God is not settling accounts now. Neither the righteous are rewarded nor the wicked judged in a final sense today. This day of grace will be followed by the day of the Lord which features early in its progress the day of wrath.

By contrast to the judgments which are inflicted upon a Christ-rejecting world, believers in this present age are promised escape from the judgment which the world richly deserves (cf. John 3:18, 36). The person who trusts in Christ is not only uncondemned in this world but he has eternal life and is a member of God's family. By contrast the unbeliever shall never see life, but abides under the wrath of God which in due time will be inflicted.

The book of Revelation discredits those who hold that God is so loving and kind that He will never judge people who have not received His Son. Though the modern mind is reluctant to accept the fact that God will judge the wicked, the Bible clearly teaches that He will. The Scriptures reveal a God of love as clearly as they reveal a God of wrath who will deal with those who spurn the grace proffered in the Lord Jesus Christ. The passage before us is a solemn word that there is inevitable judgment ahead for those who will not receive Christ by faith.

The close of chapter 6 of the book of Revelation advances the narrative to a new high in the progress of the book. In some sense chapter 6 is the outline of the important facts of the period of great tribulation, and the rest of the events of the book of Revelation are comprehended in the seventh seal introduced in chapter 8. Chapter 6 closes with a pointed question: "Who shall be able to stand?" The answer is obvious: Only those who avail themselves of the grace of God, even though they suffer a martyr's death in this future tragic period. This is brought out in the next chapter. The given revelation emphasizes the importance of partaking of the grace of God in this present age with the bright prospect of the Lord coming for His own.

[24]*Ibid.*, p. 277.

7

THE SAINTS OF THE GREAT TRIBULATION

IN CONTRAST TO CHAPTER 6 which seems to give the chronological sequence of major events of the great tribulation, chapter 7 does not advance the narrative but directs attention to two major groups of saints in the tribulation. The opening portion of the chapter pictures the 144,000 representative of the godly remnant of Israel on earth in the great tribulation. The latter part of the chapter describes a great multitude of martyred dead in heaven, those who died as a testimony to their faith from every kindred, tongue, and nation.

The question has often been asked, Will anyone be saved after the rapture? The Scriptures clearly indicate that a great multitude of both Jews and Gentiles will trust in the Lord after the church is caught up to glory. Though the children of God living on earth at the time will be translated when Christ comes for His church, immediately a testimony will be raised up to the name of Christ through new converts among Jews and Gentiles. Though these are never described by the term "church," they are constantly called saints, that is, those set apart as holy to God and saved through the sacrifice of Christ.

The presence of saved people in the world after the rapture has puzzled some because according to II Thessalonians 2:7 the one who now restrains sin, often identified as the Holy Spirit, is pictured as being removed from the world. The question then is how can people be saved in the tribulation if the Holy Spirit is taken out of the world? The answer, of course, is that the Holy Spirit is removed from the world in the same sense in which He came on the day of Pentecost. People were saved before the day of Pentecost when the Spirit of God came to indwell the church, and it should be clear from other Scriptures that the Holy Spirit is always omnipresent. He has always been in the world and always will be, in keeping with the divine attribute of omnipresence. Though the special ministries which are characteristic of the present dispensation may cease, there will be the continued ministry of the Spirit in a similar way to that which existed before Pentecost.

There is a parallel in the fact of the incarnation of Jesus Christ. Throughout the Old Testament, Christ was present in the world, but it was not His particular field of operation though He ministered as the Angel of Jehovah. In due time, according to the plan of God, Christ was born in Bethlehem and ministered as God's unique revelation of Himself to mankind. Then He ascended into heaven, yet at the same time He told His disciples, "Lo, I am with you alway" (Matt. 28:20). In other words while His special earthly work was completed with His sacrifice on the cross and His resurrection, He nevertheless continued to work in the world in His omnipresence as God.

Likewise the Holy Spirit is resident in the world now just as Christ was resident in the world between His birth and ascension. When the present age ends and the Holy Spirit is caught up with the church, the situation will return to that which was true before the day of Pentecost. The Holy Spirit will continue to be working in the world, but in some particulars in a different way. There is good reason to believe, however, that the Holy Spirit will lead people to Christ, and many will be saved during the tribulation time. A description of this is given in the seventh chapter of the book of Revelation, which is so plain that no one should question whether people will be saved after the rapture.

THE VISION OF THE FOUR ANGELS (7:1-3)

> **7:1-3** And after these things I saw four angels standing on the four corners of the earth, holding the four winds of the earth, that the wind should not blow on the earth, nor on the sea, nor on any tree. And I saw another angel ascending from the east, having the seal of the living God: and he cried with a loud voice to the four angels, to whom it was given to hurt the earth and the sea, Saying, Hurt not the earth, neither the sea, nor the trees, till we have sealed the servants of our God in their foreheads.

In the order of the vision as given to John, he sees in the opening verses of chapter 7 four angels controlling the four winds of the earth. An angel which is described as ascending from the east and possessing the seal of the living God commands the four angels not to hurt the earth and the sea until the servants of God are sealed in their foreheads. The implication is that the judgment of God is impending and that prior to its infliction on the earth, God wants to set apart and protect His servants. In the verses which follow, 12,000 from each of the twelve tribes of Israel are protected by the angelic seal. It is implied that these who are thus sealed have been saved in the time of trouble pictured in the book of Revelation and by this means are being set apart as a special divine remnant to be a testimony to God's grace and mercy during this time of judgment.

There are many precedents in Scripture for such a protection of God's own. When God sent the flood upon the earth, He separated Noah and his family from the rest of the human race and the flood did not hurt them. When God destroyed Jericho, He protected Rahab and her household. Wicked though she was, she had put her trust in God, and God protected her from the judgment that fell upon Jericho. In a similar way in the time of great tribulation protection will be given to this group of 144,000 Israelites. The matter is so significant to God that the names of the tribes and the number to be saved from each are given in detail.

THE SEALING OF THE TWELVE TRIBES (7:4–8)

7:4-8 And I heard the number of them which were sealed: and there were sealed an hundred and forty and four thousand of all the tribes of the children of Israel. Of the tribe of Juda were sealed twelve thousand. Of the tribe of Reuben were sealed twelve thousand. Of the tribe of Gad were sealed twelve thousand. Of the tribe of Aser were sealed twelve thousand. Of the tribe of Nepthalim were sealed twelve thousand. Of the tribe of Manasses were sealed twelve thousand. Of the tribe of Simeon were sealed twelve thousand. Of the tribe of Levi were sealed twelve thousand. Of the tribe of Issachar were sealed twelve thousand. Of the tribe of Zabulon were sealed twelve thousand. Of the tribe of Joseph were sealed twelve thousand. Of the tribe of Benjamin were sealed twelve thousand.

A number of significant details are mentioned in connection with the sealing of the 144,000 in Israel. This Scripture makes plain that there are twelve tribes in Israel still in existence, as the names of the different tribes are given. There are, however, some omissions. In some lists of the twelve tribes both of the sons of Joseph, Ephraim and Manasseh, are numbered as separate tribes.

In this list Manasseh is mentioned but Ephraim is not, and in place of Ephraim the name of Joseph his father is given in verse 8. No explanation is made concerning this substitution. There is also no mention of the tribe of Dan, and the Bible does not tell us why Dan should be omitted. As Alford points out, ancient interpreters accounted for this on the theory that the Antichrist would come from the tribe of Dan (cf. Gen. 49:17).[1] A more common explanation is that the tribe of Dan was one of the first to go into idolatry, was small in number, and probably was thereafter classified with the tribe of Naphtali, another son of Jacob born to the same mother as Dan.

In commenting on the twelve tribes, Walter Scott writes:

[1]Henry Alford, *The Greek New Testament*, IV, 625.

In the enumeration of the tribes throughout Scripture, of which there are about eighteen, the full representative number twelve is always given; but as Jacob has thirteen sons, one or other is always omitted. Levi is more generally omitted than any other. In the apocalyptic enumeration, Dan and Ephraim are omitted. Both these tribes were remarkable as being connected with idolatry in Israel, the probable reason for blotting out of their names here (Deut. 29:18–21). But in the end grace triumphs, and Dan is named first in the future distribution of the land amongst the tribe (Ezek. 48:2), but, while first named, it is the farthest removed from the temple, being situated in the extreme north.[2]

H. B. Swete notes:

Lists of the patriarchs or of the tribes occur in Gen. xxxv. 22 ff., xlvi. 8 ff., xlix., Exod. i. 1 ff., Num. i., ii., xiii. 4 ff., xxvi., xxxiv., Deut. xxvii. 11 ff., xxxiii. 6 ff., Josh. xiii–xxii., Judg. v., I Chron. ii–viii., xii. 24 ff., xxvii. 16 ff., Ezek. xlviii.[3]

J. B. Smith observes,

There are no fewer than 29 lists of the tribes of Israel throughout the Scriptures, thus showing the prominence accorded them in the sacred page.[4]

Though a full answer does not present itself for these omissions, it is most important that Israel is here divided into the twelve tribes. Though Israelites today do not normally know what tribe they belong to, in the mind of God there is no question. Here representatives for each of the twelve tribes are selected for the signal honor of being sealed by the angel.

The fact that the twelve tribes of Israel are singled out for special reference in the tribulation time is another evidence that the term "Israel" as used in the Bible is invariably a reference to the descendants of Jacob who was first given the name Israel. Galatians 6:16 is no exception. The prevalent idea that the church is the true Israel is not sustained by any explicit reference in the Bible, and the word *Israel* is never used of Gentiles and refers only to those who are racially descendants of Israel or Jacob.

William Kelly, in defense of the literal interpretation of the tribes of Israel, states:

On the other hand, I conceive that the specification of the tribe is inconsistent with any sense but the literal. Then again the contradistinction is as plain and positive as words can make it, between the sealed number out of Israel and the innumerable multitude from all nations and kindreds and peoples and tongues. So that the mystical

[2]*Exposition of the Revelation of Jesus Christ,* p. 166.
[3]*The Apocalypse of St. John,* p 98.
[4]*A Revelation of Jesus Christ,* p. 130.

theory, when closely examined, cannot escape the charge of absurdity; for it identifies the sealed Israelites with the palm-bearing Gentiles, in spite of the evident and expressed contrasts on the face of the chapter.[5]

This literal interpretation is held not only by the premillenarians but by representative postmillenarians such as Charles Hodge,[6] nineteenth century theologian, and amillenarians such as Hendriksen,[7] twentieth century expositor. The decision as to who are included in the term "Israel" should be reached on the basis of exegesis and usage.

Though the Bible distinguishes true Israelites from those who have forsaken their heritage, the term "Israel" is never used outside the descendants of Jacob himself. The remnant of Israel as portrayed here in the book of Revelation should not therefore be taken as meaning the church. It would be rather ridiculous to carry the typology of Israel representing the church to the extent of dividing them up into twelve tribes as was done here, if it was the intent of the writer to describe the church. It is rather a clear indication of God's continued purpose for the nation Israel and their preservation through this awful time of trouble.

The mention of the twelve tribes of Israel is likewise a refutation of the idea that the tribes of Israel are lost, as well as of the theory that the lost tribes are perpetuated in the English-speaking people of the world. Obviously none of the tribes are lost as far as God is concerned. Though genealogies have been lost, a modern Jew can be assured that he belongs to the seed of Abraham; and God knows into which tribe he should be classified. In the book of James there is reference to the twelve tribes of Israel as being in existence at the time our Lord was upon earth (James 1:1; cf. I Peter 1:1). This vision given to John, therefore, is prophetic of the fact that God has a future purpose for Israel and that in spite of satanic persecution a godly remnant will be preserved to be on earth when Christ returns.

The question has also been raised whether the "12,000" in each tribe means literally 12,000. There seems to be indication that more than 12,000 from each tribe actually will be saved. The point of this Scripture is that in any event 12,000 in each tribe are made secure. There will be other Israelites saved besides these 144,000, but many of these will die martyrs' deaths and give up their lives for their faith. The 144,000 are those who are delivered from their persecutors and brought safely through this terrible time of tribulation. In chapter 14 they are seen triumphant at the end of the tribulation when Christ returns.

[5]*Lectures on the Book of Revelation*, p. 158.
[6]*Commentary on the Epistle to the Romans*, p. 589.
[7]W. Hendriksen, *And So All Israel Shall Be Saved*, p. 33.

THE MARTYRED DEAD OF THE GREAT TRIBULATION SEEN IN HEAVEN
(7:9–10)

7:9-10 After this I beheld, and, lo, a great multitude, which no man could number, of all nations and kindreds, and people, and tongues, stood before the throne, and before the Lamb, clothed with white robes, and palms in their hands; And cried with a loud voice, saying, Salvation to our God which sitteth upon the throne, and unto the Lamb.

The second half of chapter 7 of Revelation demonstrates that not only will many be saved in Israel but also many Gentiles will come to Christ in the great tribulation. In his vision John sees a great multitude beyond human computation coming from all nations, kindreds, people, and tongues standing before the throne, clothed with white robes, with palms in their hands, ascribing salvation to God and to the Lamb. In contrast to those coming from the twelve tribes as pictured earlier in the chapter, this throng comes from all nations. The white robes mentioned seem to refer to 6:11, and the palms indicate their triumph. This great multitude is heard by John in a great symphony of praise as they ascribe salvation to God. The fact that they are martyrs is stated later in the chapter (vv. 13–14).

THE PRAISE OF THE HEAVENLY HOST (7:11–12)

7:11-12 And all the angels stood round about the throne, and about the elders and the four beasts, and fell before the throne on their faces, and worshipped God, Saying, Amen: Blessing, and glory, and wisdom, and thanksgiving, and honour, and power, and might, be unto our God for ever and ever. Amen.

Joining the multitude of the saints, the angels and all those in heaven are described as falling down before the throne to worship God in a sevenfold ascription of praise similar to that in Revelation 5. The point of this introduction, however, is to identify the presence in glory of the great multitude coming from all nations.

THE MARTYRED DEAD IDENTIFIED AS TRIBULATION SAINTS
(7:13–14)

7:13-14 And one of the elders answered, saying unto me, What are these which are arrayed in white robes? and whence came they? And I said unto him, Sir, thou knowest. And he said to me, These are they which came out of great tribulation, and have washed their robes, and made them white in the blood of the Lamb.

One of the twenty-four elders is quoted in verse 13 as asking the questions "What are these which are arrayed in white robes? and whence came they?" It is clear from these questions that the twenty-four elders are representative of a group different from those who are here pictured as the great multitude in white robes. If the elders represent the church, the multitude represents a different body of saints. In answer to the elder, John confesses that he does not know; whereupon John is informed, "These are they which came out of great tribulation." In the Greek the expression is far more specific. Literally it could be translated, "These are those who came out of the tribulation, the great one." It is undoubtedly a reference to the specific period of the great tribulation of which Christ spoke (Matt. 24:21).

The common tendency to ignore the definite terminology of the prophecies in the book of Revelation is illustrated in the interpretation which would make this throng refer to all the elect of all ages and the great tribulation as "the whole sum of the trials of the saints of God, viewed by the Elder as now complete."[8] One must not read into a passage something that is foreign to its express statement. The group here described is a particular group coming from a particular time.

Larkin attempts to explain away the reference to "great tribulation" (7:14) in order to place this company in the first half of Daniel's seventieth week. His explanation is beside the point as this seventh chapter is not necessarily in chronological order, and further, there is no reason why the great tribulation should not have already begun at this time.[9]

Ottman, because of his opposition to the view that the saints of all ages are in view here, also insists that the prophetic narrative is a projection forward to the time of the millennium itself. He bases his conclusion largely on the fact that neither death nor resurrection is mentioned regarding the Gentile multitude. He does not explain, however, the reference to the throne (7:9-13) that is clearly parallel to the throne in heaven in chapters 4-5. His objection is unnecessary, as the throng are not saints of all ages but only saints of the tribulation time who are martyred.[10] The saints, then, who are before the throne coming from every kindred, tongue, and nation, are those who have come out of the great tribulation. This passage clearly teaches that many Gentiles will be saved during the tribulation. The command to preach the gospel to every nation throughout the world (Matt. 24:14; 28:19-20) will have its ultimate fulfillment in this way before Christ comes back to establish His millennial kingdom. The concept sometimes advanced that the rapture cannot occur because all the world has not heard the gospel is a faulty conclusion. The requirement that all the world hear the gospel pertains not to the rapture but to the coming of Christ to set up His kingdom. Though the church should press on with all zeal in presenting the gospel to every

[8]Alford, IV, 628.
[9]Clarence Larkin, *Book of Revelation*, p. 67.
[10]Ford C. Ottman, *The Unfolding of the Ages*, pp. 181-89.

creature, it is not necessary for the rapture to wait until this task be completed. In spite of the difficulties, there will be worldwide preaching of the gospel during the tribulation time.

The question has been raised concerning the time pictured in this vision. Two explanations are possible; the first is that this chapter is a preview of the beginning of the millennium. Under this interpretation John is considered to be carried beyond the coming of Christ to establish His kingdom and is chronologically already in the millennial kingdom. Jennings considers this chapter a foreview of the millennial earth rather than a picture of heaven, with the passage teaching that in the millennium both Jews and Gentiles will be blessed. The difficulty with this view, however, is that the only throne and temple introduced thus far are those in heaven, seen in chapters 4 and 5; and there is little justification for arbitrarily putting this chapter in the millennium.[11] The scene here obviously is in heaven, rather than on earth, and the living tribulation saints are not caught up to heaven.

Another interpretation is therefore preferred. This view understands the passage to teach that those here described are martyrs who have sealed their testimony with their own blood. Some believe that the majority of saints in the tribulation will die as martyrs. Many will be killed by earthquakes, war, and pestilence. Others will be the object of special persecution by the world ruler. They will be hounded to death much as the Jews were in World War II. Because they will not worship the beast, they will be under a death sentence (Rev. 13:15). Those who accept Christ in that time may be faced with the solemn alternative of either renouncing their faith in Christ and worshiping the beast or being slain. The result will be multiplied thousands of martyrs.

The scene before us, then, is not earth but heaven, not the millennium but the time of the tribulation. The martyrs are before the throne and before the Lamb. The picture is similar to chapters 5 and 6. The "great multitude" represents an important portion of those mentioned in 6:9-11 who are given white robes as faithful witnesses to the Word of God and to the testimony of the Lamb. The main facts in the case are clear regardless of which interpretation is followed. During the tribulation, countless people of all nations will come to know Christ. It will be a time of salvation for them in spite of persecution and even martyrdom.

In verse 14 the significant detail is given that the martyrs have washed their robes and made them white in the blood of the Lamb. Normally one cannot make anything white with blood. The passage is talking, however, of spiritual purity. The only way sins can be washed away is through the precious blood of Christ and because of His death and sacrifice.

[11]F. C. Jennings, *Studies in Revelation,* pp. 218 ff.

The Scriptures of the Old and New Testaments speak often of blood as the symbol of life, as in Leviticus 17:14: "The life of all flesh is the blood thereof." The spiritual significance of shed blood is given prominence in both the Old and New Testaments with hundreds of references to it. According to Hebrews 9:22, "without shedding of blood is no remission." According to Acts 20:28, the church has been purchased by the blood of Christ. In Romans 3:25 Christ is declared to be the propitiation for our sins through "faith in his blood." In Romans 5:9 we are "justified by his blood," and therefore "shall be saved from wrath through him." Ephesians 1:7 states that "we have redemption through his blood." According to Colossians 1:20, Christ has "made peace through the blood of his cross."

The Apostle Peter adds his testimony in I Peter 1:18–19 when he writes, "Ye were not redeemed with corruptible things, as silver and gold, from your vain conversation received by tradition from your fathers; but with the precious blood of Christ, as of a lamb without blemish and without spot." The frequent references to blood in the book of Revelation itself begin in chapter 1:5: "Unto him that loved us, and washed us from our sins in his own blood." In the second advent itself in Revelation 19:13, Christ is described as "clothed with a vesture dipped in blood."

The emphasis in the Scripture upon the shed blood of sacrifice whether in the Mosaic law of the Old Testament or the sacrifice of Christ in the New Testament points to the necessity of His substitutionary death for the believer's redemption. Though a modern world is offended by substitutionary sacrifice and especially by the reference to sacrificial blood, from God's viewpoint, like the children of Israel in Egypt, there is no safety except for those under the blood. God promised Israel in Exodus 12:13, "When I see the blood, I will pass over you, and the plague shall not be upon you to destroy you, when I smite the land of Egypt."

Accordingly, though not suited to the sophistication of twentieth century aesthetics, the blood of Christ is exceedingly precious in the sight of the Lord and is the only cleansing agent for sin. The blood of the Lamb is the assurance of cleansing and forgiveness for these who have been martyred for their faith in Christ. Even their own sacrificial death could not atone for their sins. They, like all others, must rest alone in that sacrifice which Christ provided for them. What is true for them is true for the saints of all ages; only the blood of Christ avails to wash away sin.

The Heavenly Bliss of the Martyred Saints (7:15-17)

7:15-17 Therefore are they before the throne of God, and serve him day and night in his temple: and he that sitteth on the throne shall dwell among them. They shall hunger no more, neither thirst

147

any more; neither shall the sun light on them, nor any heat. For the Lamb which is in the midst of the throne shall feed them, and shall lead them unto living fountains of waters: and God shall wipe away all tears from their eyes.

The wonderful blessing of the martyred saints in the presence of the Lord is spelled out in these verses. They are described as being before the throne of God, that is, in a place of prominence and honor. Their special privilege is further defined as serving the Lord day and night in His temple. This expression is highly significant, for it indicates that heaven is not only a place of rest from earthly toil but also a place of privileged service. Those who have served well on earth will have a ministry in heaven. The fact that they are declared to serve "day and night" has been taken by some as an indication that this is a millennial scene rather than heaven since there is never any night in the temple of God in heaven. The expression, however, can be understood as meaning simply that they will continually serve the Lord, that is, they will not need sleep or restoration as is necessary in earthly toil. They are delivered from the limitations of this life. Their service is said to occur in the temple of God, a reference to the immediate presence of the Lord, not to any earthly temple. Further, they shall be honored by the fact that the One sitting on the throne will dwell among them; that is, they will be in wonderful fellowship with their blessed Lord.

Verse 16 reveals that they will be delivered from the afflictions of life such as hunger, thirst, and the heat of the sun. This may be an oblique reference to some of their sufferings which they endured in the tribulation. According to Revelation 13:17 it may be that they had gone hungry rather than buying food and submitting to the worship of the beast. Thirst is another form of suffering common in times of persecution. The glaring sun and burning heat and the trials which may have attended them as they fled from their enemies are far behind them in glory. Instead of such severe trials, verse 17 pictures the Lamb of God as feeding them and leading them to living fountains of water. The abundant provision of the heavenly scene is evident in this description.

The concluding statement in the chapter is that "God shall wipe away all tears from their eyes." In other words they will have the tender comfort and care of the Saviour, and the tears that once were theirs shall be wiped away. Some have attempted to draw from this passage that there will be actual tears in heaven and have implied that saints will be shedding tears because of grief over wasted lives and unconfessed sin while on earth. This passage, however, does not even suggest such a situation. The point is that the grief and tears of the past, speaking of their trials in the tribulation, will be over when they get to heaven. The

148

saints in glory will be occupied with the beauty and wonder of heaven and the worship of the Saviour. They will not have time for repentance of that which can no longer be changed. Instead, God will wipe away all tears resulting from their suffering on earth. In the glory of heaven whatever burdens and cares may have been laid upon the saints in earthly life, there will be no sorrow, no tears, and no death.

The juxtaposition of the 144,000 in the first half of this chapter immediately preceding the description of the multitude of martyred dead from among the Gentiles would seem to imply that there is a causal relationship between these two groups. The 144,000 on earth are preserved in safety through the tribulation, as a testimony to the power and grace of God and as a channel through which the gospel could come to the earth. The result of their ministry had its fruit among the Gentiles even as was true in the apostolic age with the result that great multitudes of the Gentiles were saved from whom the martyred throng in heaven were separated by death. The use of the 144,000 of Israel as a channel of witness to the earth is in keeping with the general purposes of God in relation to the Jewish nation.

Chapter 7 of the book of Revelation serves as a review of the situation described in the previous chapters and emphasizes two important facts. First, God is going to judge Israel in the period of great trial, and 12,000 from each tribe, totaling 144,000, will be protected and sealed from the judgments which will fall upon the world in general. Second, a great multitude of Gentiles will also be saved, but many of these will be martyred, and a multitude of the martyred dead are found in heaven rejoicing in the presence of the Lamb and representing every tongue and nation. It is an indication that even in the tragic closing hours prior to the second coming of Christ to the earth, countless souls will find Christ as Saviour and be saved by His grace.

8

THE SEVENTH SEAL AND THE BEGINNING OF THE TRUMPETS

THE OPENING OF THE SEVENTH SEAL (8:1)

8:1 And when he had opened the seventh seal, there was silence in heaven about the space of half an hour.

THIS CHAPTER OPENS with the announcement that the seventh seal is opened. This is the last of the seven seals marking the prophetic judgments of God. With the opening of the seventh seal the narrative is resumed from the close of chapter 6. Though simply introduced, the seventh seal is obviously the most important development up to this point.

Contained in the seventh seal are all the subsequent developments leading to the second coming of Christ, including the seven trumpets and the seven bowls of the wrath of God. Scroggie, after a careful discussion of the chronological order of the book of Revelation, concludes:

> The trumpets, therefore, do not *double back* over all or some of the Seals, but lie under the sixth Seal, and proceed from it. For this reason it is equally incorrect to speak of the Trumpets as following the Seals. They do not follow, but are the Seventh Seal.[1]

In like manner he holds that the bowls constitute the seventh trumpet:

> Therefore the Bowls do not *double back* over the Seal and Trumpet Judgments; neither is it correct to say that they follow the Trumpet visitations. They do not follow because THEY ARE THE SEVENTH TRUMPET CONTENTS.[2]

Scroggie goes on to note that the judgments of the bowls are poured out in quick succession. Alford disagrees with this conclusion stating,

> I believe all interpretation to be wrong, which regards the blowing of the seven trumpets as forming a portion of the vision accompanying the seventh seal in particular: and again . . . I place in the same category all that which regards it as taking up and going over the same ground again.[3]

[1]W. G. Scroggie, *The Book of the Revelation*, p. 167.
[2]*Ibid.*, p. 169.
[3]Henry Alford, *The Greek New Testament*, IV, 630.

Alford, however, does not give any explanation as to what the content of the seventh seal is and thus leaves his conclusion unsupported.

Blanchard believes that the seven trumpets are included in the seventh seal and that the seven bowls are included in the seventh trumpet:

> It is interesting to note that the series of three sevens are really included in one series of seven, that is, the seven trumpets are included under the seventh seal and the seven bowls are included under the seventh trumpet, so that we have in fact a single series in three movements—the first six seals opened, then the seventh seal which includes the seven trumpets blown, and then the last trumpet sounding, introducing the seven bowls and concluding the opening of the seven seals.[4]

In fitting recognition of the important character of this seal, the Scriptures record that there is silence in heaven about the space of half an hour. Though thirty minutes is not ordinarily considered a long time, when it is a time of absolute silence portending such ominous developments ahead it is an indication that something tremendous is about to take place. It may be compared to the silence before the foreman of a jury reports a verdict; for a moment there is perfect silence and everyone awaits that which will follow.

INTRODUCTION OF THE SEVEN ANGELS (8:2-6)

8:2-6 And I saw the seven angels which stood before God; and to them were given seven trumpets. And another angel came and stood at the altar, having a golden censer; and there was given unto him much incense, that he should offer it with the prayers of all saints upon the golden altar which was before the throne. And the smoke of the incense, which came with the prayers of the saints, ascended up before God out of the angel's hand. And the angel took the censer, and filled it with fire of the altar, and cast it into the earth: and there were voices, and thunderings, and lightnings, and an earthquake. And the seven angels which had the seven trumpets prepared themselves to sound.

In verse 2 John records his vision of the seven trumpets given to the seven angels standing before God. Though there has been some speculation as to the character of these angels, the best interpretation is to take the revelation in its ordinary sense, that is, that these are indeed seven angels appointed by God to direct the series of judgments symbolized by the seven trumpets. These angels are to be distinguished from those who pour out the seven vials and are not to be confused with the seven spirits of God of Revelation 5:6. The number seven is in harmony with the seven seals and the seven vials. The fact that these angels stand before God indicates a place of prominence such as is given to the angel Gabriel (cf. Luke 1:19).

[4]C. A. Blanchard, *Light on the Last Days,* p. 58.

The use of trumpets by the angels has considerable background in the Scriptures. Trumpets were used in various phases of Israel's economy. They were sounded at times of public assembly, used to direct soldiers in war and to signal important events on the calendar. Trumpets were used on the occasion of the giving of the law, were sounded on the first of the month, and served to announce almost every important occasion (cf. Exodus 19:19; Lev. 23:24; 25:9; Num. 10:2–10; Joel 2:1).

In verse 3 another angelic personage is introduced as standing before the altar with a golden censer presenting incense and the prayers of the saints before the throne. This is a beautiful picture of the prayers of the saints as seen from heaven. In the Old Testament order the priests would burn incense upon the altar of incense, and the smoke would fill the Temple or the Tabernacle and would then ascend to heaven. Incense was symbolic of worship and prayer and a reminder that intercession to the Lord has the character of sweet incense. The altar in heaven is referred to seven times in this book (6:9; 8:3a, b, 5; 9:13; 14:18; 16:7). Commentators differ as to whether the altar is the altar of burnt offering or the altar of incense, although the latter is usually preferred.[5]

Difference of opinion has also been expressed concerning whether the angel mentioned in verse 3 is actually an angel of high rank or an angelic representation of the Lord Jesus Christ. From the fact that the angel has items given to him in order to make his worship possible, some have concluded that this is only an angel designated for this work in heaven. From the nature of his work as a mediator serving in the role of a priest, others have argued that it must be the Lord Jesus Christ because this would not be a proper function of an angel. The fact that Christ appeared in the Old Testament frequently as the Angel of Jehovah lends further support to this point of view (cf. Gen. 16:7; Exodus 3:2; Num. 22:22; Judges 2:1; I Kings 19:7; Ps. 34:7; Isa. 37:36). There is no way to determine with finality which of these two views is correct though the preponderance of opinion seems to favor regarding the angel as Christ in His work as High Priest.

Though nothing is said as to the nature of the incense, it is reasonable to suppose that it fulfills the same function as incense used in Old Testament worship, composed of the four spices mentioned in Exodus 30:34-38 and regarded as so holy that the people of Israel were forbidden to use it for any common purpose. The incense speaking of the perfections of Christ is inseparably bound up with any ministry of intercession, and the believer's petitions are coupled with the worthiness of Christ in their presentation at the heavenly altar, testifying at once to the necessity of praying in the name of Christ and to the efficacy of such prayer when faithfully ministered on earth.

[5]Cf. J. B. Smith, *A Revelation of Jesus Christ*, p. 138.

Attention is also directed in verse 5 to the censer, apparently corresponding to the instrument used to offer incense in the Old Testament worship. It was made of gold (Exodus 37:25–28; Heb. 9:4), and it was used to take fire off the altar to be carried into the Holy of Holies where the incense was added. Here the angel is said to take the censer filled with fire and to cast it into the earth. The incident is followed by voices, thunderings, lightnings, and an earthquake. The clear implication is that the censer is here used as a symbol of judgment, apparently in response to the intercession and prayers of the suffering saints in the midst of the great tribulation. The scene, therefore, is set for the judgment symbolized by the seven trumpets about to sound according to verse 6.

THE FIRST TRUMPET (8:7)

8:7 The first angel sounded, and there followed hail and fire mingled with blood, and they were cast upon the earth: and the third part of trees was burnt up, and all green grass was burnt up.

In response to the sounding of the trumpet held by the first angel, a scene of desolation is spread abroad upon the earth caused by hail and fire mingled with blood. The judgment seems to be directed to vegetation, and a third part of the trees and all the green grass are burned. The tendency on the part of the expositors has been to read into this judgment a symbol of divine chastening rather than literal hail and fire. The obvious parallel, however, is found in the tenth plague in Exodus 9:18-26. Inasmuch as in the account of Exodus there was literal hail and fire, and the result of the judgment here is the burning up of the third part of trees and all the green grass, there is no solid reason for not taking this judgment in its literal sense.

The only problem which seems to remain is the meaning of the term "blood." Here we have another helpful suggestion from the plagues of Egypt. The hail was of such character according to Exodus 9:19, 25 that it destroyed not only vegetation but also men and beasts who were caught in it. Whether or not blood was actually included in the hail and fire cast on the earth, the result was bloodshed of man and beast, though the main burden of the judgment seems to be that of destroying vegetation. If, however, it is held that the hail, fire, and blood are merely symbols, the result and meaning are almost the same, as the obvious implication is that of a similar destruction to what would have been caused if hail and fire had fallen on the earth.

This judgment, great as it is, is only the introduction. Six more trumpets are to sound. In addition to the judgment mentioned in verse 7, some manuscripts add an additional phrase after the word *earth*: "and the third part of the earth was burned up." That which is implied in the

Authorized Version is thus given explicit mention. There is little justification, however, for commentators to try to designate which portion of the
earth is thus judged.[6]

As in the case of the seals, the first four trumpets form a special unit
in contrast to the last three trumpets. Alford states,

> It has been before observed, that as in the case of the seals, so here,
> the first four are marked off from the last three. . . . It is in the
> *kind* of the exercise which their agency finds, that these four trum-
> pets are especially distinguished. The plagues indicated by them are
> entirely inflicted on *natural objects:* the earth, trees, grass, sea, rivers,
> lights of heaven: whereas those indicated by the two latter are ex-
> pressly said to be inflicted on *men,* and *not* on natural objects: cf.
> ch. 9:4, 15.[7]

THE SECOND TRUMPET (8:8-9)

8:8-9 And the second angel sounded, and as it were a great mountain burning with fire was cast into the sea; and the third part of the
sea became blood; and the third part of the creatures which were in
the sea, and had life, died; and the third part of the ships were
destroyed.

At the sound of the trumpet held by the second angel, another great
judgment falls on the earth, this time dealing with the sea. John, in his
vision, sees a large object compared to a great mountain burning with
fire which is cast into the sea. A third part of the sea becomes blood, a
third part of the creatures of the sea die, and a third part of the ships are
destroyed.

As in the interpretation of the other trumpet, the tendency of expositors
is to give a symbolic meaning to this great judgment. It is not impossible,
however, to suggest a reasonable literal interpretation. It is earlier indicated in the sixth seal that the stars from heaven fall and that there
are various disturbances of this character during this period. It may
be that the great mountain, instead of being a symbol of a government,
as is sometimes the case in Scripture, is actually a large object falling
from the heavens. Again there seems to be a parallel to the plagues of
Egypt. Just as the River Nile and all other bodies of water in Egypt
were turned to blood when Aaron stretched out his rod over the waters
of Egypt, so this object apparently had a similar effect upon the sea.
Though some believe that the sea becoming blood is the language of
appearance, that is, that the sea through some chemical change turns
blood-red, the natural effect is devastating in that the judgment destroys

---

[6]Cf. the view of Walter Scott that the "western part of the prophetic earth is here
designated" (*Exposition of the Book of the Revelation of Jesus Christ,* p. 185).
[7]Alford, IV, 634–35.

a third of the ships and a third of life in the sea. The probability is that all life and all ships are destroyed in one portion of the earth, the area nearest to the impact of the great burning mountain.

The interpreter of these and later judgments is constantly faced with the problems of how far to take the literal and the symbolic. The point of view here being expressed is that these judgments should be interpreted literally insofar as this can be reasonably followed. To make the mountain a form of human government, the sea the Roman Empire, and the ships that are destroyed the church or organized religion, is to read into the passage far more than is justified. Though all questions cannot be answered, the unmistakable implication of these judgments is that God is dealing in righteous wrath with the wicked earth.

THE THIRD TRUMPET (8:10-11)

8:10-11 And the third angel sounded, and there fell a great star from heaven, burning as it were a lamp, and it fell upon the third part of the rivers, and upon the fountains of waters: And the name of the star is called Wormwood: and the third part of the waters became wormwood; and many men died of the waters, because they were made bitter.

When the third trumpet sounds, John witnesses a great star burning like a lamp falling upon rivers and fountains of water. It is named "Wormwood" and apparently causes the water to be bitter, resulting in the death of many. In interpreting this third trumpet, expositors have had a field day in assigning symbolic meaning to the components of this judgment. If the meaning is symbolic, there is no clear indication as to the interpretation of this judgment except that the great star can be assigned to some personage such as the Antichrist or Satan himself and the waters could be regarded as symbolic of the peoples of the earth.

It seems preferable, however, to view this with a reasonable literalness, as in the case of the second trumpet. The star seems to be a heavenly body or a mass from outer space, understandably burning as it enters the atmosphere of earth, and falling with contaminating influence upon the rivers and waters. The reference to wormwood seems to draw the parallel of the experience of the children of Israel at the waters of Marah (Exodus 15:23-25). There the tree cast into the bitter waters made them sweet. Here the wormwood cast into the sweet water made it bitter. Such also is the contrast between Christ on the cross atoning for sin and making that which is bitter sweet and Christ coming in judgment which turns the vain hopes and ambitions of men into bitterness and despair. The result of this trumpet is to inflict a divine judgment from God upon men themselves.

155

THE FOURTH TRUMPET (8:12–13)

8:12-13 And the fourth angel sounded, and the third part of the sun was smitten, and the third part of the moon, and the third part of the stars; so as the third part of them was darkened, and the day shone not for a third part of it, and the night likewise. And I beheld, and heard an angel flying through the midst of heaven, saying with a loud voice, Woe, woe, woe, to the inhabiters of the earth by reason of the other voices of the trumpet of the three angels, which are yet to sound!

In contrast to the first three judgments having to do respectively with land, sea, rivers, and fountains of water, the fourth trumpet relates to the heavens themselves. As John witnesses the scene, he sees a third part of the sun, a third part of the moon, and a third part of the stars darkened, an eclipse that extends to a third part of the day and a third part of the night. The symbolic interpretation of verse 12 usually regards this prophecy as portending a disruption of human government and society extending to a third part of the earth. Here again, however, it is probably preferable to interpret this literally as extending to a disruption of light from heaven as a solemn warning of other judgments which were yet to fall upon the earth. J. B. Smith comments:

> It is of considerable interest to note the progress—one third of the green trees and grass, one third of marine life and shipping, one third of the waters, and one third of the heavenly bodies. Food is destroyed; distribution is crippled; water supply is limited; production is hampered.[8]

This interpretation is given support by the next verse, which indicates that the first four trumpets are not only judgments in themselves but warnings of the last three trumpets which will be far more severe in character. John records that he both beheld and heard the loud voice of an angel pronouncing a triple woe on the inhabitants of the earth because of the three trumpets which were yet to sound. In the best manuscripts, "eagle" is substituted for "angel." Whether announced by an angel or an eagle, the effect of the trumpet is much the same. The earth is warned of judgment to come. The trumpet judgments, which have their beginning in this chapter, confirm the predictions of Christ and the Old Testament prophets of the coming time of tribulation far worse than anything the human race had ever experienced before.

The first four trumpets deal with aspects of the physical world which are taken more or less for granted. The beauty and benefit of the trees, the luxury and growth of green grass are seldom occasions for thanksgiving to the living God. In a similar way, men are prone to take for granted the blessings of water, whether it be the beauty of the sea, the

[8]Smith, p. 140.

majestic flow of great rivers, or the pure fountains and springs which abound in the natural world. These too are gifts from a loving God to an undeserving world, and they come under the blight and judgment described in the second and third trumpets.

Still another area of blessing from God is the light of the sun, moon, and stars. The handiwork of God in the heavens is mentioned frequently in Scripture as a reminder of God's power, sovereignty, and wisdom. David, in writing Psalm 19, declared, "The heavens declare the glory of God; and the firmament sheweth his handiwork. Day unto day uttereth speech, and night unto night sheweth knowledge." The very presence of these aspects of nature so essential to human life and existence is referred to by Paul in Romans 1:20 as manifesting God in His eternal power. The Prophet Jeremiah spoke of the sun and moon as tokens of God's faithfulness to His promise to the nation of Israel and as symbols of their continuance as long as the earth endures (Jer. 31:35–36). These very tokens of blessing and revelation of the glory of God are affected by the fourth trumpet. So dramatic are the judgments and so unmistakably an evidence of the power and sovereignty of God that blaspheming men on earth can no longer ignore the fact that God is dealing with them. Fearful as these judgments are, they are only the beginning of God's dealing with the earth; and as indicated in a special announcement, three great woes are still to fall. Though it is difficult in this day of grace to imagine such catastrophic judgments, the Word of God is plain, and men are called everywhere to avail themselves of grace before it is too late.

9

THE FIFTH AND SIXTH TRUMPETS:
THE FIRST AND SECOND WOES

THE FIFTH TRUMPET:
THE FALLEN STAR AND THE OPENING OF THE ABYSS (9:1-2)

9:1-2 And the fifth angel sounded, and I saw a star fall from heaven unto the earth: and to him was given the key of the bottomless pit. And he opened the bottomless pit; and there arose a smoke out of the pit, as the smoke of a great furnace; and the sun and the air were darkened by reason of the smoke of the pit.

The rising crescendo of judgments on the earth now introduces the first woe, a dramatic event described by John in the first twelve verses of this chapter. As the trumpet of the fifth angel is sounded, John records that he sees a star fallen from heaven having the key to the bottomless pit. Earlier in the book of Revelation, in connection with the sixth seal (6:12–17) and the fourth trumpet (8:12–13) record is made of unusual disturbances in the starry heavens. In chapter 6, the stars of heaven fall even as a fig tree casts her untimely figs, and heaven itself departs as a scroll when it is rolled together. In chapter 8, a great star from heaven described as "burning as it were a lamp" falls upon rivers and fountains of waters. In these instances it is probable that reference is made to material stars or fragments of them, and their falling on the earth is a form of divine judgment upon a wicked world.

The star here mentioned, however, seems to refer to a person rather than a literal star or meteor. The star is described as "fallen" in more accurate translations rather than falling, as indicated in the Authorized Version. The word *fall* is in the perfect tense which signifies completed action. For the event itself, see Revelation 12. J. B. Smith notes two passages anticipating this: Isaiah 14:12–17; Luke 10:18.[1] The person referred to as the star is given the key of the bottomless pit, or the pit of the abyss, as it is better translated. No explanation is offered in the passage itself concerning the identity of this person, but the occasion may be the aftermath of warfare in heaven mentioned in Revelation 12:7–9, where the devil is cast out into the earth. This act of God, probably at

[1] *A Revelation of Jesus Christ*, p. 142.

the beginning of the great tribulation, terminates the ability of Satan to accuse the brethren in heaven as he has been doing through previous ages. The first verse of chapter 9 does not record the fall itself, but rather the star is seen as already fallen from heaven to the earth. It would seem likely, therefore, that the person referred to as the star is none other than Satan himself. J. B. Smith believes the star is an angel:

> That a literal *star* is not meant is evident from the part that to him was given the key, that is, the authority (Matthew 16:19; Revelation 1:18), to open the bottomless pit. An intelligent being must be intended. It has been observed that a star is used as a symbol of the angel, 1:20. As early as the days of Job, there is a similar use of the word . . . (Job 38:7).[2]

To this personage is given the key of the bottomless pit, or pit of abyss. This is the first instance of this expression in Scripture mentioned three times in this chapter and four additional times later in Revelation. The "bottomless pit" (Gr., *abyssos*) is the abode of demons according to Luke 8:31. The Greek word is found seven times in Revelation (9:1, 2, 11; 11:7; 17:8; 20:1, 3). Romans 10:7 implies hypothetically that Christ descended into the spirit world between His death and resurrection.[3] From these references, it may be concluded that the pit of the abyss is none other than the place of detention of wicked angels. It is here that Satan himself is confined for a thousand years during the reign of Christ on earth (20:1-3). The opening verse of this chapter, therefore, presents Satan as having the key to the pit of the abyss with power to release those who are confined there.

The second verse records the use of the key. The pit of the abyss is opened, and out of it comes a smoke as the smoke of a great furnace which darkens the sun and the air. It is evident that this event causes that which is contained in the pit of the abyss to erupt, polluting the air and darkening the light of day. It seems to portend the spiritual corruption which will be caused by these demons released from their confinement, and it identifies the character of the judgment involved in the fifth trumpet as that of demonic and satanic oppression.

THE FIFTH TRUMPET:
DEMONIC TORMENT LOOSED UPON THE EARTH (9:3-6)

9:3-6 And there came out of the smoke locusts upon the earth: and unto them was given power, as the scorpions of the earth have power. And it was commanded them that they should not hurt the grass of the earth, neither any green thing, neither any tree; but only those men which have not the seal of God in their foreheads. And to them it was given that they should not kill them, but that they should

[2]*Ibid.*, p. 141.
[3]Cf. *ibid.*, p. 142.

be tormented five months: and their torment was as the torment of a
scorpion, when he striketh a man. And in those days shall men seek
death, and shall not find it; and shall desire to die, and death shall
flee from them.

As John continues to observe the unfolding of the fifth trumpet, he
sees locusts coming out of the smoke which are likened to scorpions. As
is borne out by the description given later, these are not natural locusts,
but a visual representation of the hordes of demons loosed upon the
earth. Peake observes:

> Now these descriptions of heaven and hell were meant by the author
> to be very literally taken. They are not figures of speech; and if we
> are to be true to the writer's thought we can scarcely represent the
> scenes to our imagination with too much realism. And similarly the
> scorpion locusts are quite literally intended; they are not heretics,
> or Goths, or Mohammedans, or the mendicant orders, or the Jesuits,
> or Protestants, or Saracens or Turks, but they are uncanny denizens
> of the abyss, locusts of a hellish species, animated by devilish instincts
> and equipped with infernal powers.[4]

Walter Scott expresses another viewpoint, "that the locust army is a
symbolical representation of judgment of a superhuman kind."[5] Scott
holds that "neither the smoke nor the locusts are literal."[6]

The locusts are commanded, probably by God or perhaps by Satan himself, not to hurt the grass of the earth or any green thing, or any tree, but
only men who do not have the seal of God on their foreheads. In the
Old Testament, locusts were a greatly feared plague because they could
strip the country of every green leaf and sprout, leaving man and beast
alike to die for lack of food. Frequently in the Bible, locusts are used by
the Lord as a divine judgment upon a wicked world. In the contest of
Moses with Pharaoh in Egypt the plagues of locusts mentioned in Exodus
10:12–20 caused Pharaoh to be quickly humbled. According to Exodus
10:16–17, when the plagues of locusts had covered Egypt, Pharaoh called
for Moses and Aaron and said, "I have sinned against the LORD your God,
and against you. Now therefore forgive, I pray thee, my sin only this
once, and entreat the LORD your God, that he may take away from me
this death only." In response to this entreaty, Moses prayed to God and
a strong west wind blew the locusts into the Red Sea. A similar plague
of locusts is mentioned in Joel 1:4–7.

The locusts in Revelation 9, however, while given this title because
their function is similar to that of a locust, represent a divine judgment
upon a wicked world. They are described as having the capacity to sting
as the scorpions of the earth and as not eating the grass or green vegeta-

[4]A. S. Peake, *The Revelation of John*, p. 181.
[5]*Exposition of the Revelation of Jesus Christ*, p. 204.
[6]*Ibid.*

tion as ordinary locusts would do. Instead, they torment men in a way comparable to the torment of a scorpion. Apparently the entire human race is open to their activity except those who are sealed by God in their foreheads. This obviously excludes the 144,000 of Revelation 7, and the protection may extend as far as this plague is concerned to all who know the Lord in that day. According to II Timothy 2:19, "the foundation of God standeth sure, having this seal, The Lord knoweth them that are his." In a similar way, believers in the present age are sealed with the Holy Spirit of promise according to Ephesians 1:13–14. It would seem improbable that any true believer in that day would be subject to the torment of the locusts; the torment is rather a judgment upon Christ-rejecting men.

The graphic description of the torment is compared to that when a scorpion strikes a man. Scorpions in all climates are fearful and painful scourges. In warm climates, they grow to such size as to make their sting not only painful but dangerous. Frequently small children die from the sting of a scorpion in tropical countries. Though the affliction here described is not actually a sting of a scorpion, it is compared to the pain and suffering caused by such a sting.

Further, the torment is said to extend for five months. Probably the best interpretation is to take this literally as a period of five months. As Alford and other commentators point out, "Five months is the ordinary time in the year during which locusts commit their ravages."[7] In contrast to the pain caused by a scorpion which would pass away in a course of hours, this continues for a long period so that in verse 6 John writes that men shall seek death and shall not find it.

Literal death is meant here. Elliott's point of view that the command not to kill in verse 5 refers to the security of the church is made impossible in view of the obvious character of death in verse 6 where men seek to die and cannot do so. As Alford notes in commenting on this,

> For it surely cannot be allowed that the *killing of men* should be said of their annihilation as a political body in one verse and their *desiring to die* in the next should be said of something totally different, and applicable to their individual misery.[8]

This is a horrible picture of domination by demons to such an extent that men lose their ability of free choice and are in agony of body and soul. What the Scriptures here convey is that in addition to the natural plagues of the first four trumpets, now wicked men are afflicted by torment of demons.

The attempts of some commentators to spiritualize this trumpet and work out an elaborate prophetic system, based on the idea that each

[7]Henry Alford, *The Greek New Testament*, IV, 641.
[8]*Ibid.*

day in the five months is a year, is totally unjustified. There is no period in history which in any sense fulfills what is portrayed in this chapter, nor is there any evidence in Scripture that the term "month" or "year" is ever used in any other sense than a literal one. Though the word *day* frequently refers to a period of time longer than twenty-four hours, and the weeks or sevens of Daniel's prophecy in Daniel 9 are evidently prophetic years rather than twenty-four-hour days, in this instance there is no justification for taking the expression to mean anything other than a literal five months. This would fit in the chronology of the tribulation time as it is elsewhere taught in the Scriptures. The introduction of the time element is to show that the torment is not a passing experience of a few days but rather a plague that extends over a considerable period of time, making its affliction a fearful experience to contemplate.

Undergoing such a strange and painful experience, it is natural that men would seek to die. The prophecy indicates, however, that though they seek death, death shall flee from them. As is common in demonic affliction as recorded in the Gospels, those in the grip of demons are not free to exercise their own will and therefore are not free to take their own lives. Even the hope of death to deliver them from their present troubles is taken away from them in that dark hour. They are left to face their trial and affliction without any way of escape.

THE FIFTH TRUMPET: THE LOCUSTS DESCRIBED (9:7–11)

9:7-11 And the shapes of the locusts were like unto horses prepared unto battle; and on their heads were as it were crowns like gold, and their faces were as the faces of men. And they had hair as the hair of women, and their teeth were as the teeth of lions. And they had breastplates, as it were breastplates of iron; and the sound of their wings was as the sound of chariots of many horses running to battle. And they had tails like unto scorpions, and there were stings in their tails: and their power was to hurt men five months. And they had a king over them, which is the angel of the bottomless pit, whose name in the Hebrew tongue is Abaddon, but in the Greek tongue hath his name Apollyon.

The description of the locusts given in these verses makes it clear that they are not ordinary locusts and are so named only because of their function as a judgment and plague from the Lord. They apparently are much larger than ordinary locusts and are compared to horses prepared for battle. Inasmuch as demons do not have physical shape, what John is seeing must symbolize demonic possession. The locusts are described as having crowns of gold on their heads, ordinarily a token of victory, but here apparently a decoration or headdress. Their faces are described as similar to the faces of men. Their hair is described as the hair of women and their teeth as the teeth of lions. This awesome combination

162

of the qualities of beasts and men depicts the utterly fearful character of these instruments of divine judgment. This is in keeping with the general character of the book of Revelation as an unmasking of the true nature of Satan and evil.

In verse 9, the locusts are declared to have breastplates of iron, implying that they are immune to destruction. They are also equipped with wings which give forth the sound of many chariots going to battle, implying speed and the impossibility of evading their attack. Particular attention is given to their tails, which are compared to those of scorpions and by which they have power to hurt men for five months. It would be difficult to describe a more fearful spectacle than these instruments of divine justice, utterly wicked in themselves, and released from the pit of the abyss to accomplish this terrifying judgment. The fact that they have power to hurt men five months is repeated in verse 10, as if to call special attention to the length of their torment.

In addition to the previous description, in verse 11 the locusts are declared to have a king who is the angel of the pit of the abyss, described both in the Hebrew and the Greek. The Hebrew name "Abaddon" and the Greek name "Apollyon" both mean "destroyer." Such is the character of Satan and those who affiliate with him as wicked or fallen angels. Though in the modern world Satan often appears as an angel of light in the role of that which is good and religious, here the mask is stripped away and evil is seen in its true character. Satan and the demons are seen as the destroyers of the souls of men and as those who can only bring affliction. When divine restraint is released, as in this instance, the true character of the evil one is manifested immediately.

ANNOUNCEMENT OF TWO MORE WOES (9:12)

9:12 One woe is past; and, behold, there come two woes more hereafter.

Fearful as is the torment inflicted by the locusts out of the pit of the abyss, it is only the first of three great judgments which conclude the trumpet period. In verse 12, we are informed that the woe described as following the fifth trumpet is now past, and two more woes are going to follow. The word *woe* refers in Scripture to some great calamity, usually a judgment from God such as Christ pronounced upon Chorazin and Bethsaida (Matt. 11:21). Desperate indeed will be the situation of those who know not Christ in these tragic hours preceding His return to judge the wicked world.

The tribulation period unmasks human wickedness and also demonstrates the true character of Satan. In our modern day while Satan is still restricted it is easy to forget the great conflict which is raging between

163

the forces of God and the forces of Satan referred to in Ephesians 6:12. In the great tribulation, and especially in the time of the fifth trumpet, with the release of the confined demons the full character of Satan will be starkly manifested. For the first time in history all those who do not know the Lord Jesus Christ as Saviour will come under demonic possession and affliction. What is true in that hour is also true in some measure today, for there is no deliverance from the power of Satan nor from his affliction apart from salvation in Christ and the delivering power of God.

THE SIXTH TRUMPET: THE LOOSING OF THE FOUR ANGELS (9:13–15)

9:13-15 And the sixth angel sounded, and I heard a voice from the four horns of the golden altar which is before God, Saying to the sixth angel which had the trumpet, Loose the four angels which are bound in the great river Euphrates. And the four angels were loosed, which were prepared for an hour, and a day, and a month, and a year, for to slay the third part of men.

With the sounding of the sixth trumpet, John hears a voice described as coming from the four horns of the golden altar before God. In 8:3, this altar is the scene of the offering of incense with the prayers of saints. Here in its final mention in the book of Revelation, it is related to the judgment of the sixth trumpet. The inference is that this judgment like those preceding is partially an answer to the prayers of the persecuted saints on earth and a token of divine response and preparation for their deliverance. The four horns seem to indicate that this altar is similar to the design of the altar of incense used in the Tabernacle and in the Temple. If the horns have significance, they refer to the sovereignty and judicial government of God.

The voice instructed the sixth angel to loose the four angels declared to be bound in the great river Euphrates. Walter Scott observes that the command to loose the four angels indicates that "these angelic ministers of judgment are under divine control; they cannot act without express command."[9]

In attempting to understand the description of this unusual event, a number of questions can be raised about the four angels. Why should they be bound in or at the river Euphrates? The answer seems to be that the vision concerns an invasion from the Orient. As Alford says, "there is nothing in the text to prevent 'the great river Euphrates' from being meant literally."[10]

These apparently are not the same four angels mentioned in 7:1, who are angels in authority over the winds of the earth. The four angels

[9]Scott, p. 210.
[10]*Ibid.*, IV, 645.

mentioned in chapter 7, holding the four winds of the earth, are instructed not to inflict their punishment until the 144,000 of Israel are sealed and protected. They seem to be holy angels or instruments of God's divine wrath upon the world. The four angels in chapter 9, however, are obviously of different character, for they are described as bound at the great river Euphrates. There is no instance in Scripture where holy angels are bound. Some of the wicked angels, however, are bound according to Jude 6. Likewise, later Satan is bound for one thousand years and cast into the pit of the abyss.

From these parallels, it may be concluded that the four angels bound in the Euphrates River are evil angels who are loosed on the occasion of the sounding of the sixth trumpet in order to execute this judgment. It is another instance of the loosing of wicked angels similar to the release of the demonic locusts earlier in the fifth trumpet. They all are prepared for their hour of activity much as the whale was prepared to swallow Jonah and effect divine discipline upon the prophet. These are wicked angels designated to execute the great judgment of the sixth trumpet but prevented from doing so until the proper moment. It is declared that the angels' function is to slay the third part of men and that they had been prepared to fulfill this purpose at the given hour.

The expression "an hour, and a day, and a month, and a year" designates not the duration of their activity but the fact that this judgment comes exactly at the hour of God's appointment. On the basis that the article is used only before the word *hour* in the Greek construction it should be translated "the hour, and day, and month, and year," to be interpreted as Alford does: "the appointed hour occurring in the appointed day, and that in the appointed month, and that in the appointed year."[11] Though the agency of men is used to accomplish the purpose of God, the time schedule is determined by God, not man, and even angels execute God's will in God's time.

The judgment here depicted, that of slaying the third part of men, is one of the most devastating mentioned anywhere in the book of Revelation prior to the second coming. Earlier in the fourth seal, a fourth of the earth's population is killed. Here an additional third is marked out for slaughter. These two judgments alone account for half of the world's population, and it is clear that in addition to these judgments there is widespread destruction of human life in other divine judgments contained in the seals, trumpets, and vials. Never since Noah has such a substantial proportion of the earth's population come under God's righteous judgment. The fact that the third part of the population of the world is killed is repeated in verse 18.

[11]Alford, IV, 645.

THE SIXTH TRUMPET:
THE ARMY OF TWO HUNDRED MILLION (9:16–19)

9:16-19 And the number of the army of the horsemen were two hundred thousand thousand: and I heard the number of them. And thus I saw the horses in the vision, and them that sat on them, having breastplates of fire, and of jacinth, and brimstone: and the heads of the horses were as the heads of lions; and out of their mouths issued fire and smoke and brimstone. By these three was the third part of men killed, by the fire, and by the smoke, and by the brimstone, which issued out of their mouths. For their power is in their mouth, and in their tails: for their tails were like unto serpents, and had heads, and with them they do hurt.

Having declared the purpose of the army, John now gives details. Most impressive is the astounding number of the army of horsemen, 200 million, or literally "twice ten thousand times ten thousand." Because the number "ten thousand times ten thousand" is often used of an innumerable company (cf. 5:11) some have held that this should not be understood as a literal number. Scott does not believe that the army of 200 million should be taken literally:

> A literal army consisting of 200 million of cavalry need not be thought of. The main idea in the passage is a vast and overwhelming army, one beyond human computation, and exceeding by far any before witnessed.[12]

H. B. Swete comments, "These vast numbers forbid us to seek a literal fulfillment, and the description which follows supports this conclusion."[13] If considered a literal enumeration of the army, it would represent the largest armed force ever known to man. Considering the millions of people in the Orient, the literal interpretation is not impossible, especially in view of the population explosion. The number of the horsemen here is comparable to the innumerable chariots of God mentioned in Psalm 68:17.

There is no direct statement as to the origin of this army, but the implication is, from the fact that the angels of verse 14 were bound "in" or at the Euphrates, that the army may come from the East. A similar and later development mentioned in Revelation 16:12 following the outpouring of the sixth vial also depicts an invasion from the East. Unless the vials and the trumpets coincide as some believe, these are two different events, possibly two different phases of the same operation. Chronologically the trumpets involved closely succeed one another and their judgments seem to fall like trip-hammer blows as the great tribulation

[12]Scott, p. 211.
[13]*The Apocalypse of St. John*, p. 122. Swete, if living today, would no doubt be astounded to read in *Time* (May 21, 1965, p. 35) that Red China alone claims to have a man-and-woman militia of 200,000,000, exactly the figure of Revelation 9:16.

comes to its close. Whether the army is held to be the literal number mentioned or not, it is clear that this is a massive force of tremendous military power as evidenced in its capacity to slay a third part of the human race. It may be that the army here described continues to fight until the time of the second coming of Christ, and the number slain is the total number involved in the conflict.

John also gives a graphic description of the horses as well as of the warriors who sit upon them. They are declared to have breastplates of fire and of jacinth and brimstone. Some have interpreted the description as John's understanding of a scene in which modern warfare is under way. Further, the heads of the horses are compared to heads of lions out of whose mouths fire, smoke, and brimstone issue. This again is a description that might be comparable to modern mechanical warfare. In verse 19 additional details are given in that the power is declared to be in their mouths and in their tails. Their tails are compared to serpents, and even the tails have heads with which they can hurt men. Whether these are symbols or the best description John can give of modern warfare, this is an awesome picture of an almost irresistible military force destroying all that opposes it. The terms "horses," "lions," and "serpents" all speak of deadly warfare. The mention of lions can be compared to that in Revelation 10:3 where lions roar, and to the description of the locusts in 9:8 as having teeth of lions, and to the beast of Revelation 13:2, which has the mouth of a lion. As king of beasts the lion speaks of victorious conquest.

Further light is cast on the character of the warfare in verse 18, where it is repeated that the third part of men are killed by the invading force; special mention is made of the means, namely, "by the fire, and by the smoke, and by the brimstone, which issued out of their mouths." This again seems to be a picture of modern warfare rather than of ancient weapons. This indicates that though there may be a disarmament in the early phases of the time period between the rapture and the second coming, by this time, namely toward the close of the tribulation, modern means of war are once again being fully used. The world that longs for peace and seeks to attain it by the worship of the beast of Revelation 13 will learn the sad lesson that there can be no peace until the Prince of Peace rules.

THE SIXTH TRUMPET: MAN STILL UNREPENTANT (9:20-21)

9:20-21 And the rest of the men which were not killed by these plagues yet repented not of the works of their hands, that they should not worship devils, and idols of gold, and silver, and brass, and stone, and of wood: which neither can see, nor hear, nor walk: Neither repented they of their murders, nor of their sorceries, nor of their fornication, nor of their thefts.

In spite of the dramatic judgment inflicted by this invading military force, those who survive are declared to be unrepentant. Such is the hardness of the human heart even though faced by worldwide destruction and divine judgment from God and a clear testimony of God's power to deal summarily with every human soul. The character of their wickedness is unfolded in these verses. They do not repent of the evil works of their hands. They do not repent of their worship of devils, or demons, and the worship of idols which their hands have formed, which John dramatically describes in the words "which neither can see, nor hear, nor walk." Their worship of idols does not change their lives, and verse 21 indicates that they do not repent of their murders, their wicked sorceries, their fornication, nor their thefts. Though the power of satanic false religion is evident in the world, it does not have the transforming, purifying, redeeming quality found only in the power and grace of God. Though men can be made to fear God by demonstration of divine power, they are not brought to the place of repentance apart from faith in Christ and divine grace. Scott observes, "The two closing verses of the chapter reveal an astounding picture of human depravity."[14]

[14]Scott, p. 214.

10

THE MIGHTY ANGEL WITH THE LITTLE BOOK

The Mighty Angel and the Seven Thunders (10:1–4)

10:1-4 And I saw another mighty angel come down from heaven, clothed with a cloud: and a rainbow was upon his head, and his face was as it were the sun, and his feet as pillars of fire: And he had in his hand a little book open: and he set his right foot upon the sea, and his left foot on the earth, And cried with a loud voice, as when a lion roareth: and when he had cried, seven thunders uttered their voices. And when the seven thunders had uttered their voices, I was about to write: and I heard a voice from heaven saying unto me, Seal up those things which the seven thunders uttered, and write them not.

BEGINNING WITH CHAPTER 10 a parenthetical section is introduced which continues through 11:14. Like chapter 7 it does not advance the narrative but presents other facts which contribute to the total prophetic scene. In the opening verses of chapter 10 a personage is introduced, described as "another mighty angel." The word *another* (Gr., *allon*) ordinarily means "another of the same kind," that is, an angel similar to othe. angels which have been previously introduced. It seems evident from the context that this angel is not the sixth angel mentioned in 9:13, nor the angel which sounds the seventh trumpet in 11:15. As no clear statement is made, the interpreter is led to determine the character of this angel by the description which follows.

Some expositors[1] of Revelation believe that the angel mentioned here, as well as the angel of 8:3, is none other than the Lord Jesus Christ. This conclusion is based on the description given of the angel as being in a position of great power over the earth and as possessing majesty. Walter Scott identifies the angel as "an *uncreated* being of divine majesty and power. . . . It is the Lord Himself."[2] Scott goes beyond the text, however, in affirming that the being is "uncreated." In the Old Testament, Christ appeared frequently as the Angel of Jehovah, the first instance being in Genesis 16:7, where the Angel of the Lord appeared to Hagar. In the book of Revelation itself, Christ is presented in several symbols, the most

[1]Cf. Walter Scott, *Exposition of the Revelation of Jesus Christ,* p. 219; J. A. Seiss, *The Apocalypse,* p. 223.
[2]*Ibid.,* p. 219.

frequent of which is the Lamb slain as in chapters 4 through 6. William Kelly identifies the angel as the Lord Jesus Christ in that he is "clothed with a cloud" which Kelly holds is "the well-known badge of Jehovah's presence."[3]

Though this is a plausible interpretation, the evidence seems to support the idea that here is a holy angel to whom has been given great power and authority. J. B. Smith believes it is an error to understand the angel here to be Christ.[4] The angel of 10:1 is declared to be "another mighty angel" and apparently refers to "the strong angel" of 5:2 who is clearly an angel and not Christ the Lamb. The angel of 10:1 is described as one who "comes down from heaven" and there is no evidence that Christ comes to earth midway in the tribulation. There are many instances of this in Revelation where angels are made the ministers of God for both the punishment of the wicked and the protection of the righteous. In chapter 12 Michael the archangel is mentioned by name as contending against Satan and the wicked angels and casting them out of heaven. Some have concluded that the description given in chapter 10 must be a reference to Michael as the chief of all the holy angels. Though the angel is presented as one having great majesty and power, there is no clear evidence that his function or his person is more than that of a created angel to whom has been entrusted great authority.

The description of the angel, however, is in very graphic terms. He is declared to be "clothed with a cloud" and has "a rainbow upon his head." His face is described as glorious as the sun and his feet compared to pillars of fire. John sees him in a most dramatic pose, with his right foot upon the sea, and his left foot upon the earth, implying a position of power and authority over the entire earth. All of this, however, is introductory to the point of primary importance that in his hand is a little book which is opened.

In Revelation 5, the Lamb has in His hands a seven-sealed book which in successive chapters is unrolled, unfolding the judgment symbolized by the seals. This book, by contrast, is already open and specifically called "a little book," referring to its small size. Some have tried to connect this book with the scroll of chapters 4 through 6, but there is no clear identification which would make these the same. The name of the book itself is different. In 5:1 the scroll is described by the Greek *biblion*, whereas here the diminutive form is used, *biblaridion*.

The contents of the little book are nowhere revealed in Revelation, but they seem to represent in this vision the written authority given to the angel to fulfill his mission. As John beholds the vision with the angel standing upon the sea and the earth, the angel cries with a loud voice

[3]*Lectures on the Book of Revelation*, p. 200.
[4]Cf. J. B. Smith, *A Revelation of Jesus Christ*, p. 153.

like a lion's roar. In answer to this cry of the angel, seven thunders are heard.

It would seem evident that the seven thunders contain a further revelation consisting of some articulate voice which John could understand. Scott relates the seven thunders to the seven times the voice of Jehovah is mentioned in Psalm 29:3-9, and states, "The seven thunders point to 'the perfection of God's intervention in judgment.' "[5] When John was about to write what he had heard, however, he was instructed not to do so, as recorded in verse 4, "I heard a voice from heaven saying unto me, Seal up those things which the seven thunders uttered, and write them not." Though the principal purpose of the vision given to John was to enable him to write the book of Revelation and thus pass on divine revelation to the church, in this instance the revelation is for John's ears and eyes only, and he is not permitted to reveal what he heard. This illustrates a divine principle that while God has revealed much, there are secrets which God has not seen fit to reveal to man at this time.

ANNOUNCEMENT OF THE END OF THE AGE (10:5-7)

10:5-7 And the angel which I saw stand upon the sea and upon the earth lifted up his hand to heaven, And sware by him that liveth for ever and ever, who created heaven, and the things that therein are, and the earth, and the things that therein are, and the sea, and the things which are therein, that there shall be time no longer: But in the days of the voice of the seventh angel, when he shall begin to sound, the mystery of God should be finished, as he hath declared to his servants the prophets.

One of the indications that the angel portrayed in this vision is not Christ Himself is the fact that he swears by God, implying that God is greater than the angel. It is, however, a very solemn oath. Attention is called to the special character of the authority of God over the earth as the One who lives forever and as the One who created all things in heaven and in earth. Thus, abruptly, is brushed aside the foolishness of men who try to create a universe out of resident forces apart from God. As the Creator, God is also the sovereign Ruler who can declare that there shall be no more time, that is, no more delay. This expression (Gr., *chronos*) has sometimes been misunderstood to mean that time will cease. The expression here, however, does not refer to time as a succession of chronological events; rather it means that time has run out, that is, that there will be no further delay. The end is now to be consummated. Even in eternity, there will be a time relationship in that one event will follow another.

Oscar Cullmann comments,

None of the New Testament expressions for time has as its object
[5]Scott, p. 221.

171

time as an abstraction. This is not even the meaning of *chronos*, "time." . . . In the New Testament we find this word for "time" used in concrete reference to the redemptive history; it may have the meaning of "season" or of "age," or it may signify simply some space of time that is to elapse. Thus even the well-known passage in Rev. 10:6, where it is said that there will be no more *chronos*, is not to be understood as if the era of timelessness were meant; rather, on the analogy of Hab. 2:3 and Heb. 10:37, we must translate: "there will be no more *delay*."[6]

J. B. Smith compares the expression "there should be time no longer" to the similar expressions "there was no more sea" (21:1); "there shall be no more death" (21:4); "neither shall there be any more pain" (21:4); "there shall be no more curse" (22:3); "there shall be no night there" (22:5). Smith observes, "In each there is the negative *no*, the verb *to be* and the word *eti* translated *more*."[7]

In explanation of the statement that there shall be no more delay, verse 7 declares that the sounding of the seventh trumpet, here referred to as the voice of the seventh angel, brings about the completion of the mystery of God as declared to His servants the prophets. Kelly identifies "the mystery of God" as

> the secret of His allowing Satan to have his own way, and man too (that is to say, the wonder of evil prospering and of good being trodden underfoot). God checks, no doubt, the evil in a measure, partly through human government and partly through His own providential dealings.[8]

The reference to the mystery of God seems to mean truth concerning God Himself which has not been fully revealed.

It is often overlooked, however, that the mystery is said to have been "declared to his servants the prophets" (v. 7). The mystery of God which is declared as subject to fulfillment is unfolded therefore in the Old Testament in the many passages which speak of the establishment of the kingdom of God on earth.

The prediction is related to the full manifestation of the divine power, majesty, and holiness of God which will be evident in the glorious return of Christ, the establishment of His millennial kingdom, and the creation of the eternal state which will follow. The ignorance of God and the disregard of His majestic person which characterize the present age as well as the great tribulation will exist no longer when Christ returns and manifests Himself in glory to the entire earth. In that day all, from the least to the greatest, will know the Lord, that is, know the important facts about Him (cf. Jer. 31:34).

[6]*Christ and Time*, p. 49.
[7]Smith, p. 157.
[8]Kelly, p. 206.

The Eating of the Little Book (10:8–11)

10:8-11 And the voice which I heard from heaven spake unto me again, and said, Go and take the little book which is open in the hand of the angel which standeth upon the sea and upon the earth. And I went unto the angel, and said unto him, Give me the little book. And he said unto me, Take it, and eat it up; and it shall make thy belly bitter, but it shall be in thy mouth sweet as honey. And I took the little book out of the angel's hand, and ate it up; and it was in my mouth sweet as honey: and as soon as I had eaten it, my belly was bitter. And he said unto me, Thou must prophesy again before many peoples, and nations, and tongues, and kings.

After the utterance of the angel, John hears another voice from heaven apparently to be identified with the same voice he heard in 4:1. John is commanded by the voice to take the book previously described as "open in the hand of the angel which standeth upon the sea and upon the earth." This is the third time in this chapter when the reader is reminded that the angel stands upon the sea and upon the earth. In each of the three instances, sea is mentioned before earth, though the normal order in the book of Revelation is to mention earth before sea (cf. 5:13; 7:1–3; 12:12; 14:7). John is more impressed by the fact that the angel stands on the sea than upon the earth, but the symbolism in either case indicates complete authority over the entire earthly situation.

In obedience to the command of the voice, John goes to the angel and requests that he be given the little book. In reply the angel instructs John, "Take it, and eat it up; and it shall make thy belly bitter, but it shall be in thy mouth sweet as honey." Verse 10 records John's obedience, and, as he eats the book, the prophecy of the angel is fulfilled. The incident of John's eating the book should be compared to the similar experiences of Ezekiel (Ezek. 2:9–10; 3:1–4, 14) and Jeremiah (Jer. 15:16–18).[9] The angel informs John, "Thou must prophesy again before many peoples, and nations, and tongues, and kings."

This experience of John naturally raises a question concerning the meaning of his eating the little book. No interpretation of the experience of John is given in the Scriptures, but it is obvious that the symbolism is supposed to convey meaning without necessary comment. John by eating the book partakes of its content, and in his act of obedience appropriates the statements, promises, and affirmations contained in the book. The book itself seems to be a symbol of the Word of God as it is delivered to men, that is, divine revelation already given. This seems to be confirmed by the word of the angel to John in the last verse of the chapter where John is commanded to prophesy to many people. The testimony to which John is called is that of faithfully delivering the Word of God as it is committed to him. Such a commission with obedience to it

[9]Cf. extended discussion, Smith, pp. 161–63.

has precisely the twofold effect mentioned. To John the Word of God is sweet, in that it is a word of promise, a word of grace, and a revelation of the love of God. Though he is on the Isle of Patmos in the flesh and experiencing the bitterness of persecution, the Word of God is a precious assurance of his eternal salvation, a basis for his present fellowship with Christ, and the ground for his hope of glory to be fulfilled in the future.

Partaking of the Word of God is indeed sweet. How precious God's written revelation should be to the child of God. As David wrote in Psalm 19:9-10, "The fear of the LORD is clean, enduring for ever: the judgments of the LORD are true and righteous altogether. More to be desired are they than gold, yea, than much fine gold: sweeter also than honey and the honeycomb."

The Word of God which is sweet to John's soul also has its bitter aspects. John is experiencing this in his exile on the Isle of Patmos and is enduring hardness as a good soldier of Jesus Christ, separated from friends, afflicted by age and discomfort, and tasting somewhat of the suffering of Christ. More particularly, however, the Word of God is bitter in that it not only contains promises of grace but, as the book of Revelation itself abundantly illustrates, it reveals the divine judgments which will be poured out on the earth as God deals in wrath with the wicked world. God who created heaven also prepared the lake of fire for the devil and his angels. It is probable that the little book in chapter 10 of Revelation is the Word of God itself. Though John as a child of God will never know the bitterness of being lost or the afflictions of eternal punishment, he knows what it is to be like his Master, despised and rejected of men.

The invitation to John to partake of the little book and eat is, of course, the invitation of God to all who would participate in the blessing of the Word of God. Though there may be trials and afflictions for the saint, like the Apostle John he has been promised eternal blessing when the Lord comes for His own. The trials during the brief span of the Christian's life in this world, as he seeks to serve the Lord, are only the prelude to the eternal blessing which will be the fulfillment of God's grace to those who trust in Christ. Like John, every saint should take and eat with the assurance that the Word will be sweet, whatever sufferings and trials he may be called upon to bear.

John is informed that he must prophesy before "many peoples." Swete commenting on "many" (Gr., *pollois*) states that the word "emphasizes the greatness of the field. It is no one Empire or Emperor that is concerned in the prophecies of the second half of the Apocalypse; not merely Rome or Nero or Domitian, but a multitude of races, kingdoms, and crowned heads."[10]

[10]Henry B. Swete, *The Apocalypse of St. John*, p. 132.

11

THE TWO WITNESSES AND THE SEVENTH TRUMPET

CAREFUL STUDENTS of the book of Revelation will probably agree with Alford that chapter 11 "is undoubtedly one of the most difficult in the whole Apocalypse."[1] A comparison of many commentaries will reveal the widest kind of disagreement as to the meaning of this chapter. Even Alford attempts to spiritualize the city, the temple, and the events portrayed in this chapter. The guiding lines which govern the exposition to follow regard this chapter as a legitimate prophetic utterance in which the terms are taken normally. Hence, the great city of 11:8 is identified as the literal city of Jerusalem. The time periods are taken as literal time periods. The two witnesses are interpreted as two individuals. The three and a half days are taken literally. The earthquake is a literal earthquake. The seven thousand men who are slain by the earthquake are seven thousand individuals who die in the catastrophe. The death of the witnesses is literal as are their resurrection and ascension. These major assumptions provide an intelligent understanding of this portion of prophecy even though the possibility of difference of opinion on the part of the reader is taken for granted in some of these judgments.

Chapter 11 of the Revelation continues the parenthetical section beginning in chapter 10 and extending through chapter 14. With the exception of 11:15-19, introducing the seventh trumpet, the narrative does not advance in these chapters and various topics are presented. In chapter 15, the chronological developments continue as the contents of the seventh trumpet, namely, the seven vials, are manifested. In 11:1-14 there is a continuation of the same subject as in chapter 10.

THE MEASURING ROD OF GOD (11:1-2)

11:1-2 And there was given me a reed like unto a rod: and the angel stood, saying, Rise, and measure the temple of God, and the altar, and them that worship therein. But the court which is without the temple leave out, and measure it not; for it is given unto the Gentiles: and the holy city shall they tread under foot forty and two months.

[1]Henry Alford, *The Greek New Testament*, IV, 655.

175

In the opening verse of chapter 11, John is given a reed compared to a rod. This reed is commonly grown in the Jordan Valley, and because of its light weight it constitutes a good measuring rod. John is instructed to measure the Temple of God, the altar, and them that worship therein. The introductory phrase, "the angel stood saying," is not in some manuscripts though found in Victorinus and in the Armenian version. As there is some question whether the angel actually says this, the phrase "it was said" could be substituted. It may actually be the voice of God rather than the voice of the angel, if the angel of chapter 10 is not Christ Himself.

This command to measure the Temple of God makes John the actor as well as the observer. The Temple of God (Gr., *naon tou theou*) refers to the Holy Place and the Holy of Holies, not the outer court of the Temple. The altar may be a reference to the brazen altar which was in the outer court although the altar in chapter 8 seems to be the altar of incense. Only priests could go into the Temple, but others who were not priests could approach the brazen altar with their sacrifices. Although John is commanded to measure the Temple and the altar and them that worship therein, he is instructed not to measure the court without the Temple. The explanation given is that this is given to the Gentiles and that the outer court as well as the entire holy city will be under Gentile dominion for forty-two months.

A number of questions can be raised concerning this symbolic picture. In Zechariah 2, a man is seen measuring Jerusalem, a scene which evidently portrays God's divine judgment on the city. Another instance is found in Ezekiel 40, where the Temple of the future kingdom is carefully measured with a reed. Still another instance is Revelation 21, where the new Jerusalem is measured (21:15–17). The act of measuring seems to signify that the area belongs to God in some special way. It is an evaluation of His property.

The Temple here is apparently that which will be in existence during the great tribulation. Originally constructed for the worship of the Jews and the renewal of their ancient sacrifices, during the great tribulation it is desecrated and becomes the home of an idol of the world ruler (cf. II Thess. 2:4; Rev. 13:14–15; Dan. 9:27; 12:11). For this reason it is most significant that John is instructed to measure not only the Temple and the altar but also the worshipers. It is saying in effect that God is the judge of man's worship and man's character and that all must give an account to Him. It also implies, inasmuch as the reed is ten feet long, that man comes far short of the divine standard. Even a person very tall would fall short of the ten-foot measuring rod. God is therefore not only claiming ownership by this measurement of the Temple and the altar but demonstrating the shortcomings of the worshipers who do not measure up to His standard.

The second verse adds further light to the situation in that instruction is given not to measure the outer court because it is given to the Gentiles along with the holy city for a period of forty-two months. Here again is the familiar three-and-one-half-year period or half of the seven-year period predicted by Daniel the prophet (Dan. 9:27) in which Israel's history will be consummated with Christ's returning at its close.

Expositors have differed as to whether the forty-two months are the first half of the seven years or the second half. The decision is complicated by the fact that in verse 3 another reference is made to the three and one-half years as the period during which the two witnesses give their testimony. On the basis of the evidence, it is not possible to be dogmatic. If the point of view is adopted, however, that Revelation is primarily concerned with the latter half of Daniel's seventieth week, this perspective would seem to give weight to the conclusion that this is the latter half of the week or the last three and one-half years prior to the second coming especially in light of the details of judgments portrayed in the seals, trumpets, and vials.

This conclusion is substantiated in verse 2 by the fact that the Gentiles have control of the outer court and the city. It would seem that under the covenant relationship between the beast and the children of Israel they are given considerable freedom in their worship for the first three and one-half years, and this would probably preclude the Gentiles trampling on the outer court, even though the holy city as such is under Gentile dominion. Since the Gentiles are said to tread the holy city underfoot only forty-two months, this ill treatment better fits the latter half of the week. If the former half were mentioned, Jerusalem would be trodden underfoot for the entire seven-year period rather than for only forty-two months. The passage seems to anticipate freedom from Gentile dominion after the three and one-half years have run their course, which would mean that the second half of the seven-year period is in view.

The statement that the holy city is under Gentile control is borne out by the prophecy of Christ in Luke 21:24 where He predicted of the people of Israel, "They shall fall by the edge of the sword, and shall be led away captive into all nations: and Jerusalem shall be trodden down by the Gentiles, until the times of the Gentiles be fulfilled." The times of the Gentiles end at the second coming of Christ when Gentile dominion is destroyed and Christ establishes His kingdom. This is predicted in the seventh trumpet revealed later in this chapter. The first two verses then signify that while God is permitting Gentile dominion and persecution of Israel, God Himself will be the judge of her persecutors.

THE PROPHECY OF THE TWO WITNESSES (11:3–6)

11:3-6 And I will give power unto my two witnesses, and they shall prophesy a thousand two hundred and threescore days, clothed in sackcloth. These are the two olive trees, and the two candlesticks standing before the God of the earth. And if any man will hurt them, fire proceedeth out of their mouth, and devoureth their enemies: and if any man will hurt them, he must in this manner be killed. These have power to shut heaven, that it rain not in the days of their prophecy: and have power over waters to turn them to blood, and to smite the earth with all plagues, as often as they will.

In verse 3, two unusual characters are introduced, described as two witnesses who shall prophesy 1,260 days. This is exactly three and one-half years or forty-two months of thirty days each, and is unquestionably related to either the first three and one-half years or the latter three and one-half years of the seven years of Daniel 9:27. Expositors have differed as to which of the two periods is in view here. From the fact, however, that the two witnesses pour out divine judgments upon the earth and need divine protection lest they be killed, it implies that they are in the latter half of the seven years when awful persecution will afflict the people of God, as this protection would not be necessary in the first three and one-half years. The punishments and judgments the witnesses inflict on the world also seem to fit better in the great tribulation period.

There has been much debate on the identity of these two witnesses.[2] Some have suggested that these represent Israel and the church, or Israel and the Word of God, as the two principal instruments of witness in the world. Arno C. Gaebelein regards the two witnesses as representative of witness in the great tribulation: "Perhaps the leaders would be two great instruments, manifesting the spirit of Moses and Elijah, endowed with supernatural power, but a larger number of witnesses is unquestionably in view here."[3] Gaebelein implies that the two witnesses are individuals but representative of a larger witness. Others like J. B. Smith are quite sure that they are Moses and Elijah, because of the similarity of judgment inflicted to those pronounced by Elijah and Moses, namely fire from heaven, turning water into blood, and smiting the earth with plagues.[4] Support for the identification of Elijah as one of the two witnesses is found in the prediction that Elijah will come "before the coming of the great and dreadful day of the Lord" (Mal. 4:5). This seems to be at least partially fulfilled by the coming of John the Baptist accord-

---

[2]For various views on the two witnesses, see John Peter Lange, *Commentary on the Holy Scriptures*, XXIV, 230–33.

[3]*The Revelation*, p. 70.

[4]*A Revelation of Jesus Christ*, pp. 169, 70; also I. M. Haldeman identifies the two witnesses as Moses and Elias who were seen together on the Mount of Transfiguration (*Synopsis of the Book of Revelation*, p. 13). This view has real problems, however, as Moses died.

ing to the discussion of Christ with His disciples (Matt. 17:10-13; Mark 9:11–13; cf. Luke 1:17). Evidence for both Moses and Elijah is found in the fact that they are related to the second coming and the transfiguration (Matt. 17:3). The dispute of Michael with the devil over the body of Moses (Jude 9) is mentioned preceding a prophecy of the second coming, but no specific connection is made between the two. All the evidence for the identification, however, is circumstantial and not clear. There are great difficulties in all points of view identifying the two witnesses with historical characters.

The use of the article with the expression "two witnesses" in verse 3 seems to signify that they are specific persons. The actions are those of people; and their resultant death and resurrection, including their bodies lying in the streets of Jerusalem for three and one-half days, can hardly refer to Israel, the church, or the Word of God. There are also difficulties, however, in defining them as any two characters such as Elijah and Moses or, as some would have it, Enoch and Elijah. Govett identifies the two witnesses as Enoch and Elijah and cites in support early tradition and apocryphal writing.[5] The fact that Enoch and Elijah did not die but were translated has been seized upon by some as a violation of the general rule of Hebrews 9:27, "It is appointed unto men once to die." But this argument is nullified by the fact that the entire living church at the time of the rapture will go to heaven without dying. If Moses is included as one of the two witnesses, there is an added difficulty in that he once died. Could he die a second time? It seems far preferable to regard these two witnesses as two prophets who will be raised up from among those who turn to Christ in the time following the rapture. Ainslie identifies the two witnesses as "two strange men" whose identity cannot now be determined who will literally have prophetic ministry for twelve hundred sixty days and then be slain.[6] Many other conservative expositors agree with Easton who takes these two witnesses "to be two men, not two companies of men, nor yet a mere symbol of 'adequate testimonies.' " He finds this confirmed in verse 10 in the expression "these two prophets." He adds, "Who they may be, can be but conjecture, and is best left in the obscurity in which God has surrounded them."[7]

Though the word *power* in verse 3 is not in the best manuscripts, it is evident that they do have power from God—such power, in fact, that they are able to witness for 1,260 days in spite of the antagonism of the world. Their unusual character as prophets of doom is symbolized in the fact that they are clothed in sackcloth (cf. Isa. 37:1-2; Dan. 9:3).

The two witnesses are described as two olive trees and two lampstands

[5]Robert Govett, *The Apocalypse*, pp. 225–50.
[6]Edgar Ainslie, *The Dawn of the Scarlet Age*, pp. 93–94.
[7]William Easton, *Gleanings in the Book of Revelation*, p. 83.

(A.V., "candlesticks") who stand before the God of the earth. This seems to be a reference to Zechariah 4, where a lampstand and two olive trees are mentioned. In answer to the question in the Zechariah incident, "What are these?" the answer is given to Zerubbabel: "This is the word of the LORD unto Zerubbabel, saying, Not by might, nor by power, but by my spirit, saith the LORD of hosts." It is evident that a similar meaning is intended in the book of Revelation. The olive oil from the olive trees in Zechariah's image provided fuel for the two lampstands. The two witnesses of this period of Israel's history, namely Joshua the high priest and Zerubbabel, were the leaders of Israel in Zechariah's time. Just as these two witnesses were raised up to be lampstands or witnesses for God and were empowered by olive oil representing the power of the Holy Spirit, so the two witnesses of Revelation 11 will likewise execute their prophetic office. Their ministry does not rise in human ability but in the power of God.

Verses 5 and 6 record the miraculous powers given to the two witnesses. Anyone who attempts to hurt them will be destroyed by fire proceeding out of their mouths. This is at once a judgment of God upon their enemies and a means of protection of the two witnesses, so that no one can lay a hand on them. A parallel is found in the prophetic ministry of Elijah, who on two occasions called fire from heaven upon the company of fifty soldiers sent to arrest him. The third company was delivered from this judgment only because they besought Elijah for their lives (II Kings 1). In a similar way, the enemies of Moses were destroyed (Num. 16:35).

Like the Prophet Elijah, the two witnesses also have power to shut up the heavens that it cannot rain. This is reminiscent of the judgment of God imposed on Israel when in answer to Elijah's prayer it did not rain for three and one-half years, curiously the same length of time as the ministry of these two witnesses in Revelation. Like Moses, they have power to turn water into blood and to bring plagues upon the earth as often as they will (cf. Exodus 7:17-19). Taking all the facts furnished, it is evident that these two witnesses have a combination of the greatest powers ever given prophets on earth, and this accounts for their ability to withstand their enemies for the entire period of 1,260 days.[8] It is only at the end of the great tribulation when their ministry has been accomplished that their enemies temporarily have the upper hand, and this is allowed by sovereign appointment of God.

[8]British Israelites interpret the 1,260 days (11:3) as so many years of Roman power. The three and one-half days the witnesses remain dead are the three and one-half years of the persecutions by Queen Mary (Feb. 1555–Nov. 1558). This ridiculous interpretation illustrates the problems of the historical interpretation of Revelation (cf. Augusta Cook, *Light from Patmos*, p. 85).

THE DEATH OF THE TWO WITNESSES (11:7–10)

11:7-10 And when they shall have finished their testimony, the beast that ascendeth out of the bottomless pit shall make war against them, and shall overcome them, and kill them. And their dead bodies shall lie in the street of the great city, which spiritually is called Sodom and Egypt, where also our Lord was crucified. And they of the people and kindreds and tongues and nations shall see their dead bodies three days and an half, and shall not suffer their dead bodies to be put in graves. And they that dwell upon the earth shall rejoice over them, and make merry, and shall send gifts one to another; because these two prophets tormented them that dwelt on the earth.

As in the case of many other great prophets of God, when their ministry is finished, God permits their enemies to overcome them. According to verse 7, the beast from the bottomless pit, which is none other than Satan himself, makes war against them and overcomes them and kills them. Of interest is the fact that this is the first of thirty-six references in Revelation to the beast (Gr., *thērion*), not to be confused with the living creatures of chapter 4. The beast out of the pit is Satan. The beast out of the sea is the world dictator (13:1). The beast out of the land is the false religious leader of that day (13:11). This unholy trinity is the satanic counterfeit of the divine Trinity, the Father, the Son, and the Holy Spirit. (For further discussion see exposition of 13:1–4; 17:7–8.)

So great is the victory over the two witnesses and so significant to their enemies that their dead bodies are allowed to lie in the street of the city described as "the great city, which spiritually is called Sodom and Egypt, where also our Lord was crucified." It is unquestionably the city of Jerusalem in which these two witnesses have their prophetic ministry as well as their martyrdom. In the effort to capitalize as much as possible on their death, their bodies are exhibited in the streets for three and one-half days contrary to all reasonable laws of humanity. Apparently great throngs of people come to witness the bodies of the two witnesses whom they so greatly feared in life.

According to verse 10, their death is the occasion for great rejoicing. The expression "they that dwell upon the earth" seems to refer to those who are not only dwelling on the earth in their physical bodies but whose hope is limited to the present life. The phrase is repeated a dozen times or more in Revelation. Apparently the celebration is worldwide. By means of television and the transmission of pictures throughout the world by communication satellites and other means, the entire earth will see graphically the dead bodies of the two witnesses, a symbol of victory for the beast and those who oppose God. They will have merry feasts and send gifts one to another, certain that their fear of God's wrath and power is no longer justified.

A righteous prophet is always a torment to a wicked generation. The two witnesses are an obstacle to wickedness, unbelief, and satanic power prevalent in that time. If their ministry is in the time of great tribulation, it is all the more a thorn in the side of the world rulers of that day; and their death symbolizes the silencing of the prophets who announce the doom of those who will not believe in God. The Word of God makes it clear that it is often possible to silence a witness to the truth by death, but such action does not destroy the truth that has been announced. The power of God will be ultimately revealed. If this is at the end of the great tribulation, only a few days remain before Christ comes back in power and great glory.

THE TWO WITNESSES RESTORED TO LIFE AND CAUGHT UP TO HEAVEN (11:11–12)

11:11-12 And after three days and an half the spirit of life from God entered into them, and they stood upon their feet; and great fear fell upon them which saw them. And they heard a great voice from heaven saying unto them, Come up hither. And they ascended up to heaven in a cloud; and their enemies beheld them.

The merrymaking of those who rejoice in the death of the two witnesses is cut short after three and one-half days by the witnesses' restoration to life. As they stand on their feet before the startled gaze of those who watch, it is recorded that great fear falls upon those who see them. Their amazement increases as they hear a voice from heaven saying to the witnesses, "Come up hither." As they watch, the two witnesses ascend up into heaven.

Though there are similarities between this event and the rapture of the church, the contrast is also evident. The rapture will take place in a moment, and apparently will not be gradual enough for people to observe. The parallel here is to the ascension of Christ on the Mount of Olives, when the disciples beheld Him ascending into heaven, and, like the two witnesses, He was received by a cloud. This is a special act of God addressed to those who reject His grace and designed as a final warning of the supreme power of God over man whether in life or in death. This act of resurrection and catching up into heaven is distinct from any other mentioned in the Bible in that it occurs after the rapture and before the resurrection in chapter 20.

From the fact that the resurrection takes place three and one-half days after the martyrdom some have attempted to construct an interpretation that the three and one-half days represent three and one-half years as in Daniel's seventieth week (Dan. 9:27) where each unit does represent a year. Under this interpretation, those who minister on the earth as the two witnesses are on earth the first three and one-half years of the seven-year period, are dead for the next three and one-half years, and then are raised at the end. Though this is a possible interpretation, it is unlikely. If the 1,260 days of verse 3 are literal days, it would seem strange to have days mentioned immediately thereafter which are to be taken in another way. It is preferable to understand the word *day* here to refer to a twenty-four-hour day. It does not seem possible to allow the bodies of the two witnesses to lie in the streets of Jerusalem for three and one-half years. The Scriptures seem to imply that it is a short period and that the people are still in the process of rejoicing when the witnesses are restored to life and caught up to be with the Lord. Just as their ministry on earth is a literal 1,260 days, so their period of experiencing death is a literal three and one-half days. Likewise also their resurrection from the dead and their being caught up to heaven are literal events.

ANNOUNCEMENT OF THE THIRD WOE (11:13-14)

11:13-14 And the same hour was there a great earthquake, and the tenth part of the city fell, and in the earthquake were slain of men seven thousand: and the remnant were affrighted, and gave glory to the God of heaven. The second woe is past; and, behold, the third woe cometh quickly.

As an aftermath to the resurrection of the two witnesses, the Scriptures record that a great earthquake occurs in which a tenth part of the city of Jerusalem falls and seven thousand men are killed. These dramatic events bring great fear to those who remain, and it is recorded that they "gave glory to the God of heaven." The reference to "the God of heaven" is one of two in the New Testament (cf. Rev. 16:11). It is a familiar phrase in the Old Testament where it is used to distinguish the true God from pagan deities. Here the significance is that they recognize the true God to the extent indicated as in contrast to their worship of the beast. Even though they recognize the power of the God of heaven, it does not seem to indicate that they have come to the point of true faith in Christ.

With this event, the second woe is brought to its completion and is evidently regarded as the final phase of the sixth trumpet. The third woe contained in the seventh trumpet is announced as coming quickly. The end of the age is rapidly approaching.

THE SEVENTH TRUMPET SOUNDS (11:15)

11:15 And the seventh angel sounded; and there were great voices in heaven, saying, The kingdoms of this world are become the kingdoms of our Lord, and of his Christ; and he shall reign for ever and ever.

When the seventh trumpet sounds, John hears great voices in heaven announcing that the kingdoms have become the kingdoms of Christ and that henceforth He shall reign forever and ever. In contrast to previous instances where a single voice makes the announcement, here there is a great symphony of voices chanting the triumph of Christ. The expression "the kingdoms of this world" in the best manuscripts is in the singular, but the meaning is much the same. The fact that earthly rule will pass into the hands of God is frequently mentioned in Old Testament prophecy (cf. Ezek. 21:26-27; Dan. 2:35, 44; 4:3, 6:26; 7:14, 26-27; Zech. 14:9). The question that remains, however, is how can the kingdoms of the world become at this point the kingdoms of Christ when, as a matter of fact, the seven vials seemingly are still to be poured out?[9] The answer as indicated previously seems to be that just as the seven trumpets are comprehended in the seventh seal so the seven vials are comprehended in the seventh trumpet. The process of destruction of earthly power is therefore already under way.[10]

A further problem is presented in the fact that Christ is declared to reign "for ever and ever." This is more than simply announcing His kingdom over the earth. The millennial reign, while it extends for only one thousand years, is in some sense continued in the new heaven and the new earth. Never again will the earth be under the control and over-lordship of man. Even the brief rebellion recorded in Revelation 20 at the close of the millennium is unsuccessful.

THE WORSHIP OF THE TWENTY-FOUR ELDERS (11:16–17)

11:16-17 And the four and twenty elders, which sat before God on their seats, fell upon their faces, and worshipped God, Saying, We give thee thanks, O Lord God Almighty, which art, and wast, and art to come; because thou hast taken to thee thy great power, and hast reigned.

The twenty-four elders, who here fall down to worship God, have previously appeared seven times in the book of Revelation in a similar context. Here they give thanks to God as the eternal One "which art, and wast, and art to come," because He has manifested His power and assumed authority over the earth. The event for which they give thanks is of course the fulfillment of Psalm 2:9, where Christ the Anointed of God reigns supreme over the earth. Twice in verse 17 mention is directed to the power of God in the word *almighty* (Gr., *pantokratōr*) and the word *power* (Gr., *dynamin*). God's power here is demonstrated in

[9]Tacy W. Atkinson like Scofield begins the great tribulation with the seventh trumpet but like most others offers no evidence whatever for this conclusion (*A Guide to the Study of Revelation*, p. 44).

[10]Norman B. Harrison identifies the seventh trumpet with the last trump, that is, the rapture, anticipated in the rapture of the two witnesses in 11:12. He holds that the rapture occurs three and one-half years before the coming of Christ in Revelation 19. This viewpoint confuses the trumps of judgment of the angels with the trump calling for the resurrection and rapture of the church. It further requires that there be no wrath prior to the seventh trumpet which is contradicted by Revelation 6:17 as well as the content of the preceding sixth trumpet (cf. *The End*, pp. 116 ff).

the sense of authority as well as in the sense of ability to accomplish His will as reflected in *dynamin*.

EVENTS MARKING THE REIGN OF CHRIST (11:18)

11:18 And the nations were angry, and thy wrath is come, and the time of the dead, that they should be judged, and that thou shouldest give reward unto thy servants the prophets, and to the saints, and them that fear thy name, small and great; and shouldest destroy them which destroy the earth.

This comprehensive statement of the main features of the transition from the kingdom of earth to the kingdom of God begins with the fact that the nations are angry at the time when the wrath of God comes. There is a play on words in the Greek which is not indicated in the Authorized Version, the same word (Gr. verb form of *orgē*) being used for "angry" as for "wrath" referring to the righteous judgment of God. The wrath of men is impotent; the wrath of God is omnipotent. The wrath of men is wicked; the wrath of God is holy. That which was anticipated in Revelation 6:16–17 as well as in Psalm 2:4 is here being fulfilled.

It is not clear from the text whether verse 18 is a continuation of the thanksgiving of the twenty-four elders or an observation made by John and given by direct revelation to him. In either case, other important events related to the judgment of God are mentioned. The dead are judged at this time. The context seems to indicate that the resurrection of the righteous dead is especially in view rather than that of the wicked dead, who are not raised until after the millennium. The comment, which follows immediately, speaks of the reward given to the prophets who are servants of God, to saints in general, and to those who fear the name of God whether small or great. The time has also come when God destroys those who destroy the earth, referring to those living on the earth at that time who rebel against God.

Another approach to the exegesis of this verse is suggested by J. B. Smith, namely, that in the first part of verse 18, three statements are made concerning the wicked: (1) the nations are angry, (2) the time of their wrath is come, and (3) the time of the judgments of the wicked dead is come. This is repeated in the threefold description of the reward to the prophets, to the saints, and to all who fear the name of God.[11] The passage itself, however, does not indicate whether the dead include the wicked dead, much less that it is restricted to them. The return to the divine judgment upon those on the earth in the latter part of verse 18 seems to destroy a strict antithesis of the wicked versus the righteous. Rather the verse teaches that in general it is a time of divine wrath, a

[11]Cf. Smith, *A Revelation of Jesus Christ,* p. 181.

time of resurrection of the dead and their reward, and a time of special dealing with those living on the earth. All of these aspects of the second coming of Christ are borne out in later prophecies in the book of Revelation.

THE OPENING OF THE TEMPLE OF GOD IN HEAVEN (11:19)

11:19 And the temple of God was opened in heaven, and there was seen in his temple the ark of his testament: and there were lightnings, and voices, and thunderings, and an earthquake, and great hail.

The opening of the temple of God in heaven seems to be related to the revelation given in chapter 12 rather than to the seventh trumpet specifically. There may be an antithesis between the temple of God in heaven (v. 19) and the temple of God in Jerusalem during the great tribulation (vv. 1–2). Though the earthly temple may have been desecrated by the beast, its counterpart in heaven reflects the righteousness and majesty of God. The heavenly ark of the covenant, which in its earthly equivalent originally contained the law, speaks of God's righteousness. Aaron's rod that budded typifies resurrection, and the golden pot that had manna represents Christ as the basis of the shed blood of the sacrifice.

With the opening of the temple in heaven, there are accompanying lightnings, voices, and thunderings, apparently in the earthly scene, as well as an earthquake and a great hail. The plain implication is that now God is going to deal in summary judgment with the earth. J. N. Darby believes what precedes verse 19 "brings the general history of the ways of God to a termination." He outlines the material which follows under three headings:

first, the causes of evil, and what proceeds from those causes; secondly, the development of Satan's power and of the moving springs of evil in the instruments he used, and which manifests itself under a very decided form; and thirdly, what God does in order to destroy the evil.[12]

Before the details of the judgment to follow are unfolded in the seven vials in chapter 16, the divine revelation turns to other important aspects which relate to this period and which chronologically precede the consummation. Apart from the outpourings of the vials, which occur in rapid succession, there is little chronological movement from this point until chapter 19 and the second coming of Christ. Events and situations are now introduced which are concurrent with the seals and the trumpets. These serve to emphasize the dramatic climax of this period in the second coming of our Lord and Saviour, Jesus Christ.

[12]J. N. Darby, *Notes on the Apocalypse*, p. 55.

12

THE CONFLICT IN HEAVEN AND EARTH

IN CHAPTERS 12 through 14 of the book of Revelation, the great actors of the tribulation time are introduced in another parenthetical section ending at 14:20. As many commentators have noted they are seven in number: (1) the woman, representing Israel, (2) the dragon, representing Satan, (3) the man-child, referring to Christ, (4) Michael, representing the angels, (5) Israel, the remnant of the seed of the woman, (6) the beast out of the sea, the world dictator, and (7) the beast out of the earth, the false prophet and religious leader of the world. About these main characters swirls the tremendously moving scene of the great tribulation. First to be introduced and of prime importance as a key to the whole situation is the woman representing Israel.

THE FIRST GREAT WONDER, THE WOMAN CLOTHED WITH THE SUN: ISRAEL (12:1-2)

12:1-2 And there appeared a great wonder in heaven; a woman clothed with the sun, and the moon under her feet, and upon her head a crown of twelve stars: And she being with child cried, travailing in birth, and pained to be delivered.

The first of the seven personages to be introduced in this section of Revelation is described as a great wonder in heaven, or, better translated, a great "sign" in heaven (Gr., sēmeion). Though what John beholds excites his wonder, he does not use the Greek word for wonder (teras), a word which does not occur in the Revelation. The main point is that it is a sign or symbol of important truth rather than merely a wonder. Subsequently, six other signs or miracles (cf. Greek) are mentioned (12:3; 13:13–14; 15:1; 16:14; 19:20). This sign in verse 1 is distinguished by being called "great." Though the sign is seen in heaven, it apparently portrays a reality on the earth, for subsequently the woman pictured is persecuted by Satan in the great tribulation. The woman is described as clothed with the sun, having the moon under her feet, and on her head a crown of twelve stars. Further, she is with child and waiting the imminent birth of her son.

187

Many explanations have been offered for the identity of this woman. The woman does not represent Christ, nor the church in general, but rather Israel as the matrix from which Christ came. By contrast, other representative women are mentioned in the Apocalypse such as Jezebel (2:20), representative of false religion as a system; the harlot (17:1-7, 15-18), the apostate church of the future; and the bride, the Lamb's wife (19:7), the church joined to Christ in glory. In the Old Testament, Israel frequently is presented as the wife of Jehovah, often in her character as being unfaithful to her husband. Here is the godly remnant of Israel standing true to God in the time of the great tribulation.[1]

The description of the woman as clothed with the sun and the moon is an allusion to Genesis 37:9-11, where these heavenly bodies represent Jacob and Rachel, thereby identifying the woman with the fulfillment of the Abrahamic Covenant. In the same context, the stars represent the patriarchs, the sons of Jacob. The symbolism may extend beyond this to represent in some sense the glory of Israel and her ultimate triumph over her enemies. This identification of the woman as Israel seems to be supported by the evidence from this chapter. Israel is obviously the source from which have come many of the blessings of God including the Bible, Christ, and the apostles. The twelve stars seem to refer to the twelve tribes. The persecution of the woman coincides with the persecution of Israel.

The woman as the nation of Israel is seen travailing in birth and awaiting delivery of her child. Frequently in Scripture the nation Israel is pictured in the tribulation time as going through great trial and affliction. Though, historically, the nation gave birth to Christ through the Virgin Mary, the implication of verse 2 is that the references are to the sufferings of Israel as a nation rather than to the historic birth of Christ. It may refer to the sufferings of the nation in general over its entire troublesome history. If strictly interpreted, it may signify the travail of Israel at the time of the first coming of Christ as borne out by verses 3 and 4.

THE GREAT RED DRAGON: SATAN (12:3-4)

12:3-4 And there appeared another wonder in heaven; and behold a great red dragon, having seven heads and ten horns, and seven crowns upon his heads. And his tail drew the third part of the stars of heaven, and did cast them to the earth: and the dragon stood before the woman which was ready to be delivered, for to devour her child as soon as it was born.

[1]As J. B. Smith points out, Israel in the Old Testament frequently is represented symbolically as a woman related to the Lord as her husband (cf. Isa. 54:3-6; Jer. 3:6-10; 31:32; Ezek. 16:32; Hosea 2:14-16; 3:1). (See *A Revelation of Jesus Christ*, p. 181.)

The second great sign appearing in heaven is described as a great red dragon having seven heads and ten horns and seven crowns upon his heads. From the similar description given in 13:1 and the parallel reference in Daniel 7:7–8, 24, it is clear that the revived Roman Empire is in view. Satan, however, is also called the dragon later in 12:9, and it is clear that the dragon is both the empire and the representation of satanic power. The color red may indicate his murderous characteristics. The seven heads and ten horns refer to the original ten kingdoms of which three were subdued by the little horn of Daniel 7:8, who is to be identified with the world ruler of the great tribulation who reigns over the revived Roman Empire.

The tail of the dragon is declared to draw a third part of the stars of heaven and cast them to the earth. This seems to refer to the gathering under his power of those who oppose him politically and spiritually involving his temporary subjugation of a large portion of the earth.

The dragon is seen awaiting the birth of the child with the intent to destroy it as soon as it is born.[2] The allusion here is unmistakably to the circumstances surrounding the birth of Christ in Bethlehem (the dragon referring to the Roman Empire at that time as dominated by Satan) and the attempts of Herod to destroy the Baby Jesus. It is significant that Herod as an Edomite was a descendant of Esau and of the people who were the traditional enemies of Jacob and his descendants. Whether motivated by his family antipathy to the Jews or by political consideration because he did not want competition in his office as king, Herod nevertheless fulfilled historically this reference to the destruction of children in Bethlehem (see Matt. 2:16–18).

THE MAN-CHILD: CHRIST (12:5–6)

12:5-6 And she brought forth a man child, who was to rule all nations with a rod of iron: and her child was caught up unto God, and to his throne. And the woman fled into the wilderness, where she hath a place prepared of God, that they should feed her there a thousand two hundred and threescore days.

The woman identified as Israel in verses 1 and 2 is said in verse 5 to bring forth a man-child who is destined to rule all nations, but who for the time being is caught up to God to the throne. Though expositors have somewhat agreed that the woman is Israel, there has been considerable difference of opinion on the identity of the man-child. Some have contended that this is the New Testament church destined to reign with Christ and that the act of being caught up to God is the rapture. Though the woman with child is identified with Israel collectively rather than with the Virgin Mary specifically, the interpretation that the man-child

[2]The Greek expression for "as soon as" is literally "whenever" (Gr., *hotan*).

is Christ Himself is far to be preferred. The Greek words for "man-child" (Gr., *hyion arsen*) with their emphasis upon his gender (*arsen* means "male") favor identification of the child as Christ rather than as the church which would be feminine. As Alford points out, the interpretation of *arsen* as neuter rather than masculine does not change its meaning nor the definite masculine character of *hyion* meaning "son."[3] Alford concludes, "The man-child is the Lord Jesus Christ, *and none other*."[4] He is described as destined to rule all nations with a rod of iron. This is an allusion to Psalm 2:9, where in connection with Christ's reign over the earth, it is declared, "Thou shalt break them with a rod of iron; thou shalt dash them in pieces like a potter's vessel." A similar expression is found in Revelation 19:15, where it is stated of Christ, "He shall rule them with a rod of iron." His rule over all nations with a rod of iron is to be distinguished from His rule over Israel which is of more benevolent character (cf. Luke 1:32–33).

The catching up of the man-child to God and to His throne seems to be a portrayal of the ascension of Christ. Alford interprets this as meaning that "after a conflict with the Prince of this world, who came and tried Him, but found nothing in Him, the Son of the woman was taken up to heaven and sat on the right hand of God. Words can hardly be plainer than these."[5] An alternative view is that the "catching up" refers to the flight to Egypt. Shortly after the birth of Christ, Joseph was instructed to flee to Egypt in order to escape the wrath of Herod. Later Joseph and his family were directed to return to Nazareth. Some accordingly have objected to the idea that the child caught up to God pictures the ascension on the ground that "was caught up" connotes being delivered from danger, which was not the case at the ascension of Christ, but which was true in the flight to Egypt.

The Greek word here (*harpazō*) sometimes is used to mean "to seize" or "to catch up" as a wild beast would its prey, as in John 10:12 where the wolf "catcheth" them and scattereth the sheep. However, the same word is used for the rapture of the church in I Thessalonians 4:17 where the church is caught up to heaven. This same word is likewise used of Paul being caught up to paradise (II Cor. 12:2, 4) and of the Spirit of God catching up Philip (Acts 8:39). If the identification of the twenty-four elders is properly to be regarded as the church in heaven, it would seem to mix metaphors to have the church represented as a male child, especially when the church is regarded in chapter 19 as the wife and bride. There is no good reason for not identifying the man-child as Christ and interpreting the drama of verse 5 as the panorama of His birth,

[3]Henry Alford, *The Greek New Testament*, IV, 668.
[4]*Ibid.*
[5]*Ibid.*, IV, 668–69.

life, and ascension. The fact that He is caught up not only to God but to "his throne" is another indication that Christ is intended.

Attention is then directed, however, to the mother of the child, again represented as Israel. Here she is seen in the time of great tribulation as fleeing into the wilderness to a place prepared of God where for 1,260 days she is cared for (again the exact length of three and one-half years). There is obviously a tremendous time lapse between verses 5 and 6, but this is not an uncommon occurrence in prophecy; the first and second comings of Christ are frequently spoken of in the same sentence. Inasmuch as Israel is in comparative tranquillity and safety in the first three and one-half years of Daniel's seventieth week (Dan. 9:27), the reference must be to the preservation of a portion of the nation Israel through the great tribulation to await the second coming of Christ.

SATAN CAST OUT OF HEAVEN BY MICHAEL THE ARCHANGEL (12:7-9)

12:7-9 And there was war in heaven: Michael and his angels fought against the dragon; and the dragon fought and his angels, And prevailed not; neither was their place found any more in heaven. And the great dragon was cast out, that old serpent, called the Devil, and Satan, which deceiveth the whole world: he was cast out into the earth, and his angels were cast out with him.

Though the conflict of the end of the age is primarily on earth, attention is directed in this section to the war which will be waged in heaven. Michael and his angels (that is, the holy angels) fight against the dragon (identified in verse 9 as the devil, Satan) and the wicked angels associated with him, with the result that Satan and his hosts are cast out of heaven. The description of Satan in verse 9 is quite significant as all of his important titles are given. He is described as "the great dragon," a term which also applies to the empire which he dominates in the end time. He is referred to as "that old serpent," a reference to the Garden of Eden and the temptation of Eve. The title "Devil" is from the Greek *diabolos,* from the verb *diaballō,* which has the meaning of "defaming" or "slandering." He is the master accuser of the brethren. The name Satan, from the Hebrew, has the meaning of "adversary." This name is mentioned fourteen times in the book of Job, and occasionally elsewhere (I Chron. 21:1; Ps. 109:6; Zech. 3:1-2). Coates observes that Satan is seen in three characterizations in opposition to Christ. As accuser of the brethren, he is in opposition to Christ as priest; as the one who brings forth the first beast, he is in opposition to Christ as king; as bringing forth the second beast, the false prophet, he is opposed to Christ as prophet.[6]

The concept that there is a spiritual warfare in the very presence of

[6]C. A. Coates, *An Outline of the Revelation,* p. 137.

God in heaven has been resisted by some expositors, preferring to regard this war as being fought in the atmospheric or the starry heaven rather than in the very presence of God.[7] The event here prophesied was predicted by Daniel the prophet in Daniel 12:1, where it is recorded that Michael shall "stand up, the great prince which standeth for the children of thy people." This event marks the beginning of the great tribulation defined in Daniel 12:1. It is undoubtedly the same event as in Revelation 12.

Of course it seems strange that Satan should have access to the very throne of God, yet this is precisely the picture of Job 1, where Satan along with other angels presents himself before God and accuses Job of fearing God because of God's goodness to him. Thus early in biblical revelation Satan is cast in the role of the accuser of the brethren, the title given him in Revelation 12:10. Beginning at this point in Revelation, therefore, Satan and his hosts are excluded from the third heaven, though their temporary dominion over the second heaven and the first heaven continues. Satan's defeat in heaven, however, is the occasion for him to be cast into the earth and explains the particular virulence of the great tribulation time. Note that even as Satan accuses the brethren before God day and night prior to his being cast out of heaven, so the four living creatures of 4:8 cease not day or night to ascribe holiness to the Lord.

The prophetic events here described must therefore be taken at their face value. Satan, described as deceiving the whole world, that is, the inhabited earth (Gr., *oikoumenē*), is now limited in the sphere of his operation. A major step is taken in his ultimate defeat. The saint of this present dispensation, who is now the object of satanic attack and misrepresentation, can rest assured of the ultimate downfall of Satan and the cessation of his ability to afflict the saints of God. Though the events of this chapter deal in general with the end of the age, it is clear that they do not come chronologically after the seventh trumpet. Rather, the fall of Satan may be predated to the time of the seals in chapter 6, or even before the first seal. His fall begins the great tribulation.

ANNOUNCEMENT OF THE COMING DAY OF SATAN'S WRATH
AND THE ULTIMATE VICTORY OF THE SAINTS (12:10–12)

12:10-12 And I heard a loud voice saying in heaven, Now is come salvation, and strength, and the kingdom of our God, and the power of his Christ: for the accuser of our brethren is cast down, which accused them before our God day and night. And they overcame him by the blood of the Lamb, and by the word of their testimony; and they loved not their lives unto the death. Therefore rejoice, ye heavens, and ye that dwell in them. Woe to the inhabiters of the earth

[7]Joseph A. Seiss, *The Apocalypse,* p. 308.

and of the sea! for the devil is come down unto you, having great
wrath, because he knoweth that he hath but a short time.

As John beholds Satan and his angels being cast from heaven, he hears
a loud voice described as saying in heaven, "Now is come salvation, and
strength, and the kingdom of our God, and the power of his Christ."
The loud voice is not identified and probably cannot be with certainty.
Some have ascribed this voice to God Himself, some to angels, some to
the twenty-four elders, some to the martyred saints in heaven mentioned
in 6:10, because they also cry with a loud voice.[8] Support for the latter
view is given in that in the same verse the loud voice mentions "the
accuser of our brethren." This would seem to eliminate angels and indicate saints in heaven. The "loud voice" may very well be the shout of
triumph of the tribulation saints longing for and anticipating their ultimate victory and triumph.

The salvation mentioned as now impending refers not to salvation from
the guilt of sin but to salvation in the sense of deliverance and completion
of the divine program. The reference to strength (Gr., *dynamis*) implies
that now God is going to strengthen His own and manifest His own
strength. The declaration that the kingdom of our God is now impending
refers to the millennial kingdom when Christ will reign on the earth.
Coupled with this is the power or authority (Gr., *exousia*) of Christ.
The expression "his Christ," also mentioned in 11:15, parallels "his
anointed" in Psalm 2:2, against whom the kings of the earth rebel but
under whose sway they are certain to come.

The victory of the saints in that hour is revealed in verse 11, where
it is declared that they overcame Satan by the blood of the Lamb, by
the word of their testimony, and by the fact that they loved not their
lives unto death. The accusations of Satan are nullified by the blood of
the Lamb which renders the believer pure and makes possible his spiritual victory. The word of the saints' testimony opposes the deceiving
work of Satan in that the preaching of the gospel is the power of God
unto salvation. The saints' dedication to their task in which many of
them die as martyrs is recognized by the statement "They loved not their
lives unto the death." The word for "loved" is the word for profound love
(Gr., *agapaō*). Though they do not foolishly seek a martyr's death, they
do not regard their own lives (literally "souls"; Gr., *psychē*) as precious.
They follow the instruction given to the church in Smyrna (2:10) of being
faithful unto death as well as the example of the Saviour who laid down
His life for the sheep (John 10:11, 15; cf. Matt. 16:25).

The voice from heaven continues, exhorting the listeners, especially
those in the heavens, to rejoice because of this great victory. At the same
time the voice pronounces a solemn woe upon the inhabitants of the

[8]Smith, p. 186.

earth and of the sea. The awfulness of the hour ahead is attributed to the fact that the devil has been cast into the earth and has great wrath because he knows his hour of confinement is near. The word for "wrath" (Gr., not *orgē*, but *thymos*) means a strong passion or emotion but carries less weight than *orgē*. It is an emotional rather than a rational state of mind and stems from his own awareness that his days are numbered. The short time or season (Gr., *kairos*) refers to the time of the great tribulation after which Satan will be bound for the duration of the millennial kingdom. Though many of the judgments of God inflicted on the earth during the great tribulation originate in divine power rather than satanic influence, the afflictions of the inhabitants of the earth spring largely from the activities of Satan, resulting in the martyrdom of countless saints and in widespread human suffering of every kind.

THE PERSECUTION OF ISRAEL IN THE GREAT TRIBULATION (12:13–16)

12:13-16 And when the dragon saw that he was cast unto the earth, he persecuted the woman which brought forth the man child. And to the woman were given two wings of a great eagle, that she might fly into the wilderness, into her place, where she is nourished for a time, and times, and half a time, from the face of the serpent. And the serpent cast out of his mouth water as a flood after the woman, that he might cause her to be carried away of the flood. And the earth helped the woman, and the earth opened her mouth, and swallowed up the flood which the dragon cast out of his mouth.

The immediate aftermath of Satan's being cast out of heaven is his persecution of the woman which brought forth the man-child. This apparently is the beginning of the great tribulation of which Christ warned Israel in Matthew 24:15–22. This had its foreshadowing in Herod's slaughter of the infants following the birth of Christ (Matt. 2:16). It seems here to refer specifically to the great tribulation which is yet future. The persecution of Israel is a part of the satanic program to thwart and hinder the work of God. As far as Israel is concerned this had its beginning in the delay in the birth of Isaac which was overcome by the miraculous intervention of God. This hindrance continued in the delay in the birth of Jacob and in countless means used thereafter to persecute the descendants of Jacob, including the effort in the time of Esther to blot them out completely. Israel is hated by Satan not because of any of its own characteristics but because she is the chosen of God and essential to the overall purpose of God for time and eternity.

Into this scene of satanic persecution is injected the divine intervention of God. The woman is described as being given two wings of a great eagle in order to enable her to fly into the wilderness into her place. This figure of speech seems to be derived from Exodus 19:4 and Deuteronomy 32:11–12 and similar passages where God uses the strength of an eagle to illustrate His faithfulness in caring for Israel. The same flight is indicated in Matthew 24:16 where Christ exhorts those in Judea to flee to the mountains. Some have felt that the reference here is to some specific place such as Petra, where at least a portion of Israel might be safe from her persecutors. Verse 14 implies that there is some supernatural care of Israel during this period such as that which Elijah experienced by the brook Cherith, or that which Israel experienced during the forty years she lived on the manna in the wilderness. Whether natural or supernatural means are used, it is clear that God does preserve a godly remnant, though acccording to Zechariah 13:8, two-thirds of Israel in the land will perish.

The time element of Israel's suffering is described as "a time, and times, and half a time." This again seems to be a reference to the three and one-half years, the mention of time being one unit, the second reference to times, being two units, which the addition of one-half a time would make three and one-half units. A parallel reference is found in Daniel 7:25 and 12:7 referring to the same period of great tribulation. The dragon is here called a serpent (Gr., *ophis;* cf. Matt. 10:16; John 3:14 where the word is used in other contexts; Rev. 12:9, 14–15; 20:2 where "serpent" is used in connection with the devil).

In the persecution of Israel, the serpent is described in verse 15 as casting water as a flood out of his mouth that the woman might be carried away. Verse 16 reveals that the earth helps the woman by swallowing the flood. Various interpretations have been given to this description. Some, like J. B. Smith, prefer to take this literally as a flood of water let loose to sweep away Israel down some valley.[9] In this case, the earth would be either naturally or supernaturally enabled to swallow the water to prevent it from overtaking the Israelites. However, the contour of the Holy Land, and the fact that Israel would probably not all flee in the same direction combine to make a physical interpretation, such as Smith offers, improbable.[10]

It is more plausible that this passage should be understood in a symbolic way. The flood cast after Israel is the total effort of Satan to exterminate the nation, and the resistance of earth is the natural difficulty in executing such a massive program. The nature of the terrain in the Middle East, including many areas not heavily populated, provides countless places of refuge for a fleeing people. Whether the exact meaning of these two verses can be determined with certainty, the implication is that Satan strives with all his power to persecute and exterminate the people of Israel. By divine intervention, both natural and supernatural means

[9] *Ibid.,* p. 191.
[10] *Ibid.*

are used to circumvent this program and to carry a remnant of Israel
safely through their time of great tribulation.

THE PERSECUTION OF THE GODLY REMNANT OF ISRAEL (12:17)

12:17 And the dragon was wroth with the woman, and went to
make war with the remnant of her seed, which keep the commandments of God, and have the testimony of Jesus Christ.

The last verse of chapter 12 states that the dragon is especially angry
with those within the nation Israel who "keep the commandments of
God, and have the testimony of Jesus Christ." While the program of
Satan is against the Jewish race as such, anti-Semitism as a whole will
reach its peak against Jewish *believers* during this period. There is a
double antagonism against those in Israel who turn to Christ as their
Messiah and Saviour in those critical days and maintain a faithful witness. Undoubtedly many of them will suffer a martyr's death, but others
will survive the period including the 144,000 sealed in chapter 7.

The remnant mentioned here (Gr., *tōn loipōn*), literally "the rest," is
not the same term for "remnant" used elsewhere as in Romans 9:27 (Gr.,
hypoleimma) and in Romans 11:5 (Gr., *leimma*). However, all these
words come from the verb *leipō*, but normally when used of a remnant
the prefix *hypo* is added. Though the word, therefore, is a different form,
the similarity is such that there is no good reason for denying that this is
indeed the godly remnant. Smith attempts to build a distinction between
the woman in verse 14 as Israel in Judea and the remnant in verse 17 as
Israel elsewhere in the world.[11] But there does not seem to be sufficient
evidence to make this distinction. Rather than a geographic contrast,
the difference seems to be between the nation as a whole symbolized
by the woman and the godly remnant in the nation who turn to Christ.

Taken as a whole, chapter 12 is a fitting introduction to the important
revelations given in chapter 13. Here are the principal actors of the great
tribulation with the historic background which provides so much additional information. Israel, Satan, Christ, the archangel, and the godly
remnant figure largely in the closing scenes of the age. Next the two
principal human actors are introduced: the beast out of the sea and the
beast out of the earth, the human instruments which Satan uses to direct
his program during the great tribulation.

[11]*Ibid.*, pp. 191–92.

13

THE BEASTS AND THE FALSE PROPHET

THE EMERGENCE OF THE BEAST OUT OF THE SEA (13:1–2)

13:1-2 And I stood upon the sand of the sea, and saw a beast rise up out of the sea, having seven heads and ten horns, and upon his horns ten crowns, and upon his heads the name of blasphemy. And the beast which I saw was like unto a leopard, and his feet were as the feet of a bear, and his mouth as the mouth of a lion: and the dragon gave him his power, and his seat, and great authority.

IN THE FIRST TEN VERSES of chapter 13, a character is introduced of central importance to the events of the great tribulation. This passage is first of all a revelation of the revived Roman Empire in its period of worldwide dominion, but more especially this paragraph directs attention to the evil character who exercises satanic power as the world dictator. The revelation is introduced by the expression "And I stood upon the sand of the sea," which in some versions is included in the last verse of chapter 12, instead of the first verse of chapter 13.

A textual difficulty also appears in the expression "I stood." Some manuscripts read, "he stood," the change being effected by the dropping of one letter *nun* from the end of the verb *estathē*. If the letter is properly dropped, it indicates that the dragon himself stood upon the sand of the sea. If the letter is added, it means that John stood upon the sand of the sea. The difference is not of great moment, but inasmuch as it is more likely that a letter be dropped than a letter added to the text, some scholars continue to feel that the Authorized Version is correct and that John stood upon the sand of the sea. The reading supporting the translation "he stood," that is, the dragon himself contemplates the scene, has better manuscript testimony and seems to fit well into the context. Chapter 13 would then be the next action following the act of the dragon in chapter 12.

As John watches the scene, he sees a beast coming up out of the sea having seven heads and ten horns. Ten crowns are seen on the horns, and on the seven heads names of blasphemy are written. The identity of this beast is quite clear in its reference to the revived Roman Empire, as the

197

description is similar to that found in Daniel 7:7–8 and in Revelation 12:3 and 17:3, 7. The stage of the empire depicted by the beast is the period after the emergence of the little horn, the future world ruler, displacing three of the horns (Dan. 7:8). The description fits the time of the empire during the great tribulation. The fact that the beast rises out of the sea is taken by many to indicate that he comes from the great mass of humanity, namely the Gentile powers of the world. Others take it as a reference to the Mediterranean, namely, that the beast will arise from the Mediterranean area. Probably both are true in that the beast is a Gentile and does come from the Mediterranean scene.

E. B. Elliott, in keeping with his historical view of Revelation, identifies the beast out of the sea and his associate, the beast out of the land, as Roman popes and the papal empire. The reference to the sea portrays the invading Goths descending on the Roman Empire.[1] The difficulty with this historical view as with other historical interpretations of the book of Revelation is its lack of uniformity, with literally dozens of explanations on a given symbol depending on the time and circumstances of the expositor.

The monstrosity of seven heads and ten horns probably refers to the remnants of the confederacy which formed the Roman Empire in the beginning, namely, the ten nations of which three were overthrown by the little horn of Daniel 7:8. The ten crowns, therefore, refer to the diadems or symbols of governmental authority. The fact that they have the names of blasphemy ("names" is properly plural) indicates their blasphemous opposition to God and to Christ.

Some consider the seven heads as successive phases of governmental and political history during this period. Others believe that they are simultaneous kings who are subrulers under the beast. The successive idea seems to be borne out by Revelation 17:10–12 where the heads are indicated to be successive rulers. The difficulty can be resolved by regarding the heads as successive, referring to kings or emperors, and the horns as kings who will reign simultaneously receiving their power from the beast (cf. Rev. 17:12). John may be seeing the beast in both its historic and prophetic characters.

The beast is further described as being comparable to a leopard with the feet of a bear and the mouth of a lion, and as receiving his power, throne, and authority from the dragon, that is, from Satan. The selection of these three animals is related to the similar revelation given in Daniel 7, where the successive world empires are described by the lion, referring to Babylon, the bear, referring to Medo-Persia, and the leopard, referring to the Alexandrian Empire. The fourth empire gathers all these elements and characteristics in itself and is far more dreadful in its power and

[1]*Horae Apocalypticae*, III, 92–93.

blasphemy than the preceding empires. The beasts selected, as many have pointed out, are typical of the revived Roman Empire in the great tribulation, having the majesty and power of the lion, the strength and tenacity of a bear, and the swiftness of the leopard, so well illustrated in the conquest of Alexander the Great. In addition to these natural symbols of strength is the added factor of satanic power coming from the dragon, Satan himself.

THE DEADLY WOUND OF THE BEAST (13:3)

13:3 And I saw one of his heads as it were wounded to death; and his deadly wound was healed: and all the world wondered after the beast.

John in his vision sees one of the heads of the beast as wounded unto death, and the apparent parallelism is to the slain Lamb, described in 5:6. John further observes that the deadly wound (literally "plague") is healed and that the entire earth marvels at the beast. Countless views have been offered in the interpretation of this verse, one of the very common ones being to identify the person wounded to death and healed as some historic character. Among the more common suggestions are Nero, Judas Iscariot, and in modern times such personages as Mussolini, Hitler, and Stalin. The multiplicity of suggestions seems to be evidence in itself that these explanations are not the meaning of the passage.

The wounding of one of the heads seems instead to be a reference to the fact that the Roman Empire as such seemingly died and is now going to be revived. It is significant that one of the heads is wounded to death but that the beast itself is not said to be dead. It is questionable whether Satan has the power to restore to life one who has died, even though his power is great. Far more probable is the explanation that this is the revived Roman Empire in view. As Alford states, "This seems to represent the Roman pagan Empire, which having long been a head of the beast, was crushed and to all appearance exterminated."[2] It is questionable, however, whether Alford is right in saying that "the establishment of the Christian Roman Empire" was the stroke which caused the death.[3]

The identification of a head with the government over which he has authority is not a strange situation. The person is often the symbol of the government, and what is said of the government can be said of him. Although verse 3 will continue to be a subject of controversy, the theological reasons for resisting an actual resurrection of a historical character to head the revived Roman Empire are so great as to render it improbable even though such personages as Nero and Judas Iscariot will continue to attract the attention of modern students of the book of

[2]Henry Alford, *The Greek New Testament*, IV, 675.
[3]*Ibid.*

Revelation. The beast is both personal and the empire itself; so also is the head. The revival of the future empire is considered a miracle and a demonstration of the power of Satan.

THE WORSHIP OF SATAN BY ALL THE WORLD (13:4)

13:4 And they worshipped the dragon which gave power unto the beast: and they worshipped the beast, saying, Who is like unto the beast? who is able to make war with him?

The final form of apostasy is not simply the worship of some pagan deity but the worship of Satan himself who in his whole program seeks to be "like God" (Isa. 14:14). Because men worship Satan, they also worship the beast, that is, the man who rules over the revived Roman Empire. He is Satan's substitute for Christ as King of kings and Lord of lords, and to him the world as a whole flocks to give homage, indicated in the questions "Who is like unto the beast? who is able to make war with him?" The point in history where this takes place is apparently at the beginning of the great tribulation when the head of the revived Roman Empire, described here as the beast, is able to assume authority over the entire world. The basis for this authority is undoubtedly power given to him by Satan himself which is aided by a world situation in which there is no serious contender for his office. It may be that the battle of Ezekiel 38 and 39, predicting the destruction of the northern confederacy, takes place just before this, thereby removing the threat of eastern and northern powers to his authority and reign. The answer to the question, however, is to be Christ Himself manifested in His power at His second coming, who will cast the beast into the lake of fire. Until that time the beast is allowed to reign and fulfill his place in human destiny.

THE BLASPHEMOUS CHARACTER OF THE BEAST AS WORLD RULER (13:5-6)

13:5-6 And there was given unto him a mouth speaking great things and blasphemies; and power was given unto him to continue forty and two months. And he opened his mouth in blasphemy against God, to blaspheme his name, and his tabernacle, and them that dwell in heaven.

The evil character of the world ruler of that day is shown in his boasting and blasphemy. A similar description of the same character is given in Daniel 7:8, 11, 25. His authority continues for forty-two months, again the familiar three and one-half years of the great tribulation. It is probable that the person who heads the revived Roman Empire comes into power before the beginning of the entire seven-year period of Daniel 9:27, and as such enters into covenant with the Jewish people. His role as world ruler over all nations, however, does not begin until the time of the great tribulation. From that point, he continues forty-two months until the second coming of Christ terminates his reign. It is evident that blasphemy is not an incidental feature of his kingdom but one of its main features, and he is described in verse 6 as blaspheming against God, against the name of God, and against the Tabernacle of God, as well as against them that dwell in heaven. As Satan's mouthpiece he utters the ultimate in unbelief and irreverence in relation to God. If the king of Daniel 11:36-45 is the same individual, as some believe, he does so in total disregard of any god because he magnifies himself above all (Dan. 11:37).

THE UNIVERSAL DOMINION OF THE BEAST (13:7)

13:7 And it was given unto him to make war with the saints, and to overcome them: and power was given him over all kindreds, and tongues, and nations.

As is anticipated in Daniel 7:23, where the beast devours "the whole earth," here the worldwide extent of his power is indicated. The expression "it was given to him" refers to the satanic origin of his power. Acting as Satan's tool, the beast is able to wage war against the saints throughout the entire globe and to overcome them. (Cf. Dan. 7:25; 9:27; 12:10; Rev. 7:9-17.) In the will of God, many believers in Christ among both Jews and Gentiles perish as martyrs during this awful time of trial, while others are preserved in spite of all the beast can do. The ultimate in worldwide authority is indicated in verse 7, in that "power was given him over all kindreds, and tongues, and nations." The dream of countless rulers in the past of conquering the entire world is here finally achieved by this last Gentile ruler.

The universal authority of the beast over the entire earth is stated specifically in the latter part of the verse. The word *peoples* should be inserted after the word *kindred* as in the best texts, making the verse read "power was given him over all kindreds, peoples, and tongues, and nations." As the nouns are properly singular, the clause is better rendered "and authority was given to him over every tribe and people and tongue and nation." Such authority was anticipated by Daniel (Dan. 7:23) where it is stated that the fourth beast "shall devour the whole earth, and tread it down, and break it in pieces." The dream of world conquest achieved in part by the Babylonian, Medo-Persian, Macedonian, and Roman empires is now for the first time realized completely and is the satanic counterfeit of Christ's millennial reign permitted by God in this final display of the evil of Satan and wicked humanity.

The time of this universal sway is clearly indicated in verse 5 as being forty-two months, namely the last three and one-half years preceding the return of Christ. This period is otherwise described as the great tribulation. It is apparent, however, that as the period moves on to its end a gigantic world war is under way continuing to the time of the return of Christ. This war is in the form of a rebellion against the universal sway of the beast and comes at the very end of the tribulation time. A universal kingdom and a world war could not coexist, since one is the contradiction of the other. The alternative view of J. B. Smith, that all passages speaking of conflicts between the nations must precede the time of tribulation, that is, refer to the first half of the seven-year period, is without proper justification.[4] This would put the natural development of the end of the age in an unwarranted stricture.

THE UNIVERSAL WORSHIP OF THE BEAST (13:8)

13:8 And all that dwell upon the earth shall worship him, whose names are not written in the book of life of the Lamb slain from the foundation of the world.

Just as the entire world is under the political domination of the beast, so all the world except the saints will worship him. Some like J. B. Smith have read into the phrase "dwell upon the earth" a particular class of people.[5] It may be that they are contrasted to those who worship the true God in heaven. Rather than designating a particular class of people, however, the intention is to include everyone dwelling upon the earth, excluding only those who are saints. Walter Scott defines the term as meaning that "*all* save the elect are referred to."[6] These who thus worship the beast are described as not having their names written in the book of life, a book frequently mentioned in the Revelation (3:5; 17:8; 20:12, 15; 21:27; 22:19; cf. Luke 10:20; Phil. 4:3). Those worshiping the beast are the unsaved of both Jews and Gentiles in contrast to saved Jews and Gentiles whose names are written in the book of life.

A further description of the book of life is given as belonging to the "Lamb slain from the foundation of the world." The translation here follows the order of the Greek. Most expositors have taken the expression "from the foundation of the world" to refer to the writing of the names in the book, rather than to the slaying of the Lamb which occurred on Calvary. This verse presents a number of problems.

Some references to the book of life seem to indicate it is the book of the living, namely, of all born in the world, and that those who do not trust in Christ are blotted from it leaving only those who are saved (cf. Rev. 3:5; 22:19). The reference to 22:19, however, in the best texts,

[4]*A Revelation of Jesus Christ,* p. 119.
[5]*Ibid.,* p. 199.
[6]*Exposition of the Book of the Revelation of Jesus Christ,* p. 277.

concerns the *tree* of life rather than the *book* of life, and it seems preferable not to distinguish between the book of life belonging to the Lamb and the book mentioned in 3:5, as Walter Scott does, referring to the latter as the book of profession.[7] The simplest explanation here seems the best, namely, that their names were written in the book of life from eternity past. This was made possible by anticipation of the future dying of the Lamb on their behalf. Though somewhat involved, the ultimate meaning is simply that all who are not saved will worship the beast and that those who are saved will not worship him. The reference to "the foundation of the world" cannot be limited, as J. B. Smith does, to the beginning of the Old Testament,[8] but rather, as the Greek indicates, to the beginning of the "cosmos," that is, the ordered events which predate human history.

EXHORTATION TO HEAR (13:9-10)

13:9-10 If any man have an ear, let him hear. He that leadeth into captivity shall go into captivity: he that killeth with the sword must be killed with the sword. Here is the patience and the faith of the saints.

It is clear from verse 8 that the universal worship of the beast will achieve at long last the characteristics of a world religion in that it will be ecumenical. The desire to have all Christian churches unite, or to even go one step further and unite all religions of the world, has been advanced as a desired goal. It is questionable whether this will be achieved prior to the end of the church age. However, in the great tribulation as here described, a world religion will be advanced which will have as its focal point the worship of a man chosen and empowered by Satan himself. In that day, true believers on Christ will be separated from this world religion and will be the objects of its fearful persecution. From a biblical point of view, the concept of a world religion prior to the second coming of Christ will be far removed from a true recognition of God.

The invitation "If any man have an ear, let him hear" emphasizes the preceding relation as a matter of great moment to which any man should give attention. Here, as in the Gospels where a similar expression is found frequently (Matt. 11:15; 13:9, 43; Mark 4:9, 23; 7:16; Luke 8:8; 14:35), the invitation concludes the revelation on which the exhortation is based. A close parallel as well as a contrast is also observable between this invitation and the invitation to the seven churches of Revelation 2 and 3 where the exhortation is to "hear what the Spirit says unto the churches." The omission of the phrase "unto the churches" in 13:9 is

[7]*Ibid.*, p. 277.
[8]Smith, p. 200.

most significant and tends to support the teaching that the church, the body of Christ, has previously been raptured and is not in this period. This instruction is not addressed to the churches. The exhortation in Revelation 13 is much wider. It is to anyone who will listen, and the message is not addressed to the church as such but to the entire world.

Reinforcing the exhortation is the warning of the ultimate sovereign justice of God which will be brought to bear upon this scene of wickedness. A number of variations occur in the text of verse 10, but the general meaning is clear. The best texts seem to read, "If any man is for captivity, into captivity he goes. If any man is to be killed by the sword, he must be killed by the sword." In a word, it is the law of divine retribution. Those who persecute the saints and lead them into captivity must in turn suffer the righteous wrath of God. In this ultimate triumph and judgment upon wicked men lie the patience and faith of the saints in their hour of trial. The Scriptures frequently mention this final vindication (Gen. 9:6; Matt. 5:38; 26:52; Rom. 12:19; Gal. 6:7). The same truth which serves as an encouragement to the saints acts as a warning to their persecutors. Their ultimate doom is assured as in this case at the end of their brief period of power (Rev. 13:5; 16:6; 18:2-3, 5-8, 20; 19:20).

Taken as a whole, the first ten verses of Revelation 13 predict a future world government which from God's point of view will be a continuation of the ancient Roman Empire expanded ultimately to cover not only the area of the ancient empire but the entire world. This government will be empowered by Satan, and its primary objective will be forcing the whole world to worship Satan and his human representative, the world dictator.

The purpose of Satan to take the place of God in this future great tribulation is the motivating power behind Satan's activities today. Satan's desire to be like God originally plunged the universe into sin (Isa. 14:14). His program has never changed, and he is seeking today as throughout his career to lure men to obey him instead of God. In the great tribulation this purpose will be transparently clear, and after its manifestation it will be brought into divine judgment.

THE SECOND BEAST (13:11-12)

13:11-12 And I beheld another beast coming up out of the earth; and he had two horns like a lamb, and he spake as a dragon. And he exerciseth all the power of the first beast before him, and causeth the earth and them which dwell therein to worship the first beast, whose deadly wound was healed.

After the revelation of the first beast, John now beholds another beast coming up out of the earth and occupying a secondary role supporting the activities of the first beast. In contrast to the first beast which comes out of the sea, the second beast is said to come out of the earth. He is of similar nature to the first beast. The same word for beast (Gr., *thērion*) is used as well as the word "another" (Gr., *allo*) meaning "one like in kind." Though some have interpreted the word *earth* as referring to the Holy Land, it is the general word for the earth (Gr., *gē*). If the sea, mentioned as the source of the first beast, represents the mass of humanity indicating the racial background of the first beast as a Gentile, the reference to the second beast as coming out of the earth indicates that this character, who is later described as a false prophet (Rev. 19:20), is a creature of earth rather than heaven. To argue that the earth means Palestine and that therefore this character is a Jew is reading into the passage more than it says. His geographic origin and his racial connection are not mentioned. He is pictured, however, as having two horns like a lamb and as speaking like a dragon. The description of him as a lamb seems to indicate that he has a religious character, a conclusion supported by his being named a prophet. His speaking as a dragon indicates that he is motivated by the power of Satan who is "the dragon."

As a supporting character to the first beast, he is active on behalf of the first beast and exercises his authority. Verse 12 translated literally reads, "He exerts [Gr., *poieō*, 'to do'] all the authority of the first beast in his presence." Using his satanic power, he causes (Gr., *poieō*) the earth, that is, those who dwell in the earth, to worship the first beast whose wound unto death was healed according to verse 3. There is some evidence pointing to the conclusion that the second beast is the head of the apostate church during the first half of Daniel's seventieth week. With the rise of the first beast to a place of worldwide dominion, the apostate church is destroyed according to Revelation 17:16, and the worship of the whole world is directed to the beast out of the sea. The second beast, however, survives the destruction of the church which had been under his control, and he assists the beast in making the transition. Facilitating this change into the final form of apostate religion, the beast out of the earth causes men to worship the first beast.

The identification of the second beast as the head of the apostate church is indicated in many ways in the book of Revelation. It is obvious that he is associated with the first beast in a religious way in that his miracles and activities tend to cause men to worship the image of the first beast (cf. 13:13–17). It is also clear that he shares prominence and leadership with the first beast throughout the great tribulation as they both are cast alive into the lake of fire at its close (19:20).

Alford's extended remarks on the character of the second beast are worthy of mention:

It may be well to premise a few remarks, tending to the right understanding of this portion of the prophecy. 1) These two beasts are identical as to genus: they are both *thēria*, ravaging powers, hostile to
God's flock and fold. 2) They are diverse in origin. The former came
up out of the sea, that is, if we go back to the symbolism of Daniel,
was an empire, rising up out of confusion into order and life: the latter comes out of the earth: i.e., we may not unreasonably say, arises
out of human society and its progress: which as interpreted by the
context, will import its origin and gradual development during the
reign and progress of the secular empire denoted by the former beast.
3) The second beast is, in its zeal and action, entirely subsidiary to
the first. It wields its authority, works miracles in its support, causes
men to make and to worship its image; nay, itself is lost in the splen-
dour and importance of the other. 4) An important distinction exists
between the two beasts, in that this second one has two horns like a
lamb. In other words, this second beast puts on a mild and lamb-like
appearance, which the other did not. But it speaks as a dragon: its
words, which carry its real character, are fierce and unrelenting: while
it professes that which is gentle, its behests are cruel. And now I may
appeal to the reader, whether all these requisites do not meet in that
great wasting Power which arose, not out of anarchy and conquest,
but out of men's daily life and habits, out of and in the presence of
the last form of the secular power, which was the Empire of Pagan
Rome; I mean, the *sacerdotal persecuting power*, which, gentle in its
aspect and professions, was yet cruel in its actions; which did all the
deeds of the Empire, in its presence, which kept up its image, its
laws, its formulae, its privileges; which, coming in as it did by a corrupt and ambitious priesthood, deceived by its miracles the dwellers
on earth, and by them maintained the image of the despotic secular
power? Surely it is this Latin Christianity, in its ecclesiastico-secular
form, not identical with, but as preparing the way for, the great apostasy, helping, so to speak, to place the woman on the beast, as in
chapter XVII, that is here depicted before us. It is this which, owing
its power in the main to imposture and unwarrantably assumed spiritual authority, deserves best the name of *the false prophet*, expressly
given to this second beast in chapter 19:20.[9]

Although the primary reference of this passage is to the period just prior
to the second advent, it is foreshadowed undoubtedly in history as Alford
indicates. While resisting the historical school of interpretation, Alford
is nevertheless unduly influenced by it.

THE DECEPTIVE MIRACLES OF THE FALSE PROPHET (13:13–14)

13:13-14 And he doeth great wonders, so that he maketh fire come
down from heaven on the earth in the sight of men, And deceiveth
them that dwell on the earth by the means of those miracles which
he had power to do in the sight of the beast; saying to them that dwell
on the earth, that they should make an image to the beast, which had
the wound by a sword, and did live.

[9]Alford, IV, 678–79.

The first miracle accomplished by the false prophet is described as a great wonder, literally, one of many "great signs." The frequent use of *poieō* in the present tense seems to indicate repeated action, of which fire coming down from heaven in the sight of men is an illustration. The miracle may be an imitation of Pentecost (Acts 2:3), or it may be regarded as similar to Elijah's miracles (II Kings 1:10–12), or to the destructive fire coming out of the mouths of the two witnesses (Rev. 11:5). The Scriptures indicate that the devil does have power to do miracles and that by their use he deceives people into worshiping the beast.

The deceptive power of the beast is mentioned specifically in verse 14. By means of this power he performs miracles in the sight of the first beast. On the basis of this power and the impression it makes upon men described as "them that dwell on the earth," the second beast urges them to make an image of the first beast, described for the third time in this chapter as one which had the wound by a sword and did live. The beast is both the empire and its ruler. As ruler he is the symbol of the empire and the executor of its power. Though the wound by the sword apparently refers to the decline of the historic Roman ,Empire and its revival is indicated by the expression "did live," the man who serves at the head of the empire is the symbol of this miraculous restoration. The image made to the beast is not necessarily an image of the beast but, like the image of Nebuchadnezzar in Daniel 3, is the symbol of his power and majesty. Though the Scriptures do not say so, it is apparent that this suggestion is followed through, and the image, whatever its character, becomes the center of the false worship of the world ruler. This image, referred to three times in the chapter, is mentioned seven more times in the book of Revelation (14:9, 11; 15:2; 16:2; 19:20; 20:4). The image is the center of the false worship and the focal point of the final state of apostasy, the acme of the idolatry which has been the false religion of so many generations.

ALL REQUIRED TO WORSHIP THE BEAST (13:15-17)

13:15-17 And he had power to give life unto the image of the beast, that the image of the beast should both speak, and cause that as many as would not worship the image of the beast should be killed. And he causeth all, both small and great, rich and poor, free and bond, to receive a mark in their right hand, or in their foreheads: And that no man might buy or sell, save he that had the mark, or the name of the beast, or the number of his name.

Translated literally, the expression "he had power to give life unto the image of the beast" is properly rendered "It was given to him to give spirit to the image of the beast." The word translated "life" (Gr., *pneuma*) as in the Authorized Version, is obviously an incorrect translation, as *pneuma*, commonly translated "spirit" or "breath," is quite different from *zōē*, which means "life." Expositors usually hold that the extraordinary powers given by Satan to the false prophet do not extend to giving life to that which does not possess life, because this is a prerogative of God alone. The intent of the passage seems to be that the image has the appearance of life manifested in breathing, but actually it may be no more than a robot. The image is further described as being able to speak, a faculty easily accomplished by mechanical means. In ancient times religious ventriloquism was sometimes used to give the impression of supernatural speech, a practice confirmed by archaeological excavations in Corinth. In Acts 16:16 the slave girl possessed of a demon was able to bring gain to her masters by soothsaying. She also supernaturally recognized Paul and his companions as "servants of the most high God, which shew unto us the way of salvation" (Acts 16:17). Her power of speech was under demonic control. Whether completely natural in its explanation, or whether some supernatural power is used to create the impression of life, the image apparently is quite convincing to the mass of humanity and helps to turn them to a worship of the first beast as their god.

The absolute authority of both the first and second beasts is such that those who will not worship the image of the beast are sentenced to be killed. J. B. Smith attempts to ridicule the interpretation that this verse means what it actually says because some saints obviously survive the period of the great tribulation.[10] This is a needless objection, however, as a decree that all who fail to worship the beast should be killed is one thing, and its execution another. Even in Germany under Hitler, it took many months to execute condemned Jews, and the task was never completed. How much greater the difficulty to extend a decree of this sort to the entire world. A countless multitude will undoubtedly be martyred according to Revelation 7:9–17, but the disorder which attends the latter half of the great tribulation as the world empire begins to break up makes it impossible for full execution of this decree. Swete goes so far as to suggest that no decree to kill nonworshipers of the beast is actually issued, but that the beast only causes the image to *suggest* that this be done. Swete says,

> As they stand, the words can only mean that the ventriloquist used his opportunity to make the image suggest that all who refused to worship to the image of Caesar should be put to death.[11]

If the latter part of verse 15 records the words of the image, it would appear that verse 16 refers to the false prophet himself. The regulation

[10]Smith, p. 205.
[11]Henry B. Swete, *The Apocalypse of St. John*, p. 172.

is issued that all classes of people who worship the beast are to receive a mark in their right hands or in their foreheads and that possession of this identification is necessary to buy or sell. All classes are included in three contrasting pairs: the small and the great, referring to status; the rich and the poor, alluding to possessions; and the free and bond, referring to their state in society. To try to read into this an evil trinity or significance from the fact that six classes are mentioned is to read more into the passage than it intends.[12] There has been much speculation concerning the mark (Gr., *charagma*) which is affixed to the right hand or to the forehead. George W. Davis observes that the mark of the beast is in mimicry of the seal of the Holy Spirit on the true believer.[13] The mark itself seems to vary according to verse 17 as in some cases being the name of the beast and in others the number of his name. There is no need for a complicated explanation. The mark is simply a token that they are beast worshipers, and it serves as an identification necessary to conduct business and to purchase the necessities of life. It is another device to force all people to worship the beast.

THE NUMBER OF THE BEAST (13:18)

13:18 Here is wisdom. Let him that hath understanding count the number of the beast: for it is the number of a man; and his number is Six hundred three score and six.

Special attention is given in verse 18 to the number of the beast, 666. The number is introduced by the phrase "Here is wisdom," and the appeal is made to those of understanding to count the number of the beast which is the number of a man. There has been endless speculation concerning the meaning of this number. In attempting to solve the riddle of this verse, some have considered the phrase to represent Caesar, others Nero or Caligula.

The explanation is rather complicated. Letters in Hebrew, Latin, and Greek had numerical equivalents. The name Caesar Nero spelled Kaisar Neron if written with Hebrew endings (as John does in some other proper names such as Abaddon, Apollyon, Armageddon) has a corresponding numerical value in that K equals 100, S equals 60, R equals 200, N equals 50, R equals 200, O equals 6, and N equals 50. Using the letters that would be Hebrew consonants in their numerical value it would add up to 666. Accordingly, J. B. Smith concludes that Nero is the one who is intended, with the reference purposely obscure to avoid persecution.[14]

A number of other suggestions are made in that the six Roman numerals, that is, I, V, X, L, C, D, add up to 666. J. B. Smith says, "This alludes

[12]Cf. Smith, p. 205.
[13]*The Patmos Vision*, p. 209.
[14]Smith, p. 207.

to the possibility of a Roman being the antichrist."[15] Smith also adds, "All the numerals from 1 to 36 total 666. *Beast* in the evil sense occurs exactly 36 times (6×6) in Revelation."[16] Speculation continues ad infinitum using the letter equivalents for numbers in Hebrew, Greek, or Roman numerals. The very variety of the suggestions, however, and the unlikely and unprecedented supposition that someone would rise from the dead to take active part in earthly affairs leaves serious question as to all these imaginative explanations.

Reading the number as 616 instead of 666, others find it referring specifically to Caligula (Gaius Caesar) as the Antichrist. The 616 is derived from the numerical equivalents of the Greek letters for Gaius Caesar written in the style of Caligula. Or if the Latin equivalents are used, the number 616 is reached by dropping the final *n*.[17] The connection is made with Antichrist on the similarity of these Roman rulers to the future Antichrist.

Beckwith holds that the number 666 refers to Nero and to the first century tradition that he would be raised from the dead. He holds, "No valid objection can be found here to the Neronic explanation of the number." Whether or not the final Antichrist is actually Nero or not, he will in effect be a Nero reincarnate.[18] All of these interpretations are based on speculation which reduces the numbers to their equivalents, either in Hebrew or Greek letters or in Roman numerals.[19] Regarding the number 666, J. N. Darby writes,

> I confess my ignorance as to the number six hundred and sixty-six. I cannot present you with anything satisfactory to myself. We find, answering to the number six hundred and sixty-six, the words *apostasy* and *tradition;* but I cannot say anything positive on the point.[20]

Probably the simplest explanation here is the best, that the triple six is the number of a man, each digit falling short of the perfect number seven. Six in the Scripture is man's number. He was to work six days and rest the seventh. The image of Nebuchadnezzar was sixty cubits high and six cubits broad. Whatever may be the deeper meaning of the number, it implies that this title referring to the first beast, Satan's masterpiece, limits him to man's level which is far short of the deity of Jesus Christ.

Chapter 13, taken as a whole, is one of the great prophetic chapters of Scripture and is the only passage which presents in any detail the two principal evil characters of the end of the age who form with Satan an

[15]*Ibid.*
[16]*Ibid.*
[17]Swete, p. 176.
[18]Isbon T. Beckwith, *The Apocalypse of John*, pp. 400–408.
[19]Cf. Smith, pp. 226–67; Swete, pp. 174–76; Scott, pp. 285–87.
[20]*Notes on the Apocalypse*, p. 68.

unholy trinity. Here is clearly presented the fact that the head of the revived Roman Empire ultimately becomes the ruler of the entire world. Dominated by Satan, he is Satan's masterpiece and substitute for Christ, and is aided and supported by the second beast called the false prophet. Many have alluded to the contrast of this evil trinity with the heavenly Trinity, Satan corresponding to God the Father, the first beast corresponding to Christ, and the second beast corresponding to the Holy Spirit. George W. Davis expresses a common view that this is a false trinity: "This trinity will consist of Satan as God, Antichrist, the counterfeit of Christ, as Christ, and the false prophet, a travesty on the Holy Spirit."[21]

Expositors have not agreed entirely as to the identity of these two characters as revealed in other passages of Scripture. The preferable view seems to be that the first beast in Revelation 13 is the "little horn" of Daniel 7:8, "the prince that shall come" of Daniel 9:26, the willful king of Daniel 11:36–45, and the man of sin, or the lawless one, of II Thessalonians 2:3. Some prefer to identify the willful king of Daniel 11 and the man of sin in II Thessalonians 2 as the second beast of Revelation 13. The term "antichrist" is variously assigned either to the first or second beast or by some to neither. Among premillennial expositors, the trend seems to be to identify all of these terms with the first beast and relegate the second beast to a subordinate role as a religious rather than a political ruler.

There is no evidence that either of the beasts is a Jew. The expression "the God of his fathers" in Daniel 11:37 which would seem to make the king in that passage a Jew is better translated "gods" in keeping with the Hebrew *elohim* which removes any specific Jewish character from the phrase. The Hebrew *elohim* is in many places properly translated in the singular, but it is not specifically singular and therefore could be translated plural. The appeal often made to the phrase "his fathers," while it is a familiar one in reference to Israel, obviously cannot be limited to the Israelite race, as others have predecessors also; and in the case of the heathen their gods could be referred to as "the gods of their fathers." It is significant that in many cases where the God of Israel is referred to, "LORD" is added to make clear that the God of their fathers is Jehovah. For instance in Exodus 3:15 the expression is found "the LORD God of your fathers." Similar expressions are found frequently (cf. Deut. 1:11, 21; 4:1; 6:3; 12:1; 26:7; 27:3; 29:25; Joshua 18:3; Judges 2:12; etc.). The customary form of reference included the name "LORD," and its omission in Daniel 11:37 is most significant and points to the conclusion that this is not the God of Israel, and hence, that the king

21Davis, pp. 205–6.

is not a Jew. It would seem quite unlikely that either of the two beasts of Revelation 13 will be a Jew inasmuch as they both persecute the Jewish people and are the final Roman rulers of the times of the Gentiles.

The general character of the great tribulation, however, is graphically portrayed in this chapter. It will be a time of absolute rule, and Satan will have his way. The ultimate in false religion will sweep the entire world in a manifestation of evil never before seen on the earth. The fact will be demonstrated beyond question that man is not able to solve his own problems and only God can bring righteousness and peace to the earth. The present attempts at unification of ecclesiastical and political power seem to be the forerunner and preparation for this end-time situation.

14

THE VICTORY OF THE LAMB
AND HIS FOLLOWERS

CHAPTER 14 brings to a conclusion the material found in the section of chapters 12 through 14. Chapter 12 deals with the important characters of the period, chapter 13 with the wicked rulers of the period, and chapter 14 with the ultimate triumph of Christ. All of this material is not chronological but prepares the way for the climax which begins in chapter 15. Chapter 14 consists of a series of pronouncements and visions assuring the reader of the ultimate triumph of Christ and the judgment of the wicked. Much of the chapter is prophetic of events that have not yet taken place, but which are now impending. The chapter begins with the assurance that the Lamb will ultimately stand in triumph on Mount Zion with his followers, and it concludes with a series of pronouncements of judgments upon the wicked.

THE LAMB AND THE 144,000 ON MOUNT ZION (14:1–5)

14:1-5 And I looked, and, lo, a Lamb stood on the mount Sion, and with him an hundred forty and four thousand, having his Father's name written in their foreheads. And I heard a voice from heaven, as the voice of many waters, and as the voice of a great thunder: and I heard the voice of harpers harping with their harps: And they sung as it were a new song before the throne, and before the four beasts, and the elders: and no man could learn that song but the hundred and forty and four thousand, which were redeemed from the earth. These are they which were not defiled with women; for they are virgins. These are they which follow the Lamb whithersoever he goeth. These were redeemed from among men, being the firstfruits unto God and to the Lamb. And in their mouth was found no guile: for they are without fault before the throne of God.

The chapter begins with the unusual phrase used several previous times: "And I looked, and, lo." This expression, which could also be translated "And I saw, and, behold," introduces the vision of the Lamb standing on Mount Zion accompanied by 144,000. The expositors are faced with a number of important decisions in the understanding of this passage among which is the meaning of Mount Zion. J. B. Smith joins with Bengel and Hengstenberg in interpreting Mount Zion as the figurative expression referring to heaven, finding a similar usage in Hebrews 12:22.[1] Smith holds that the expression "mount Sion" always refers to the heavenly Jerusalem whereas "Sion" without "mount" always refers to the earthly city, a rather arbitrary conclusion.

To interpret this as a heavenly city, however, involves numerous problems which Smith and others do not take into consideration. If this group is the same as the 144,000 of chapter 7, they are specifically said to be sealed and kept safely through the tribulation. In this case, they move on into the millennial earth without going to the third heaven, since this is the meaning of the seal (cf. 7:3).

Further, the argument that the 144,000 must be in heaven as they hear the song before the throne may be disputed. There is no statement to the effect that they hear the song, only the declaration that they alone can learn it. The reasons for making Mount Zion a heavenly city in this passage are therefore lacking a sure foundation. Preferable is the view that this is a prophetic vision of the ultimate triumph of the Lamb following His second coming, when He joins the 144,000 on Mount Zion at the beginning of His millennial reign.

The determination of the place of this action is also correlated with the question whether the 144,000 in chapter 14 are the same group as in chapter 7. Walter Scott expresses the opinion without giving any substantiation that the 144,000 of chapter 14 are of the tribe of Judah and therefore to be distinguished from the 144,000 in chapter 7.[2] There is no evidence whatever in the passage that this group is limited to Judah, and it would be most strange to have two groups of exactly 144,000 in the end time, especially when 12,000 of those in chapter 7 are also of the tribe of Judah. The preferable view, therefore, seems to be that the 144,000 in this chapter are the same as in chapter 7. In their first mention they are seen at the beginning of the great tribulation. In their second mention in chapter 14, they are seen still intact, preserved by God through the fearful days of persecution and standing triumphantly with the Lamb on Mount Zion at the beginning of the millennial reign.

The best manuscripts indicate that the expression "having his Father's name written in their foreheads" should be "having his name, and the name of his Father, written on their foreheads." By this expression they are clearly identified as belonging to both the Father and the Son. In chapter 7, the seal is mentioned as simply being the seal of God, whereas here we have more detail. There is no good ground for imagining that the seal here is a later development and dissimilar to the earlier seal. J. B. Smith offers this view on the theory that in chapter 7 the 144,000 are not

[1]A Revelation of Jesus Christ, p. 208.
[2]Exposition of the Revelation of Jesus Christ, p. 293.

Christians and do not become Christians until chapter 14.[3] There is little to support this conclusion. The difference in the two descriptions is that one is general and the other specific. As Seiss points out, their identification with the Father is their mark of being saved Jews; their identification with the Lamb reveals their salvation through faith in Christ; their position on Mount Zion a place of security, blessing, and glory in the earthly Jerusalem in the millennial kingdom.[4]

In verse 2, a new facet of the vision is given to John and he records hearing a voice from heaven. The voice is described in most majestic terms as being similar to the sound (Gr., *phōnē*) of many waters and comparable to the sound of a great thunder. John also hears the voice of harpers harping with their harps (lyres). In verse 3 they are described as singing a new song before the throne and before the four living creatures and the elders. This scene seems reminiscent of chapters 4 and 5 though the expression "from heaven" is not in some manuscripts. The preponderance of evidence seems to indicate that this is indeed a heavenly scene which John is seeing "in the Spirit" while his body is on earth. If the 144,000 are on earth in Zion, who then are the company in heaven? Though the natural questions concerning their identity are not clearly answered in the text, the heavenly group are probably the martyred saints of the tribulation, in contrast to the 144,000 who are on earth and do not suffer martyrdom. Both groups, however, experience the trials of the great tribulation and therefore are alone worthy to enter into the song of redemption recounting their victory over their enemies and praising God for His grace which has numbered them among the redeemed.

Chronologically, the song John hears is their hymn of praise in heaven during the time of the great tribulation, but the same song is echoed by the 144,000 who stand triumphantly on Mount Zion after the tribulation. As is true of the rest of the vision in this chapter, the chronological order is not maintained, but rather different subjects are brought into view pertaining to the general theme of the ultimate triumph of God. There seems to be a definite connection between the new song that is sung and the ascription of praise (7:10) in which the martyred dead cry out to God, "Salvation to our God which sitteth upon the throne, and unto the Lamb." Different in character but also a new song is that of the twenty-four elders in 5:9–10. In chapter 14, the song is sung before the four living creatures and the elders; in chapter 5 the elders themselves sing the song. In the reference to the 144,000 as redeemed from the earth, the thought seems to be that both those in heaven and on earth have been redeemed, that is, purchased by the blood of Christ and de-

[3]Smith, pp. 208-9.
[4]Joseph A. Seiss, *The Apocalypse*, pp. 353–54.

livered from their enemies, one group through martyrdom, the other group by divine preservation through the tribulation.

Returning to the subject of the 144,000 in verse 4, John describes them as "not defiled with women, for they are virgins." This description is not explained in the context but has been taken variously as referring to necessary abstinence from marriage in the critical days of the tribulation when a normal marital life for a person true to God is impossible, or as referring to spiritual purity, that is, they are not defiled by love of the world or compromise with evil, but keep themselves pure in a world situation which is morally filthy. In like manner Israel is referred to frequently in the Bible as "the virgin the daughter of Zion" (II Kings 19:21; Isa. 37:22), as the "virgin daughter of Zion" (Lam. 2:13), and as the "virgin of Israel" (Jer. 18:13; 31:4, 21; Amos 5:2). In the New Testament also, the term "virgin" is used of both men and women as in II Corinthians 11:2 in reference to the church as a bride.

The possibility that their virgin character signifies their spiritual purity primarily is indicated in the next statement describing them as those "which follow the Lamb whithersoever he goeth." Here again it is obviously in the earthly scene, as the 144,000 of Israel do not ever go to heaven during their natural lifetime. The third statement also introduced by "these," as the two previous affirmations, repeats the thought that these are redeemed from among men as the firstfruits to God and to the Lamb. Again the word for redeemed is a form of *agorazō*, as in verse 3, meaning "to purchase." In what sense is this company "firstfruits" (Gr., *aparchē*)? The term "firstfruits" seems to refer to the beginning of a great harvest, here to the beginning of the millennial kingdom. The 144,000 are the godly nucleus of Israel which is the token of the redemption of the nation and the glory of Israel which is to unfold in the kingdom.

The description of the 144,000 closes with the statement that they are without guile and without fault. In saying that they have no guile (Gr., *pseudos*), the thought is that there is no falsehood or especially no false religion in them (cf. use of the word *pseudos* in Rom. 1:25; Rev. 21:27; 22:15). This large number have been kept utterly clean from the false religion of the great tribulation. They are also described as without fault, that is, blameless and without stain, in contrast to those who are apostates, described as "faults" or "blemishes" using the same root (Gr., *amōsos*) as in II Peter 2:13. How important this makes the life and testimony of any believer who seeks to emulate these who in this most trying time are found in no compromise with error and no defilement of their purity. Christians in the present age are exhorted to be "without blame before him" (Eph. 1:4), "without blemish" (Eph. 5:27; I Peter

1:19), "unblameable" (Col. 1:22), "without spot" (Heb. 9:14), and "faultless" (Jude 24). All of this is in the sight of God, though the expression in verse 5 "before the throne of God" is not in the best manuscripts.

THE ANGEL WITH THE EVERLASTING GOSPEL (14:6-7)

14:6-7 And I saw another angel fly in the midst of heaven, having the everlasting gospel to preach unto them that dwell on the earth, and to every nation, and kindred, and tongue, and people, Saying with a loud voice, Fear God, and give glory to him; for the hour of his judgment is come: and worship him that made heaven, and earth, and the sea, and the fountains of waters.

The next phase of the vision given to John in this chapter introduces "another angel" flying in the midst of heaven, literally "in mid-heaven," having the everlasting gospel to preach to the entire world. The reference to "another" seems to be to an angel in addition to the seven angels introduced in 8:2 and also in contrast to "another angel" in 8:3 and 10:1. J. B. Smith notes that the remaining portion of the chapter "presents a sevenfold division consisting of the appearance of six angels including a vision of the Son of man between two groups of three angels each."[5]

The expression "the everlasting gospel," actually without the article ("everlasting gospel") is an arresting phrase. It is everlasting in the sense that it is ageless, not for any specific period. Ordinarily, one would expect this to refer to the gospel of salvation. In verse 7, however, the content of the message is quite otherwise, for it is an announcement of the hour of judgment of God and the command to worship Him.

Some expositors use the term "gospel" to include all the revelation God has given in Christ and hence conclude that there is only one gospel with various phases of truth belonging to this gospel. There are others who prefer to distinguish various messages in the Bible as gospel or "good news" even though they contain only one aspect of divine revelation, hence, the expression "gospel of grace," referring to the goodness of grace, or to the gospel of the kingdom, dealing with the good news of the kingdom of God. The everlasting gospel seems to be neither the gospel of grace nor the gospel of the kingdom, but rather the good news that God at last is about to deal with the world in righteousness and establish His sovereignty over the world. This is an ageless gospel in the sense that God's righteousness is ageless. Throughout eternity God will continue to manifest Himself in grace toward the saints and in punishment toward the wicked. To refer to the gospel of grace as an everlasting gospel is to ignore the context and usage of the term.

[5]Smith, p. 211.

PROPHECY OF THE COMING FALL OF BABYLON (14:8)

14:8 And there followed another angel, saying, Babylon is fallen, is fallen, that great city, because she made all nations drink of the wine of the wrath of her fornication.

The pronouncement of verse 8 is by another angel, apparently also flying in mid-heaven, saying the great city of Babylon has fallen. The repetition of the phrase "is fallen" is for emphasis. Prophetically, "Babylon" sometimes refers to a literal city, sometimes to a religious system, sometimes to a political system, all stemming from the evil character of historic Babylon. The announcement here is prophetic as the actual fall of Babylon probably comes later if the reference is to the physical city. There is some evidence, however, that the woman referred to as "MYSTERY, BABYLON THE GREAT" in chapter 17, referring to the apostate church which will hold sway in the first half of the seventieth week of Daniel, is actually destroyed at the beginning of the great tribulation in preparation for the worship of the beast. The destruction of the city of Babylon itself, whether a reference to Rome, as is commonly held, or to a rebuilt city of Babylon on the ancient site of historic Babylon, does not take place until the end of the great tribulation. Inasmuch as the context here seems to deal primarily with the end of the great tribulation and the beginning of the millennial kingdom, the reference seems to be to the literal city.

The fall of Babylon is occasioned by her iniquity, which in the best manuscripts is described in these words: ". . . made all the nations to drink of the wine of the wrath of her fornication." Some expositors feel the text originally read "have drunk" instead of "made . . . to drink." In either reading the peculiar expression "the wine of the wrath of her fornication" has been variously interpreted but seems to be a shortened expression of the two phrases "the wine of the wrath of God" (14:10) and "the wine of her fornication" (17:2). The resultant meaning is that the nations who participate in the spiritual corruption induced by Babylon ultimately share her divine condemnation and judgment. Like the pronouncement of the previous angel and the other prophecies of this chapter, the promise of judgment upon the iniquitous Babylonian system is designed to bring comfort to those in trial in that period.

THE DOOM OF THE WORSHIPERS OF THE BEAST (14:9-11)

14:9-11 And the third angel followed them, saying with a loud voice, If any man worship the beast and his image, and receive his mark in his forehead, or in his hand, The same shall drink of the wine of the wrath of God, which is poured out without mixture into the cup of his indignation; and he shall be tormented with fire and brimstone in the presence of the holy angels, and in the presence of the Lamb:

And the smoke of their torment ascendeth up for ever and ever: and they have no rest day nor night, who worship the beast and his image, and whosoever receiveth the mark of his name.

The third angel adds immediately to the pronouncement of the previous angel by proclaiming with a great voice the sad doom of those who worship the beast. Anyone who receives the mark of the beast as required in 13:17 shall also partake of the judgment of God. As he drinks of the wine of spiritual fornication, so he also shall drink of the wine of the wrath of God. It is described in most dramatic terms as wine that is unmixed, that is, untempered by the mercy and grace of God; and these worshipers are declared to be "tormented with fire and brimstone in the presence of the holy angels, and in the presence of the Lamb." The same Scripture which assures all Christians of the love of God and the grace of God as extended to those who trust in Christ is unequivocal in its absolute statements of judgment upon the wicked.

Concerning the destiny of the wicked, J. B. Smith writes,

> Anyone disposed to discredit the Biblical teaching on the eternal destiny of the wicked should be reminded that Jesus and His beloved disciple said more in regard to this doctrine than all the remaining contributors to the New Testament record.

This is supported by the fact that Jesus referred to hell (*gehenna*) eleven out of the twelve occurrences, made twelve out of nineteen references to hell fire, and used other similar expressions more than any other person in the New Testament.[6]

The righteousness of God is as inexorable as the love of God is infinite. The love of God is not free to express itself to those who have spurned Jesus Christ. Their torment is not a momentary one, for it is described in verse 11 as continuing forever, literally "into the ages of ages," the strongest expression of eternity of which the Greek is capable. To emphasize the idea of continued suffering, they are declared to have no rest day or night. In describing the worshipers of the beast, the word *worship* as well as the word *receive* in verse 11 is in the present tense emphasizing continued worship of the beast over a long period of time, the worshipers spurning the testimony of the godly remnant and plunging blindly to their doom. The same present tense is used in describing their torment. As the worship of the beast is not interrupted by repentance, so their torment is not interrupted when repentance is too late. How dangerous it is for men to trifle with false religions, which dishonor the incarnate Word and contradict the written Word.

THE BLESSING OF THE SAINTS (14:12–13)

14:12-13 Here is the patience of the saints: here are they that keep

[6]*Ibid.,* p. 216.

> the commandments of God, and the faith of Jesus. And I heard a voice from heaven saying unto me, Write, Blessed are the dead which die in the Lord from henceforth: Yea, saith the Spirit, that they may rest from their labours; and their works do follow them.

The stern warning addressed to all worshipers of the beast is also an encouragement to those who put their trust in Christ in the time of great tribulation. Though some of them will face martyrdom and others will need to go into hiding, they are assured that their lot is far preferable to those who accept the easy way out and worship the beast. The saints are described in verse 12 as those who "keep the commandments of God, and the faith of Jesus." Here is the proper link between works and faith so necessary in all ages but especially in the great tribulation.

In verse 13, John hears a voice from heaven pronouncing a blessing on those who die in the Lord. Four times previously there is a record of a voice from heaven (10:4, 8; 11:12; 14:2). Again in 18:4 and 21:3 a voice is heard, a direct communication from God as contrasted with communication through an angel. The implication is that this is unusually important and a direct divine pronouncement. The reference to the blessing of those who die in the Lord from this time on is not a general reference to all saints who die, but specifically to those who die in this period, that is, as martyrs of the faith. It is far better to be dead at the hand of the beast than to have favor as his worshiper. This is followed by the expression "Yea, saith the Spirit." The implication is that the voice from heaven is none other than the voice of the Holy Spirit. Those who die in the Lord are described as resting from their labors with the rewards of their work following them. This verse is the second beatitude in Revelation (cf. 1:3; 16:15; 19:9; 20:6; 22:7, 14).

THE JUDGMENT OF THE SON OF MAN (14:14–16)

> **14:14-16** And I looked, and behold a white cloud, and upon the cloud one sat like unto the Son of man, having on his head a golden crown, and in his hand a sharp sickle. And another angel came out of the temple, crying with a loud voice to him that sat on the cloud, Thrust in thy sickle, and reap: for the time is come for thee to reap; for the harvest of the earth is ripe. And he that sat on the cloud thrust in his sickle on the earth; and the earth was reaped.

Following the reassurance of the saints' ultimate reward, a further revelation is given graphically in the closing portion of this chapter. John in his vision beholds One like the Son of man sitting on a white cloud wearing a golden crown and having in his hand a sharp sickle. The revelation is introduced by the familiar phrase "And I looked, and behold," indicating another major advance in the revelation. Though the one described is said to be like the Son of man, it is probable that this is none other than Christ Himself participating in the divine judgments of God upon a wicked world. This probability is reinforced by the golden crown speaking of His glorified state and His royal dignity. Alford says, "This clearly is our Lord Himself."[7] The sharp sickle indicates this is the time of harvest, referring to the climactic judgments relating to the second coming.

As John beholds the vision of the Son of man having a sharp sickle, he sees another angel come out of the Temple crying to the Son of man to thrust in His sickle and reap, declaring that the harvest of the earth is ripe. It is remarkable that an angel should thus address the Son of man, but it should be regarded as an entreaty of a holy angel to Christ as the Son of man in His position as judge of men (cf. John 5:22, 27). The fact that the angel comes from the Temple seems to allude to this judgment as proceeding from the righteousness of God. Further, the angel urges judgment at this time because, in God's sovereign plan as made known to the angel, it is the time for judgment. The expression "the harvest of the earth is ripe" seems to imply that judgment is overdue. The verb form "is ripe" (Gr., *exēranthē*), meaning "to become dry or withered," has a bad connotation (cf. Matt. 21:19–20; Mark 3:1, 3; 11:20; Luke 8:6; Rev. 16:12). The picture here is of a fruit or vegetable that has become so ripe that it has begun to dry up and wither. The rotten moral condition of the world is dealt with now with a sharp sickle. Verse 16 indicates that the Son of man does as the angel requests, possibly using angelic means to accomplish this end as in Matthew 13:30, 39–42.

Some commentators like Alford distinguish between the figure of reaping in verses 14–16 and the vision of reaping which follows, holding that the first harvest is that of the saints in contrast to the second harvest which is obviously of the wicked. As Alford states,

> The verdict of Commentators is very much divided. There are circumstances in the context which tell both ways. The parallelism with the vintage which follows, seems to favour a harvest of the wicked: but then on the other hand, if so, what is the distinction between the two ingatherings? And why do we read of the casting into the wine-press of God's wrath in the second case, and of no corresponding feature in the other? Again, why is the agency so different—the Son of man on the white cloud with a golden crown in the one case, the mere angel in the other? Besides, the two gatherings seem quite distinct. The former is over before the other begins. On the whole then, though I would not pronounce decidedly, I must incline to think that the harvest is the ingathering of the saints, God's harvest, reaped from the earth: described here thus generally, before the vintage of wrath which follows.[8]

[7]Henry Alford, *The Greek New Testament*, IV, 690.
[8]*Ibid.*, p. 691.

As Alford himself notes, the passage itself does not tell us what the first harvest is. There is no distinct event in this sequence of prophecies which clearly presents a harvest of saints, and it is probably preferable to consider the first harvest as the judgments in general which characterize the period and the second harvest as the final climactic one.

THE ANGEL WITH THE SHARP SICKLE (14:17–20)

14:17-20 And another angel came out of the temple which is in heaven, he also having a sharp sickle. And another angel came out from the altar, which had power over fire; and cried with a loud cry to him that had the sharp sickle, saying, Thrust in thy sharp sickle, and gather the clusters of the vine of the earth; for her grapes are fully ripe. And the angel thrust in his sickle into the earth, and gathered the vine of the earth, and cast it into the great winepress of the wrath of God. And the winepress was trodden without the city, and blood came out of the winepress, even unto the horse bridles, by the space of a thousand and six hundred furlongs.

The use of angels to assist in the harvest of the earth is now stated explicitly in verse 17. Though not enumerated, the angel of verse 17 is the fifth to appear in this chapter and, like the angel of verse 15, comes from the Temple in heaven. Like the Son of man he has a sharp sickle indicating the severity of the judgment. This angel is exhorted in verse 18 by another angel, the sixth in the chapter, to thrust in his sharp sickle. The angel making this request is described as coming from the altar and having power over fire. These allusions seem to indicate that the angel is acting in response to the prayers of the saints for divine judgment on wickedness in the earthly scene, and the fact that he has power over fire indicates the purging judgment of which he is capable.

The figure of divine judgment as a harvest is here enlarged. Twice the sharp sickle is mentioned in this verse and the clusters of the vine of the earth are described as grapes fully ripe. The expression "fully ripe" (Gr., *ēkmasan*) is a different expression from the verb (Gr., *exēranthē*) used in the description of the harvest in verse 15. Here it pictures grapes fully grown in their prime almost bursting with juice. Though the figure is somewhat different, the spiritual meaning is the same. The time has come for the final harvest. The use of the vine in a figurative way, frequently found in the Bible in relation to Israel (Ps. 80:8, 14–15; Isa. 5:2–7; Jer. 2:21; Ezek. 17:5–8; Hosea 10:1), is also used of the church in John 15:1–6. Just as Israel and the church were to bear fruit of righteousness to the Lord, so here we have the vine producing the fruit of wickedness and corruption.

In verse 19 the angel, in response to the entreaty, thrusts or "casts" (Gr., *ebalen*) his sickle into the earth and harvests its vintage casting it into what is described as "the great winepress of the wrath of God."

This action is actually fulfilled in Revelation 19:15, where the same figure of speech is used. In verse 20, the winepress is described as trodden without the city, and blood is said to come even to the bridles of the horses as far as 1,600 furlongs. This is obviously a picture of ultimate judgment of the wickedness of men at the time of the second coming of Christ. Alford interprets it: "A tremendous final act of vengeance is denoted."[9] This passage speaks prophetically of that which will chronologically follow the return of Christ to the earth.

The spurting of the grape juice from under the bare feet of those treading the grapes in the winepress is compared to the spurting of blood and speaks of the awful human carnage of Revelation 19:17-19, 21. The unusual expression that the blood spatters to "the horse bridles" for "a thousand six hundred furlongs" has intrigued expositors. The scene of this event is apparently the city of Jerusalem outside which the judgment takes place. It seems quite impossible that the blood will flow in depth as high as the horses' bridles, and it is better to understand this simply as a liberal spattering of blood.

As Alford states, "It is exceedingly difficult to say what the meaning is, further than that the idea of a tremendous final act of vengeance is denoted."[10] This interpretation is confirmed by the parallel in Isaiah 63:3. The area covered, 1,600 furlongs, is approximately 200 miles, and specifies that the area within a 200-mile radius from Jerusalem will be the center of the final carnage where the armies of the world will be gathered at the time of the second coming of Christ. The land of Israel covers about 200 miles from the north to the south, and the reference to distance may mean that this area is in view rather than the more extensive territory of 200 miles in all directions from Jerusalem.

Alford objects to a literal distance, as the holy land is actually only 160 miles north and south, and prefers a symbolic meaning of the distance. He concludes, however, "This is one of the riddles of the Apocalypse to which not even an approximate solution has ever yet been given."[11] There is no reason, however, for limiting the battle to the precise boundary of the holy land, and there is really no serious problem here in taking the distance literally. The terrible picture here given of the bloodletting which will mark the end of the age may include various phases of the battle taking place in the great tribulation and the climax of Christ's victory when He judges the nations at its end.

William Kelly regards this chapter as the outline of the end of the age:

In this chapter, then, we have the full outline of the dealings of God in the latter-day crisis. There are seven divisions of it. First, there is

[9]Ibid., p. 693.
[10]Ibid.
[11]Ibid.

the full remnant of godly Jews associated with the Lamb on mount Sion, in sympathy with His sufferings and waiting for the kingdom. Secondly, a testimony to the Gentile nations scattered all over the world as well as to those seated on the prophetic earth. Thirdly, the fall of Babylon. Fourthly, the fearful doom, both in this world and in the next, of such as should worship the beast and his image, or receive the mark of his name. Fifthly, the blessedness from that time of those that die in the Lord. Sixthly, the discriminating process of the harvest. And seventhly, the awful infliction of vengeance on religious apostasy; the first, at least, of these two last acts of judgment being executed by the Son of man, which necessarily supposes the very close of the age; the wrath, not of God only, but of the Lamb.[12]

Taken as a whole, chapter 14 of Revelation emphasizes first that the 144,000 of Israel seen at the beginning of the great tribulation will be preserved triumphantly through it. Second, the rest of the chapter is devoted to various pronouncements of divine judgment upon a wicked world, reassuring the saints of that day that, though they may suffer and even be martyred, God's ultimate justice will triumph, the wicked will be judged, and the saints will be rewarded. This chapter reassures the saints after the two preceding chapters speak of the gigantic conflict that will have its consummation in the great tribulation. The implications of the message for today are only too plain. Today is a day of grace; but what is true of the tribulation is also true today, namely, that God will ultimately judge all men. Today, however, the invitation is still open to those who will trust in Christ and who thereby can avail themselves of the grace of God and be saved from entering this awful period which may be impending for this present generation.

---

[12]*Lectures on the Book of Revelation*, p. 330.

15

THE VISION OF THE SEVEN LAST PLAGUES

THE SIGN OF THE SEVEN ANGELS WITH THE PLAGUES (15:1–2)

15:1-2 And I saw another sign in heaven, great and marvellous, seven angels having the seven last plagues; for in them is filled up the wrath of God. And I saw as it were a sea of glass mingled with fire: and them that had gotten the victory over the beast, and over his image, and over his mark, and over the number of his name, stand on the sea of glass, having the harps of God.

CHAPTERS 15 and 16 of Revelation bring to consummation the chronologically ordered events leading up to the second coming of Christ described in chapter 19. These are introduced in this chapter as "the seven last plagues" which are the divine judgments preceding the second coming of Christ. As previously indicated, the chronological order of events in Revelation is presented basically in the seven seals (6:1–17; 8:1). The seventh seal includes all of the seven trumpets (8:1–9:21; 11:15–19). The seven vials or bowls of divine judgment are included in the seventh trumpet. From this it can be seen that the order of events is one of dramatic crescendo, the seventh seal being all-inclusive of the end-time events including the seven trumpets, and the seventh trumpet including the events described in the seven vials. The second coming of Christ follows this order of events immediately after the seventh vial. The intervening sections such as 10:1–11:14; 13–14; 17–19 do not advance the narrative chronologically. Chapter 19 of Revelation follows immediately after chapter 16 in the chronological development.

The final series of the seven last plagues is introduced by the vision in which John sees "another sign in heaven." The word *another* refers to the two preceding signs of chapter 12, namely, the woman who appeared as "a great wonder in heaven," literally "a great sign in heaven" (12:1), and the "great red dragon" (12:3), signifying the empire of the beast under Satan's control. The three signs taken together represent important elements in the prophetic scene: (1) Israel, that is, the woman; (2) the final world empire under the control of Satan and the beast, that is, the great red dragon; and (3) the seven angels having the seven

last plagues, that is, the divine judgment upon the satanic system and
political power of the beast.

The sign in heaven is described as "great and marvellous" (Gr., *mega
kai thaumaston*). These words appear together only here and in verse 3
(the description of the works of God) in the entire New Testament,
though they appear separately elsewhere.

Central in the vision given to John are seven angels, apparently another
group of seven angels not to be confused with any other group of seven,
as the article is not used with the expression. This new group of seven
angels is described as having the seven last plagues. As in the trumpets
and seals, the number of completion, seven, is used. It is most significant
that they are described as "last," more emphatic in the Greek (literally
"having seven plagues, the last ones"). This implies that the previous
judgments unfolding in the breaking of the seals and the blowing of the
trumpets were also plagues, that is, divine judgments of God pouring
out affliction upon a wicked world. (Cf. other divine judgments in 9:18,
20; 11:6; 13:3, 12, 14. "Wound" is "plague" in the original. Cf. also
16:7-9; 18:8; 19:2; 22:18.) That they are described as the last plagues
shows that they are the final judgments preceding the second coming
itself.

The seven plagues are further described as acts of judgment which
"filled up the wrath of God." The concept of "filled up" (Gr., *etelesthē*)
means to bring to conclusion or to the ultimate goal, that is, a fulfillment
of divine purpose. The word for "wrath" is not *orgē* but *thymos*, often
translated "anger." In view is not divine wrath as an attitude, but divine
judgment as the expression of God's wrath. The word *orgē* is used in
Revelation 16:19 in the final judgment upon Babylon extending from the
seventh vial. As Arndt and Gingrich observe, the combination of *thymos*
and *orgē* connotes the strongest kind of outpouring of divine judgment.
The word *thymos* is defined as "anger, wrath, rage."[1] It may be concluded, therefore, that the anger of God is the preliminary expression,
the wrath of God is the final expression of divine righteousness.

The scene in heaven is described thus by John: "as it were a sea of
glass mingled with fire." This seems to be an allusion to the same situation as in 4:6 where a "sea of glass like unto crystal" is "in the midst of
the throne." Alford observes,

> The fact, that the personages of the former heavenly vision are still
> present, ver. 7, seems to remove all doubt of this being *the same sea*
> of glass as that before described, Ch. iv. 6.[2]

Here the sea of glass has two variations. The sea of glass is said to be

[1]Arndt and Gingrich, *A Greek-English Lexicon of the New Testament,* p. 366.
[2]Henry Alford, *The Greek New Testament,* IV, 693-94.

"mingled with fire," the statement qualified by the phrase "as it were" (Gr., *hōs*). In both instances it is obvious that John does not see an ordinary sea because the heavenly hosts stand upon it. The symbolism, however, is rich. The sea is designed to reflect the glory of God. In chapter 4 its description "like unto crystal" speaks of the holiness of God. Here the sea mingled with fire speaks of divine judgment proceeding from God's holiness. The fact that the saints are able to stand upon it reflects the faithfulness of God in upholding His own in keeping with His divine character. Some suggest that the sea is specifically the Word of God with its many precious promises to the saints.[3]

Upon this sea stand an innumerable company of those who "had gotten the victory over the beast, and over his image, and over his mark, and over the number of his name." These unmistakably are the martyred dead destroyed by the beast of Revelation 13:1–10 whose number is given in 13:18. Their triumph consists in the fact that they remained faithful to death instead of yielding to the blasphemous demand of the beast. Their resurrection and reward are described in 20:4–6. These have "harps of God" (no article before "harps" [lyres] in original). The harp (lyre) and the trumpet are the only musical instruments mentioned in the book of Revelation. Though possessed by this group of saints, the harps apparently are not given to all the martyred dead (cf. absence of harps in 7:9–17). The harpers' privileged position before the throne contributing to the heavenly harmony of the chorus of the redeemed is their reward for refusing to worship the beast, receive his mark, bow to his image, or be identified with his number. They clearly belong to saints martyred during the time of great tribulation, confirming that the time schedule is near the end of the period and contrasting them to saints of other ages.

THE SONG OF MOSES AND THE SONG OF THE LAMB (15:3-4)

15:3-4 And they sing the song of Moses the servant of God, and the song of the Lamb, saying, Great and marvellous are thy works, Lord God Almighty; just and true are thy ways, thou King of saints. Who shall not fear thee, O Lord, and glorify thy name? for thou only art holy: for all nations shall come and worship before thee; for thy judgments are made manifest.

The hymn of praise sung by the martyred saints in glory is identified as "the song of Moses the servant of God, and the song of the Lamb." The fact that "song" (Gr., *ōdēn*) is repeated with a definite article in both cases would lead to the conclusion that two songs are in view rather than one, both being sung by the martyred throng. The former recounts the faithfulness of God to Israel as a nation in recognition that a large number of Israelites are among these martyred dead. The song

[3]Cf. H. A. Ironside, *Lectures on the Revelation*, pp. 271–72.

of the Lamb speaks of redemption from sin made possible by the sacrifice of the Lamb of God, and would include all the saints.

There has been difference of opinion as to what song is meant by "the song of Moses." Walter Scott follows the traditional interpretation in referring it to the song of Exodus 15 sung by Moses and the children of Israel on the occasion of their triumph over the host of Pharaoh at the Red Sea.[4] The alternative view advanced by J. B. Smith has much to commend it, however.[5] He suggests that the song of Moses is the one recorded in Deuteronomy 32, a song personally written and spoken to the children of Israel by Moses himself at the close of his career. It is a comprehensive picture of God's faithfulness to Israel and His ultimate purpose to defeat their enemies. This latter song more nearly corresponds to the situation found here in Revelation 15. Both passages, however, ascribe praise to God and are similar in many ways to the hymn here recorded.

Praise ascribed to God begins with the statement "Great and marvellous are thy works, Lord God Almighty." The unusual expression of verse 1 is carried over here to the works of God as "great" in extent and "marvellous" or wonderful, that is, arousing wonder or astonishment, which could apply to the works of God in the past, but more probably anticipates the great work just ahead. The verb is omitted and could be past, present, or future, though the thought seems to be the present tense with a futuristic intent. God is also described as "just and true" in His ways. He is just, in that He is perfectly righteous. He is true, in that He keeps His promises. The expression closing verse 3, "King of saints," is in the better manuscripts properly "King of the nations." God, the sovereign ruler of all men, is shortly to manifest this sovereignty and divine judgment to the wicked world.

The futuristic context of this ascription of praise is indicated in the question of verse 4, "Who shall not fear thee, O Lord, and glorify thy name?" Though the nations neither fear God nor glorify Him in their mad unbelief during the great tribulation, the day is to come soon when they will both fear Him and be forced to acknowledge Him as God. A similar question is found in Jeremiah 10:7: "Who would not fear thee, O King of nations?" (Cf. also Rev. 14:7.) The prospect of all nations worshiping the Lord, a familiar theme of the prophets, is brought out in the next statement: "For thou only art holy: for all nations shall come and worship before thee" (cf. Ps. 2:8-9; 24:1-10; 66:1-4; 72:8-11; 86:9; Isa. 2:2-4; 9:6-7; 66:18-23; Dan. 7:14; Zeph. 2:11; Zech. 14:9).

The concluding phrase in the song speaks of the divine judgments which are revealed, speaking of the application of divine righteousness

[4]*Exposition of the Revelation of Jesus Christ,* p. 315.
[5]*A Revelation of Jesus Christ,* pp. 224-26.

to the wicked earthly situation. The righteous judgment from God proceeds from what He is as described in this song: the God who is almighty, righteous, true, holy, just, and worthy of worship.

THE TABERNACLE OF THE TESTIMONY IN HEAVEN OPENED (15:5-6)

15:5-6 And after that I looked, and, behold, the temple of the tabernacle of the testimony in heaven was opened: And the seven angels came out of the temple, having the seven plagues, clothed in pure and white linen, and having their breasts girded with golden girdles.

Another vision now introduced by John as a later development constitutes the immediate introduction of the judgments represented in the vials. Our attention is arrested by the phrase "I looked, and, behold." This expression always introduces something dramatically new. As John observes, the Holy of Holies in the heavenly Tabernacle is opened. The expression "the temple" (Gr., naos) refers to the inner holy place of the Tabernacle, the design of which God gave to Israel during the wilderness wandering. The expression "the tabernacle of the testimony" is a reference to the whole tentlike structure, a portion of which contained the Holy of Holies. It is described as "the tabernacle of the testimony" because of the presence of the tables of stone containing the ten commandments which were placed in the ark of the testimony in the Holy of Holies (cf. Exodus 32:15; Acts 7:44) and is mentioned frequently in the Old Testament (Exodus 38:21; Num. 1:50, 53; 10:11; 17:7-8; 18:2).

As John looks intently on the scene, the sanctuary is opened, that is, the curtain is parted, and seven angels are seen coming out of the sanctuary. The holy place, into which the high priests alone could go and only after proper sacrifices, does not exclude holy angels who have no sin. Each of the angels is carrying one of the vials containing the seven plagues and is described as being clothed in pure white linen and girded with a golden girdle.

The whole scene is most symbolic of what is about to happen. The angels coming out of the sanctuary indicate that the judgments to be poured out stem from the holiness of God and are properly required of God who must do all things right. The suggestion of J. B. Smith that the clothing of linen requires that these be regarded as the seven angels of the churches of Revelation 2 and 3 is rather farfetched.[6] Linen here, as in the garment of the wife of the Lamb (19:8), represents righteousness in action, certainly proper of holy angels and not requiring in their use the cleansing of redemptive blood. The symbolism of the golden girdles is less clear, except that they bind the linen. If gold reflects the glory of God, it would point to the conclusion that these angels pouring out righteous judgments on the earth thereby bring glory to God.

6*Ibid.*, p. 226.

SEVEN GOLDEN VIALS GIVEN TO THE ANGELS (15:7-8)

15:7-8 And one of the four beasts gave unto the seven angels seven golden vials full of the wrath of God, who liveth for ever and ever. And the temple was filled with smoke from the glory of God, and from his power; and no man was able to enter into the temple, till the seven plagues of the seven angels were fulfilled.

The seven angels described as already having the seven plagues in verse 6 are given seven golden vials or bowls described as full of the wrath of God in verse 7. The reference to plagues in verse 6 may be prophetic, or the bestowal of the vials may be the authorization to use them. The extent of the divine judgment is indicated by the word *full* indicating the devastating character of this divine judgment. The word for "wrath" is *thymos*, literally "anger," rather than *orgē*, properly "wrath." The solemn reminder that God lives forever and ever gives a solemn cast to the wrath that is to be poured out to be inflicted forever and ever upon those who perish.

As the angels emerge from the sanctuary, it is filled with smoke proceeding from the glory of God and His power, a pointed reminder of the ineffable holiness of God. The scene can be compared to that when the cloud filled the Tabernacle in Exodus 40:34-35. Access into the sanctuary is made impossible by the smoke until the judgments contained in the seven plagues are fulfilled. It is an ominous sign of impending doom for those who persist in their blasphemous disregard of the sovereignty and holiness of God.

16

THE VIALS OF THE WRATH
OF GOD

THE COMMAND TO POUR OUT THE VIALS (16:1)

16:1 And I heard a great voice out of the temple saying to the seven angels, Go your ways, and pour out the vials of the wrath of God upon the earth.

THE SEVEN ANGELS to whom were given the seven plagues symbolized in the seven vials are now commanded to pour out their divine judgment upon the earth. The voice is undoubtedly the voice of God which is described as coming out of the Temple and as being a "great" voice (Gr., *megalēs*), a word which occurs frequently in this chapter. The word *great* is mentioned again in connection with the great voice (v. 17), great heat (v. 9), the great river Euphrates (v. 12), that great day of God Almighty (v. 14), a great earthquake, "so mighty an earthquake, and so great" (v. 18), the great city (v. 19), great Babylon (v. 19), a great hail (v. 21), and the "exceeding great" plague (v. 21). As J. B. Smith expresses it, "This is the *great* chapter of the Bible."[1]

The seven vials thus introduced and itemized in this chapter have often been compared to the seven seals and to the seven trumpets, especially the latter. One form of interpretation has been to view the vials as merely an enlargement on the trumpet judgments corresponding numerically to them. There is undoubtedly much similarity between the trumpet judgments and the judgments inflicted by the pouring out of the vials of the wrath of God. In both the trumpets and the vials, the first in the series deals with the earth, the second with the sea, the third with rivers and fountains of water, the fourth with the sun, the fifth with darkness, the sixth with the Euphrates River, and the seventh with lightnings, thunders, and a great earthquake. The principle is often overlooked, however, that similarities do not prove identity. A careful study of the seven vials as compared to the seven trumpets will reveal numerous differences. The first four trumpet judgments deal only with one-third of the earth, while the vial judgments seem to be universal in their application and greater in intensity. The position is therefore taken in this ex-

[1] *A Revelation of Jesus Christ,* p. 228.

231

position that the vial judgments are subsequent to the trumpet judgments and proceed out of and constitute the seventh trumpet. The judgments described in the trumpet pronouncements and the vial pronouncements fall in rapid succession like trip-hammer blows, and they all will be consummated within a short period of time toward the close of the great tribulation. The vial judgments, the climax of God's divine dealings with a blasphemous earth, lead up to the second coming of the Lord and Saviour Jesus Christ.

Alford in commenting on the phrase "the seven last plagues" writes, "There can then be no doubt here, not only that the series reaches on to the time of the end, but that the whole of it is to be placed close to the same time."[2]

THE FIRST VIAL (16:2)

16:2 And the first went, and poured out his vial upon the earth; and there fell a noisome and grievous sore upon the men which had the mark of the beast, and upon them which worshipped his image.

With the pouring out of the first vial, a terrible judgment falls upon men who have the mark of the beast. There is a notable contrast between the first vial and the first trumpet, in that the first trumpet (8:7) burns up a third part of the trees and all the green grass. Here the judgment is specifically upon men and is directed to a particular group of men, namely, the beast worshipers who have received the mark of the beast. The judgment is described as a sore or ulcer (Gr., *helkos*) which is bad (Gr., *kakos*) and evil or malignant (Gr., *poneros*). The judgment is in the form of a physical affliction of unusual severity bringing widespread suffering. Smith notes that *helkos* used here to describe the sore is the word selected by the translators of the Old Testament into Greek (the LXX) for the boils inflicted on the Egyptians in Exodus 9:9–11.[3]

Confirmation that the vial judgments occur late in the great tribulation is given in the record that the first vial judgment falls on those who are worshipers of the beast's image. This image apparently is established in the early part of the great tribulation, the last half of the seven-year period preceding the second coming (13:14–17). Almost everyone seems to comply with the demand that all men worship the beast and receive his mark. The vial judgment, therefore, follows this edict. The only ones who escape the judgment are those who have refused to obey the edict of the beast, the few individuals who trust in Christ in those evil days. From 13:8 it would appear that only a small fraction of the earth's population resists the blandishments of the beast. The warning given in 14:9–

[2]Henry Alford, *The Greek New Testament*, IV, 696.
[3]Smith, p. 229.

11 is now reinforced in a preliminary judgment which anticipates the ultimate doom of the beast worshipers.

THE SECOND VIAL (16:3)

16:3 And the second angel poured out his vial upon the sea; and it became as the blood of a dead man: and every living soul died in the sea.

The second vial is poured out upon the sea with the result that the sea becomes as blood (literally "it became blood as of a dead man"), and every living soul in the sea dies. As in the second trumpet in 8:8, the analogy seems to be to the first of the ten plagues in Egypt (Exodus 7:20–25) which killed all the fish in the Nile River and made the water unfit to drink. In all these cases it is possible that the sea does not become literally human blood but that it corresponds to it in appearance and loathsomeness.[4] The area of the judgment is similar to that of the second trumpet where one-third of the sea is turned to blood and one-third of the creatures of the sea die. Here the judgment is universal. The reference to the sea may be limited to the Mediterranean, but the same word would be used if the judgment extended to all large bodies of water. In the latter event, a major portion of the earth would be involved in the judgment as most of the earth is covered with water.

THE THIRD VIAL (16:4-7)

16:4-7 And the third angel poured out his vial upon the rivers and fountains of waters; and they became blood. And I heard the angel of the waters say, Thou art righteous, O Lord, which art, and wast, and shalt be, because thou hast judged thus. For they have shed the blood of saints and prophets, and thou hast given them blood to drink; for they are worthy. And I heard another out of the altar say, Even so, Lord God Almighty, true and righteous are thy judgments.

The third in the series of judgments extends the turning of water into blood to rivers and fountains, apparently with the same devastating effect, though the results of the judgment are not mentioned. Though some have taken rivers and fountains to be symbolic, there is no reason for not taking this in the literal sense as the sea in the second vial and the men in the first vial. The physical affliction stems from spiritual apostasy.

At this point John hears one described as "the angel of the waters" deliver a justification of God for this judgment. The angel is apparently a holy angel who has some jurisdiction over water. There is a remarkable variety of ministries assigned to angels as recorded in Revelation. The angel declares that because men have shed the blood of saints and prophets, God is righteous in judging them in kind in that they are given

[4]Cf. Alford, IV, 697-98.

blood to drink. Even as the saints are worthy of rest and reward, so the wicked are worthy of divine chastening and judgment. The bloodletting during the great tribulation, as saints are slaughtered by the thousands, is without parallel in the history of the race. Christ Himself declares it will be a time of trouble without precedent (Matt. 24:21). The multitude of martyrs in heaven is revealed in chapter 7. The eternal God, the One which is, and was, and shall be (v. 5), though awaiting the proper time, is inexorable in His judgment of those who persecuted the saints.

The statement of the angel of the waters is confirmed by another voice out of the altar, another angel who declares that God, who is almighty, true, and righteous, manifests these attributes in His divine judgments. The phrase "another out of" in verse 7, though omitted in some manuscripts, is obviously the meaning of the verse, as the utterance must come from a being rather than from the altar itself. Combining the judgment of the second and third vials, it appears that all water is turned into blood, constituting a universal testimony to all men that God will avenge his martyred saints.

THE FOURTH VIAL (16:8–9)

16:8-9 And the fourth angel poured out his vial upon the sun; and power was given unto him to scorch men with fire. And men were scorched with great heat, and blasphemed the name of God, which hath power over these plagues: and they repented not to give him glory.

Like the fourth trumpet, the fourth vial is a judgment which affects the starry heaven, specifically the sun. In the fourth trumpet the judgment extends to a third part of the sun, moon, and stars, resulting in the darkening of a third part of the day and of the night. By contrast, the fourth vial relates only to the sun and increases rather than decreases the sun's intensity with the result that men are scorched with fire. The divine judgment thus inflicted, apparently upon the entire earth, does not bring men to repentance but only increases their blasphemy, even though they recognize that the plague comes from the God whom they reject. The expression "and power was given unto him to scorch men with fire" is rendered, according to the best manuscripts, "and it was given to him [the sun] to scorch the men with fire." The use of the article with "men" seems to refer the judgment to the same class as in verses 2, 5, and 6. The article is also used in connection with the men mentioned in verse 9 (literally "the men"). The implication is that saints in this period who are true believers in the Lord Jesus Christ will not suffer from this plague, and possibly creatures other than men may also escape. The wishful thinking of some that men would repent if they only knew the power and righteous judgment of God is shattered by frequent mention in this chapter of the hardness of the human heart in the face of the most stringent and evident divine discipline (cf. vv. 11, 21).

THE FIFTH VIAL (16:10–11)

16:10-11 And the fifth angel poured out his vial upon the seat of the beast; and his kingdom was full of darkness; and they gnawed their tongues for pain, And blasphemed the God of heaven because of their pains and their sores, and repented not of their deeds.

The fifth judgment resulting from the pouring out of the fifth vial is directed to the throne of the beast and his subjects. The result of the judgment is darkness, pain, and the accumulated effect of the preceding judgment when sores were inflicted as in the first vial. The noun clause "the seat of the beast" is more accurately "the throne of the beast" (Gr., *thronos*). The beast is probably the first beast of Revelation 13. As in the fifth trumpet and in the ninth plague of Egypt (Exodus 10:21–23), there is darkness over the earth, but this is only part of the divine judgment. As in both trumpet and vial judgments, there is also pain and torment. The wicked in their suffering are declared to gnaw their tongues for pain, a description of severe agony. The sores inflicted in the first vial were, in this judgment, aggravated and increased. Again, we have the sad note that they blasphemed God as the author of these judgments and did not repent of their deeds. Though they are declared once more in verse 21 to have blasphemed God, this is the last reference to their failure to repent (cf. 2:21; 9:20–21; 16:9). The Scriptures plainly refute the notion that wicked men will quickly repent when faced with catastrophic warnings of judgment. When confronted with the righteous judgment of God, their blasphemy is deepened and their evil purpose is accentuated.

THE SIXTH VIAL (16:12–16)

16:12-16 And the sixth angel poured out his vial upon the great river Euphrates; and the water thereof was dried up, that the way of the kings of the east might be prepared. And I saw three unclean spirits like frogs come out of the mouth of the dragon, and out of the mouth of the beast, and out of the mouth of the false prophet. For they are the spirits of devils, working miracles, which go forth unto the kings of the earth and of the whole world, to gather them to the battle of that great day of God Almighty. Behold, I come as a thief. Blessed is he that watcheth, and keepeth his garments, lest he walk naked, and they see his shame. And he gathered them together into a place called in the Hebrew tongue Armageddon.

The sixth vial has occasioned more comment on the part of expositors than any of the preceding vials, and numerous interpretations have been offered. As the sixth vial is poured out, its particular objective is the great Euphrates River. As the result of judgment, the water of the river is dried up and the way of the kings of the East is thereby prepared. The most natural explanation is the best, namely, that this is the judgment which actually dries up the great Euphrates River, thereby preparing for an invasion from the East.

The river Euphrates here called "the great" is one of the prominent rivers of the world and forms the eastern boundary of the ancient Roman Empire as well as the prophesied eastern boundary of the land which God promised to the seed of Abraham (Gen. 15:18; Deut. 1:7; 11:24; Joshua 1:4). In Genesis 15:18, Deuteronomy 1:7, and Joshua 1:4, it is called "the great river Euphrates" as it is here. These references seem to establish unmistakably the geographic usage in this passage. In Isaiah 11:15 and Zechariah 10:11 there is a similar prediction of the drying up of the Euphrates River, though the name of the river is not mentioned.

Alford interprets the passage in this way:

> In order to understand what we have read, we must carefully bear in mind the context. From what follows under this same vial, we learn that the kings of the whole earth are about to be gathered together to the great battle against God, in which He shall be victorious, and they shall utterly perish. The time is now come for this gathering: and by the drying up of the Euphrates, the way of those kings who are to come to it from the East is made ready. This is the only understanding of these words which will suit the context, or the requirements of this series of prophecies. For to suppose the conversion of Eastern nations, or the gathering together of Christian princes, to be meant, or to regard the words as relating to any auspicious event, is to introduce a totally incongruous feature into the series of vials, which confessedly represents the "seven last *plagues*."[5]

The purpose of the drying up of the Euphrates is indicated as a preparation for "the way of the kings of the east." Through the centuries, commentators particularly of the postmillennial and the historical schools have guessed at the identity of the kings of the East, and as many as fifty different interpretations have been advanced.[6] The very number of these interpretations is their refutation. The passage is best understood as referring to the kings of the East, literally, of the "sunrising," referring to Oriental rulers who will descend upon the Middle East in connection with the final world conflict described a few verses later. The reasons seem to be weak for taking this prediction in other than its literal meaning. The rising power of parts of the Orient in our day in countries such as Japan, China, India, as well as lesser nations, makes such an invasion a reasonable prediction.

[5]*Ibid.*, IV, 700.
[6]This conclusion is based on a survey of 100 commentaries on the book of Revelation.

In verses 13–16 John has an additional vision introduced by the phrase "and I saw" which is parenthetical in nature but a commentary upon the sixth vial and somehow related to it. In his vision he sees three unclean spirits like frogs in appearance coming out of the mouth of the dragon and out of the mouth of the beast and out of the mouth of the false prophet. The source of these unclean spirits is the world ruler specified as the beast, his associate the beast who is the false prophet, and the dragon himself which is Satan (cf. 12:9; 13:1–8, 11–18). There is no need for speculation as to the identity of the three unclean spirits, as too many commentators have done, attempting to link these spirits to some contemporary personage. They are specified in verse 14 as spirits of demons (Gr., *daimoniōn*) and should be so interpreted. These wicked spirits are declared to work miracles (cf. 13:12–15) and are commissioned to gather the kings of the entire earth to the battle described as "the battle of that great day of God Almighty." As such, they are the emissaries of the unholy trinity of verse 13, namely, the dragon, the beast, and the false prophet, a counterfeit of the true triune God.

While many commentators have agreed that this is the prelude for the great battle climaxing in the second coming of Christ, some have been confused as to the details. The battle (Gr., *polemos*) is probably better translated "war" in contrast to *machē*, which is properly a battle or fighting (cf. James 4:1 where both words are used). What is in view here is something more than a military engagement. It is rather a major war. The evidence, however, seems to point to the conclusion that this is a climax of a series of military events described in Daniel 11:40–45, where the reference to the "tidings out of the east" (Dan. 11:44) may have this invasion in view.

The major problem is how a war is possible when there is a world government under the control of Satan and the beast. Some have interpreted this as a gathering of forces in anticipation of the second coming of Christ. More probably, it reflects a conflict among the nations themselves in the latter portion of the great tribulation as the world empire so hastily put together begins to disintegrate. The armies of the world contending for honors on the battlefield at the very time of the second coming of Christ do all turn, however, and combine their efforts against Christ and His army from heaven when the glory of the second coming appears in the heavens. It will be the final challenge to divine sovereignty and power as the military might of the world of that day will be engaged in fighting on the very day that Christ returns (cf. Zech. 14:1–3). It is significant that the battle itself bears the name of "that great day of God Almighty." In the battle the omnipotence of God will be fully demonstrated. The phrase "unto the kings of the earth and of the whole world" is best rendered according to the Greek text "unto the kings of the whole inhabited earth" (Gr., *oikoumenē*).

The utterance of verse 15 is apparently a direct quotation from God Himself, though the text does not indicate it specifically. The pronouncement is made, "Behold, I come as a thief." The expression is used of a sudden, unexpected coming which will result in judgment or loss on the part of the person overtaken. In Matthew 24:43 and Luke 12:39 the second coming of Christ is compared to the coming of a thief who will overtake those who do not watch. A similar warning is given to the church in Sardis (Rev. 3:3). In II Peter 3:10 and in I Thessalonians 5:2, 4 the day of the Lord is said to come as a thief. The unifying factor in all these passages is that the coming in view results in loss for those who are not ready.

The contrast between those who are overtaken by the Lord at His coming and those who are prepared by faith in Christ is expressed in the beatitude "Blessed is he that watcheth, and keepeth his garments, lest he walk naked, and they see his shame." (For previous beatitudes, see 1:3 and 14:13.) The symbolism of preservation of garments is not entirely clear from the passage. Some have construed this symbolism as the garments of salvation, but more probably the righteousness of the saints is symbolized, as expressed in their life and testimony (cf. 19:8). The saints will thus be protected from spiritual nakedness at the coming of the Lord. The saints in view here are evidently those still on earth who have been able to escape martyrdom even though remaining true to their Lord. It is probable that the beast will not be able to enforce his edict of death on those who are located in the outer reaches of his empire, and that he will not find all those who are in hiding (cf. Matt. 24:16).

The conclusion of the combined action of the sixth vial and the enticement of the demons is that the armies of the earth are gathered in the Middle East in a place described as Armageddon. Though the armies are lured by the demons under the direction of Satan, they nevertheless fulfill the Word of God. It is probable that the "he" of verse 16 refers to God Himself.

There has been considerable discussion concerning the meaning of the term "Armageddon," taken by some to mean "Mount of Slaughter." Geographically, it relates to the Mount of Megiddo located adjacent to the plain of Megiddo to the west and the large plain of Esdraelon to the northeast. *Megiddo* is the Hebrew word corresponding to the Greek word *Armageddon*. This area was the scene of many of the great battles of the Old Testament such as that of Barak and the Canaanites in Judges 4 and the victory of Gideon over the Midianites in Judges 7. Here also occurred the deaths of Saul and Josiah. The area, though it is a large one, is not sufficient for the armies of all the world, though the valley of Esdraelon is fourteen miles wide and twenty miles long. What this Scripture seems to indicate is that this area is the central point for the military conflict which ensues. Actually the armies are deployed over a 200-mile area up and down from this central location (cf. 14:20). At the time of the second coming, some of the armies are in Jerusalem itself (Zech. 14:1-3).

The difficulty of the historical interpretation of the book of Revelation is illustrated in the identification of Armageddon with World War I. Alexander Hardie, for instance, stated, "The last Great War of 1914–1918 which convulsed and disgraced humanity, was doubtless the predicted Armageddon."[7] History alone has proved countless theories of the historical school to be in error. In view of the fact that the second coming which brings this battle to a climax is still future, it is far better to regard this entire conflict as relating to the latter stages of the great tribulation.

The relationship between the drying up of the Euphrates and the battle that follows has sometimes been connected with the sixth trumpet in 9:13-21. In the sixth trumpet an army of 200 million men is loosed to slay a third part of men (9:15). This army is related to the Euphrates River even as the army of the kings of the East. Probably the best explanation is that the seven vials follow very rapidly after the trumpets and that the events such as a great invasion are pictured in their early stages in the sixth trumpet with a statement of their ultimate purpose that is actually realized in the sixth vial. The time sequence here may be in terms of days rather than months or years.

THE SEVENTH VIAL (16:17-21)

16:17-21 And the seventh angel poured out his vial into the air; and there came a great voice out of the temple of heaven, from the throne, saying, It is done. And there were voices, and thunders, and lightnings; and there was a great earthquake, such as was not since men were upon the earth, so mighty an earthquake, and so great. And the great city was divided into three parts, and the cities of the nations fell: and great Babylon came in remembrance before God, to give unto her the cup of the wine of the fierceness of his wrath. And every island fled away, and the mountains were not found. And there fell upon men a great hail out of heaven, every stone about the weight of a talent: and men blasphemed God because of the plague of the hail; for the plague thereof was exceeding great.

The vial of the seventh angel is declared to be poured out into the air and the resulting action is catastrophic. It is accompanied by a great voice out of the Temple in heaven and from the throne stating in emphatic

[7] *A Study of the Book of Revelation*, p. v.

terms, "It is done!" In the Greek, the statement is one word, *gegonen,* in the perfect tense, indicating action accomplished. It is the final act of God preceding the second coming of Christ.

There has been speculation as to why this vial should be poured into the air, inasmuch as Satan as the prince of the power of the air has already been cast down from heaven. The fact that Satan has been cast out of the third heaven, however, does not mean that he still does not have great power in the atmospheric heavens which are here in view. It is also clear in our modern day that the control of the air as well as space has become increasingly important in military matters. Undoubtedly air and space travel will increase rather than decrease as the end of the age comes upon the world. Some have compared this prophecy to Ezekiel 38:9, 16 where the host from the north is said to "ascend and come like a storm" and "like a cloud to cover the land." While this may imply an air attack, it is perhaps reading too much into the passage to assume this. In any event the seventh vial, which is poured out in the air, has its principal resulting action on the earth as the verses which follow indicate. The solemn accompaniment of the affirmation "It is done" by the great voice from the Temple in heaven and from the throne is a most ominous introduction to this final judgment.

As in the case of the final seal and the seventh trumpet (8:5; 11:19) the final vial is introduced by the sound of voices, thunderings, lightnings, and a great earthquake. The earthquake is declared to be greater than any previous earthquake. The earth literally convulses as the times of the Gentiles come to an end. The voices, thunders, and lightnings are the prelude to the earthquake which is the express judgment from God.

Verse 19 declares that "the great city" is split into "three parts" and that the other cities of the Gentile world fall. It is a picture of awesome destruction. The question has been raised as to the reference to the great city, inasmuch as Babylon is specifically mentioned later in the verse. Some have taken both references to indicate Babylon, others have identified the first great city of the verse as Jerusalem. In 11:8 Jerusalem is referred to as "the great city, which spiritually is called Sodom and Egypt, where also our Lord was crucified." It is also clear that great topographical changes will take place around Jerusalem in connection with the judgments at the end of the age (cf. Zech. 14:4). There is therefore some justification for considering Jerusalem as a possible interpretation. There does not, however, seem to be any clear evidence that Jerusalem is destroyed with the judgments which overtake the earth at the end of the great tribulation. Babylon, however, according to Scripture, is destined to be completely destroyed. Whether this refers to Rome which is spiritual Babylon or, as some have understood it, to a rebuilt city of Babylon on the Euphrates, it is clear in any case that Babylon is the special object of the judgment of God, expressed graphically in the statement "to give unto her the cup of the wine of the fierceness of his wrath." Here the word for "wrath" is *orgē*, a strong word often related to *thymos* which refers to divine anger.[8] This is the final judgment of this wicked city. The fact that the judgment is an earthquake seems to indicate that a literal city is in view, either Rome or rebuilt Babylon, and that the judgment results in its physical destruction. The time is just prior to the second coming of Christ.

Not only does every city of the world come under terrible judgment as a result of the great earthquake which leaves all monuments of men's ingenuity in shambles, but the Scriptures also indicate great changes in the topography of the entire world. The sweeping statement is made in verse 20 that every island is affected and mountains disappear. The fierceness of the wrath of God in verse 19, literally the anger of His wrath, is manifested in the entire physical earth. The movement of the islands and mountains mentioned in 6:14 as stemming from the sixth seal is here carried to a more violent conclusion with apparently the entire earth radically changing its appearance. Such a judgment undoubtedly causes great loss of life and disruption of such world organization as may have remained up to this time. There does not seem to be any good reason for taking this verse in other than its literal meaning, coming as it does at the climax of the great tribulation when many other Scriptures indicate changes in topography including an entirely new appearance of the holy land itself.

In addition to mentioning the great earthquake which is the primary means of divine judgment in the seventh vial, verse 21 records a great hail with every stone about the weight of a talent. Though the talent in different periods of history varied in weight, the reference here seems to be to the talent weighing about 100 pounds and representing all that a man could normally carry. Such a hail from heaven falling upon men would have a devastating effect and would destroy much that was still left standing by the earthquake. It is a judgment compared to that of the destruction of Sodom and Gomorrah but here extending over the entire earth. Although the judgment and its demonstration of the power and sovereignty of God are great, men are still unrepentant, and verse 21 concludes with the sad statement that "men blasphemed God because of the plague of the hail; for the plague thereof was exceeding great." Chronologically the next event is that prophesied in 19:11 where Christ Himself descends from heaven to take over His kingdom on earth.

Though from the contemporary point of view all the details of these

[8]Cf. discussion of 14:8.

dramatic judgments are not immediately understood, the unmistakable impression of the Scriptures is that the whole world is being brought to the bar of justice before Christ as King of kings and Lord of lords. There is no escape from divine judgment except for those who avail themselves of the grace of God in that day by faith in Jesus Christ. The utter perversity of human nature, which will reject the sovereignty of God in the face of such overwhelming evidence, confirms that even the lake of fire will not produce repentance on the part of those who have hardened their hearts against the grace of God.

17

THE DESTRUCTION OF ECCLESIASTICAL BABYLON

THE INVITATION TO VIEW THE JUDGMENT OF THE GREAT HARLOT (17:1–2)

17:1-2 And there came one of the seven angels which had the seven vials, and talked with me, saying unto me, Come hither; I will shew unto thee the judgment of the great whore that sitteth upon many waters: With whom the kings of the earth have committed fornication, and the inhabitants of the earth have been made drunk with the wine of her fornication.

CHAPTERS 17 and 18 of Revelation are dedicated to the description of the final destruction of Babylon in both its ecclesiastical and political forms. It is evident from these chapters that the events described therein, especially those in chapter 17, precede by some considerable period the events represented in the seven vials. In fact, it is probable that the events of chapter 17 occur at the beginning of the great tribulation. The revelation is given to John, however, subsequent to the revelation of the vials. It must be remembered that from John's point of view all of the events of the book of Revelation were future, and it pleased God to reveal various aspects of future events in other than their chronological order.

Any interpretation of Revelation 17 and 18 is difficult because expositors have not agreed as to the details of their interpretations. In general, however, it is helpful to consider chapter 17 as dealing with Babylon as an ecclesiastical or spiritual entity and chapter 18 as dealing with Babylon as a political entity. It is also helpful in chapter 17 to distinguish the vision in verses 1 through 6 from the interpretation in verses 7 through 18.

John is shown the vision of the destruction of Babylon, as representing false religion, by one of the seven angels which had the seven vials, and is invited to behold the judgment of a woman, the symbol of Babylon, described as the great whore (Gr., *pornē*, usually translated "harlot"), who is seen sitting on many waters. The interpretation of "waters" is that these are the many nations ruled by Babylon.. The woman is further described as having committed fornication (Gr., *porneuō*,

243

verb form of *pornē*). The inhabitants of the earth are declared to have been made drunk with the wine of her fornication. The picture of the woman as utterly evil signifies spiritual adultery, portraying those who outwardly and religiously seem to be joined to the true God but who are untrue to this relationship. The symbolism of spiritual adultery is not ordinarily used of heathen nations who know not God, but always of people who outwardly carry the name of God while actually worshiping and serving other gods. The concept of spiritual adultery is frequently used in describing the apostasy of Israel (cf. Ezek. 16 and 23; all of Hosea). Characteristically, the Jehovah of the Old Testament is the husband of Israel (cf. Isa. 54:1–8; Jer. 3:14; 31:32). In the New Testament the church is viewed as a virgin destined to be joined to her husband in the future (II Cor. 11:2), but she is warned against spiritual adultery (James 4:4).

The alliance of the apostate church with the political powers of the world during this future period of time not only debauches the true spiritual character of the church and compromises her testimony in every way but has the devastating effect of inducing religious drunkenness on the part of the inhabitants of the earth. False religion is always the worst enemy of true religion, and the moral wickedness involved in the union of the church with the world imposes a stupefying drunkenness as far as spiritual things are concerned. The hardest to win to Christ and the most difficult to instruct in spiritual truth are those who have previously embraced false religion with its outward show of a worship of God. The concept here presented, enlarging on the previous revelation in 14:8, makes plain that the apostate church has eagerly sought and solicited the adulterous relation with the world political powers and therefore is primarily to be blamed.

THE VISION OF THE WOMAN ON THE BEAST (17:3–4)

17:3-4 So he carried me away in the spirit into the wilderness: and I saw a woman sit upon a scarlet coloured beast, full of names of blasphemy, having seven heads and ten horns. And the woman was arrayed in purple and scarlet colour, and decked with gold and precious stones and pearls, having a golden cup in her hand full of abominations and filthiness of her fornication.

Accepting the invitation of the angel, John is carried away in the spirit, that is, in a spirit of ecstacy, into a place described as the wilderness or literally "wilderness" (no article in the original). From this vantage point John is able to see the woman previously introduced as the great harlot. She is seen seated on a scarlet-colored beast which is full of the names of blasphemy and which has seven heads and ten horns. The scarlet beast is the same one described in 13:1 where the beast is the revived Roman Empire in its character as the center of the world government of Gentile power in that day. The fact that the woman is riding the beast and is not the beast itself signifies that she represents ecclesiastical power as distinct from the beast which is the political power. Her position, that of riding the beast, indicates on the one hand that she is supported by the political power of the beast, and on the other that she is in a dominant role and at least outwardly controls and directs the beast.

The situation here described is apparently prior in time to that described in Revelation 13, where the beast has already assumed all power and has demanded that the world should worship its ruler as God. The situation, therefore, seemingly is in the first half of Daniel's seventieth week before the time of the great tribulation which is the second half. While such a relationship has many parallels in the past history of the Roman church in relation to political power, the inference is that this is a future situation which will take place in the end time. The significance of the seven heads and the ten horns is revealed subsequently in this chapter, the seven heads apparently referring to forms of government which are successive, and the ten horns to kings who reign simultaneously in the end time. The fact that the woman, representing the apostate church, is in such close association with the beast, which is guilty of utter blasphemy, indicates the depth to which apostasy will ultimately descend. The only form of a world church recognized in the Bible is this apostate world church destined to come into power after the true church has been raptured.

The description of the woman as arrayed in purple and scarlet and decked with gold, precious stones, and pearls is all too familiar to one acquainted with the trappings of ecclesiastical pomp today and especially of high officials in the Roman Catholic and Greek Orthodox churches. Purple and scarlet, symbolically so rich in their meaning when connected with true spiritual values, are here prostituted to this false religious system and designed to glorify it with religious garb in contrast to the simplicity of pious adornment (cf. I Tim. 2:9-10). Alford states, "I do not hesitate therefore . . . to maintain that interpretation which regards papal and not pagan Rome as pointed out by the harlot of this vision."[1] The most striking aspect of her presentation, however, is that she has a golden cup in her hand described as "full of abomination and filthiness of her fornication." The Word of God does not spare words in describing the utter filthiness of this adulterous relationship in the sight of God. Few crimes in Scripture are spoken of in more unsparing terms than the crime of spiritual adultery of which this woman is the epitome. As alliance with the world and showy pomp increase, so spiritual truth and purity decline.

[1]Henry Alford, *The Greek New Testament,* IV, 705.

THE NAME OF THE WOMAN (17:5)

17:5 And upon her forehead was a name written, MYSTERY, BABYLON THE GREAT, THE MOTHER OF HARLOTS AND ABOMINATIONS OF THE EARTH.

Upon the forehead of the woman was written her name described as "MYSTERY, BABYLON THE GREAT, THE MOTHER OF HARLOTS AND ABOMINATIONS OF THE EARTH." The word *mystery* is a descriptive reference to the title, not a part of the title itself as implied by the capitalization in the Authorized Version. This can be seen by comparing the name given to the woman in 16:19 and 18:2. It has been commonly held that the title "Babylon the Great" assigned to this woman is not a reference to Babylon as a city or to Babylonia as a nation but a religious designation, namely, that the woman corresponds religiously to what Babylon was religiously. The meaning is made clear by her description as "the mother of harlots and abominations of the earth." It has been noted by many writers that the iniquitous and pagan rites of Babylon crept into the early church and were largely responsible for the corruptions incorporated in Roman Catholicism from which Protestantism separated itself in the Middle Ages.

The subject of Babylon in the Scripture is one of the prominent themes of the Bible beginning in Genesis 10, where the city of Babel is first mentioned, with continued references throughout the Scriptures climaxing here in the book of Revelation. From these various passages, it becomes clear that Babylon in Scripture is the name for a great system of religious error. Babylon is actually a counterfeit or pseudo religion which plagued Israel in the Old Testament as well as the church in the New Testament, and which, subsequent to apostolic days, has had a tremendous influence in moving the church from biblical simplicity to apostate confusion. In keeping with the satanic principle of offering a poor substitute for God's perfect plan, Babylon is the source of counterfeit religion sometimes in the form of pseudo Christianity, sometimes in the form of pagan religion. Its most confusing form, however, is found in Romanism.

In Genesis 10 and 11 it is recorded that Nimrod was the founder of Babel, later called Babylon. In chapter 11 is recorded the rebellion of men against God in attempting to make a city and a tower that would reach to heaven. The history of the ancient world reveals that it was a common practice to build huge mounds (ziggurats) of sun-dried bricks of which the most ancient illustration has been discovered at Erech, a place mentioned in Genesis 10:10 and dated more than 3,000 years before Christ. The tower of Babel was apparently a forerunner of later towers dedicated to various heathen deities. There was no stone with which to build, and therefore bricks were used with mortar binding them together.

The tower of Genesis 11 was a monument to human pride and an express act of rebellion against the true God.

In judging this act God confounded the language of the people and gave the city the name of "Babel," meaning "confusion" (cf. Gen. 11:9). The city, later named Babylon, had a long history. It became prominent under Hammurabi (1728–1686 B.C.) who was the guiding light to the empire during the Old Babylonian period. Babylon's greatest glory was achieved under Nebuchadnezzar who lived during the Neo-Babylonian period about 600 years before Christ. Daniel the prophet wrote his book at that time. The story of the city and empire has been deciphered from thousands of cuneiform tablets unearthed by archaeologists.

Of primary importance in the study of Babylon is its relation to religion as unfolded in Revelation 17. In addition to materials given in the Bible itself, ancient accounts indicate that the wife of Nimrod, who founded the city of Babylon, became the head of the so-called Babylonian mysteries which consisted of secret religious rites which were developed as a part of the worship of idols in Babylon. She was known by the name of Semiramis and was a high priestess of the idol worship. According to extrabiblical records which have been preserved, Semiramis gave birth to a son who she claimed was conceived miraculously. This son, given the name of Tammuz, was considered a savior of his people and was, in effect, a false messiah, purported to be the fulfillment of the promise given to Eve. The legend of the mother and child was incorporated into the religious rites and is repeated in various pagan religions. Idols picturing the mother as the queen of heaven with the babe in her arms are found throughout the ancient world, and countless religious rites were introduced supposedly promising cleansing from sin. Though the rites which were observed in the Babylonian false religion differed greatly in various localities, there usually was a priestly order which furthered the worship of the mother and child, practiced the sprinkling of holy water, and established an order of virgins dedicated to religious prostitution. Tammuz, the son, was said to have been killed by a wild beast and afterward brought back to life, obviously a satanic anticipation of the resurrection of Christ.

In the Scriptures themselves, though many of these facts are not mentioned, there are a number of allusions to the conflict of the true faith with this pseudo religion. Ezekiel protests against the ceremony of weeping for Tammuz in Ezekiel 8:14. Jeremiah mentions the heathen practices of making cakes for the queen of heaven (Jer. 7:18) and offering incense to the queen of heaven (Jer. 44:17–19, 25). The worship of Baal, characteristic of pagan religion in Canaan, was another form of this same mystery religion originating in Babylon. Baal is considered identical to

Tammuz. The doctrines of the mystery religions of Babylon seem to have permeated the ancient world, giving rise to countless mystery religions, each with its cult and individual beliefs offering a counterfeit religion and a counterfeit god in opposition to the true God revealed in the Scriptures. Babylon as an evil woman is portrayed in the prophecy of Zechariah 5:1–11 where the woman of verse 7 is described as personifying wickedness in verse 8.

The Babylonian cult eventually made its way to other cities including Pergamos, the site of one of the seven churches of Asia. The chief priests of the Babylonian cult wore crowns in the form of the head of a fish, in recognition of Dagon the fish god, with the title "Keeper of the Bridge," that is, the "bridge" between man and Satan, imprinted on the crowns. The Roman equivalent of the title, *Pontifex Maximus*, was used by the Caesars and later Roman emperors, and was also adopted as the title for the bishop of Rome. In the early centuries of the church in Rome, incredible confusion arose; and attempts were made to combine some of the features of the mystery religion of Babylon with the Christian faith, a confusion which has continued down to the present day. In this chapter in Revelation, the last stage of counterfeit religion is revealed as it will be in existence in the period before the return of the Lord to earth.

It is a sad commentary on contemporary Christendom that it shows an overweening desire to return to Rome in spite of Rome's evident apostasy from true biblical Christianity. In fact, modern liberalism has far outdone Rome in its departure from the theology of the early church, thus has little to lose by a return to Romanism. Apostasy, which is seen in its latent form today, will flower in its ultimate form in this future superchurch which will apparently engulf all Christendom in the period after the rapture of the church.

THE WOMAN DRUNKEN WITH THE BLOOD OF MARTYRS (17:6-7)

17:6-7 And I saw the woman drunken with the blood of the saints, and with the blood of the martyrs of Jesus: and when I saw her, I wondered with great admiration. And the angel said unto me, Wherefore didst thou marvel? I will tell thee the mystery of the woman, and of the beast that carrieth her, which hath the seven heads and ten horns.

The woman is pictured not only as the source of all evil in apostate Christendom but also as the one who is actively engaged in the persecution of the true saints. Her wickedness in this regard is demonstrated by the description that she is drunken with the blood of the saints and with the blood of the martyrs of Jesus. Here the primary reference is not to ancient Babylon but to Babylon perpetuated in apostate Christendom especially in its future form. The history of the church has demonstrated that apostate Christendom is unsparing in its persecution of those who attempt to maintain a true faith in Jesus Christ. What has been true in the past will be brought to its ultimate in this future time when the martyrs will be beyond number from every kindred, tongue, and nation. The blood shed by the apostate church is exceeded only by that of the martyrs who refuse to worship the beast in the great tribulation. As John contemplates the woman, he records, "I wondered with great admiration," or more literally, "I wondered with great wonder" (the verb in the Greek, *thaumazō*, has the same root as the noun *thauma*, both meaning "to regard with wonder or astonishment").

The angel, perceiving that John wonders at what he sees, states that he will declare the mystery of the woman and of the beast. He does so, however, by describing the beast first in detail, then the woman and subsequent action relating to her. Few passages in Revelation have been the subject of more dispute among scholars who have attempted to interpret them than this explanation of the angel. Great care, therefore, must be exercised in determining precisely the component parts of the divine revelation herein given.

THE ORIGIN OF THE BEAST (17:8)

17:8 The beast that thou sawest was, and is not; and shall ascend out of the bottomless pit, and go into perdition: and they that dwell on the earth shall wonder, whose names were not written in the book of life from the foundation of the world, when they behold the beast that was, and is not, and yet is.

The angel first gives a detailed description of the beast in his general character. The beast is explained chronologically as that which was, is not, and is about to ascend from the abyss and go into perdition. "The bottomless pit" (Gr., *abyssos,* meaning "bottomless," or "the abyss") is the home of Satan and demons and indicates that the power of the political empire is satanic in its origin as is plainly stated in 13:4. The word *perdition* (Gr., *apōleia*) means "destruction" or "utter destruction," referring to eternal damnation. The power of the political empire in the last days is going to cause wonder as indicated in the questions in 13:4: "Who is like unto the beast? who is able to make war with him?" The overwhelming satanic power of the final political empire of the world will be most convincing to great masses of mankind.

There is a confusing similarity between the descriptions afforded Satan who was apparently described as the king over the demons in the abyss (9:11), "the beast that ascendeth out of the bottomless pit" (11:7), the beast whose "deadly wound was healed" (13:3), and the beast of 17:8. The solution to this intricate problem is that there is an identification to some extent of Satan with the future world ruler and identification of the world ruler with his world government. Each of the three entities is described as a beast. Only Satan himself actually comes from the abyss. The world government which he promotes is entirely satanic in its power and to this extent is identified with Satan. It is the beast as the world government which is revived. The man who is the world ruler, however, has power and great authority given to him by Satan. The fact that Satan and the world ruler are referred to in such similar terms indicates their close relationship one to the other.

While many have attempted to demonstrate from this verse that the final world ruler is some resurrected being such as Judas Iscariot,[2] Nero,[3] or one of the more recent world rulers, it would seem preferable to regard the "eighth" beast as the political power of the world government rather than its human ruler. What is revived is imperial government, not an imperial ruler (cf. Rev. 13:3). That which seemingly went out of existence in history never to be revived is thus miraculously resuscitated at the end of the age.

THE SEVEN HEADS OF THE BEAST (17:9–11)

17:9-11 And here is the mind which hath wisdom. The seven heads are seven mountains, on which the woman sitteth. And there are seven kings: five are fallen, and one is, and the other is not yet come; and when he cometh, he must continue a short space. And the beast that was, and is not, even he is the eighth, and is of the seven, and goeth into perdition.

The explanation of the beast introduced by the unusual phrase "here is the mind which hath wisdom" anticipates the difficulty and complexity of the revelation to follow. The reader is warned that spiritual wisdom is required to understand that which is unfolded. The first key to the revelation is in the statement "The seven heads are seven mountains on which the woman sitteth." Many expositors refer this to Rome. Seven hills formed the nucleus of the ancient city on the left bank of the Tiber. These hills received the names of Palatine, Aventine, Caelian, Esquiline, Viminal, Quirinal, and Capitoline.[4] As Rome grew, however, the hill Janiculum on the other side of the river Tiber was often included among the seven, as Alford does, omitting the Capitoline.[5] Later the hill Pincian to the north of the ancient city was also included in the hills of Rome as the city developed and moved north.[6] This passage in Revelation is taken, therefore, to indicate that the seat of the ecclesiastical power will be in Rome geographically rather than in Babylon. Throughout its

[2]Cf. Kenneth Wuest, *Prophetic Light in Present Darkness*, pp. 67–70.
[3]H. H. Rowley, *The Relevance of the Apocalyptic*, pp. 130, 132.
[4]William Smith, *Dictionary of Greek and Roman Geography*, II, 719-21.
[5]Alford, IV, 710.
[6]Smith, *ibid.*

history Rome has been described as the city of seven hills as indicated in coins which refer to it in this way and in countless allusions in Roman literature. Victorinus, one of the first to write a commentary on the book of Revelation, identified the seven mountains as the city of Rome.[7]

The seven heads of the beast, however, are said to be symbolic of seven kings described in verse 10. Five of these are said to have fallen, one is in contemporary existence, that is, in John's lifetime, the seventh is yet to come and will be followed by another described as the eighth, which is the beast itself. In the Greek there is no word for "there," thus translated literally, the phrase is "and are seven kings." The seven heads are best explained as referring to seven kings who represent seven successive forms of the kingdom. Because the seven heads are identified with kings in verse 10, some prefer to divorce the meaning from the city of Rome entirely and center the ultimate fulfillment in a rebuilt Babylon on the site of ancient Babylon.

Seiss marshals a convincing array of evidence that the seven mountains of 17:9 refer not to the seven hills of Rome but rather to successive imperial governments. An extensive quotation of Seiss on this important point is necessary to present the matter fully:

> John further saw this Woman sitting upon a scarlet Beast, full of names of blasphemy, having seven heads and ten horns. This Beast is the same described in chapter 13. He is referred to here, not so much to make us better acquainted with him, as to give us a full understanding of the Great Harlot and her relationships. The "wisdom" or inner sense and meaning of the presentation is, that "the seven heads are seven mountains, where the Woman sitteth upon them, and are seven kings." These are the words which are supposed to fix the application of the picture to the city of Rome, as Rome is called a city of seven hills. But a flimsier basis for such a controlling and all-conditioning conclusion is perhaps nowhere to be found. The seven *hills* of the city of Rome, to begin with, are not *mountains*, as every one who has been there can testify; and if they were, they are more characteristic of the situation of Rome than the seven hills are characteristic of Jerusalem. But the taking of them as literal hills or mountains at all is founded upon a total misreading of the angel's words.
> A *mountain*, or prominent elevation on the surface of the earth, is one of the common scriptural images, or representatives of a kingdom, regal dominion, empire, or established authority. So David, speaking of the vicissitudes which he experienced as the king of Israel, says: "Lord, by Thy favour Thou didst make *my mountain* to stand strong" —margin, "settled strength for *my mountain*," meaning his kingdom and dominion. (Ps. 30:7.) So the Lord in His threat against the throne and power of Babylon said: "I am against thee, O destroying *mountain*, which destroyest all the earth; and I will stretch out mine hand upon thee, and will roll thee down from the rocks, and will make

[7]Cf. J. B. Smith, *A Revelation of Jesus Christ*, p. 245.

thee a burnt *mountain.*" (Jer. 51:25.) So the kingdom of the Messiah is likened to "a stone, which became a great *mountain,* and filled the whole earth." (Dan. 2:35.) And this is exactly the sense in which the angel uses the word here, as he himself tells us. He does not say, "the seven heads are seven mountains, where the Woman sitteth upon them," and there leave off; but he adds immediately, *"and they are seven kings,"* or *personified kingdoms.* The mountains, then, are not piles of material rocks and earth at all, but royal or imperial powers, declared to be such by the angel himself. The description, therefore, so far from fixing the application to the Papacy, or to the city of Rome, decisively settles that it cannot possibly apply to either, for neither has seven such mountains. The late Albert Barnes has written in his *Notes* that "all respectable interpreters agree that it refers to Rome; either Pagan, Christian, or Papal." Of course he is one of the "respectable interpreters," but then he should be able to tell which of the objects he names it is, for it cannot be all three. Most people assign Dr. E. W. Hengstenberg, the great Berlin professor, a place among "respectable interpreters," but Hengstenberg says Rome cannot possibly be meant by these seven heads. The angel says they are seven regal mountains, seven kings, seven great ruling powers. Rome Papal cannot be meant, for Rome Papal has no such count of seven regal powers. Rome Christian cannot be meant, for Rome Christian, as distinguished from Rome Papal, never supported and carried the great Harlot in any possible sense, and could not without ceasing to be Christian. Rome Pagan cannot be meant, for Rome Pagan ceased with the conversion of the throne, and no count of emperors or kings can be found in it to "respectably" fill out the angel's description. The succession of the forms of administration, enumerated as *Kings, Consuls, Dictators, Decemvirs, Military Tribunes,* and *Emperors,* were not seven kings or regal mountains. Prior to the empire most of these administrations were less than anthills in the history of the world, and furnished rather slender ponies for the great purple-clad and pearl-decked mother of harlots to ride on in her majesty. Rome surely comes into the count of these seven mountains of empire; but to make Rome the whole seven, including also the eighth, requires a good deal more "respectability" of interpretation in that line than has thus far appeared. Barnes is sure the whole thing applies to Rome because this Woman "hath rule or kingdom upon the kings of the earth, and there was no other empire on the earth to which this could be properly applied." But this assumes that the Woman is an empire, for which there is not a particle of evidence. The Woman is *not* an empire any more than the Church of Christ is an empire. She rides upon empires, kings, and powers of the world, and inspires, leads, and controls them; but she herself is not one of them, and is above all of them so that they court her, and are bewitched and governed by her—governed, not with the reins of empire, but with the lure of her fornication. This Woman is longer-lived than any one empire. We have seen that she bears the name of Babylon, and is not destroyed until the day of judgment. The seven imperial mountains on which she rides must therefore fill up the whole interval; or there was a time, and the most of her history, when she did not ride at all, which is not the fact. Seven is itself the number of fulness, which includes the whole of its kind. The reference here is to kings, to mountains of temporal dominion, to empires. It must therefore take in all of them. And when men once get over their "respectability," and rise to the height of range of the interpreting angel's view of things, they will have no difficulty in identifying the mountains, or the times to which they belong.

Of these seven regal mountains, John was told *"the five are fallen,"* dead, passed away, their day over; *"the one is,"* that is, was standing, at that moment, was then in sway and power; *"the other is not yet come, and when he shall come, he must continue a little time."* What regal mountain, then, was in power at the time John wrote? There can be no question on that point; it was the Roman empire. Thus, then, we ascertain and identify the sixth in the list, which shows what sort of *kings* the angel meant. Of the same class with this, and belonging to the same category, there are five others—five which had then already run their course and passed away. But what five imperial mountains like Rome had been and gone, up to that time? Is history so obscure as not to tell us with unmistakable certainty? Preceding Rome the world had but five great names or nationalities answering to imperial Rome, and those scarce a school-boy ought to miss. They are Greece, Persia, Babylon, Assyria, and Egypt; no more, and no less. And these all were imperial powers like Rome. Here, then, are six of these regal mountains; the seventh is not yet come. When it comes it is to endure but a short time. This implies that each of the others continues a long time; and so, again, could not mean the dictators, decemvirs, and military tribunes of the early history of Rome, for some of them lasted but a year or two. Thus, then, by the clearest, most direct, and most natural signification of the words of the record, we are brought to the identification of these seven mountain kings as the seven great world-powers, which stretch from the beginning of our present world to the end of it. Daniel makes the number less; but he started with his own times, and looked only down the stream. Here the account looks backward as well as forward. That which is first in Daniel is the third here, and that which is the sixth here is the fourth in Daniel. Only in the commencing point is there any difference. The visions of Daniel and the visions of John are from the same Divine Mind, and they perfectly harmonize, only that the latest are the amplest.

By these seven great powers then, filling up the whole interval of this world's history, this great Harlot is said to be carried. On these she rides, according to the vision. It is not upon one alone, nor upon any particular number of them, but upon all of them, the whole seven-headed Beast, that she sits. These seven powers, each and all, support the Woman as their joy and pride; and she accepts and uses them, and sways their administrations, and rides in glory by means of them. They are her devotees, lovers, and most humble servants; and she is their patronizing and most noble lady, with a mutuality of favours and inter-communion belonging to her designation. This is the picture as explained by the angel. But, to say that the Romish Papacy was thus carried, nurtured, and sustained by the ancient empires of

Greece, Persia, Babylon, Assyria, and Egypt, would be a great lie on history. It was not so. In the nature of things it could not be so. By no means then can this Harlot be the Papacy alone, as maintained by all *"respectable* interpreters." Furthermore, it is a matter of fact, that as surely as Rome in John's day, and Greece, Persia, Babylon, Assyria, and Egypt, before Rome, existed and bore sway on earth as regal mountains, so surely and conspicuously were they each and all ridden by this great Harlot. They were each and all the lovers, supporters, and defenders of organized falsehood in religion, the patrons of idolatry, the foster friends of all manner of spiritual harlotry. Nimrod, the hunter of the sons of men and author of despotic government, established his idolatrous inventions as the crown and glory of his empire, and intertwined the worship of idols with the standards of his power. It was the same with Egypt, whose colossal remains, unfading paintings, and mummy scrolls confirm the Scripture portraitures of her disgusting devotions, and tell how the priests of these abominations were honoured by the throne, of which they were the chief advisers. It was so with Assyria, as the recent exhumations of Nineveh abundantly attest. It was so with the Babylon of Nebuchadnezzar, as Daniel, who lived amid it all, has written. It was so with Persia, as her various records all declare. It was so with Greece, as her own most cherished poets sung, her mightiest orators proclaimed, and all her venerated artists and historians have set forth. It was so with Rome, as all her widespread monuments still show, and all the Christian testimonies, with her own, render clear and manifest as the sun. And it will be so with the last, which is yet to come, as declared in the apocalyptic foreshowings, and in all the prophecies in the Book of God upon the subject. It requires but a glance at history to see that spiritual harlotry has ever been the particular pet and delight of all the Beast-powers of time. If ever the worship and requirements of the true God won their respect and patronage, they soon corrupted it to their own selfish and ambitious ends, or never were easy until freed from the felt restraint.[8]

The final form of world government, symbolized by the eighth beast itself, is the world empire of the great tribulation time. The revived Roman Empire which will be in sway immediately after the rapture of the church is apparently indicated by the seventh head, while the beast, described in verse 11 as the eighth, is the world empire, which is destroyed by Jesus Christ at His second coming. In summation, what is described in verses 8 through 11 is the final form of Gentile world power in alliance with apostate religion symbolized by the harlot.

THE TEN HORNS OF THE BEAST (17:12-14)

17:12-14 And the ten horns which thou sawest are ten kings, which have received no kingdom as yet; but receive power as kings one hour with the beast. These have one mind, and shall give their power and strength unto the beast. These shall make war with the Lamb,

[8]Joseph A. Seiss, *The Apocalypse*, pp. 391–94.

and the Lamb shall overcome them: for he is Lord of lords, and King of kings: and they that are with him are called, and chosen, and faithful.

Further detail is given concerning the final stage of the world empire as having a nucleus of ten kings apparently joined in a confederacy represented by the ten horns. These kings in contrast to the seven heads of the beast are kings who rule not in succession but simultaneously at the end time. By comparison with chapter 13, it will be seen that this is the form of the Roman Empire just preceding the world empire. The ten horns' rule as kings is subject to that of the beast itself, and their sphere of power is brief. They are a phase of the transmission of power from the various kingdoms to that of the beast itself. This is shown by verse 13 where it is said that these have one mind and shall give their power and strength to the beast. They are further described as making war with the Lamb, a reference to the Lord Jesus Christ, and their ultimate subjugation under the Lamb is destined to be fulfilled at the second coming. A brief anticipation of this triumph is indicated in verse 14 where the Lamb is prophesied to overcome them as Lord of lords and King of kings. Those on the side of the Lamb are called, chosen and faithful.

THE EXPLANATION OF THE WATERS (17:15)

17:15 And he saith unto me, The waters which thou sawest, where the whore sitteth, are peoples, and multitudes, and nations, and tongues.

In the first verse of the chapter the harlot is seen sitting upon many waters. Here the description and the symbolic meaning of the waters are given as referring to people, multitudes, nations, and tongues. Generally speaking, when water is mentioned in Revelation, it should be taken literally. The fact that a symbolic meaning is specifically assigned to it here indicates that this is the exception to the usual rule. The situation described here is one of great political power on the part of the beast but a sharing of rule with the woman who controls the multitudes of the world.

THE DESTRUCTION OF THE WOMAN (17:16-18)

17:16-18 And the ten horns which thou sawest upon the beast, these shall hate the whore, and shall make her desolate and naked, and shall eat her flesh, and burn her with fire. For God hath put in their hearts to fulfil his will, and to agree, and give their kingdom unto the beast, until the words of God shall be fulfilled. And the woman which thou sawest is that great city, which reigneth over the kings of this earth.

Verse 16 reveals a most remarkable development in the vision which is also the climax and the purpose of the preceding description. Here the ten horns, previously seen as ten kings, destroy the woman riding the beast in a most graphic action. The best reading indicates that both the ten horns and the beast combine in this effort. The expression "upon the beast" is most accurately translated according to the better manuscripts "and the beast." The action of this verse is cast in the future tense which must be understood as future from John's point of view. The destruction of the harlot reduces all her pomp and gorgeous robes to naught. She is stripped of them, her flesh is eaten, and she is burned with fire. These graphic words clearly picture the downfall of the apostate world church of the future.

By comparison with other scriptures, the time of the event may be placed approximately at the midpoint of the seven years of Daniel's seventieth week, which leads up to and climaxes in the second coming of Christ. During the first half of the seven years, apostate Christendom flowers and establishes its power over all the world. During this period there is a measure of religious freedom as indicated by the fact that the Jews are allowed to worship and renew their sacrifices (Dan. 9:27). There may be widespread preaching of the gospel in this same period, as it would hardly seem possible to extend religious freedom to the Jews without doing the same for all. However, the triumph of the ecumenical movement is simultaneous with this final effort. All religions of the world, apart from the true faith in Christ, gather in one great world church. Only those who are truly saved, whose names are written in the Lamb's book of life and who know Jesus Christ as Saviour and Lord, seem to escape this movement toward unification. The climax of this series of events is seen in the early portion of chapter 17 where the woman in all her pomp and wickedness is riding the beast.

However, with the beginning of the second half of the week, the ruler of the revived Roman Empire, who is the political head of the world empire and is himself designated also as "the beast," is able to proclaim himself dictator of the whole world. In this capacity he no longer needs the help and power of the church. He therefore destroys the world church and substitutes for this ecclesiastical apostasy the final form of wickedness in the area of religion, the worship of himself. According to 13:8, all men shall worship the beast except true believers in Christ. Many find a parallel revelation in Daniel 11:36-39 where the willful king likewise puts aside all other deities in favor of the worship of himself.

The divine judgment inflicted upon apostate Christendom follows a pattern which can be observed in other judgments upon wicked nations and ungodly rulers. Ancient Babylon was used to bring affliction upon the people of Israel, as were also the governments of Assyria and Egypt. But in due time the same nations who inflicted divine judgment were themselves the objects of God's wrath. The principle involved is plainly stated in verse 17. Their action, though inspired by a blasphemous attempt to institute a world religion utterly contrary to divine revelation, nevertheless fulfills God's will that the kingdoms of the world should come under the domain of the beast in fulfillment of prophecy until the end of the age, indicated in the phrase "until the words of God shall be fulfilled." Thus the plan of the ages unfolds majestically, and Scripture indicates that God sovereignly permits the increment of wickedness until the cup of iniquity overflows.

At the close of the chapter, the woman is again identified with the great city which reigned over the kings of the earth, referring to the ecclesiastical power and control of the political which characterized portions of church history in the past and will have its climax in this future period. The "great city" is obviously a reference to Babylon in its religious rather than its historical significance. The influence of Babylon on Roman Christianity was partly responsible for the assumption by Rome of political power, namely, the authority of the church over the state. Just as ancient Babylon conquered kings in a political way, so its religious counterpart would dominate political states during the period of Roman papal power.

The interpretation that this is a reference to pagan political Rome as advanced by the historical school of interpretation or that it refers to a future literal city of Babylon is wrong. The city here according to verse 5 is a mystery, not a literal city. The entire context of chapter 17 supports this interpretation, distinguishing as it does between the city identified with the woman and the political power referred to as the beast and the ten horns.[9]

After the disposal of Babylon in its religious form by its destruction at the hands of the beast, the prophetic revelation in chapter 18 then deals with Babylon as a political force also destined for destruction at a later date.

[9]Cf. Alford, IV, 711–12.

18

THE FALL OF BABYLON

The Fall of Babylon Announced (18:1–3)

18:1-3 And after these things I saw another angel come down from heaven, having great power; and the earth was lightened with his glory. And he cried mightily with a strong voice, saying, Babylon the great is fallen, is fallen, and is become the habitation of devils, and the hold of every foul spirit, and a cage of every unclean and hateful bird. For all nations have drunk of the wine of the wrath of her fornication, and the kings of the earth have committed fornication with her, and the merchants of the earth are waxed rich through the abundance of her delicacies.

THE OPENING PHRASE of chapter 18, "after these things," marks a later revelation than that given in chapter 17. John declares, "I saw another angel come down from heaven." The phrase "another angel" makes clear that the angel of chapter 18 is a different angel from that of 17:1. Though the angel is described as "having great power; and the earth was lightened with his glory," it is evident that this is a literal angel and not a theophany, nor Christ in the form of an angel. The term "another" (Gr., *allon*) makes clear that this angel is the same in kind as the angel of 17:1. And the facts that the angel has great power and that the earth is lighted with the glory of the angel lead to the conclusion that the angel is delegated to do a great work on behalf of God. The announcement by the angel given in verses 2 and 3 declares that Babylon the great is fallen. The repetition of the verb "is fallen," found in the aorist tense, indicates a sudden event viewed as completed, though the context would indicate a future event. Seiss believes that the repetition of the phrase "is fallen" is intended to describe

> two separate parts or stages of the fall, answering to the two aspects in which Babylon is contemplated, referring first to Babylon in mystery, as *a system* or spirit of false worship, and second to Babylon as *a city*, in which this system or spirit is finally embodied.[1]

The announcement of chapter 18 coming so closely after the destruction of the harlot in chapter 17 has, however, raised a question as to whether the two are one and the same event.

[1]Joseph A. Seiss, *The Apocalypse*, p. 407.

There are a number of reasons for believing that chapter 18 is a subsequent event, though described in similar terms. The woman who is destroyed in chapter 17 is made desolate, naked, and burned with fire by the beast with the ten horns. From this it may be concluded that the destruction of the harlot in chapter 17 is the fall of Babylon in its ecclesiastical or religious sense and that it probably occurs when the beast assumes the role of God at the beginning of the great tribulation. The world church is destroyed in favor of a world religion honoring the political dictator, the beast out of the sea of chapter 13.

In chapter 18, the context seems to indicate that Babylon here is viewed in its political and economic character rather than in its religious aspect. The term "Babylon" in Scripture is more than a reference to the false religious system which stemmed from the false religion of ancient Babylon. Out of ancient Babylon also came the political power represented in Nebuchadnezzar and fulfilled in the first world empire. In some sense this is continued in the commercial system which came from both the religious and the political Babylons. It seems that chapter 17 deals with the religious aspect and chapter 18 with the political and economic aspects of Babylon.

According to verse 9 the kings of the earth as well as the merchants will mourn the passing of the Babylon of chapter 18. There is apparently no mourning connected with the destruction of the woman in chapter 17. The destruction of Babylon in chapter 18 should be compared with the preceding announcement in 16:19 where the great city is divided and the cities of the Gentiles fall. This event comes late in the great tribulation, just prior to the second coming of Christ, in contrast to the destruction of the harlot of chapter 17 which seems to precede the great tribulation and paves the way for the worship of the beast (13:8).

The downfall of the city of Babylon in 18:2 is followed by its becoming the habitation of demons, the "hold" or "prison" of every evil spirit, and the "cage," the same word in the Greek as "hold" (*phylakē*), of every unclean and hateful bird. The threefold description of the inhabitants of fallen Babylon is a reference to fallen angels in their various characteristics as demons and evil spirits, symbolized by the bird (cf. "birds," Isa. 34:11–15; Matt. 13:32). This abandonment of destroyed Babylon to demons is a divine judgment stemming from the utter wickedness of its inhabitants described in verse 3. Babylon in her political character has had evil relationships with "all nations" described as "fornication." In this, they have been led by the rulers, "the kings of the earth." The resulting evil association has made the merchants of the earth rich. Just as the church had grown rich in proportion as it had been wicked, so the nations have likewise prospered, as they have abandoned God and sought to accumulate wealth of this world. The wealth originally collected through the influence of the apostate church is taken over by the political system in the great tribulation which with universal political power is able to exploit to the full its accumulation of wealth.

A CALL TO SEPARATION FROM BABYLON (18:4-5)

18:4-5 And I heard another voice from heaven, saying, Come out of her, my people, that ye be not partakers of her sins, and that ye receive not of her plagues. For her sins have reached unto heaven, and God hath remembered her iniquities.

As John contemplates the announcement of the fall of Babylon, he hears another voice from heaven addressed to the people of God instructing them to come out of Babylon. In a similar way the people of God were urged to leave Babylon in ancient days (Jer. 51:45). Seiss explains the phrase "come out of her," citing Jeremiah 50:4-9 where the children of Israel are urged to "remove out of the midst of Babylon" (Jer. 50:8), and the command "Flee out of the midst of Babylon, and deliver every man his soul" (Jer. 51:6).[2] Alford compares the command to come out of Babylon to the warning to Lot to leave Sodom (Gen. 19:15-22).[3] The purpose of leaving Babylon is twofold: first, by separation from her they will not partake of her sin, and second, they will not have her plagues inflicted on them. The reference to plagues refers to the vials of chapter 16, especially the seventh vial which falls upon Babylon itself (16:17-21). This is further evidence that the event of chapter 18 is subsequent to the seventh vial and therefore in contrast to the destruction of the harlot in chapter 17.

In verse 5 the sins of Babylon are declared to reach to the heavens with the result that God remembers, that is, judges her iniquities (cf. Jer. 51:9). The fact that her sins have reached (Gr., *kollaō*, literally "glued" or "welded together," i.e., piled one on another as bricks in a building) unto heaven is an allusion to the tower of Babel which began the wicked career of ancient Babylon (Gen. 11:5-9). Though God permits the increment of sin, its ultimate divine judgment is inescapable.

THE INDICTMENT AGAINST BABYLON (18:6-8)

18:6-8 Reward her even as she rewarded you, and double unto her double according to her works: in the cup which she hath filled fill to her double. How much she hath glorified herself, and lived deliciously, so much torment and sorrow give her: for she saith in her heart, I sit a queen, and am no widow, and shall see no sorrow. Therefore shall her plagues come in one day, death, and mourning, and famine; and she shall be utterly burned with fire: for strong is the Lord God who judgeth her.

[2]*Ibid.*, p. 408.
[3]Henry Alford, *The Greek New Testament*, IV, 715.

In keeping with the enormity of her sin, the voice from heaven now calls on God to reward Babylon even as she rewarded the people of God. The verb (Gr., *apodidōmi*) means literally "to pay a debt" or "to give back that which is due." It is the law of retribution sometimes called *lex talionis*. Divine justice exacts the "eye for an eye" and the "tooth for a tooth."

The normal law of retribution, however, is here doubled in recognition of the enormity of the sin of Babylon. Accordingly the voice demands, "Double unto her double according to her works." In keeping with this principle, the cup of iniquity which Babylon filled is now to be filled twice with the measure of her judgment. There is no mercy for the utter apostasy found in Babylon in all her phases of operation. The verb (Gr., *kerannymi*) translated "fill" is literally "mix" or "mingle" as in the preparation of a drink. The same verb is used in 14:10 in connection with the wine of the wrath of God.

The same law of retribution is indicated in verse 7 where the standard of her judgment is compared to her luxurious living in which she was given to self-glorification. The expression "lived deliciously" (Gr., *estrē-niasen*) means "to be wanton" or "to revel" and comes from a word meaning "hardheaded" or "strong." Her willful sin against God is now to be rewarded with torment and sorrow. The "torment" (Gr., *basanis-mon*) refers to trial by torture with its resultant mental anguish and grief (Gr., *penthos*). Her wishful thinking in which she said, "I sit a queen, and am no widow, and shall see no sorrow" is going to be rewarded by sudden destruction from the Lord which according to verse 8 will come in one day in the form of plagues, death, mourning, and famine, resulting in her utter destruction by fire. Her vaunted strength is as nothing compared to the power of God. Like the church at Laodicea, her wealth has brought a sense of false security (3:17). Her claim to not being a widow has only the faulty foundation of her illicit love affairs with the kings of the earth (17:2). The fact that her judgment comes in one day, emphasized in the Greek by being placed first in the sentence, is reminiscent of the fall of Babylon in Daniel 5, which fell in the same hour that the finger traced its condemning words upon the wall. Before morning, the ancient power of Babylon has been destroyed. In a similar way, the rich fool of Luke 12:16–20 lost his barns and his soul in one night. When it is time for God's judgment, it descends with unwavering directness.

THE LAMENT OF THE KINGS OF THE EARTH (18:9-10)

18:9-10 And the kings of the earth, who have committed fornication and lived deliciously with her, shall bewail her, and lament for her, when they shall see the smoke of her burning, Standing afar off

for the fear of her torment, saying, Alas, alas, that great city Babylon,
that mighty city! for in one hour is thy judgment come.

The destruction of Babylon in its political and economic aspects described in the preceding verses is now the subject of a lament by the
kings of the earth. These kings are a wider designation than the ten
kings of 17:12, 16, who participated in the destruction of the harlot. Here
there is lament over the destruction of that which remained. The time is
the second coming of Christ at the end of the great tribulation. The very
kings who participated in the wickedness and wealth of Babylon now
mourn her passing, symbolized in the burning of the capital city. The
lament of the kings over Babylon is most emphatic in the Greek by the
repetition of the article: literally "the city the great, Babylon the city
the mighty." It was great in its extent of power and accomplishment and
mighty in the strength of its rule. In spite of its greatness and strength
(Gr., *megalē* and *ischyra*), it nevertheless falls in one hour.

Some believe that ancient Babylon is to be rebuilt as the capital of the
world empire in the great tribulation period and that Babylon in this
chapter refers to ancient Babylon rather than to Rome. According to
Isaiah 13:19–22, Babylon was to be completely destroyed and not inhabited. This seems also the teaching of Jeremiah 51:24–26, 61–64. It is
argued that ancient Babylon as a city was not destroyed for hundreds of
years after the fall of the empire and therefore these prophecies have not
been literally fulfilled.

The destruction of Babylon according to Jeremiah 51:8 was to be sudden. This is confirmed by Revelation 18:17–19. As far as the physical
city of Babylon was concerned, this was not true of ancient Babylon as
it continued for many years after its political downfall. Further, it is
pointed out that the prophecy of Isaiah 13:6, 9–11, which formed the
context of Isaiah 13:19–22, indicates that the destruction of Babylon
would be in the day of the Lord.[4] Hence, it is held that Babylon will be
rebuilt and then destroyed by Christ at His second coming.

Others identify Babylon as Rome, the seat of the apostate church as
described by the seven mountains of 17:9 and also the political city as
elsewhere described.[5] It is possible that Rome might be the ecclesiastical
capital and rebuilt Babylon the political and commercial capital. It is
also conceivable that Rome might be the capital in the first half of the
last seven years and Babylon in the second half—in the world empire
phase. Haldeman holds that Babylon will be rebuilt. He states, "Rome
will be the political, Babylon the commercial, capital of Antichrist's king-

[4]See the extended discussion presenting evidence for the futurity of the final judgments on Babylon in B. W. Newton, *Babylon and Egypt, Their Future History and
Doom*, pp. 1–30.
[5]Cf. previous discussion of Rev. 17:9–11; also cf. Seiss, pp. 397-415.

dom."[6] On the other hand Hoste observes, "I do not think there is any necessity that Babylon should be rebuilt, for another city has, as we see in this chapter, taken her place."[7]

Those who deny that Babylon will be rebuilt do so on the principle that the prophecy of destruction refers to ecclesiastical and political power symbolized in Babylon but not embodied in an actual city. The city of Babylon politically therefore is now destroyed historically. The power and religious character of Babylon are destroyed at the second coming. The ultimate decision depends upon the judgment of the expositor, but in many respects it is simpler to postulate a rebuilt Babylon as fulfilling literally the Old Testament prophecies as well as that embodied in this chapter.

Regardless of location, the burning of the city is a symbol of the fall of its political and economic might, and the kings of the earth marvel at the destruction of the seemingly infinite power of the capital of the world empire. The twofold lament involved in the words *bewail* and *lament* indicates to vocally lament (bewail) and to beat the breast (lament, Gr., *kopsontai*). Their vocal lament, "Alas, alas" (Gr., *ouai*) is probably better translated "Woe, woe" because it is much more emphatic than the English "alas." The word is mournful in both its sound and meaning and is reminiscent of the hopeless wailing of those who mourn the passing of loved ones. Their mourning is also characterized by fear lest they have the same judgment which has overcome the city, and for this reason they stand afar off. How sad is the hour of judgment when it is too late for mercy.

THE LAMENT OF THE MERCHANTS OF THE EARTH (18:11-19)

18:11-19 And the merchants of the earth shall weep and mourn over her; for no man buyeth their merchandise any more: The merchandise of gold, and silver, and precious stones, and of pearls, and fine linen, and purple, and silk, and scarlet, and all thyine wood, and all manner vessels of ivory, and all manner vessels of most precious wood, and of brass, and iron, and marble, And cinnamon, and odours, and ointments, and frankincense, and wine, and oil, and fine flour, and wheat, and beasts, and sheep, and horses, and chariots, and slaves, and souls of men. And the fruits that thy soul lusted after are departed from thee, and all things which were dainty and goodly are departed from thee, and thou shalt find them no more at all. The merchants of these things, which were made rich by her, shall stand afar off for the fear of her torment, weeping and wailing, And saying, Alas, alas that great city, that was clothed in fine linen, and purple, and scarlet, and decked with gold, and precious stones, and pearls! For in one hour so great riches is come to nought. And every ship-

[6]I. M. Haldeman, *A Synopsis of the Book of Revelation*, p. 21.
[7]William Hoste, *The Visions of John the Divine*, p. 129.

master, and all the company in ships, and sailors, and as many as trade
by sea, stood afar off, And cried when they saw the smoke of her
burning, saying, What city is like unto this great city! And they cast
dust on their heads, and cried, weeping and wailing, saying, Alas, alas
that great city, wherein were made rich all that had ships in the sea
by reason of her costliness! for in one hour is she made desolate.

The economic character of the city of Babylon is indicated in the fact
that the merchants also weep and mourn for her. Their grief is occasioned
by the loss of their trade with the city. The rich and varied character of
the merchandise is itemized in verses 12 and 13, beginning with precious
stones and costly metals characteristic of wealth and luxury. Next in
order are the fine fabrics used in their clothing, composed of fine linen
and silk in the luxurious colors of purple and scarlet. Precious stones,
versatile metals, and fine fabrics which constituted the wealth of the
ancient world are here itemized as the treasure of Babylon in the hour
of her destruction. The luxury of their apparel is matched by the rich
furnishings of their homes including articles of thyine and other precious
wood, ivory, brass, iron, and marble. Thyine was a fragrant wood corresponding to cypress and was used for expensive furniture in Roman
times along with other precious materials. The use of vessels made of
ivory, brass, iron, and marble as well as precious wood was symbolic of
the luxury and wealth of Babylon before its destruction.

In verse 13 expensive perfumes and spices are mentioned, such as cinnamon, unspecified odors (Gr., *amōmon*, from an odiferous shrub of
which an ointment was made, translated "spice" in the A.R.V.), and ointments (Gr., *myron*, an unguent made of an aromatic juice). Some manuscripts add "incense" between "odours" and "ointments" (Gr., *thymia-
mata*). The last luxury item to be listed is frankincense. All of these
could be afforded only by the wealthy. Next is mentioned the abundance
of foods, such as wine, oil, fine flour, wheat, cattle, and sheep. The word
beasts (Gr., *ktēnē*), used as a general word for property in the form of
animals, probably refers to cattle. Verse 13 closes with reference to the
means of transportation employed by the wealthy, namely, horses and
chariots, and finally, the slaves they possessed in body and soul. The
combined picture is one of complete abandonment to the wealth of this
world and total disregard of God who gave it.

Verse 14 tells of the sweeping removal of all these precious possessions
described as "the fruits that thy soul lusted after" and "all things which
were dainty and goodly." The inhabitants of Babylon addressed as "thou"
are no longer able to find these things. Like the kings of the earth who
stood afar off and watched the ascending smoke of the burning of Babylon,
so the merchants also shall fear to go near the city. Weeping and wailing,
that is, crying out loud and mourning, they also repeat their sad "alas"

(Gr., *ouai*). All the great riches of the city, described again as fine linen, purple and scarlet, gold, precious stones, and pearls, are brought to nothing.

Those in ships, apparently standing off from shore on the sea, witness the scene and join in the mourning as they see the smoke of the city ascending. They cry saying, "What city is like unto this great city!" In expression of their grief, they cast dust on their heads and join other merchants in weeping and wailing. For the third time in the passage, the mourning cry *"Ouai ouai"* is heard. Their mourning is not for the city, however, but because their wealth derived from trade in shipping is now at an end. Christ warned against coveting the wealth of this world when He said,

> Lay not up for yourselves treasures upon earth, where moth and rust doth corrupt, and where thieves break through and steal: But lay up for yourselves treasures in heaven, where neither moth nor rust doth corrupt, and where thieves do not break through nor steal: For where your treasure is, there will your heart be also (Matt. 6:19-21).

In contrast to the transitory wealth and glory of this world, which are here consumed by a great judgment from God, are the true riches of faith, devotion, and service for God laid up in heaven beyond the destructive hands of man and protected by the righteous power of God. The destruction of Babylon also ends the nefarious control of the souls of men mentioned last in the list of commodities in verse 13. No longer can ancient Babylon control the world religiously, politically, or economically.

REJOICING IN HEAVEN OVER THE FALL OF BABYLON (18:20)

18:20 Rejoice over her, thou heaven, and ye holy apostles and prophets; for God hath avenged you on her.

In contrast to the grief overtaking worldly rulers and merchants by the destruction of Babylon, those in heaven, who are mentioned later in 19:1, are called upon to rejoice at the righteous judgment of God. The address is to "the saints and the apostles and the prophets" rather than to the "holy apostles," with the article repeated each time. The expression "hath avenged" is literally "God hath judged your judgment on them," that is, "God hath inflicted your judgment on them," thus bringing to bear upon Babylon the righteous recompense for her martyrdom of the saints. It is another case where the righteous ultimately triumph as victory follows suffering.

THE UTTER DESTRUCTION OF BABYLON (18:21-24)

18:21-24 And a mighty angel took up a stone like a great millstone, and cast it into the sea, saying, Thus with violence shall that great city Babylon be thrown down, and shall be found no more at all. And the voice of harpers, and musicians, and of pipers, and trumpeters, shall be heard no more at all in thee; and no craftsman, of whatsoever craft he be, shall be found any more in thee; and the sound of a mill-stone shall be heard no more at all in thee; And the light of a candle shall shine no more at all in thee; and the voice of the bridegroom and of the bride shall be heard no more at all in thee: for thy merchants were the great men of the earth; for by thy sorceries were all nations deceived. And in her was found the blood of prophets, and of saints, and of all that were slain upon the earth.

John in his vision now sees a "mighty angel" (cf. 5:2; 10:1) throw a stone like a great millstone into the sea, portraying the violent downfall of the great city. A similar instance is found in Jeremiah 51:61–64. In this passage in Jeremiah, Seraiah, a prince who accompanied Zedekiah into Babylon, is instructed after reading the book of Jeremiah to bind a stone to it and cast it into the midst of the Euphrates with the words "Thus shall Babylon sink, and shall not rise from the evil that I will bring upon her: and they shall be weary." In the similar instance portrayed in Revelation, the millstone is cast into the sea instead of the Euphrates. The symbolism is the same. It represents the destruction of the great city, which like a stone cast into the sea will be found no more. The ultimate end of Babylon in all its forms will be accomplished by God's judgment at the end of the great tribulation. Babylon will be found "no more at all" (cf. vv. 14, 22–23). The expression occurs seven times with minor variations.

The angel now enlarges on the cessation of activity in this great city. That which characterized its life and featured its luxurious existence, such as the voices of harpers and musicians, of pipers and trumpeters, who added to the fanfare and public display of both the religious and political Babylon, is now silent. Similarly, the fine craftsmen who produced the ultimate in luxurious goods are no longer to be found. The sound of the millstone grinding out the grain is silent. In like manner, the light of the candle is now out, the city cold and dead, and no longer do its streets ring with the voices of the bridegroom and the bride. Of the nine different features mentioned, seven are described as "the voice" (Gr., *phōnē*, literally "sound") of harpers, musicians, pipers, trumpeters, millstone ("sound" same as "voice" in Greek), bridegroom, and bride. The very silence of the city is a testimony to God's devastating judgment.

Verses 23 and 24 provide another brief summary of the extent of Babylon's sins and greatness. Her merchants were "great men of the earth." All nations were deceived by Babylon's sorceries. Here too was the martyred blood of prophets and saints. The greatness that was the secret of her rise in power and influence makes her downfall all the more impressive. Babylon is declared to be guilty of the blood of prophets and saints, reference in part to the martyrs of the great tribulation.

There is an obvious parallel in the rise and fall of Babylon in its varied forms in Scripture. As introduced in Genesis 11:1-9, Babylon, historically symbolized by the tower reaching to heaven, proposed to maintain the union of the world through a common worship and a common tongue. God defeated this purpose by confusing the language and scattering the people. Babylon, ecclesiastically symbolized by the woman in Revelation 17, proposes a common worship and a common religion through uniting in a world church. This is destroyed by the beast in Revelation 17:16 who thus fulfills the will of God (Rev. 17:17). Babylon, politically symbolized by the great city of Revelation 18, attempts to achieve its domination of the world by a world common market and a world government. These are destroyed by Christ at His second coming (Rev. 19:11-21). The triumph of God is therefore witnessed historically in the scattering of the people and the unfinished tower of Genesis 11 and prophetically in the destruction of the world church by the killing of the harlot of Revelation 17 and in the destruction of the city of Revelation 18. With the graphic description of the fall of Babylon contained in chapters 17 and 18, the way is cleared for the presentation of the major theme of the book of Revelation, the second coming of Christ and the establishment of His glorious kingdom.

19

THE SECOND COMING OF CHRIST

THE ALLELUIA OF THE SAINTS IN HEAVEN (19:1-3)

19:1-3 And after these things I heard a great voice of much people in heaven, saying, Alleluia; Salvation, and glory, and honour, and power, unto the Lord our God: For true and righteous are his judgments: for he hath judged the great whore, which did corrupt the earth with her fornication, and hath avenged the blood of his servants at her hand. And again they said, Alleluia. And her smoke rose up for ever and ever.

IN RESPONSE to the invitation of 18:20, John next hears "a great voice of much people in heaven." The chronological relationship of these experiences is obvious, with the voice in heaven following the destruction of Babylon in all its forms. The time, therefore, must be just before the second coming of Christ. J. Vernon McGee mentions that chapter 19

> marks a dramatic change in the tone of Revelation. The destruction of Babylon, the capital of the Beast's kingdom, marks the end of the Great Tribulation. The somber gives way to song. The transfer is from darkness to light, from black to white, from dreary days of judgment to bright days of blessing. This chapter makes a definite bifurcation in Revelation, and ushers in the greatest event for this earth—the Second Coming of Christ. It is the bridge between the Great Tribulation and the Millennium.[1]

The reference to "much people" (Gr., *ochlou pollou*) is to the same group as in 7:9 where "a great multitude" is a translation of precisely the same Greek words. Though the general reference may be to all people in heaven, the allusion seems to be to the martyred dead of the great tribulation. This multitude is heard saying, "Alleluia." The English translation is a transliteration of the Greek word *allēlouia*, the Greek equivalent for *hallelujah*, the similar Hebrew word in the Old Testament. The four instances of "alleluia" in the New Testament are found in this chapter (vv. 1, 3, 4, 6). Luther Poellot points out that "Rev. 19:1-6 is the New Testament Hallelujah Chorus."[2] The saints here speak with a "loud voice" (cf. 7:10). In addition to the introductory alleluia they express

[1]*Reveling Through Revelation*, II, 66.
[2]*Revelation*, p. 240.

praise to the Lord in three great words: *salvation* (Gr., *sōtēria*), *glory* (Gr., *doxa*), and *power* (Gr., *dynamis*). A fourth word, *honor* (Gr., *timē*), is found in some texts between *glory* and *power* but omitted in others. *Power* is followed by *tou theou hēmōn* (genitive), literally "of our God." As Scott has expressed it, "The first of the three terms signified *deliverance,* the second God's *moral* glory in judgment, and the third His *might* displayed in the execution of the judgment upon the harlot."[3] The article occurs before each of the words: "the salvation, and the glory, and the power of our God."

The judgments of God upon Babylon are declared to be true and righteous (Gr., *alēthinai kai dikaiai*). God is praised for having judged the great harlot and having avenged the blood of His servants shed by her hand. The ascription of praise is followed by a second alleluia and the statement that the smoke of Babylon will continue to rise forever. This cannot refer to the city itself, but will be fulfilled by a perpetual judgment of the people who engaged in her wicked deeds. Thus is answered the appeal of the martyred saints in 6:10 for God's righteous judgment on those who shed their blood.

THE ALLELUIA OF THE TWENTY-FOUR ELDERS (19:4)

19:4 And the four and twenty elders and four beasts fell down and worshipped God that sat on the throne saying, Amen; Alleluia.

The twenty-four elders first introduced in chapter 4 along with the four living creatures then fall down and worship God and add their "Amen; Alleluia." The fact that the twenty-four elders and the four living creatures ("beasts") are introduced as worshiping God in a separate way from the great multitude seems to confirm the earlier suggestion that the great multitude are the martyred dead of the great tribulation who suffered immediately from the wickedness of Babylon in its form just prior to the second coming of Christ. If the twenty-four elders represent the church, they are witnesses of these events from heaven even though they have not participated in quite the same way.

THE FINAL ALLELUIA OF THE GREAT MULTITUDE (19:5-6)

19:5-6 And a voice came out of the throne, saying, Praise our God, all ye his servants, and ye that fear him, both small and great. And I heard as it were the voice of many waters, and as the voice of mighty thunderings, saying, Alleluia: for the Lord God omnipotent reigneth.

Joining the praise of the tribulation saints, the twenty-four elders, and the four beasts, a voice is now heard coming out of the throne calling upon the servants of God to praise the Lord. It is probable that this is a voice of an angel rather than the voice of God or the voice of the

[3]Walter Scott, *Exposition of the Revelation of Jesus Christ,* p. 375.

saints. The occasion for the praise of God is His judgment against wicked
men who have oppressed the people of God. The expression "his servants"
does not refer to a particular group such as the tribulation saints, as
J. B. Smith suggests,[4] but rather as the passage itself says, to "all ye
his servants." In other words, this is an occasion for every true servant of
God to praise the Lord. The following expression, "ye that fear him, both
small and great," is another descriptive phrase applying to the same
group. This seems to be supported by the Greek text which links the
phrases in apposition without a connective "and" as in the Authorized
Version. Hence it reads, "Keep on praising our God, all his servants who
fear him, small and great." The verb "praise" is in the present tense and
is therefore a command to "keep on praising" the Lord.

In antiphonal response to this call to praise, John hears the voice of
the great multitude, that is, the same as in verse 1, accompanied by the
majestic sound of many waters and mighty thunderings, saying for the
fourth time in this passage, "Alleluia: for the Lord God omnipotent
reigneth."

THE MARRIAGE SUPPER OF THE LAMB ANNOUNCED (19:7-8)

19:7-8 Let us be glad and rejoice, and give honour to him: for the
marriage of the Lamb is come, and his wife hath made herself ready.
And to her was granted that she should be arrayed in fine linen, clean
and white: for the fine linen is the righteousness of saints.

Continuing the praise of the Lord their God, the great multitude now
announce a major feature of the Lord's reign upon earth, namely, His
marriage to His bride. In verse 7, the great multitude express their joy
that the marriage of the Lamb has come and that His wife has made
herself ready. William R. Newell is certain that the marriage of the
Lamb occurs in heaven. He writes, "Where is the marriage, with its
attending marriage supper, celebrated? The answer can only be—in
heaven; for the scene is wholly heavenly. No one can read verse 6 without coming to this conclusion."[5] The text, of course, does not say where
the marriage takes place. It merely announces that the marriage of the
Lamb is come. This event is obviously subsequent to the destruction of
Babylon, but, if this occurs at the end of the great tribulation which is
immediately climaxed and succeeded by the second coming of Christ, the
more normal presumption would be that the supper would take place on
earth in connection with the second coming to the earth itself.

It is most significant and in keeping with the concept of a pretribulational rapture that those in the great multitude composed of tribulation
saints should thus regard the wife of the Lamb as an entity other than

[4]*A Revelation of Jesus Christ*, p. 260.
[5]*The Book of Revelation*, p. 295.

themselves. The word for "marriage" is the same as that translated in verse 9 "marriage supper" (Gr., *gamos*).

Though marriage customs varied in the ancient world, usually there were three major aspects: (1) The marriage contract was often consummated by the parents when the parties to the marriage were still children and not ready to assume adult responsibility. The payment of a suitable dowry was often a feature of the contract. When consummated, the contract meant that the couple were legally married. (2) At a later time when a couple had reached a suitable age, the second step in the wedding took place. This was a ceremony in which the bridegroom accompanied by his friends would go to the house of the bride and escort her to his home. This is the background of the parable of the virgins in Matthew 25:1-13. (3) Then the bridegroom would bring his bride to his home and the marriage supper, to which guests were invited, would take place. It was such a wedding feast that Christ attended at Cana as recorded in John 2:1-12.

The marriage symbolism is beautifully fulfilled in the relationship of Christ to His church. The wedding contract is consummated at the time the church is redeemed. Every true Christian is joined to Christ in a legal marriage. When Christ comes for His church at the rapture, the second phase of the wedding is fulfilled, namely, the Bridegroom goes to receive His bride. The third phase then follows, that is, the wedding feast. Here it is significant to note that the bride is already the wife of the Lamb, that is, the bridegroom has already come for His bride prior to His second coming described in 19:11-16. That which is here announced is not the wedding union but the wedding feast. This has been variously interpreted as relating to the wonderful fellowship in heaven following the rapture or to the millennium itself. Of primary importance at this point, however, is the order of events. The third phase of the wedding is about to take place, namely, the feast, which presumes the earlier rapture of the bride. The translation would be much improved in verse 7 if it would read "for the marriage feast of the Lamb is come."

Another problem of interpretation is the proper inclusion of the term "wife." In the biblical use of the figure of marriage, variations can be observed in both the Old and New Testaments. Frequently in the Old Testament, as for instance in the book of Hosea, Israel is described as the unfaithful wife of Jehovah to be restored to her position as a faithful wife in the future millennial reign. While marriage is often used as an illustration of various truths, the norm for the doctrine is that Israel is already married to Jehovah and has proved unfaithful to her responsibility as a wife. By contrast, in the New Testament the church is pictured as a virgin waiting for the coming of her bridegroom (II Cor. 11:2). In this case the wedding union is still future as well as the wedding feast. The dispensational distinction between the saints of the present age belonging to the church, the Body of Christ, and saints of other ages, such as those in the Old Testament or those in the future tribulation, therefore seems to be observed in this passage where the wife is distinguished from the great multitude identified in chapter 7 as martyrs out of the great tribulation. The "marriage of the Lamb" is properly the marriage supper of the Lamb, the final aspect of the marriage relationship between Christ and His church.

In verse 8 a beautiful picture is drawn of the holiness and righteousness of the church in that hour, for the bride is described as arrayed in "fine linen, clean and white." We are not left to imagine what this means, for the interpretation is given: "for the fine linen is the righteousness of saints." The word for "righteousness" (Gr., *dikaiōmata*) is the word for righteous deeds and is in the plural. The reference, therefore, seems to be not to justification by faith but rather to the righteousness wrought in the lives of the saints who comprise the wife of the Lamb. It seems that this is the sense of the unusual phrase "his wife hath made herself ready."

In Ephesians 5:26–27 Christ is said to be carrying on a present work with His church "that he might sanctify and cleanse it with the washing of water by the word" with a view to the future presentation in glory as stated in verse 27: "That he might present it to himself a glorious church, not having spot, or wrinkle, or any such thing; but that it should be holy and without blemish." The present work of sanctification of the church must be distinguished from justification. Justification by its nature is an act of God by which a believer is declared righteous, in contrast to sanctification, as in Ephesians 5:26, which is the work of God in the believer to bring his spiritual state up to the level of his position in Christ. The righteousness thus wrought in the life of the believer is pictured here as the fine linen which adorns the wife of the Lamb. Though even this righteousness is a product of the grace of God, it is distinguished as being related to human works, an experience, rather than to a divine fiat. The fine linen may, in some sense, be a part of the reward given at the judgment seat of Christ to those who have served the Lord, here seen collectively in the wife of the Lamb.

THE BLESSEDNESS OF THOSE CALLED TO THE MARRIAGE SUPPER
(19:9–10)

19:9-10 And he saith unto me, Write, Blessed are they which are called unto the marriage supper of the Lamb. And he saith unto me, These are the true sayings of God. And I fell at his feet to worship him. And he said unto me, See thou do it not: I am thy fellowservant, and of thy brethren that have the testimony of Jesus: worship God: for the testimony of Jesus is the spirit of prophecy.

Following the praise to the Lord and the announcement of the marriage of the Lamb by the multitude, John is now instructed to write that those who are invited to the marriage supper are truly blessed. In this verse, as in verses 7 and 8, the wife of the Lamb is distinguished from the attendants at the wedding, the wife apparently being the church, and the attendants at the wedding the saints of past and future ages. The unfounded notion that God treats all saints of all ages exactly alike is hard to displace in the theology of the church. The fact that the divine purpose is not the same for Israel, the Gentile believers, or the church of the present age is plainly written in the Word of God. Such distinctions, however, should not be made greater than they really are. God does not deal with Israel on the same plane as He does the Gentiles, nor does He deal with the church on the same plane as He does the Gentile saints or Israel. Each has its peculiar advantages and particular place in the divine program. Just as no two individuals have exactly the same destiny, so no two nations or groups in God's program are treated exactly alike. In all these relationships God is completely sovereign, righteous, and wise.

The angel speaking the words of verse 9 is apparently the same one who on other occasions has informed John that he should write (cf. 14:13, but contrast 21:5 where the command is from God). The beatitude here expressed, the fourth beatitude of the book, is enforced by the statement "These are the true sayings of God." While this fact is rather obvious in the context, its statement reinforces the sovereign character of this divine revelation. So awesome is the revelation that, according to verse 10, John falls at the feet of the angel in an attitude of worship. Such a reaction, however, is not appropriate for an angel, and John is rebuked with the statement that the one speaking is "thy fellowservant, and of thy brethren that have the testimony of Jesus." The word for "servant" (Gr., *syndoulos*) could be translated "fellow slave." It is most significant that not only men who are redeemed are by this token bond-slaves of Jesus Christ, but the angels also have a similar obligation of implicit obedience to the Lord. Together they form the body that bears testimony to Jesus. The command "Worship God" means that only God should be worshiped.

The concluding phrase of verse 10 is most significant: "the testimony of Jesus is the spirit of prophecy." This means that prophecy at its very heart is designed to unfold the beauty and loveliness of our Lord and Saviour Jesus Christ. In the present age, therefore, the Spirit of God is not only to glorify Christ but to show believers things to come as they relate to His person and majesty (cf. John 16:13–15). Christ is not only the major theme of the Scriptures but also the central theme of prophecy.

273

The statement introduces the passage which follows on the second coming of Christ in glory to the earth.

At this point in the book of Revelation the climax of the revelation is reached with the presentation of Jesus Christ as the glorified King of kings and Lord of lords. In keeping with the subject of the book itself, "a revelation of Jesus Christ," all which precedes Revelation 19:11 is in some sense introductory and that which follows is an epilogue.

The revelation of Jesus Christ presented in the book of Revelation is in contrast to the Christ of the Gospels where He is revealed in rejection, humiliation, suffering, and death. His return is to be one of triumph, glory, sovereignty, and majesty. This is anticipated in the judgment upon Babylon in chapters 17 and 18 and in the dramatic introduction of the second coming in 19:1–10. In many respects the scene which now follows, namely, the second coming of Christ, is not only the high point of the book of Revelation but in many respects the high point of all history. Here is the manifestation of the Son of God in glory, the demonstration of the sovereignty of God, and the beginning of the end of human rebellion. How poverty-stricken is any Christian theology which minimizes the second coming of Christ and how limited the Christian hope which does not include this glorious climax to God's announced program of exalting His Son and putting all creation under His control (cf. Ps. 2).

THE REVELATION OF THE KING OF KINGS (19:11–13)

19:11-13 And I saw heaven opened, and behold a white horse; and he that sat upon him was called Faithful and True, and in righteousness he doth judge and make war. His eyes were as a flame of fire, and on his head were many crowns; and he had a name written, that no man knew, but he himself. And he was clothed with a vesture dipped in blood: and his name is called The Word of God.

This passage contains one of the most graphic pictures of the second coming of Christ to be found anywhere in Scripture. Merrill C. Tenney describes the revelation of Christ in His second coming as following

the pattern of a Roman triumphal procession. When a general returned from a successful campaign, he and his legions were granted the right to parade up the Via Sacra, the main street of Rome that led from the Forum to the Temple of Jupiter on the Capitoline Hill. Mounted on a white horse, the general rode at the head of his troops, followed by the wagonloads of booty that he had taken from the conquered nation, and by the chained captives that were to be executed or sold in the slave markets of the city. The chief captives or rebels were remanded to the Mamertine Prison, where they were usually executed, while sacrifices of thanksgiving were offered in the temple.[6]

6*The Book of Revelation,* p. 94.

Even a casual study should make evident the remarkable contrast between this event and the rapture of the church. At the rapture Christ meets His own in the air, and there is no evidence of immediate judgment upon the earth. By contrast, Christ here is coming to the earth with the specific purpose of bringing divine judgment and establishing His righteous rule.

Many Scriptures in both the Old and New Testaments anticipate this scene. Zechariah 14:3-4 revealed the event in these words:

> Then shall the lord go forth, and fight against those nations, as when he fought in the day of battle. And his feet shall stand in that day upon the mount of Olives, which is before Jerusalem on the east, and the mount of Olives shall cleave in the midst thereof toward the east and toward the west, and there shall be a very great valley; and half of the mountain shall remove toward the north, and half of it toward the south.

According to Zechariah's prophecy, when Christ returns He will come to the Mount of Olives, the point of His departure on the occasion of His ascension into heaven recorded in Acts 1. His return to the Mount of Olives, however, will be dramatic, as the mountain will split in half in evidence of His power and authority. The Mount of Olives today has two high points, and what seems to be a natural division between them will be transformed into a great valley stretching toward the east from Jerusalem and extending down to Jericho at the Jordan River. No such event will take place at the rapture of the church.

The second coming of Christ is likewise described in Matthew 24:27–31:

> For as the lightning cometh out of the east, and shineth even unto the west; so shall also the coming of the Son of man be. For wheresoever the carcase is, there will the eagles be gathered together. Immediately after the tribulation of those days shall the sun be darkened, and the moon shall not give her light, and the stars shall fall from heaven, and the powers of the heavens shall be shaken: And then shall appear the sign of the Son of man in heaven: and then shall all the tribes of the earth mourn, and they shall see the Son of man coming in the clouds of heaven with power and great glory. And he shall send his angels with a great sound of a trumpet, and they shall gather together his elect from the four winds, from one end of heaven to the other.

As is made clear in these prophecies, the second coming of Christ will be a glorious event which all the world will behold, both believers and unbelievers. It is compared to lightning that shines from the east to the west, in other words, illuminating the whole heaven. The second coming will be preceded by the sun being darkened and the moon not giving her light, stars falling from heaven, and other phenomena not only mentioned in Matthew 24 but vividly revealed in the Revelation. The climax to all these events will be the return of Christ Himself in the clouds of heaven with power and great glory and accompanied by the saints. The final revelation of this event is found in Revelation 19.

The dramatic presentation of this awe-inspiring scene is introduced by John's statement "I saw heaven opened." In the vision he beholds a person who can be no other than the Lord Jesus Christ on a white horse. In contrast to the pseudo ruler of the world (6:2), Christ is presented here as the true ruler. The plea of Isaiah as recorded in 64:1-2 is now fulfilled:

> Oh that thou wouldest rend the heavens, that thou wouldest come down, that the mountains might flow down at thy presence, As when the melting fire burneth, the fire causeth the waters to boil, to make thy name known to thine adversaries, that the nations may tremble at thy presence!

The opening of the heavens is dramatic in itself and to this is added the symbolism of a rider on a white horse drawn from the custom of conquerors riding on a white horse as a sign of victory or triumph. The rider on the white horse in Revelation 6 is described as one who "went forth conquering, and to conquer." Now the true King of kings and Lord of lords is going to triumph over those who blasphemously assumed control over the world. The titles given here to Christ are in keeping with the divine judgment which follows. He is declared to be faithful and true, and to judge and make war in righteousness. This is to be the demonstration of the sovereignty and righteousness of God even as Christ in His first coming demonstrated grace and truth. The titles here ascribed to Christ are previously given in Revelation 1:5 and 3:7, and were anticipated in the prophecies of Isaiah 11:3-4.

H. A. Ironside points out the significance of the three names given to Christ:

> "A Name written that no man knew but He Himself" speaks of His essential glory as the Eternal Son, concerning which He declared that "no man knoweth the Son but the Father." . . . The second name is "The Word of God." [The third title is] "KING OF KINGS AND LORD OF LORDS." In these three names we have set forth, first, our Lord's dignity as the Eternal Son. Second, His incarnation—the Word became flesh. And, lastly, His second advent to reign as King of kings and Lord of lords.[7]

These attributes are demonstrated in the appearance of Christ as described in the following verses. In verse 12 His eyes are as a flame of fire, a term previously used to describe Christ in 1:14 and 2:18. This

---

[7]*Lectures on Revelation,* pp. 326-27.

speaks of His righteous judgment upon sin. His head is crowned with many crowns, or diadems, the symbol of sovereignty. He possesses a name which no man knows, as yet unrevealed. His vesture is declared to be "dipped in blood," as if anticipating the bloodshed to come (cf. Isa. 63:2–3; Rev. 14:20). Christ as the slain Lamb in Revelation speaks of redemption by blood; here blood represents divine judgment upon wicked men. The name given to Christ in verse 13 is "The Word of God" (Gr., *ho logos tou theou*). The Word of God, who according to John 1:1–3 is the Creator, is here also the Judge of man.

THE COMING OF THE KING OF KINGS (19:14–16)

19:14-16 And the armies which were in heaven followed him upon white horses, clothed in fine linen, white and clean. And out of his mouth goeth a sharp sword, that with it he should smite the nations: and he shall rule them with a rod of iron: and he treadeth the wine-press of the fierceness and wrath of Almighty God. And he hath on his vesture and on his thigh a name written, KING OF KINGS, AND LORD OF LORDS.

Accompanying Christ on His second coming are those described as "the armies which were in heaven." Some, such as J. B. Smith, have limited this army to the church, the Bride of Christ, on the basis that it is described as clothed in fine linen, white and clean.[8] There is, however, no reason to limit this to the church, though the church is arrayed in fine linen. The church is not alone in having righteousness in the form of righteous deeds, and it is more probable that here not only the saints but also the holy angels are meant. It is well not to impose limitations upon a Scripture text which are not implicit in the text itself. The spectacle, however, of Christ on a white horse with a vesture dipped in blood accompanied by innumerable heavenly beings clothed in fine linen is a demonstration that now at long last the filthy, blasphemous situation in earth is going to be wiped clean with a divine judgment of tremendous character.

A further description is given of Christ, adding to the picture of divine judgment. Out of His mouth goes a sharp sword, which according to the text will be used to smite the nations and bring them under His rule. The word for "sword" (Gr., *hromphaia*) indicates a long Thracian sword or one unusually large and longer than most swords. The same word is sometimes used to describe a javelin, a sword sufficiently light and long to be thrown as a spear. Here the word is used symbolically to represent a sharp instrument of war with which Christ will smite the nations and establish His absolute rule. The expression of ruling "with a rod of iron" is also found in Psalm 2:9 and Revelation 2:27, with a similar expression,

[8]Smith, p. 264.

"the rod of his mouth," in Isaiah 11:4. It represents unyielding, absolute government under which men are required to conform to the righteous standards of God.

The divine act of judgment is also described in the latter part of verse 15 in the words "he treadeth the winepress of the fierceness and wrath of Almighty God." This is another view of divine judgment portrayed in a similar way in 14:19-20 and anticipated in Isaiah 63:1-6. All of these passages point to the sad conclusion that in the day of judgment it is too late for men to expect the mercy of God. There is nothing more inflexible than divine judgment where grace has been spurned. The scene of awful judgment which comes from this background is in flat contradiction of the modern point of view that God is dominated entirely by His attribute of love.

The concluding description of Christ reveals that on His vesture, previously described as dipped in blood, and also on His thigh a name is written, "KING OF KINGS, AND LORD OF LORDS." Here at last has come One who has a right to rule the earth, One whose power and majesty will demonstrate His authority as He brings to bear His sovereign judgment on a wicked world. It is in anticipation of this ultimate triumph that God the Father holds the nations of the world in derision in their rebellion against the Lord's Anointed (Ps. 2:1-4). God will indeed break the nations with a rod of iron and dash them in pieces and give the uttermost parts of the earth to His Son as His rightful possession. In view of this consummation, how pertinent is the invitation of Psalm 2:10-12 to serve the Lord and kiss the Son while there is yet time to claim the blessing of those who put their trust in Him.

THE BATTLE OF THE GREAT DAY OF GOD ALMIGHTY (19:17-19)

19:17-19 And I saw an angel standing in the sun; and he cried with a loud voice, saying to all the fowls that fly in the midst of heaven, Come and gather yourselves together unto the supper of the great God; That ye may eat the flesh of kings, and the flesh of captains, and the flesh of mighty men, and the flesh of horses, and of them that sit on them, and the flesh of all men, both free and bond, both small and great. And I saw the beast, and the kings of the earth, and their armies, gathered together to make war against him that sat on the horse, and against his army.

Following the vision of Jesus Christ and His return to earth, the Apostle John sees an angel standing in the sun. Though some have taken this as a very unusual phenomenon, the most natural explanation is that the angel is standing in the light of the sun with the angel himself possibly shining with even greater brilliance. The image is one of brilliant light speaking of the glory of God. The angel John sees cries with a

278

loud voice, signifying something important as impending (cf. 6:10; 7:2, 10; 10:3; 14:15; 18:2). The message of the angel is addressed to the fowls that fly in the midst of the heaven, literally "in mid-heaven" (Gr., *en mesouranēmati*). The birds thus addressed are invited to gather themselves to the supper of the great God. The contrast to this is found in 19:9 where the saints other than the church are invited to the marriage supper of the Lamb. The word for "supper" (Gr., *deipnon*), referring to the principal meal of the day, is the same word used in both verses, but the events are in sharp contrast. The birds are invited in verse 18 to eat the flesh of those killed in the battle, that is, the army of the beast. The various classes of men are described in detail as kings, captains, mighty men, including both free and bond, small and great. Even the horses of these men are mentioned. The divine judgment upon the wicked is no respecter of persons or station, and is the great equalizer of all.

There is an evident parallel in this passage to the prediction of Ezekiel 39:17–20 as far as the description is concerned. However, the Ezekiel passage seems to refer to an earlier battle, when the army from the North invaded Israel, whereas in this battle God is contending with the armies of the entire world. The resultant destruction of human flesh and the consumption of it by birds are similar. The actual parallel to the scene in Revelation is found in Matthew 24:28, where reference is made to the carcasses of those who fall in battle and the gathering of the birds to eat them. Care must be exercised in interpreting passages so similar by following the rule that similarities do not necessarily prove identity. Birds of prey are always in evidence where there is death.

The destruction of the armies of the beast, however, is the prelude to the destruction of the beast himself and his associates. John in his vision sees not only the carnage but also the beast, referring to the world ruler, the kings of the earth associated with him, and their armies, all of whom gather to make war against Christ and His army from heaven. The beast is to be identified with the one of Revelation 13:1–10, and the kings with the ten kings immediately associated with the beast as well as others who participate in this final battle. There is some evidence that a struggle is going on between the various segments of the world empire at the time of the second coming of Christ; but with the appearance of the Lord in glory and the procession of the armies of heaven accompanying Him, these armies of earth forget their differences and join in battle against the King of kings and Lord of lords.

THE DOOM OF THE BEAST AND THE FALSE PROPHET (19:20)

19:20 And the beast was taken, and with him the false prophet that wrought miracles before him, with which he deceived them that had received the mark of the beast, and them that worshiped his image. These both were cast alive into the lake of fire burning with brimstone.

The consummation of the battle with victory for Christ and the armies of heaven is described in verse 20. The beast of Revelation 13:1–10 is taken and with him the false prophet, the second beast of Revelation 13:11–16. The false prophet is identified as the one who wrought miracles and deceived them that received the mark of the image (cf. 13:12–15). The doom of the beast and the false prophet culminates in their being cast alive into the lake of fire burning with brimstone. The lake of fire thus introduced is mentioned again in 20:15. By comparison with other scriptures, it seems that the beast and the false prophet are the first to inhabit the lake of fire. Unsaved who die prior to this time are cast into Hades, a place of torment, but not into the lake of fire, which is reserved for those who have been finally judged as unworthy of eternal life.

Alford observes: "These only, and not the Lord's human enemies yet, are cast into eternal punishment. The latter await the final judgment, ch. xx 11 ff."[9] These who were Satan's masterpieces precede Satan himself to this final place of everlasting punishment into which he is cast a thousand years later (20:10). The rest of the wicked dead after being judged at the great white throne will follow the beast, the false prophet, and the devil into this eternal doom.

Ironside comments on the capture of the beast and the false prophet in these words:

Two men, be it noted, are taken alive. They are the two arch-conspirators who have bulked so largely in this book—the beast and the false prophet, the civil and religious leaders of the last league of nations, which will be Satan-inspired in its origin and Satan-directed until its doom. These two men are "cast alive into the lake burning with fire and brimstone," where a thousand years later they are still said to be "suffering the vengeance of eternal fire," thus incidentally proving that the lake of fire is not annihilation, and that it is not purgatorial either, for it neither annihilates nor purifies these two fallen foes of God and man after a thousand years under judgment.[10]

THE DOOM OF THE ARMY OF THE BEAST (19:21)

19:21 And the remnant were slain with the sword of him that sat upon the horse, which sword proceeded out of his mouth: and all the fowls were filled with their flesh.

In bringing to conclusion the battle of the great day of God Almighty, those not killed in the first stage of the conflict and in the capture of the

[9]Henry Alford, *The Greek New Testament*, IV, 730.
[10]Ironside, p. 330.

beast and the false prophet are now put to death. The evidence seems to be that the entire army of the wicked are killed. According to verse 21, "the remnant," that is, the rest, are slain by the sword of Christ, the one mentioned as proceeding out of His mouth (19:15). This act of judgment seems to be exercised by the immediate power of Christ rather than by the armies which accompany Him. There is no evidence that the armies of earth prevail in any sense against the armies of heaven, but there is total defeat of man at the height of his satanic power when brought into conflict with the omnipotence of God. The chapter concludes with a graphic note that all the fowls were filled with their flesh. Such is the abundance of the dead that the fowls are satiated as they consume the fruits of the battle.

The Word of God makes plain that God so loved the world that He gave His Son, and that all who avail themselves of the grace of God are immeasurably blessed in time and eternity. On the other hand, the same Word of God states plainly that those who spurn God's mercy must experience His judgment without mercy. How foolish it is to rest in the portions of the Word of God that speak of the love of God and reject the portions that deal with His righteous judgment. The present age reveals the grace of God and suspended judgment. The age to come, while continuing to be a revelation of the grace of God, will give conclusive evidence that God brings every evil work into judgment and that those who spurn His grace must experience His wrath.

20

THE REIGN OF CHRIST

THIS IS ONE of the great chapters of the Bible. It presents in summary the tremendous series of events which relate to the millennial reign of Christ on earth. In this future period of one thousand years, many expositors believe that hundreds of Old Testament prophecies will be fulfilled, such as that of Jeremiah 23:5-6:

> Behold, the days come, saith the LORD, that I will raise unto David a righteous Branch, and a King shall reign and prosper, and shall execute judgment and justice in the earth. In his days Judah shall be saved, and Israel shall dwell safely: and this is his name whereby he shall be called, THE LORD OUR RIGHTEOUSNESS.

A bewildering array of diverse interpretations greets the student of this passage. Generally speaking, however, expositions fall into a number of principal categories.

E. B. Elliott points out that there have been four explanations of this millennial passage: (1) the literal and premillennial interpretation followed by Papias, Justin Martyr, Irenaeus, and Tertullian. This holds to a literal period of a thousand years preceded and followed by resurrection and judgment. (2) The amillennial view that the resurrection is spiritual, that is, the new birth, and the millennium began with the first coming of Christ, a view popularized by Augustine. (3) The view of Grotius and Hammond that the resurrection referred to the revival of the church beginning at the time of Constantine when paganism was overthrown. (4) The postmillennial idea introduced by Whitby and advocated by Vitringa which understands the resurrection

> to signify a resurrection of the principles, doctrine, spirit, and character of the Christian martyrs and saints departed: being thus one in part *spiritual*, in part *ecclesiastical*, and indeed in part too national; inasmuch as it is supposed that the Jews will be then nationally restored, as well as converted, to take a share of it.[1]

Elliott much prefers the postmillennial view, that of Whitby, and argues his case for it at length. As Elliott notes, the most important divisions arise from the interpretation of the thousand years, and the three major views are: the premillennial, amillennial, and postmillennial inter-

---

[1] E. B. Elliott, *Horae Apocalypticae*, IV, 180; cf. 175-219.

pretations. Each of these, however, has many variations and subdivisions which need to be understood in a proper interpretation of Revelation 20.

Premillennial interpretation. All premillennial interpreters consider the second advent of Christ as preceding His thousand-year reign on the earth. They differ, however, in their interpretation of preceding passages in the book of Revelation as well as in their concept of the millennium itself. Three important types of premillennialism can be observed:

1. Premillenarians of the historical school tend to interpret Revelation 6 through 19 as largely fulfilled in history but hold that chapter 20 and following are future and are to be interpreted somewhat literally. An illustration of this form of premillennialism is found in E. H. Horne who believes that symbolism to a large extent ceases in chapter 20 and specific prophecy is given. Horne states:

> The symbolic language in which previous chapters have been written is here dropped, and certain predictions are made in plain words, though they contain allusions to the Dragon and the Beast, which are symbolic figures. The meaning of the Dragon is *here* so carefully explained, as "the old serpent, which is the Devil and Satan," that all of symbolism is removed: and the Beast is only indirectly referred to at all. The change in style is no doubt due to the change of subject; though the predictions found in this chapter relate to the consequences of the Second Advent, and that event will remove all need of concealment of things future.[2]

Horne's position is that all the prophecies of Revelation are future from John's point of view but that much of the material through chapter 18 has already been largely fulfilled and will be climaxed with the second coming of Christ and a literal millennium.

2. A second form of premillennialism emphasizes the soteriological character of the millennium. This point of view is usually advocated by covenant theologians who are premillennial and by others such as George Ladd in his work *Jesus and the Kingdom*. The millennium is considered by them as primarily an aspect of God's soteriological program, and the political character of the kingdom and the prominence of the nation Israel are subordinated. For this reason, some like Ladd attempt a synthesis of the amillennial and premillennial points of view by finding some prophecies relating to the future kingdom as being fulfilled in the present age.

3. The most popular form of premillennialism in the twentieth century is supported by premillenarians who consider the millennium an aspect of God's theocratic program, a fulfillment of the promise given to David that his kingdom and throne would continue forever over the house of Israel. Advocates of this position include many twentieth century premillennial scholars such as Lewis Sperry Chafer, Alva McClain, Charles

[2]Edward H. Horne, *The Meaning of the Apocalypse*, pp. 283–84.

Feinberg, Charles Ryrie, Wilbur Smith, and Merrill Unger, and many popular writers and Bible teachers such as C. I. Scofield, A. C. Gaebelein, H. A. Ironside, William Pettingill, and numerous others. Advocates of this view hold that the millennium is a period in which Christ will literally reign on earth as its supreme political leader and that the many promises of the Old Testament relating to a kingdom on earth in which Israel will be prominent and Gentiles will be blessed will have complete and literal fulfillment. Because the distinctive character of this millennial reign of Christ is maintained in contrast to the present age, this view is sometimes designated as the dispensational interpretation. In the interpretation of the book of Revelation, they consider all material 'from 4:1 on as future, and are often named futurists. See note at 4:1.

Amillennial interpretation. The amillennial interpretation is essentially a denial that there will be a millennial reign of Christ after His second advent. It is amillennial or nonmillennial because it denies such a literal reign of Christ on earth. Although there is a great variety of amillennial interpretations, adherents of this view also form several subdivisions.

1. The historic Augustinian form of amillennialism is based on Augustine's work *The City of God.*[3] In his discussion of the millennium, Augustine advanced the theory that the thousand years fall in the interadvent period and will terminate with the second advent. Because this denied a future millennium after the second advent, his interpretation has in modern times been called amillennial.

Augustine was an advocate of the view, common in his day, that human history would be completed in 6,000 years. Unlike some early premillenarians who held the same point of view but believed that the millennium would be the seventh millennium of history, Augustine felt that the seventh millennium was the eternal state. As Augustine followed what is known as the septuagint chronology which began the sixth millennium several centuries before Christ, he considered that the final millennium was well along at the time of his writing. Augustine tended to interpret the one thousand years as literal, but he was not emphatic on this point and left the question somewhat open. In order to accommodate his point of view to Revelation 20, he held that "the first resurrection" is a spiritual resurrection which occurs when a person is regenerated by faith in Christ, while the second resurrection described in Revelation 20 occurs at the time of the second advent. Augustinian amillennialism is very important because most schools of thought which oppose premillennialism are derived in some measure from Augustinian theology. Many modern scholars hold with some minor variations to Augustinian amillennialism.

Harry Buis, an amillenarian belonging to the preterist school of inter-

[3]Augustine, *The City of God, The Fathers of the Church,* translated by Gerald G. Walsh and Grace Monahan (New York: Fathers of the Church, Inc., 1952).

pretation, believes that the thousand years of the millennium describe the period between the first and second advents of Christ. His reasons for holding this position are typical of the amillennial position:

> 1. No other passage of Scripture mentions such a thousand-year period. Obscure passages are to be interpreted in the light of less obscure passages, and not vice versa. 2. The entire book is one filled with symbolism; therefore any doctrine based on insisting upon a literal thousand-year period is building on a weak foundation. 3. The amillennial position agrees most fully with the interpretation that the primary application of the beast was the Roman Empire. 4. The creeds of the church such as the Apostles' Creed make no mention of such a literal period between this age and the eternal kingdom. The greatest Bible scholars of all times, the Reformers, were not premillenarian.[4]

Premillenarians usually have objected to this type of argument as being inconclusive. The six mentions of "a thousand years" in the passage are sufficient to establish the doctrine as scriptural. In general the premillennial answer to arguments of this kind is that they do not have sufficient weight to alter the ordinary meaning of the passage.

Another well-known advocate of Augustinian amillenarianism is Abraham Kuyper who, in attempting to demonstrate the untenability of the premillennial interpretation of Revelation 20, nevertheless makes this confession:

> In every other writing the construction of the first ten verses of chapter 20 would require a literal interpretation, but as in Revelation the idea "thousand" is *never* taken literally, and also here merely expresses the exceeding fulness of the divine action, the precise, literal and historical understanding can not be imputed to God, and the exegete is duty bound to interpret what as Divine language comes to us according to the claim of the exegesis that is adaptable to it.[5]

What Kuyper overlooks, of course, is that the term "thousand" is never used alone anywhere else in the book of Revelation. Where it is used in combination with numbers, as the 12,000 of each tribe of Israel, there is no proof whatever that other than the literal sense is intended, and this is also true in the entire New Testament.

Lenski also follows traditional Augustinianism when he states, "These 1,000 years thus extend from the incarnation and the enthronement of the Son (12, 5) to Satan's final plunge into hell (20, 10), which is the entire New Testament period."[6]

Typical of the Roman Catholic interpretation of the millennium is that by R. J. Loenertz, who makes the millennium the present age between

[4]*The Book of Revelation,* 107–8.
[5]*The Revelation of St. John,* p. 277.
[6]R. C. H. Lenski, *The Interpretation of St. John's Revelation,* pp. 568–69.

the two advents and makes the millennium equal to the three and one-half years of the great tribulation. The period when the two witnesses of Revelation 11 lie dead in the streets of Jerusalem for three and one-half days is made equivalent to the period when Satan is loosed at the end of the millennium. The contemporary Roman Catholic interpretation is an extension of the Augustinian amillennialism which equates the millennium with the present age.[7]

2. A modified Augustinian interpretation of the millennium is probably the most popular amillennial viewpoint today. Advocates include capable twentieth century scholars such as Louis Berkhof, William Hendriksen, Oswald Allis, Floyd Hamilton, Gerhardus Vos, and many others. Like Augustine, they believe that Revelation 20 parallels the earlier chapters of the book of Revelation and constitutes a recapitulation. Unlike Augustine, however, they believe the millennium refers to the saints reigning in heaven with Christ. In contrast to Augustine, they do not make any attempt to make the thousand years a literal period. As this was made impossible after A.D. 1000 had come to pass, their "millennium" accordingly runs from the death of Christ to His second coming. The binding of Satan is considered to be partial, consisting in Christ's triumph over him, first in His temptations and later in every triumph which stems from Christ. The first resurrection occurs when the Christian's soul is taken from earth to heaven at his death. The second resurrection relates to the resurrection of all men.

A variation of this point of view is found in B. B. Warfield who to some extent follows an earlier suggestion of Duesterdieck and Kliefoth that the millennium is the intermediate state.[8] In contrast to Hendriksen, however, Warfield is more optimistic, hence is usually classified as a postmillenarian. His interpretation of Revelation 20, however, is very similar to Hendriksen's. Robert Culver comments on Warfield's view:

> While his theories are ingenius, they are not convincing. I know of no prominent writer who has heartily endorsed and adopted his views of Revelation 20. . . . Except that his view was expressed by a noted scholar, whose expositions in Christian doctrine and some other areas are justly famous, it is doubtful that his view of the Millennium would have made an impression on the Christian public.[9]

Still another variation within modern amillennialism is the form of preterist interpretation advanced by H. B. Swete in *The Apocalypse of Saint John* in which he follows the earlier suggestion of Grotius and Hammond that the millennium started with the triumph of Christianity at

---

[7]R. J. Loenertz, *The Apocalypse of Saint John*, pp. 130–33.
[8]B. B. Warfield, *Biblical Doctrines*, pp. 643-64.
[9]*Daniel and the Latter Days*, p. 202.

the time of Constantine when Christianity began to be a major force in opposing paganism. This view, also advanced by Albertus Pieters, combines various views of amillennialism, premillennialism, and postmillennialism. Like the amillennialists, these men view the millennium as being in the present age and of indeterminate length, following Augustine in this. Like postmillennialism, amillennialism is optimistic in viewing the church as moving triumphantly to victory. Like premillennialism, it recognizes the continuity of chapters 19 and 20 of Revelation in that the binding of Satan, the first resurrection, and the thousand years are chronologically subsequent to chapter 19. Amillennialism recognizes also that the destruction of the beast is the downfall of Rome as a pagan power. Swete states, "St. John has in view the moment of the overthrow of the Beast and the False Prophet, i.e., the final breakup of the Roman world-power and its ally, the pagan system of priestcraft and superstition."[10] Swete describes the millennium as "the age of the Martyrs, however long it might last," and continues that this period "would be followed by a far longer period of Christian supremacy during which the faith for which the Martyrs died would live and reign."[11] Swete declares that this "is the essential teaching of the present vision."[12] The millennium will conclude with the war of Gog and Magog which Swete considers the climax of the present age.

3. The interpretation that the millennium is purely a descriptive term is followed by still other amillenarians. Milligan, for instance, believes that the millennium does not indicate any time period at all.

> The fundamental principle to be kept clearly and resolutely in view is this, that the thousand years express no period of time. Like so many other expressions of the Apocalypse, their real meaning is different from their apparent meaning. They are not to be taken literally. They embody an idea; and that idea, whether applied to the subjugation of Satan or to the triumph of the saints, is the idea of *completeness*. Satan is bound for a thousand years— i.e., he is completely bound. The saints reign for a thousand years—i.e., they are introduced into a state of perfect and glorious victory.[13]

C. Anderson Scott expresses hearty agreement with Milligan that the thousand years express no period of time at all but rather simply an idea that Satan is completely bound.[14]

William Bruce expresses the opposition to a literal interpretation of the millennium of all expositors who consider Revelation as purely descriptive rather than predictive:

[10]Henry B. Swete, *The Apocalypse of St. John*, p. 266.
[11]*Ibid.*
[12]*Ibid.*
[13]William Milligan, *Lectures on the Apocalypse*, p. 211.
[14]*The Book of the Revelation*, pp. 295–96.

> The theory of a personal reign of Christ upon earth, with the risen saints for His subjects, is founded on a literal apprehension of a prophecy that was never intended to be literally understood, and which is impossible to be literally fulfilled.[15]

Like most others who adopt a descriptive interpretation of Revelation, Bruce considers it self-evident that literal prediction is impossible as well as literal fulfillment.

Ames, in keeping with his view that the millennium is the present age and not of exact duration, holds as a normal principle that in the entire book of Revelation "numbers are taken as symbols of epics, not as a measurement of duration."[16] On the contrary, it may be observed that while numbers have symbolic value, there is no solid evidence that any of the numbers of the Revelation referring to time periods are other than literal.

Vaughan believes like Ames:

> I am not aware of any instance in which that particular duration (one thousand years) is used in Scripture literally. We are all familiar with the phrases, *A thousand years in Thy sight are but as yesterday. One day is with the Lord as a thousand years, and a thousand years as one day.* The application of the expressions is always vague, not strict: it denotes a period protracted, prolonged, but indefinite.[17]

Vaughan, as is typical of other writers, fails to recognize that when Scriptures speak of "a thousand years" as in Psalm 90:4, a literal thousand years is meant. A thousand years with a man is only a moment with God, but this does not deny that it is actually a thousand years with man. Again, when II Peter 3:8 states that one day is with the Lord as a thousand years, the meaning is clear that one day with God is as a literal thousand years with man—that is, the day has great detail in God's plan. When the verse goes on to say a thousand years are as one day, it is speaking of a literal thousand years with man as being as one day with the Lord. In none of these references is the literalness of a thousand years questioned.

Some consider the millennial teaching of Revelation 20 a complete enigma and are therefore amillennial to the extreme. This view is usually followed by modern liberals who do not take prophecy seriously.

Postmillennialism. One of the most recent points of view, at least in its modern definition, is the interpretation of Revelation from the postmillennial view. Adherents of this position regard the thousand-year reign as being completed prior to the second coming of Christ. It is very similar to amillennial interpretations such as that of Swete and Pieters in that it views the millennium as the final triumph of the gospel in the present age.

---

[15]*Commentary on the Revelation of St. John,* pp. 353–54.
[16]A. H. Ames, *The Revelation of St. John the Divine,* p. 217.
[17]C. J. Vaughan, *Lectures on the Revelation of John,* II, 215–16.

It is usually more specifically a literal view, however, and considers the millennium to be a thousand years. Adherents to this postmillennial position are largely nineteenth century scholars such as Charles Hodge, A. H. Strong, C. A. Briggs, and David Brown. Most of them trace their view to that of Daniel Whitby, seventeenth century controversialist. With variations, they consider the gospel as being triumphant during the last one thousand years of the present age which most of them consider as being still future, although not all insist that it is a literal period of that length.

A variation of postmillennialism, advanced by certain liberal scholars in the nineteenth and early twentieth centuries, connected postmillennialism with the theory of evolution. Such writers paid little attention to the precise details advanced in Revelation 20 and often stretched the millennium to millions of years that they felt still were required to bring humanity to its full flower.[18] This point of view has had little influence on contemporary discussion of the millennial doctrine.

With the occurrence of the two world wars, postmillennialism suffered a severe reversal. However, a recent writer, Loraine Boettner, in his work *The Millennium*, has revived the view of Charles Hodge that the millennium is still ahead, a thousand years in which the gospel will be triumphant, a period climaxed by the return of Christ.

With the great variety of interpretations of Revelation 20 with their corresponding influence on eschatology, the task of giving an exposition of this chapter is greatly complicated. The confusion of so many interpretations, however, is dispelled if the events of this chapter are allowed to follow in their natural chronological sequence, with the return of Christ and the conquest of the beast and the false prophet serving as the introduction to the millennium. The opening events of the twentieth chapter then become a natural outgrowth of the battle in which the beast and the false prophet and his armies are destroyed, leading to the next step, the judgment of Satan himself. The repeated phrase "And I saw" (cf. 19:11, 17, 19; 20:1, 4, 11, 12) marks the major steps of the progress of the revelation.

The sequence of events is supported not only by the chronological order itself (note the "when" of 20:7) but by the logical dependence of one event upon the preceding event. This is strong evidence for chronological order in this section and, if this is granted, the millennial kingdom follows the second coming as described in 19:11–16. The only reason for denying such a conclusion would be to avoid premillennialism. There is no evidence in the passage at all which would give ground to question that from 19:1 to 21:8 a strict chronological order is observed.

---

[18]Cf. James H. Snowden, *The Coming of the Lord*, p. 79.

Many expositors would extend the chronological sequence to the end of the book of Revelation. Accordingly, though Revelation as a whole is not strictly in chronological order, as some chapters are parenthetical or summary in character, chapters 19 and 20 constitute a unit and form one continued prophetic strain. The folly of attempting to find historic fulfillment in chapters 6 through 20 is well illustrated in Hengstenberg who, following the conservative postmillennial point of view, begins the millennium at Christmas Eve A.D. 800, when the pope crowned Charlemagne. Hengstenberg believed Christ would return at the end of approximately 1,000 years from that date, namely, in his own lifetime.[19]

THE BINDING OF SATAN (20:1–3)

20:1-3 And I saw an angel come down from heaven, having the key of the bottomless pit and a great chain in his hand. And he laid hold on the dragon, that old serpent, which is the Devil, and Satan, and bound him a thousand years, And cast him into the bottomless pit, and shut him up, and set a seal upon him, that he should deceive the nations no more, till the thousand years should be fulfilled: and after that he must be loosed a little season.

The next phase of the prophetic program is introduced by another vision of an angel (cf. 7:2; 8:1; 10:1; 14:6, 8, 9, 15, 17, 18; 17:1; 18:1; 19:17). Though some have understood the angel of 20:1 to be Christ Himself, in lieu of specific proof it is better to assume that this is another great angel operating at the command and in the authority of God. As John witnesses the scene, he observes the angel coming down from heaven possessing the key of "the bottomless pit," that is, "the abyss" (cf. 9:1, 2, 11; also "the deep," Luke 8:31; Rom. 10:7). This is the home of demons and unclean spirits. The angel is also observed to have a great chain in his hands. In verse 2 the angel is seen laying hold of Satan and binding him for 1,000 years after which, in verse 3, Satan is cast into the abyss and its door is shut. A seal is placed upon Satan himself making it impossible for him to deceive the nations until a thousand years have elapsed, after which, the angel declares, Satan must be loosed for a little while.

The dramatic prophecy contained in these three verses has been the subject of endless dispute because to some extent the whole controversy between premillenarians and amillenarians hangs upon it. The passage yields to patient exegesis, and there is no solid reason for taking it in other than its ordinary sense. According to the prediction the angel is empowered for six functions: (1) to lay hold on the dragon, (2) to bind him for 1,000 years, (3) to cast him into the abyss, (4) to shut him up,

[19]E. W. Hengstenberg, *The Revelation of St. John*, II, 275.

that is, to use the key which will lock up the abyss, (5) to set a seal upon Satan which will render him inactive in his work of deceiving the nations, (6) to loose him after the thousand years. At every point, however, the prediction has been disputed.

Encell, in keeping with his historical interpretation of Revelation, finds the chain with which Satan was bound a symbol of "the chain of evidence that has been coming to life for nearly a hundred years past, but mostly within the last half century, and is still coming to life, corroborating the truths of the Bible." By this he means archaeological evidence confirming the Bible record. He continues:

> We are living in the time when the many lengths of this chain are being brought forward for which to bind Satan; when he is securely bound a happy state of things will prevail, as for a long period of time, is indicated by the expression "a thousand years." How long a period of time is symbolized no mortal knows.[20]

The difficulty with this symbolic interpretation is that it fails to satisfy the passage. The mounting evidence for Christianity does not seem to have bound Satan in the twentieth century.

The question has been raised as to how an angel who is an immaterial being can lay hold on Satan who is also an immaterial being. Such a query is born of unbelief. Certainly the qualities belonging to a physical body are frequently attributed to angels and to Satan; and God, the Creator of angels, can also deal with them in a physical way. Particular objection has been raised to the idea of binding Satan with a chain, again on the grounds that an immaterial being such as an angel or Satan cannot be bound with a physical chain.

In considering this problem, we must bear in mind that we have here the language of appearance, that is, that John saw the angel with a chain in his hands. The word *chain* here (Gr., *halysis*) is the same as found in Mark 5:3 relating to the man possessed of demons who had been bound with chains. It is also used for the chains which fell off Peter (Acts 12:7) and for Paul's chains (Acts 28:20; II Tim. 1:16). Different words, however, are used in II Peter 2:4 referring to the chains of darkness binding the wicked angel, and for the everlasting chains of Jude 6. These are more general terms for being bound. The four instances in Scripture of the word for "chain" in Revelation 20:1 give no reason for interpreting the word in other than its ordinary sense.

Whatever the physical character of the chain, the obvious teaching of the passage is that the action is so designed as to render Satan inactive. The intention is not to represent Satan as merely restricted but as rendered completely inactive. In confirmation of this, verse 3 states that he

[20]J. G. Encell, *The Exiled Prophet*, pp. 231-32.

is cast into the abyss, which by its character is a place of confinement. The angel uses the key and shuts him up in the abyss. If God wanted to show that Satan was totally inactive and out of touch with the world, how could He have rendered it more specifically than He has done in this passage? The fact that Satan is bound for a thousand years is confirmed by the multitude of passages dealing with the kingdom period in which Satan is never found working in the world.

Of major importance, however, is the decision whether this scene refers to the future millennium or to the present age as is taught by the amillenarians. It should be made clear from this passage that if the millennium is the interadvent period between the first and second comings of Christ, as held by amillenarians (the common Augustinian viewpoint of the interadvent age), then Satan must be bound during the present age. There are few theories of Scripture which are less warranted than the idea that Satan was bound at the first coming of Christ. Amillenarians often refer to Luke 10:18, as does Augustine, where Christ said to the seventy witnesses returning in triumph from their period of witness and miracles, "I beheld Satan as lightning fall from heaven." From this it has been inferred that the fall of Satan occurred at the first coming of Christ instead of in relationship to the second coming.

Opposed to the amillennial interpretation, however, is the uniform revelation of the New Testament which shows that Satan in the present age is a very active person. If anything, he is more active than in preceding ages and is continuing an unrelenting opposition to all that God purposes to do in the present age.

In Luke 22:3, Satan is said to have entered "into Judas surnamed Iscariot, being of the number of the twelve" with the result that he went out to betray Christ. Satan is revealed to have attempted to dominate Simon Peter as recorded in the Lord's saying in Luke 22:31: "The Lord said, Simon, Simon, behold, Satan hath desired to have you, that he may sift you as wheat." It was only the prayer of the Lord Jesus Christ, not the binding of Satan, which prevented the defeat of Peter.

Throughout the rest of the New Testament similar references are found. In Acts 5:3 Ananias and Sapphira are said to be filled with Satan and motivated to lie to the Holy Spirit regarding the extent of their gift to the church. In II Corinthians 4:3-4, Paul records that Satan is active in blinding the minds of those who hear the gospel: "But if our gospel be hid, it is hid to them that are lost: In whom the god of this world hath blinded the minds of them which believe not, lest the light of the glorious gospel of Christ, who is the image of God, should shine unto them."

In II Corinthians 11:14 Satan is declared to be transformed into an angel of light thereby deceiving the church through false teachers. The unsaved, according to Ephesians 2:2, live "according to the prince of the power of the air, the spirit that now worketh in the children of disobedience." Paul writes in I Thessalonians 2:18 that Satan had hindered his coming to them. More dramatically, in II Timothy 2:26, unsaved people are declared to be taken captive by the devil at his will and are rescued only by the grace of God. The capstone to this series of references to the activity of Satan is found in I Peter 5:8 which should settle the matter beyond dispute. In this passage Christians are told, "Be sober, be vigilant; because your adversary the devil, as a roaring lion, walketh about, seeking whom he may devour." This passage, instead of saying that Satan is bound and unable to deceive the nations, pictures him as a lion which has been loosed, walking about, roaring, seeking someone to devour. That Satan is hindered by the protective power of God is evident throughout the Scriptures as in the case of Job. There is no evidence whatever that Satan is bound today, but rather the mounting evil in the world and in the church would seem to demonstrate that he is more active than ever. The nations of the world are being deceived today and saints are being opposed by the ceaseless activity and deceptive power of Satan.

Much has been made of the fact that these verses are found in a book largely given to symbolic presentation and visions. It is true that John is seeing a vision in these early verses of chapter 20. The passage reveals, however, something more than what he saw. John visually saw the angel bind Satan and cast him into the pit. John could not see visually how long Satan was to be in the pit nor could he see the purpose, namely, that the devil should deceive the nations no more and that he should be loosed again after the thousand years. This purpose had to be given to John by divine revelation which constituted an interpretation of the vision. If the record had given only what he saw without any indication as to the meaning of the passage, it might have lent itself to diverse interpretation. But with the vision recorded as it is, accompanied by the divine interpretation, expositors are not free to inject their own preconceived ideas but must accept the plain statements and interpretations of the passage as given.

It is most important to observe that while the thousand years are mentioned in verses 4 and 5 in the vision of John, they are also mentioned in verse 6 in the interpretation. The expositor is not free to spiritualize the interpretation of the vision but must accept the interpretation in its ordinary and literal meaning. If this is done, there is no other alternative than the premillennial interpretation which holds that at the second coming of Christ, Satan will be bound for a thousand years. This will constitute one of the major features of Christ's righteous rule upon the earth and in fact will make possible the peace and tranquillity and absence of spiritual warfare predicted for the millennial kingdom. The period before Satan is bound, that is, the great tribulation, and the period at the close of the millennium, when Satan is again loosed, stand in sharp contrast to the tranquillity of the thousand years in between. The fact is that the only period in all human history in which Satan will not execute his work of deception will be the thousand years in which Christ will reign.

This passage also introduces, for the first time in Scripture, the exact length of the mediatorial kingdom of Christ. Six times in this passage the fact is stated that the period is a thousand years or a millennium.

The idea that the future millennium would be 1,000 years has been suggested by apocalyptic writers before Christ. In the *Book of the Secrets of Enoch*, 32:2; 33:1-2 Enoch holds the idea that the history of man will run for seven thousand years, the last millennium of which will be one of great blessedness and will precede the eighth millennium, which is eternity.[21] According to R. H. Charles, Enoch's view can be explained as follows:

> As the world was made in six days, so its history will be accomplished in 6,000 years, and as the six days of creation were followed by one of rest, so the 6,000 years of the world's history would be followed by a rest of 1,000 years. On its close would begin the eighth eternal day of blessedness when time should be no more, xxxii. 2—xxxiii. 2.[22]

While evidence points to the conclusion that it was commonly believed that the kingdom reign of Christ would be a thousand years even before this scripture was written, possibly originating in direct revelation from God through His prophets although not recorded in Scripture, here scriptural authority is given for this concept.

Much of the opposition to the futurist interpretation has been leveled at this concept of a literal thousand years. Barnes, more than a century ago, in commenting on the phrase "a thousand years," stated that it should be understood "either (a) literally; or (b) in the prophetic use of the term, where a day would stand for a year, thus making a period of three hundred and sixty thousand years; or (c) figuratively, supposing that it refers to a long but indefinite period of time." Barnes seems to prefer the interpretation that the millennium is 360,000 years in duration. He further holds that Revelation 20 should not be taken literally, and interposes the words "as if" before the judgment and resurrection

[21]R. H. Charles (ed.), *The Apocrypha and Pseudepigrapha of the Old Testament*, II, 451.
[22]*Ibid.*, II, 430.

of 20:4 as well as with the binding of Satan. This would seem to be adding to the book, so strongly forbidden in 22:18.[23]

Baldinger, like many others, rejects completely the prophetic character of Revelation and dismisses the thousand-year reign of Christ in these words:

> This mooted passage is, therefore, nothing more than a word of encouragement to those Christians who are facing martyrdom for refusing to bow before the image of the beast or burn incense to Caesar. . . . a man who brings an unprejudiced mind to this passage will find not a scintilla of evidence for two resurrections. . . . We believe it [the millennium] refers merely to a great period of time of unknown length, in which evil will be more and more restrained and the gospel increasingly triumphant.[24]

There is no good reason for taking the thousand years in other than their literal sense. Even Augustine, living in the fourth and fifth centuries, though he denied many other aspects of the literal reign of Christ on earth in his attempt to accommodate it to the interadvent age, was favorable to the concept of a literal thousand years. It was only after the second thousand years of the interadvent age had passed that questions began to be raised concerning the literalness of this event in an attempt to harmonize it with the interadvent period. It is evident that much has to take place which will require time, including the repopulation of the world after its decimation in the great tribulation.

While Scripture sometimes uses the term "day" in other than a literal sense, never in the Bible is a month or a year used in other than its literal sense. Even the word *day* used of a period of time in reference to "the day of the Lord" is used literally throughout the book of Revelation. It may also be faithfully held that all numbers in the Revelation are literal. About the only number that can even be reasonably questioned is that of the army of two hundred million in 9:16. Even here it is probable that the number is intended to be taken literally as is the "ten thousand times ten thousand" of 5:11. Certainly there is nothing inherently impossible in a thousand-year period in which Christ should reign upon the earth.[25]

THE JUDGMENT AND RESURRECTION OF TRIBULATION SAINTS (20:4)

> 20:4 And I saw thrones, and they sat upon them, and judgment was given unto them: and I saw the souls of them that were beheaded for the witness of Jesus, and for the word of God, and which had not worshipped the beast, neither his image, neither had received his mark

[23]Albert Barnes, *Notes, Explanatory and Practical, on the Book of Revelation*, pp. 260–61.
[24]Albert H. Baldinger, *Sermons on Revelation*, pp. 240-41.
[25]For further discussion of various theories on the millennium, see John Peter Lange, *Commentary on the Holy Scriptures*, Vol. XXIV: *Revelation*, pp. 342–46.

upon their foreheads, or in their hands; and they lived and reigned with Christ a thousand years.

The interpretation of verse 4 is complicated by a lack of specificity. John in his vision records that he saw thrones but refers to those sitting on the thrones as "they" (the subject "they" supplied by the translator as implied in the third person plural of the verb). Who are these sitting on thrones and what is meant by the judgment given to them? One possibility is that the subject of the verb "sat" includes Christ and all the saints related to Him including both the church and Israel. Possible confirmation of this is found in 22:5 where the servants of the Lord are said to reign with Christ.

The most probable interpretation is that they are the twenty-four elders who are said to reign on earth (5:10). This correlates with the prophecy of Christ recorded in Luke 22:29–30: "And I appoint unto you a kingdom, as my Father hath appointed unto me; That ye may eat and drink at my table in my kingdom, and sit on thrones judging the twelve tribes of Israel." These words addressed to the twelve disciples indicate that they will share with Christ His rule over the world and especially will judge Israel at the beginning of the kingdom. Inasmuch as the twelve apostles are members of the church, the Body of Christ, they represent the church as such. A parallel passage is found in Matthew 19:28.

The judgment here predicted may be considered a general one involving several phases of divine judgment at this stage in world history. According to Matthew 25:31–46, the nations or the Gentiles will be judged following the return of Christ. In a similar manner the house of Israel is judged according to Ezekiel 20:33–38. The implication in the latter part of verse 4 is that the tribulation saints resurrected from the dead are also judged and rewarded. If the saints of the Old Testament are raised at this time, they too may be the objects of divine judgment and reward.

Specific mention, however, is made of those described as "beheaded for the witness of Jesus, and for the word of God, and which had not worshipped the beast, neither his image, neither had received his mark upon their foreheads, or in their hands." This detailed description fits only one class of saints, namely, the tribulation saints who in refusing to worship the beast are martyred. Here we learn that they are beheaded, first, for their positive witness for Christ and the Word of God, second, because they refuse to worship the beast and receive his mark. The background of this experience is found in Revelation 13:15–17. Included in the number of tribulation saints are the two witnesses of chapter 11, the "souls of them that were slain for the word of God, and for the testimony which they held" (6:9), and the martyrs referred to in 12:11. The group as a whole is seen in heaven in 7:9–17.

These who were the special objects of Satan's hatred and the beast's persecution are now exalted, rewarded, and blessed. They are declared to have "lived and reigned with Christ a thousand years." The verbs are in the past tense but are obviously prophetic from John's perspective because he is looking at these events from the viewpoint of eternity future as if already accomplished. The expression "they lived" implies that they are resurrected and live again, similar to the meaning of Christ's statement in John 11:25: "I am the resurrection and the life: he that believeth in me, though he were dead, yet shall he live." It is the resurrection of life mentioned in John 5:29.

The tribulation saints are also declared to reign with Christ a thousand years. This has troubled some who have considered the church as properly reigning with Christ, which implies that saints of other ages will be the subjects of the kingdom. It should be evident from this passage that others will share places of prominent rule with the church as the Body of Christ in the millennial kingdom as is also revealed in verse 6. There is a sense, of course, in which saints participate in the present spiritual kingdom of God. This explanation is quite inadequate to support the teaching that we are now reigning with Christ in any real sense. The order is rather that we suffer now and reign in the future (II Tim. 2:12). Such a reign with Christ would require Christ to be in the present earth in a physical way participating directly in the government of the world.

Most important also in verse 4 is the expression "they lived" (Gr., *ezēsan*), used in the sense of coming to life. Amillenarians who equate this with spiritual resurrection or regeneration point out that the verb does not actually mean to be resurrected, but only *to live*. While the word itself is not specific, it is the context which designates it as a bodily resurrection. Verse 5 states, "But the rest of the dead lived not again until the thousand years were finished." The resurrection at the end of the millennium is obviously a bodily resurrection as it includes the unsaved. The context therefore invests the word with the necessary content of bodily resurrection. This is confirmed by the fact that the same verb is used of Christ in 1:18 where He states, "I am he that liveth, and was dead; and, behold, I am alive for evermore." The same expression is found also in 2:8. As Culver has pointed out, if the saints are going to reign with Christ, they will need to be alive in the same sense that He is, namely, having a resurrection body.[26]

The most important truth introduced in verse 4 is the evident fact that a thousand years separate the resurrection of the martyred dead from

[26]Culver, p. 211.

the resurrection of the wicked dead. This is borne out in the passage which follows.

THE FIRST RESURRECTION (20:5–6)

20:5-6 But the rest of the dead lived not again until the thousand years were finished. This is the first resurrection. Blessed and holy is he that hath part in the first resurrection: on such the second death hath no power, but they shall be priests of God and of Christ, and shall reign with him a thousand years.

In order to clarify the exact distinctions observed in this passage, John mentions now that in contrast to the martyred dead raised at this time, the rest of the dead do not live again until the thousand years are finished. The resurrection at the beginning of the millennium is therefore characterized as "the first resurrection." In what sense can the tribulation saints in their resurrection be labeled "the first resurrection"?

It is obvious that Christ was the first one raised from the dead with a resurrection body as He was the firstfruit from the dead (I Cor. 15:20). On the occasion of the resurrection of Christ, Matthew mentions that at the death of Christ, "the graves were opened" and that later "many bodies of the saints which slept arose, And came out of the graves after his resurrection, and went into the holy city, and appeared unto many" (Matt. 27:52-53). This difficult passage is best explained as an actual resurrection of a token number of saints in keeping with the symbolism of the feast of the firstfruits, when a handful of grain, not just one stalk, was presented to the priest. There is no evidence that the resurrection of Matthew 27 included all the righteous saints up to that time, as Daniel 12:2 seems to place the resurrection of the Old Testament saints immediately after the great tribulation described in Daniel 12:1. In any event, there was a genuine resurrection on the occasion of the resurrection of Christ.

In describing the resurrection of the saints here, the familiar word for "resurrection" (Gr., *anastasis*) is used, a word occurring about forty times in the New Testament. This word is almost always used of bodily resurrection. The only exception seems to be in Luke 2:34. The fact that practically all instances of *anastasis* refer to physical resurrection makes it improbable that it means here what amillenarians frequently interpret it to mean, namely, a spiritual resurrection or regeneration. It is just as unnatural to deny that it means bodily resurrection here as in the case of the resurrection of Christ Himself. Hence, it may be concluded that this resurrection is not different in kind from other resurrections which are included in the designation "the first resurrection."

At the end of the church age the rapture of the church will take place.

and the dead in Christ will be raised. At the end of the great tribulation, the tribulation saints will also be raised from the dead. It would seem clear from these facts that the term "the first resurrection" is not an event but an order of resurrection including all the righteous who are raised from the dead before the millennial kingdom begins. They are "first" in contrast to those who are raised last, after the millennium, when the wicked dead are raised and judged. Just as there are two kinds of physical death, namely, the first death which results in burial, and the second death which is described as being cast into the lake of fire (20:14), so there are two kinds of resurrection, a first resurrection having to do with the resurrection of the righteous, and a second resurrection having to do with the wicked. They are separated by at least one thousand years. Just as the first death did not occur to all in one moment but is experienced individually by those who die over a long period of time, so the first resurrection is fulfilled according to the groups that are in view.

A further question can be raised concerning the special mention of the martyred dead of the tribulation. In view of the fact that they are publicly humiliated and suffer as no preceding generation of saints have suffered, so God selects them for public triumph on the occasion of the establishment of His kingdom in the earth.

The blessedness of those who take part in the first resurrection regardless of classification is summarized in verse 6 in the words "Blessed and holy is he that hath part in the first resurrection." Their estate is a happy and holy one. They are delivered from the power of the second death; they are given the special status of priests of God and of Christ, and are privileged to reign with Him for the thousand years. As previously indicated in verse 4, the privilege of reigning with Christ is not exclusively the reward of the church, but the righteous saints in general are given privileged places of service. This does not mean that classifications of saints are ignored, but each saint is rewarded according to his individual relationship to the sovereign will of God.

An illustration of the differing capacities in which saints can reign is afforded in the book of Esther. Esther, as queen, reigned with Ahasuerus as his wife and queen, while Mordecai, her uncle, reigned as the chief political officer of the king. Both reigned but in different senses and in different offices. If the church is afforded the special place of being the Bride of Christ and reigning in this sense, other resurrected people will also reign and enjoy privileges and rewards. They will apparently not only share in the political aspects of the kingdom but also in its religious life, for they are declared to be "priests of God and of Christ," a designation of a privileged rank similar to that which the church enjoys in this present age under Christ our High Priest. The expression "shall reign"

(Gr., *basileusousin*) is future in the best manuscripts. Inasmuch as this is future in relationship to the martyred dead who die in the tribulation and are raised in the second advent, it provides added proof for the premillennial interpretation.

The main burden of this passage, however, is to demonstrate beyond any question that there will be a thousand-year period between the resurrections of the righteous and the wicked. Passages such as Daniel 12:2 and John 5:28–29, which refer in general to the resurrection of both the righteous and the wicked, must be interpreted as declaring the fact of resurrection rather than that the two events take place at the same time, even though the word *hour* is used of both events. The significance seems to be that the time will come when both the righteous and the wicked will be raised without designating exactly when it will occur. J. B. Smith attempts to establish an unnecessarily complicated system of rules relative to the mention of the righteous and their resurrection.[27] The main facts of this passage are clear when the general rule is applied that that which is plain should interpret that which is obscure.

In considering Revelation 20:1–6 as a whole, there is much to commend its normal and literal interpretation. Alford writes pointedly:

> Those who lived next to the Apostles, and the whole Church for 300 years, understood them in the plain literal sense: and it is a strange sight in these days [1860] to see expositors who are among the first in reverence of antiquity, complacently casting aside the most cogent instance of consensus which primitive antiquity presents. As regards the text itself, no legitimate treatment of it will extort what is known as the spiritual interpretation now in fashion. If, in a passage where *two resurrections* are mentioned, where certain *psychai ezēsan* at the first, and the rest of the *nekrōn ezēsan* only at the end of a specified period after that first,—if in such a passage the first resurrection may be understood to mean *spiritual* rising with Christ, while the second means *literal* rising from the grave;—then there is an end of all significance in language, and Scripture is wiped out as a definite testimony to anything. If the first resurrection is spiritual, then so is the second, which I suppose none will be hearty enough to maintain: but if the second is literal, then so is the first, which in common with the whole primitive Church and many of the best modern expositors, I do maintain, and receive as an article of faith and hope.[28]

THE LOOSING OF SATAN AND THE FINAL REVOLT (20:7-9)

20:7-9 And when the thousand years are expired, Satan shall be loosed out of his prison, And shall go out to deceive the nations which are in the four quarters of the earth, Gog and Magog, to gather them together to battle: the number of whom is as the sand of the sea. And they went up on the breadth of the earth, and com-

[27]*A Revelation of Jesus Christ*, p. 273.
[28]Henry Alford, *The Greek New Testament*, IV, 732–33.

passed the camp of the saints about, and the beloved city: and fire
came down from God out of heaven, and devoured them.

Before considering the climax of the thousand years as revealed in this
passage, a brief survey of the Scripture bearing upon the millennial kingdom described here will serve to emphasize and justify the literal interpretation of the thousand years. John in his vision in Revelation does
not occupy himself with the details of the millennial kingdom but only
with the fact and duration of it. The character of Christ's reign on earth
is fully described in many Old Testament passages such as Isaiah 2:2–4;
11:4–9; Psalm 72, and many others. From these scriptures it may be seen
that Jerusalem will be the capital of the millennial kingdom (Isa. 2:3)
and that war will be no more (Isa. 2:4). Isaiah 11 describes the righteous reign of Christ and the peace and tranquillity of His kingdom.
There will be justice for all, the wicked will be punished, and even
the natural ferocity of beasts will be abated. The character and extent
of the kingdom are summarized in Isaiah 11:9: "They shall not hurt nor
destroy in all my holy mountain: for the earth shall be full of the knowledge of the Lord, as the waters cover the sea." In the latter portion of
Isaiah 11, Israel is revealed to be regathered from the various parts of
the earth and brought back to her ancient land rejoicing in the fulfillment
of God's prophetic word.

Psalm 72 gives a similar picture of the righteous reign of Christ, describing righteousness as flourishing and abundance of peace as continuing
as long as the moon endures. The dominion of Christ is stated to be from
sea to sea with all kings bowing down before Him, all nations serving
Him, and the earth being filled with the glory of the Lord. Then will be
fulfilled the desire of the nations for peace and righteousness, for the
knowledge of the Lord, for economic justice, for deliverance from satanic
oppression and evil. For the whole period of one thousand years the earth
will revel in the immediate presence of the Lord and His perfect divine
government. Israel will be exalted and Gentiles also will be blessed. The
major factors of the millennium, therefore, include a perfect and righteous
government with Christ reigning in absolute power over the entire earth.
Every nation will be under His sway, and God's purpose in originally
placing man in charge of the Garden of Eden will have its ultimate fulfillment in the Last Adam, the Lord Jesus Christ, who will reign over the
earth.

The prominence of Israel in the millennial scene is evidenced in many
passages of the Old Testament. After the purging experience of the great
tribulation, those who survive become the citizens of the kingdom after
the rebels are purged out (Ezek. 20:34–38). Israel then is rejoined to
God in the symbol of marriage, being transformed from an unfaithful

wife to one who reciprocates the love of Jehovah. Gentiles who share in the kingdom blessings have unparalleled spiritual and economic benefits, and the thousand-year reign of Christ is a time of joy, peace, and blessing for the entire earth. Though problems in understanding this period persist due to the fact that there is not a complete revelation on all details, the major facts are sufficiently clear for anyone who is willing to accept the authority and accuracy of Scripture and interpret language in its ordinary sense.

John passes quickly over all these details as if it is unnecessary to repeat them at this point and takes us directly to the conclusion of the millennial kingdom when Satan again is loosed from his prison. The word for *expired* (v. 7) is from *teleō*, meaning "brought to the goal or the end," hence "finished." The same word is translated "fulfilled" in 20:3, and "finished" in 20:5. The prison referred to is, of course, the abyss into which Satan is cast at the beginning of the millennium.

On being relieved from his confinement, Satan loses no time in resuming his nefarious activities and plunges into his campaign to deceive the nations of the entire earth. These who are tempted are the descendants of the tribulation saints who survive the tribulation and enter the millennium in their natural bodies. B. F. Atkinson believes infants born during the millennium will live to its conclusion and will not be required to make a choice between the devil and Christ until the end.[29] The children of those entering the millennium far outnumber the parents, and undoubtedly the earth is teeming with inhabitants at the conclusion of the thousand-year reign of Christ. Outwardly they have been required to conform to the rule of the king and make a profession of obedience to Christ. In many cases, however, this was mere outward conformity without inward reality, and in their inexperience of real temptation they are easy victims of Satan's wiles.

Hoste comments:

> The golden age of the kingdom will last a thousand years, during which righteousness will reign, and peace, prosperity, and the knowledge of God be universally enjoyed. But this will not entail universal conversion, and all profession must be tested. . . . Will not a thousand years under the beneficent sway of Christ and the manifested glory of God suffice to render men immune to his [Satan's] temptations, will they not have radically changed for the better, and become by the altered conditions of life and the absence of Satanic temptations, children of God and lovers of His will? Alas! It will be proved once more that man whatever his advantages and environment, apart from the grace of God and the new birth, remains at heart only evil and at enmity with God.[30]

[29]*The Revelation of Jesus Christ*, pp. 177–78.
[30]William Hoste, *The Visions of John the Divine*, pp. 160-61.

Govett suggests four reasons why Satan must be loosed after a thousand years: (1) to demonstrate that man even under the most favorable circumstances will fall into sin if left to his own choice; (2) to demonstrate the foreknowledge of God who foretells the acts of men as well as His own acts; (3) to demonstrate the incurable wickedness of Satan; (4) to justify eternal punishment, that is, to show the unchanged character of wicked people even under divine jurisdiction for a long period of time.[31]

In describing the nations, the term "Gog and Magog" is used without any explanation. From the context it would seem that this is not the same event as that described in Ezekiel 38 and 39 where Gog and Magog are prominent; and the battle which follows is entirely different and separated by at least a thousand years from that of Ezekiel's prophecy. Baines contrasts this battle with that of Ezekiel in these words:

> Gog and Magog are here used in a wider sense than in Ezekiel, and their invasion differs in time and details, though agreeing in character and object, with that which he foretells. Ezekiel predicts an incursion by a great northern power called Gog, which, from certain geographical indications, is easily identified with Russia. In the Revelation, however, Gog and Magog are used to designate the nations, not merely from the north, but from all parts, "the four quarters of the earth." Again, the invasion named by Ezekiel is at the beginning of Christ's reign; that in the Revelation at the end. The hosts in Ezekiel, too, fall on the mountains, and their bodies are buried; whereas the forces assembled in the Revelation are devoured by fire from heaven. The judgment is instantaneous. Christ's reign is a reign of righteousness, during which evil is not tolerated as now, but promptly crushed.[32]

While many explanations have been made, one of the intriguing ones is that Gog refers to the ruler and Magog to the people as in Ezekiel 38. Hence, what the passage means is that the nations of the world follow Satan, including the rulers (Gog) and the people (Magog) under the rulers. Another plausible explanation is that the expression is used much as we use the term "Waterloo" to express a disastrous battle, but one not related to the historic origination of the term. Many contrasts can be observed between this battle and that of Ezekiel in that Satan is prominent in this whereas he is not mentioned in Ezekiel 38-39. The invasion of Ezekiel comes from the north whereas this invasion comes from all directions. Ezekiel's battle probably occurs previous to the battle of the great day of God Almighty before the millennium, whereas this occurs after the thousand years have been finished. The number of those who rebel against God and follow Satan is described as innumerable "as the

---

[31]Robert Govett, *The Apocalypse Expounded*, pp. 506–8.
[32]T. B. Baines, *The Revelation of Jesus Christ*, pp. 270–71.

sand of the sea." Thus the last gigantic rebellion of man develops against God's sovereign rule in which the wicked meet their Waterloo.

As the battle is joined in verse 9, the great host led by Satan and coming from all directions compasses the camp of the saints. The word for "camp" (Gr., *parembolē*) refers to those engaged in battle and who are in battle array, hence a "camp," "fortress," or "citadel." Here the term seems to refer to the city of Jerusalem itself which is described as "the beloved city" (cf. Ps. 78:68; 87:2). Apparently Christ permits the army to assemble and encircle the capital city. No sooner has the army of Satan been assembled, however, than fire comes down from God out of heaven, and the besiegers are destroyed, like the destruction of Sodom and Gomorrah. Thus is shattered the last vain attempt of Satan to claim a place of prominence and worship in attempted usurpation of the prerogatives of God. Thus ends also the false theory that man under perfect environment will willingly serve the God who created and redeemed him. Even in the ideal situation of the millennial reign of Christ, innumerable hosts immediately respond to the first temptation to rebel. This is the end of the road for the nations who rebel against God as well as for the career of Satan.

THE DOOM OF SATAN (20:10)

20:10 And the devil that deceived them was cast into the lake of fire and brimstone where the beast and the false prophet are, and shall be tormented day and night for ever and ever.

Following the destruction of the armies of Satan, the devil is cast into the lake of fire. Attention is called to the fact that he is the deceiver. Satan, who was first self-deceived in launching his career to be like God (Isa. 14:14) and then began his career by deceiving Eve in the garden, is still the same character at the time of his final judgment. There is no sanctifying grace for fallen angels. In the divine act of judgment which casts Satan into the lake of fire, he joins the beast and the false prophet who preceded him by one thousand years. The text should be understood as teaching that both the beast and the false prophet are still in the lake of fire when Satan joins them, a thousand years after being cast into it. It is most significant that the verb *basanisthēsontai* is in the third person plural, indication that the verb should be understood as having for its subjects not only Satan but also the beast and the false prophet. It could be translated "They shall be tormented day and night for ever and ever." Thus the Word of God plainly declares that death is not annihilation and that the wicked exist forever, though in torment. There would be no way possible in the Greek language to state more emphatically the everlasting punishment of the lost than that used here in mentioning both day and night and the expression "for ever and ever" (Gr., *eis tous aiōnas ton aiōnōn*), literally "to the ages of ages." The lake of fire prepared for the devil and the wicked angels is also the destiny of all who follow Satan.

THE ESTABLISHMENT OF THE GREAT WHITE THRONE (20:11)

20:11 And I saw a great white throne, and him that sat on it, from whose face the earth and the heaven fled away; and there was found no place for them.

The familiar phrase "And I saw" introduces the next phase of the prophetic revelation. John sees a great white throne with One sitting on it of such great majesty that earth and heaven flee away from before Him. In 4:2 John had beheld "a throne . . . set in heaven" with a description of the One sitting on the throne. Thereafter in the book of Revelation "the throne" is mentioned more than thirty times. In this verse, however, it is "a great white throne" and is probably to be distinguished from any previously mentioned throne in the book.

Though there is no specific mention made of the person sitting on the throne, it is proper to assume that it is God and more specifically Christ Himself as in 3:21. This is according to John 5:22: "For the Father judgeth no man, but hath committed all judgment unto the Son." In keeping with this, other passages speak of Christ judging (cf. Matt. 19:28; 25:31; II Cor. 5:10). The majesty of the person sitting on the throne results in the earth and heaven fleeing away, that is, the throne is in space rather than in heaven as in II Corinthians 5:10 or on earth as in Matthew 25:31. The time is clearly at the end of the millennium in contrast to the other judgments which precede the millennium.

The most natural interpretation of the fact that earth and heaven flee away is that the present earth and heaven are destroyed and will be replaced by the new heaven and new earth. This is also confirmed by the additional statement in 21:1 where John sees a new heaven and a new earth replacing the first heaven and the first earth which have passed away. Frequent references in the Bible seem to anticipate this future time when the present world will be destroyed (Matt. 24:35; Mark 13:31; Luke 16:17; 21:33; II Peter 3:10). According to this last reference, II Peter 3:10, "The heavens shall pass away with a great noise, and the elements shall melt with fervent heat, the earth also and the works that are therein shall be burned up." Peter goes on to say, "Seeing then that all these things shall be dissolved, what manner of persons ought ye to be in all holy conversation and godliness?" (II Peter 3:11).

J. B. Smith offers the rather astonishing conclusion "that the language employed does not signify 'the vanishing of the former heaven and earth into nothing'" and offers the following passages as proof: II Corinthians

5:17; James 1:10; Romans 8:19–23; II Peter 3:10, 13.[33] Even a casual reading of these passages, however, offers no evidence whatever that Revelation 20:11 should not be understood as a destruction of the present earth and heaven. It would be difficult to find a more explicit statement than that contained here in Revelation 20:11 and in II Peter 3:10–11. Further, it would be most natural that the present earth and heaven, the scene of the struggle with Satan and sin, should be displaced by an entirely new order suited for eternity. The whole structure of the universe is operating on the principle of a clock that is running down. Though many billions of years would be required to accomplish this, the natural world would eventually come to a state of total inactivity if the physical laws of the universe as now understood should remain unchanged. What could be simpler than for God to create a new heaven and a new earth by divine fiat in keeping with His purposes for eternity to come?

THE RESURRECTION OF THE WICKED DEAD (20:12-13)

20:12-13 And I saw the dead, small and great, stand before God; and the books were opened: and another book was opened, which is the book of life: and the dead were judged out of those things which were written in the books, according to their works. And the sea gave up the dead which were in it; and death and hell delivered up the dead which were in them: and they were judged every man according to their works.

Before the great white throne, John sees the dead described as "small and great" standing before God awaiting their judgment. From the context it may be assumed that these are the wicked dead, who are not raised in the first resurrection (cf. Dan. 12:2; John 5:29; Acts 24:15; Rev. 20:5). The phrase "small and great" used previously in Revelation (11:18; 13:16; 19:5, 18) indicates that those appearing before the throne come from all walks of life and degrees of greatness. Their standing posture means that they are now about to be sentenced. This is a fulfillment of the principle of Hebrews 9:27, "It is appointed unto men once to die, but after this the judgment." Their judgment is made on the basis of the books which are opened, being in two classifications. The book of life evidently refers to the roll of those who are saved and have eternal life. The other books mentioned as plural are the divine records of their works. The dead are judged on the basis of the records, and as in other final judgments, the sum of their works is now examined. It is noteworthy that all the final judgments are judgments of works. In the case of the judgment seat of Christ (II Cor. 5:10–11) believers are judged according to their works and rewarded. In Matthew 25:31–46 the Gentiles are judged according to their works in the sense that the works distinguish those who are saved,

[33]Smith, p. 278.

that is, the sheep, from those who are lost, the goats. Here the works evidently are such that salvation is not the issue but rather the degree of punishment, as there is no indication that any righteous are found in this judgment.

The question has been raised concerning the judgment of those who die in the millennium. It is clear that the unsaved who die in the millennium are included in this judgment. The Scriptures are silent, however, concerning any rapture or translation of saints who survive the millennium and concerning the resurrection of saints who may die in the millennium. Both events may be safely assumed, but are not the subject of divine revelation, probably on the principle that this truth is of no practical application to saints now living. Further light may be cast upon this in the millennium itself as the truth of God is made known.

The absolute justice of God is revealed in this judgment of works. Even for those who have spurned the Lord Jesus Christ there is differentiation in degrees of wickedness and apparently variation in punishment. While works are never a ground of salvation, they are, nevertheless, considered important before God. Smith finds forty-two instances in Scripture where man is said to be judged according to his works with the following references in Revelation (2:23; 18:3–6; 20:13; 22:12).[34] Though men are judged according to their works, the book of life is introduced as the deciding factor as to where they will spend eternity.

In verse 13 the resurrection of the wicked dead is described, with special mention of those who are raised from the sea where they did not have normal burial. Those who died normal deaths and went to hell, or Hades, are also presented at this judgment. In the Authorized Version, *Sheol* in the Old Testament and *Hades* in the New Testament are incorrectly translated by the English word *hell*. Both *Sheol* and *Hades* refer to the intermediate state or, as some believe, in certain instances to the grave. These terms *never* refer to the eternal state of punishment; therefore they should not have been translated in any instance by the word *hell*. Hell properly refers to the eternal state of punishment, described as the lake of fire, or Gehenna.

Careful distinction, therefore, must be made between Hades as the intermediate state, in which the unsaved suffer prior to the judgment of the great white throne, and the eternal punishment which follows the great white throne, the lake of fire in this passage, which apparently is identical to Gehenna (cf. Matt. 5:22, 29–30; 10:28; 18:9; etc.), properly referring to the Valley of Hinnom extending to the south of Jerusalem but representing eternal punishment. *Hades* is never used in reference to the eternal state. The meaning of verse 13 speaking of "death and hell"

[34]*Ibid.*, p. 279.

as delivering up their dead is that those in the intermediate state in Hades are now raised from the dead in order to be judged and given their final destiny.

A special problem is introduced by the resurrection of those who were cast into the sea with the presumption that their bodies have disintegrated and have been scattered over a wide area geographically. The special mention of the sea is occasioned by the fact that resurrection usually implies resurrection from the grave. The resurrection of the dead from the sea merely reaffirms that all the dead will be raised regardless of the condition of their bodies The expression is, however, somewhat unusual in that bodily resurrection is referred to in relation to the sea whereas the delivering of the spirits of the unsaved dead is in view in deliverance from Hades unless the word *death* refers to the body. Any obscurity which this passage may have does not alter the fact of the universal resurrection of all men in their order. Here is foretold the resurrection of the wicked dead.

The resurrection of the wicked dead is in sharp contrast to the resurrection of the righteous dead. Although the passage does not state so explicitly, the implication in this judgment is that there are no saved. Nothing is said here of the reward of the righteous. Apparently there is a separate resurrection of any righteous who may have died in the millennium, although this teaching is not presented anywhere in the Word of God. The righteous are given bodies like the holy, immortal, and incorruptible body of Christ in His resurrection. The wicked dead are given resurrection bodies suited for eternal punishment.

When every man is judged according to his works, he thus becomes subject to the perfect righteousness of God. The peculiar construction of the closing clause of verse 13, "they were judged every man," uses a third person plural for the verb, but a first person singular in the masculine for the term "every man" or "each" (Gr., *ekastos*). The meaning is that while they are judged as a group, the resulting judgment, nevertheless, is individual.

THE LAKE OF FIRE (20:14–15)

20:14-15 And death and hell were cast into the lake of fire. This is the second death. And whosoever was not found written in the book of life was cast into the lake of fire.

The summary judgment is pronounced in verse 14 that "death and hell were cast into the lake of fire." In a word, this means that all who died physically and were in Hades, the intermediate state, are here found unworthy and cast into the lake of fire. This is then described as "the second death," which stands in antithesis to the first resurrection, or the eternal state of bliss, enjoyed by the saved. Both the wicked and the righteous in the eternal state are thus permanently assigned to their respective destinies. The basis for the judgment is declared in verse 15 to be whether their names were found written in the book of life. The phrase "whosoever was not found written in the book of life" connotes the careful search of the records to be sure that no mistake is made.

If the point of view be adopted that the book of life was originally the book of all living from which have been expunged the names of those who departed from life on earth without salvation, it presents a sad picture of a blank space where their names could have been written for all eternity as the objects of divine grace. Though they are judged by their works, it is evident that their destiny is determined primarily by their lack of spiritual life. When the fact is contemplated that Jesus Christ in His death reconciled the world to Himself (II Cor. 5:19) and that He died for the reprobate as well as for the elect, it is all the more poignant that these now raised from the dead are cast into the lake of fire. Their ultimate destiny of eternal punishment is not, in the last analysis, because God wished it but because they would not come to God for the grace which He freely offered.

Many attempts have been made to escape the obvious meaning of this passage by spiritualizing the lake of fire as a mere symbol that is not as bad as it seems, or, on the other hand, to represent it as the annihilation of the wicked rather than the beginning of their eternal punishment. It may be conceded that the lake of fire is a symbol, but the symbol corresponds to reality. The rich man in Luke 16 gave his testimony: "I am tormented in this flame" (Luke 16:24). If unsaved souls in Hades, the intermediate state, are tormented by flames, it is not unreasonable to assume that the lake of fire connotes the same type of punishment. It cannot safely be assumed that there is any important difference between the physical and the spiritual reality embodied in the term "lake of fire." It is an awful destiny in either case.

Further, it seems very clear, according to Revelation 20:10 as well as other passages, that those cast into the lake of fire are not thereby annihilated. The beast and the false prophet are still alive and still tormented a thousand years after they are cast into it, and the Scriptures make plain that along with Satan they will be tormented forever. Not only is no termination of eternal punishment recognized in the Bible, but explicit statements are made to the contrary in the strongest possible language. It is difficult for creatures of earth, born in sin and never completely extricated from it even though experiencing God's sanctifying grace, to enter into the fact of God's inexorable righteousness and inflexible justice which insist that judgment be administered when the grace of God has been spurned.

Even Bible-believing Christians have tended to tone down the awfulness of eternal death to somehow reconcile the destiny of the lost with the prospect of the saved of being eternally in the presence of the Lord. A thorough appreciation of eternal punishment, however, will in the end enhance the doctrine of the grace of God and make the love of God all the more wonderful for those who enter into its truth. The fact of eternal punishment is not limited to this passage of Scripture, for Christ Himself speaks of the destiny of the wicked in many passages (Matt. 13:42; 25:41, 46; etc.). Earlier in Revelation itself (14:11) eternal punishment is predicted for those who receive the mark of the beast. A confirming note is also added in Revelation 21:8. The only revelation that has been given concerning the eternal state recognizes two destinies only: one of blessedness in the presence of the Lord, the other of eternal punishment.

21

THE NEW HEAVEN AND THE NEW EARTH

THE NEW HEAVEN AND THE NEW EARTH PRESENTED (21:1)

21:1 And I saw a new heaven and a new earth: for the first heaven and the first earth were passed away; and there was no more sea.

FOLLOWING THE JUDGMENT of the great white throne depicted in the closing verses of chapter 20, John's attention is next directed to the new heaven and the new earth which replace the old heaven and the old earth which fled away (20:11). The expression "And I saw" is the first of three such statements in this chapter marking the major elements of the revelation (cf. 21:2, 22). The new heaven and new earth presented here are evidently not simply the old heaven and earth renovated, but an act of new creation (cf. discussion at 20:11). No description is given of either the new heaven or the new earth in verse 1 except for the cryptic statement "There was no more sea." There is remarkably little revealed in the Bible concerning the character of the new heaven and the new earth, but it is evidently quite different from their present form of existence. Most of the earth is now covered with water, but the new earth apparently will have no bodies of water except for the river mentioned in 22:2.

Only a few other passages in the Bible deal with the subject of the new heaven and the new earth, and these are often in a context dealing with the millennium (cf. Isa. 65:17; 66:22; II Peter 3:13). The fact that millennial truths are mentioned in the same context in all three of these major references has often confused expositors. However, it is a common principle in prophecy to bring together events that are distantly related chronologically, such as frequent reference to the first and second comings of Christ, actually separated by thousands of years (Isa. 61:1–2; cf. Luke 4:17–19). In a similar way there is mention of the resurrection of the righteous and of the wicked in the same verse, as in Daniel 12:2, events separated by a thousand years. And Malachi 4:5 speaks of the second coming of the Lord followed by verse 6 referring to His first coming. Second Peter 3:10–13 refers to the day of the Lord beginning before the millennium, as well as to the destruction of the heavens and the earth

with fire at the end of the millennium. If all the passages are put together, the sequence of events becomes plain, and the allusions to the
new heaven and the new earth are clearly set forth in the book of
Revelation as following the millennial kingdom and immediately preceded by the destruction of the old earth and heaven, as previously mentioned. J. B. Smith's objection to the first heaven and the first earth passing away is not substantiated by any of the proof texts which he cites.[1]

The eternal state is clearly indicated in the absence of sea, for frequent
mention of bodies of water occur in millennial passages (cf. Ps. 72:8;
Isa. 11:9, 11; Ezek. 47:10, 15, 17, 18, 20; 48:28; Zech. 9:10; 14:8). The
evidence of Revelation 21:1 is so specific that most commentators do not
question that the eternal state is here in view.

FIRST VISION OF THE NEW JERUSALEM (21:2)

21:2 And I John saw the holy city, new Jerusalem, coming down
from God out of heaven, prepared as a bride adorned for her husband.

Though John is impressed with the new heaven and the new earth, his
attention is immediately directed to that which is central in the vision,
"the holy city, new Jerusalem, coming down from God out of heaven,
prepared as a bride adorned for her husband."[2] The expression "the holy
city, new Jerusalem" is in antithesis to the earthly Jerusalem, which spiritually was referred to as Sodom in 11:8. Earlier in the writing of the
New Testament canon, the earthly Jerusalem is referred to as "the holy
city" (cf. Matt. 4:5; 27:53). In Revelation 3:12 the new Jerusalem is
anticipated and referred to not only by this title but as "the city of my
God, which is new Jerusalem, which cometh down out of heaven from
my God."

Most important, however, is the fact that the city is declared to come
down from God out of heaven. In the Greek, the expression "out of
heaven" precedes the phrase "from God," just the reverse of the Authorized
Version order. Nothing is said about the new Jerusalem being created at
this point and the language seems to imply that it has been in existence
in heaven prior to this event (for further discussion, see 21:9). Nothing
is revealed concerning this in Scripture unless the expression of John
14:2, "I go to prepare a place for you," refers to this. If the new Jerusalem
is in existence throughout the millennial reign of Christ, it is possible that
it is a satellite city suspended over the earth during the thousand-year
reign of Christ as the dwelling place of resurrected and translated saints
who also have access to the earthly scene. This would help explain

---

[1]*A Revelation of Jesus Christ,* p. 281.
[2]For various views on the new Jerusalem, see John Peter Lange, *Commentary on the Holy Scriptures.* Vol. XXIV: *Revelation,* pp. 389–92, and Robert Govett, *The Apocalypse Explained,* pp. 549-610.

an otherwise difficult problem of the dwelling place of resurrected and translated beings on the earth during a period in which men are still in their natural bodies and living ordinary lives. If so, the new Jerusalem is withdrawn from the earthly scene in connection with the destruction of the old earth, and later comes down to the new earth.

As presented in Revelation 21 and 22, however, the new Jerusalem is not seen as it may have existed in the past, but as it will be seen in eternity future. The possibility of Jerusalem being a satellite city over the earth during the millennium is not specifically taught in any scripture and at best is an inference based on the implication that it has been in existence prior to its introduction in Revelation 21. Its characteristics as presented here, however, are related to the eternal state rather than to the millennial kingdom.

The only description of the new Jerusalem given in verse 2 is embodied in the phrase "prepared as a bride adorned for her husband." Because of the fact that the church, the Body of Christ, is considered under the symbolism of a bride in the New Testament in contrast to Israel as the wife of Jehovah, some have attempted to limit the new Jerusalem as having reference only to the church. Snell argues at length that the new Jerusalem is specifically the bride, that is, the saints of the present dispensation, the church. He believes rather than a literal, physical city in the eternal state that the new Jerusalem represents the church as the people of God. The church is seen in this section as in the millennium rather than in the eternal state.[3] Van Ryn also takes a common position when he says, "This city is apparently a symbolic description of the Bride herself."[4]

The use of the marriage figure, however, in both the Old and New Testaments is sufficiently frequent so that we cannot arbitrarily insist that figures are always used in precisely the same connotation. The subsequent description of the new Jerusalem in this chapter makes plain that saints of all ages are involved and that what we have here is not the church per se but a city or dwelling place having the freshness and beauty of a bride adorned for marriage to her husband.

F. W. Grant holds that the new Jerusalem will contain the saints of all ages. On the basis of Hebrews 11:10, 16 where Abraham is said to look for a heavenly city, Grant concludes that while it is the bride-city, it nevertheless has other occupants:

> Why should it not be the bride-*city*, named from the bride-*church*, whose home it is, and yet contains other occupants? . . . the heavenly city, the dwelling-place of God, permitting none of the redeemed to be outside of it but opening its gates widely to all.[5]

[3]H. H. Snell, *Notes on the Revelation*, pp. 231-45.
[4]August Van Ryn, *Notes on the Book of Revelation*, p. 218.
[5]*The Revelation of Jesus Christ*, p. 231.

Jennings likewise includes the saints of all ages in the heavenly Jerusalem:

> But since thus all saints of the olden times, be they prior to any distinction, as Enoch; or Gentile, as Job; or Jewish, as Abraham, may have their place in this city, she [the new Jerusalem] must by no means be accounted as characteristically Jewish. The Jerusalem of the Jews is ever and always on the earth, nor does she come out of heaven at all, since she has never left the earth; but the glory of the Lord rises upon her there (Isa. 60:1). . . . Every child of God through all the ages, whose earthly tabernacle has been dissolved, shall be at this time in his heavenly house, and thus together form the heavenly city.[6]

GOD TO DWELL WITH MEN (21:3-4)

21:3-4 And I heard a great voice out of heaven saying, Behold, the tabernacle of God is with men, and he will dwell with them, and they shall be his people, and God himself shall be with them, and be their God. And God shall wipe away all tears from their eyes; and there shall be no more death, neither sorrow, nor crying, neither shall there be any more pain: for the former things are passed away.

As John beheld the vision of the new heaven and the new earth and the lovely new Jerusalem, he heard a great voice from heaven giving the spiritual significance of this scene. This is the last of twenty-one times that "a great voice" or "a loud voice" is mentioned in the book of Revelation. The fact that the voice is great connotes that the subsequent revelation is important and authoritative. The voice declares, "Behold, the tabernacle of God is with men." This tabernacle (Gr., *skēnē*) is in contrast to the Tabernacle of God in the wilderness in which God dwelt and also to the tabernacle of God in heaven (13:6; 15:5). It symbolizes that God is now present with men in the new earth and in the new Jerusalem. The verse itself explains the meaning in the words "he will dwell with them, and they shall be his people, and God himself shall be with them, and be their God." The word for "dwell" (Gr., *skēnoō*) is the verb form for the noun translated "tabernacle" (cf. John 1:14; Rev. 7:15; 12:12; 13:6). The presence of God in Scripture frequently connotes fellowship and blessing. Here it is stated that the inhabitants of the new Jerusalem will be the people of God and that God will not only be with them but will also be their God, a thought which is often repeated in the Scripture. J. B. Smith finds twenty-one instances.[7] Some manuscripts add an *s* to "people," but the Authorized Version reading is preferred.

The presence of God assures an entirely new state for those who inhabit the new Jerusalem. In contrast to their former suffering which included going through the tribulation for many of these saints, God is

[6]F. C. Jennings, *Studies in Revelation*, pp. 566–67.
[7]Smith, p. 283.

stated to "wipe away all tears from their eyes." The expression "all tears" is singular in the Greek, literally "every tear" (Gr., *pan dakruon*), as if God wipes away every single tear. There is no just ground for imagining from this text that the saints will shed tears in heaven concerning the failures of their former life on earth. The emphasis here is on the comfort of God, not on the remorse of the saints. The tears seem to refer to tears shed on earth as the saints endured suffering for Christ's sake, rather than tears shed in heaven because of human failure. This is in keeping with the rest of the passage which goes on to say that other aspects of human sorrow such as death, sorrow, crying, or pain will also be no more in existence. The summary given at the end of the verse is "The former things are passed away." The "crying" mentioned refers to vocal response to sorrow in contrast to tears which are a silent response. The new situation is the consummation of divine grace and is the assurance of the estate of ineffable blessedness for those who were once lost sinners. The Scriptures make plain that not only the old earth and heaven pass away but also all the details and associations that belong to it which would mar the situation in the new heaven and the new earth.

ALL THINGS MADE NEW (21:5-6)

21:5-6 And he that sat upon the throne said, Behold, I make all things new. And he said unto me, Write: for these words are true and faithful. And he said unto me, It is done. I am Alpha and Omega, the beginning and the end. I will give unto him that is athirst of the fountain of the water of life freely.

As if in contrast to the great voice out of heaven in verse 3, verse 5 specifies that the One sitting upon the throne now speaks. It is probably too much to infer from the use of the singular "he" that God the Father is specifically meant here and not Christ the Son, though it is true that the mediatorial aspect of the kingdom is surrendered at the end of the millennium (cf. I Cor. 15:24-28). The Son will share the throne in this situation much as He has done in the past. The special character of His rule over the earth and His contest with the wicked, however, will be ended. An announcement is made: "Behold, I make all things new." Like the announcement of verse 3, this is introduced by the term "behold" (Gr., *idou*), the imperative form of *horaō*, meaning "to look" or "to see." The word introduces the great pronouncement "I make all things new." The verb "make" (Gr., *poieō*) means "to make, form, or construct" and is a common verb occurring many times in the New Testament for a work of accomplishment. To argue, as some have done, however, that this proves that there is no new heaven or earth created at this time because the specific word *create* is not used is building too much on too little. The same word *poieō* is used in Matthew 19:4 where God is said to have "made" Adam and Eve using both the word *create* (Gr., *ktizō*) and the word *made* (Gr., *poieō*) for the same act. Everything, of course, is not created on the occasion of the new heaven and the new earth, as all the saints involved have come from the old creation; but all things are made new in the same sense that Eve was made a new creature though formed from the rib of Adam. The word for "new" (Gr., *kainos*) means to be both new in character and new in the sense of recently made. It connotes a drastic change.

John is so astounded by the announcement and all the previous revelation that he has to be reminded, "Write, for these words are true and faithful." The message from the throne continues in verse 6 with the utterance "It is done. I am Alpha and Omega, the beginning and the end." The reference is to the work accomplished throughout the whole drama of human history prior to the eternal state. This statement does not mean that there are no future works of God but that a major work has been brought to completion and that the works now relating to the eternal state are beginning. The speaker now introduces Himself as the "Alpha and Omega, the beginning and the end." It is by this precise title that Christ is introduced in 1:8, and the phrase is again found in 22:13. While the expression is appropriate for God the Father, the fact that it is introduced in 1:8 in reference to Christ seems to confirm the idea that Christ is also in view in this passage as sitting on the throne. With the beginning of the eternal state, there is a difference in the divine undertaking but not a difference in the divine majesty of the Second Person. The first of three promises made in verses 6 and 7 then follows, where water from the fountain of the water of life is promised in abundance to the one who is thirsty. A similar assurance is given to the martyred throng of tribulation saints in 7:17. It refers to the abundant character of eternal life and the blessings which flow from it and is a fulfillment of the invitation of Isaiah 55:1 as well as that of Christ in John 4:10, 13–14.

THE BLESSINGS OF THE OVERCOMER (21:7–8)

21:7-8 He that overcometh shall inherit all things; and I will be his God, and he shall be my son. But the fearful, and unbelieving, and the abominable, and murderers, and whoremongers, and sorcerers, and idolaters, and all liars, shall have their part in the lake which burneth with fire and brimstone: which is the second death.

Another promise now extended to the glorified saints described as overcomers is that they shall inherit all things. This in turn is an extension of the additional promises to each saint that God will be his God and that in glory he shall be "my son." Frequently in Scripture, particular promises are given those who triumph in faith, but here the generous provision is made that they shall inherit "all things" rather than some

316

particular aspect of the divine provision (cf. Matt. 5:5; 19:29; 25:34; I Cor. 6:9–10; Heb. 1:14; 9:15; I Peter 1:4; 3:9; I John 5:5). Promises to overcomers are included in the messages to the seven churches and are anticipated in I Corinthians 3:21–23.

In contrast to the abundant blessings on the child of God is the sad inheritance of unbelief outlined in verse 8, where the unsaved are characterized as "fearful," "unbelieving," "abominable," "murderers," "whoremongers," "sorcerers," "idolaters," and "all liars," whose destiny is to be burned with fire and brimstone, which is the second death. The unsaved are here pictured in their principal characteristics. A similar list is found in 21:27 and another in 22:15. Some of the saved were guilty of like offenses but availed themselves in proper time of the grace of God through faith in Christ. No true believer could be categorized by this list of sins. While there is further mention of the fate of the unsaved later in the book of Revelation, this is the last mention of the lake of fire and of the second death specifically.

THE NEW JERUSALEM AS THE BRIDE (21:9–11)

21:9-11 And there came unto me one of the seven angels which had the seven vials full of the seven last plagues, and talked with me saying, Come hither, I will shew thee the bride, the Lamb's wife. And he carried me away in the spirit to a great and high mountain, and shewed me that great city, the holy Jerusalem, descending out of heaven from God, Having the glory of God: and her light was like unto a stone most precious, even like a jasper stone, clear as crystal.

With this survey of the eternal state and its blessings before him, John is now invited by one of the seven angels who had poured out the seven vials of the wrath of God to behold the bride, the Lamb's wife. This angel may have been the one mentioned in 17:1 who showed John the vision of Babylon, the harlot, but it is impossible to prove that it is the same one of the seven. In keeping with the earlier revelation of 21:2, the holy city, the new Jerusalem, is here characterized as "the bride, the Lamb's wife." Since a city is not a bride nor a wife, the truth here represented is that the city, the residence of the saints of eternity future, is to be compared to a bride for beauty and is intimately related to Jesus Christ the Lamb.

Expositors have differed as to whether the vision here introduced is chronologically subsequent to the scene of 21:1–8, or whether it is a retrospect of the millennial situation. Though the book of Revelation is not written in strict chronological style in that the events in certain chapters such as 17 actually occur before some of the preceding chapters, the decision can be reached only by a study of the contents. Those who consider this a millennial scene hold that after the preview of the new heaven and the new earth, John returns to consider the new Jerusalem as descending to the millennial earth. Those who follow this form of interpretation believe that the new Jerusalem during the millennial reign of Christ will be suspended above the earth and will be the habitation of the resurrected dead. William Kelly gives an extended defense of the interpretation that the narration returns to the millennial scene beginning here.[8] In his later work, *Exposition of Revelation,* he takes a similar position.[9]

Arno C. Gaebelein likewise believes that beginning in verse 9 the millennial state is once more introduced.[10] Edward Bennett also believes 21:9 through 22:5 is descriptive of the holy Jerusalem during the millennium rather than in the eternal state. He finds confirmation of this especially in 22:2 relative to the use of the leaves of the tree "for the healing of the nations."[11] He does not seem aware of the possible explanation of this problem, namely, the translation "health" instead of "healing" which would be in harmony with the eternal state.

Other expositors, however, have concluded that there is not sufficient justification for returning to the millennial scene after the tremendous events portraying the close of the millennium and the introduction of the new heaven and the new earth. For these scholars Revelation 21:9 through 22:7 is a description of the new Jerusalem as it will be established in the new earth in eternity to come. In other words this passage would refer to eternity rather than to the millennium.

A number of considerations support the conclusion that the eternal state is in view in Revelation 21:9 through 22:7. There is good reason for concluding that the order of Revelation beginning in chapter 19 is chronological; a retrogression in time would violate the structure of the last great section of the book. The description of the holy city as given in 21:2 is obviously identical to the description in 21:9. As most expositors grant that 21:2 is the eternal state, it would follow that 21:9 should be considered the same. The implication of 21:2 and 21:10-11 is that the holy city arrives on the new earth. Prophecies governing the millennial earth do not allow for such a city on earth. The apportionment of the Holy Land and the description of the Temple as found in Ezekiel's description of the millennial earth (Ezek. 40–48) are entirely different. The heavenly city is obviously seen as it will appear in the eternal state in the entire passage beginning with 21:1.

Hoste supports the idea that this is the eternal state rather than a reversion to the millennium: "The usual interpretation of a certain school,

[8]*Lectures on the Book of Revelation,* pp. 459 ff.
[9]*Exposition of Revelation,* pp. 248 ff.
[10]*The Revelation,* pp. 158 ff.
[11]*The Visions of John in Patmos,* pp. 278–99.

that the closing description of the Heavenly Jerusalem merely reverts to a millennial scene, seems untenable, if carefully considered."[12] Hoste admits that there are similar reversions in the Apocalypse but states that in each case previously there have been clear indications which are not found here. He notes that references to the nations, to the kings of the earth, and to the healing of the nations, and other expressions which seem to refer to the millennial earth all have a satisfactory explanation and relate to the eternal state.

Ottman concludes that this section deals with the eternal state and not the millennium:

> This expanded vision of the New Jerusalem does not, for its inter-
> pretation, demand a return in thought to the conditions existing dur-
> ing the Millennium. . . . A return to the Millennial earth in this vision
> of John would be incongruous and perplexing. There may be diffi-
> culties in the way of harmonizing what is implied in the terms of this
> vision with our own thoughts of eternity, but this should not discour-
> age us, for eternal conditions may be altogether at variance with our
> ideas of them. The all-important question is, What does the Word of
> God say? We must again insist upon the fact that the New Jerusalem
> that descends from God is a literal city, built by Him, and is to be
> forever the link between the new heaven and the new earth.[13]

As demonstrated in the exposition of this passage, there is insufficient support for chronologically placing this scene as contemporaneous with the millennium. The new Jerusalem apparently is seen here as it will be in eternity future after the millennium has been completed. However, as previously intimated, there is a possibility that the holy city will also be in existence during the millennium and, though not described in that character in this passage, may indeed be the dwelling place of the resurrected and translated saints during the thousand-year reign of Christ on earth. The problem passages of this section, which are offered by some to equate it with the millennium, upon examination prove to yield another conclusion, that eternity future is in view here.

In interpreting the description of the heavenly city, the problem of symbolic interpretation comes to the fore perhaps more than in any other section of the book of Revelation. Even the most conservative scholars are not necessarily in agreement on the extent to which this description should be taken literally. The problem depends ultimately upon the human judgment of the expositor. Certain guidelines, however, can be laid down.

John actually saw what he recorded, and what he saw is to some extent interpreted to him. Obviously what he saw transcended any earthly ex-

[12]William Hoste, *The Vision of John the Divine*, pp. 176–78; cf. Lewis S. Chafer, *Systematic Theology*, IV, 131.
[13]Ford C. Ottman, *The Unfolding of the Ages*, pp. 458–59.

perience, and it was necessary for him to describe what he saw in terms that were meaningful to him. This must not be construed, however, as an inaccurate description because John was guided by the Holy Spirit when he wrote, and the description must be viewed as accurate insofar as it is possible to communicate. The passage itself, however, as in the description of the gold, implies that the material substances were different from what exists in this present earth.

Of major importance are the facts that John actually saw a city, that this city was inhabited by saints of all ages, and that God Himself was present in it. Until further light is given, it is probably a safe procedure to accept the description of this city as corresponding to the physical characteristics attributed to it.

Responding to the angel's invitation, John is carried away in spirit to a great and high mountain. The inference is that he is not actually transported, but only experiences what follows as if he had been taken to a vantage point where he could see the entire scene. A similar experience was afforded him in 17:3. As John beholds, he sees "that great city, the holy Jerusalem, descending out of heaven from God." Again the contrast is evident between this city and Babylon of Revelation 17 and 18. A similar description is given in 21:2 where the city is declared to be holy and to have come from God out of heaven. It is to be distinguished both from Babylon and from the earthly city of Jerusalem which in its history had also fallen into evil ways.

In verse 11 a general description of the new Jerusalem is given. The city is characterized as having "the glory of God." It should be noted that the heavenly city is introduced in verses 1 and 2 as "holy," then as "new," "out of heaven," and "from God." Most of these details are repeated in verse 10, and in verse 11 the city is said to have the glory of God, and to have a brilliant light. As the glory of God is the sum of His infinite perfections in their manifestations, so the new Jerusalem reflects all that God is.

The city is ablaze with light compared to the brightness of a precious stone such as jasper, and clear as crystal. The stone here described as a jasper has its name transliterated from a similar word in the original (Gr., *iaspis*), a name used for stones of various colors, but here specifying the qualities "precious" and "clear as crystal." The mention of this stone which is costly to men but used lavishly in the new Jerusalem (cf. 21:19) is designed to manifest the glory of God. Later in the passage (v. 23), the fact is revealed that the city does not originate its light or radiance, but all illumination comes from the Lamb. The believer in Christ does not generate the light of Christ, but he should both reflect and transmit its glory without blurring the beauty and loveliness of Christ.

THE WALL AND THE GATES OF THE CITY (21:12–14)

21:12-14 And had a wall great and high, and had twelve gates, and at the gates twelve angels, and names written thereon, which are the names of the twelve tribes of the children of Israel: On the east three gates; on the north three gates; on the south three gates; and on the west three gates. And the wall of the city had twelve foundations, and in them the names of the twelve apostles of the Lamb.

The scene which John sees is tremendously impressive. After giving the general appearance of the city, he now itemizes the specific details. Expositors have differed as to the degree in which this description should be taken literally, some believing that the city is actually nonexistent and presented only as a symbolic presentation of the blessings of the saints in eternity future. Such a view, however, is difficult to harmonize with the specific details given which are nowhere explained in other than the literal sense in the Bible. There does not seem to be any solid objection to the concept that the saints in the new heaven and the new earth will have as their home precisely such a city, glorious in every aspect, reaching to tremendous heights into the new heaven, and embodying characteristics to remind them of their spiritual heritage.

The first important fact mentioned by John in verse 12 is the wall of the city, described as "great and high," an obvious symbol of exclusion of all that is unworthy to enter the city. Though countless saints will enjoy its glory, there is this reminder that only those qualified may enter. In the wall are twelve gates guarded by twelve angels and inscribed with the names of the twelve tribes of Israel. In keeping with the square shape of the city, the gates are located on each of the four sides as specified in verse 13. In the description of the new Jerusalem, the number twelve is very prominent as seen in the twelve gates and twelve angels in this passage, the twelve tribes of Israel (21:12), twelve foundations (21:14), twelve apostles (21:14). twelve pearls (21:21), and twelve kinds of fruit (22:2). The height, length, and width of the city are described as 12,000 furlongs each, or 1,342 miles (21:16) and the wall's height is said to measure twelve times twelve cubits, that is, 144 cubits, or over 200 feet (21:17).

The twelve angels mentioned are apparently apportioned one angel to each gate and serve in this capacity as an honor guard. The book of Revelation does not indicate the particular name of each gate. In the description of the city of Jerusalem which will be on earth during the millennium, Ezekiel gives the names of the twelve tribes of Israel as inscribed on the gates of the city at that time. The new Jerusalem that descends from heaven, however, is an entirely different city from that of Ezekiel and is much larger in every dimension.

It may be, however, that names are assigned to the gates of the new

Jerusalem in a similar way as those on the gates of the earthly city of Jerusalem in the millennium. If so, the names of these gates will correspond to the twelve tribes according to Ezekiel 48:31–34 in the following pattern: on the north side, going east to west, Levi, Judah, and Reuben; on the east side, going from north to south, Joseph, Benjamin, and Dan; on the west side, going from north to south, Naphtali, Asher, and Gad; on the south side, going from east to west, Simeon, Issachar, and Zebulun. The order of the gates on each side is derived from the fact that Ezekiel seems to proceed from the northwest corner eastward, then southward, then westward, and then northward. It can only be assumed, however, that the same arrangement is true of the new Jerusalem. The implication from the fact of gates on each side of the city, however, is that those properly qualified have freedom to go in and out. The new Jerusalem will have the distinction of being the residence of the saints, but it is implied that they will be able to travel elsewhere on the new earth and possibly also in the new heaven.

Also prominent in connection with the wall and the gates are twelve foundations, mentioned in verse 14, inscribed with the names of the twelve apostles of the Lamb. There has been much speculation as to why the names of the twelve apostles are used in this connection, but the most obvious answer is that they have a prominent place in the program of God in relation to the new Jerusalem. The twelve apostles on the one hand were of Israel and were called out of Israel to be leaders in the church in the New Testament. They are, in some sense, representative of both Israel and the church, though their primary significance seems to be that the saints of the church age are included in this eternal city.

It is noteworthy, however, that not only are the twelve apostles represented but also the twelve tribes of Israel. This should settle beyond any question the matter of the inclusion of Old Testament saints. It apparently is the divine intent to represent to the reader that the new Jerusalem will have among its citizens not only the church, or saints of the present age, but also Israel, or saints of other ages, whether in the Old Testament or in the tribulation period. Later on there is mention also of Gentiles. The careful expositor, therefore, on the one hand will not confuse Israel and the church as if one were the other. On the other hand, he will not deny to both their respective places of privilege in God's program. The anticipation of Hebrews 12:22–24 is specifically that the heavenly Jerusalem will include not only God and an innumerable company of angels but also the general assembly and church of the firstborn, that is, the saints of the present age and the spirits of just men made perfect, that is, all other saints. As far as this scripture is concerned, there is only one eternal resting place for the saints, and that is the new Jerusalem.

All saints, therefore, must necessarily participate in the city, just as many of them did also in the millennial scene without destroying the distinction between different companies of saints.

The Dimensions of the City (21:15-17)

21:15-17 And he that talked with me had a golden reed to measure the city, and the gates thereof, and the wall thereof. And the city lieth foursquare, and the length is as large as the breadth; and he measured the city with the reed, twelve thousand furlongs. The length and the breadth and the height of it are equal. And he measured the wall thereof, an hundred and forty and four cubits, according to the measure of a man, that is, of the angel.

Having introduced John to the wall, gates, and foundations of the city, the angel next measures the major dimensions of the new Jerusalem. Using a reed, a measure about ten feet long, the unit of measure common among the Jews, with which to measure the city, its gates, and its walls, the angel finds that the city is square, its length and breadth being the same, twelve thousand furlongs. Since a furlong is equal to 582 feet, the measured distance is equivalent to 1,342 miles, often spoken of roughly as 1,500 miles.

According to verse 16, the tremendous dimension of the city's length and breadth is equaled by its height which towers an equal distance into the heavens. Nothing is said as to the shape of the city except as the reader is guided by its square dimensions. Some have assumed it to be a cube. J. B. Smith, for instance, considers any other view as "reducing it to dimensions far inferior to those indicated by divine inspiration."[14] Inspiration, however, does not indicate the shape; it also could be in the form of a pyramid with sides sloping to a peak at the height indicated. Hoste believes the city is in the form of a pyramid.[15] This would have certain advantages, not necessarily because smaller, but because this shape provides a vehicle for the river of life to proceed out of the throne of God, which seems to be at the top, to find its way to the bottom, assuming our experience of gravity will be somewhat normal also in the new earth.

McGee, assuming that the city is in space, offers another suggestion, namely, that the city is a cube within a crystal sphere. He writes:

Several times attention is called to the fact that the city is like a crystal-clear stone or crystal-clear gold. This emphasis leads us to believe that the city is seen through the crystal. We live *outside* the planet called earth, but the Bride will dwell *within* the planet called the New Jerusalem. The glory of light streaming through this crystal-clear

[14]Smith, p. 289.
[15]Hoste, p. 178.

prism, will break up into a polychromed rainbow of breath-taking beauty.[16]

Whatever its shape, a city of large dimensions would be proper, if it is to be the residence of the saved of all ages including infants who died before reaching the age of accountability. It is not necessary, however, to hold that everyone will live continually within its walls throughout eternity. The implications are that there is plenty of room for everyone and that this city provides a residence for the saints of all ages.

In addition to measuring the city itself, the angel measures the wall which by comparison is much smaller, namely 144 cubits or, assuming that a cubit is 18 inches, a height of 216 feet. This measurement is described as being "the measure of a man, that is, of the angel." A. T. Robertson interprets this phrase: "Though measured by an angel, a human standard was employed, man's measure which is the angel's (Bengel)."[17] Robertson identifies the word *measure* (Gr., *metron*) as "the accusative case of general reference in apposition with the verb *emetrē-sen*."[18] The implication of this statement is that whether man or angel measured it, the measurement would be the same.

The city taken as a whole is pictured as descending from heaven to the new earth, and the fact that it has foundations and comes from heaven to the earth seems to imply that it rests on the new earth itself. This also is implied in the fact that people go in and out of the gates, which fact is difficult to visualize unless the gates themselves rest upon the earth.

THE BEAUTY OF THE CITY (21:18–21)

21:18-21 And the building of the wall of it was of jasper: and the city was pure gold, like unto clear glass. And the foundations of the wall of the city were garnished with all manner of precious stones. The first foundation was jasper; the second, sapphire; the third, a ϕhalcedony; the fourth, an emerald; The fifth, sardonyx; the sixth, sardius; the seventh, chrysolyte; the eighth, beryl; the ninth, a topaz; the tenth, a chrysoprasus; the eleventh, a jacinth; the twelfth, an amethyst. And the twelve gates were twelve pearls; every several gate was of one pearl: and the street of the city was pure gold, as it were transparent glass.

With the dimensions of the city graphically given, John next describes the glory of the city. The wall is said to be of jasper in keeping with the general description of verse 11 and probably clear as crystal also. The city as a whole is portrayed as made of pure gold like clear glass. This description would indicate that it is gold in appearance but like clear

[16]J. Vernon McGee, *Reveling Through Revelation*, II, 104–5.
[17]*Word Pictures in the New Testament*, VI, 474.
[18]*Ibid.*

glass in substance, namely, glass with a gold cast to it. Employing the language of semblance, John is endeavoring to give a description of a scene which in most respects transcends earthly experience. The constant mention of transparency indicates that the city is designed to transmit the glory of God in the form of light without hindrance.

Attention is next directed to the foundation of the city which is said to be garnished with all kinds of precious stones. This is a sight of indescribable beauty with the light of the city playing upon the multicolored stones. The city's first foundation is again the familiar jasper stone mentioned twice previously. The various foundations are represented as layers built upon each other, each layer extending around all four sides of the city. On top of the jasper stone is a second foundation, the brilliant sapphire, a stone similar to a diamond in hardness and blue in color. The third foundation is chalcedony, an agate stone from Chalcedon (in Turkey), thought to be sky-blue with stripes of other colors running through it. The fourth foundation, an emerald, introduces a bright green color. The fifth, the sardonyx, is a red and white stone. The sixth foundation, the sardius stone, refers to a common jewel of reddish color also found in honey color which was considered less valuable. The sardius is used with the jasper in Revelation 4:3 in describing the glory of God on the throne.

The seventh foundation is formed of chrysolyte, a transparent stone golden in color according to the ancient writer Pliny,[19] and therefore somewhat different from the modern pale-green chrysolyte stone. The eighth foundation, the beryl, is sea-green. The topaz, the ninth foundation, is yellow-green and transparent.[20] The tenth foundation, the chrysoprasus, introduces another shade of green. The eleventh foundation, the jacinth, is a violet color. The last stone, the amethyst, is commonly purple.

Though the precise colors of these stones in some cases are not certain, the general picture here described by John is one of unmistakable beauty, designed to reflect the glory of God in a spectrum of brilliant color. The light of the city within shining through these various colors in the foundation of the wall topped by the wall itself composed of the crystal-clear jasper forms a scene of dazzling beauty in keeping with the glory of God and the beauty of His holiness. The city is undoubtedly far more beautiful to the eye than anything that man has ever been able to create, and it reflects not only the infinite wisdom and power of God but also His grace as extended to the objects of His salvation.

Built in the walls are the twelve gates described as each being made

[19]William F. Arndt and F. Wilbur Gingrich, A Greek-English Lexicon of the New Testament, p. 897.
[20]"Topaz," Unger's Bible Dictionary, p. 746.

of one huge pearl, leading to the streets of the city described as pure gold transparent as glass, that is, golden in color and appearance but having the translucency of glass. The word *street* (Gr., *plateia*) is in the singular but is used generically to describe all the streets of the city.

THE TEMPLE OF THE CITY (21:22)

21:22 And I saw no temple therein: for the Lord God Almighty and the Lamb are the temple of it.

The next phase of the vision is introduced with the familiar clause "And I saw," indicating a new and important phase of the divine revelation. John, as he searches the city, finds no temple therein. This is in contrast to the situation in the Old Testament where Israel first had the Tabernacle and then the Temple. This is also a sharp contrast to the millennial situation where a temple is built for the worship of God. Here the shadows are dispelled and, as the Scripture indicates, the Lord God Himself and the Lamb are the temple of the new city. No longer is the structure necessary, for the saints are in the immediate presence of the Lord with no need for an earthly mediator or for shadows of things eternal. The word for "temple" (Gr., *naos*) is the word used for the sanctuary, or God's dwelling place, the Holy of Holies, in the Temple of Israel. Believers now have access to the most sacred, intimate fellowship with the Lord their God in fulfillment of the many promises given to the saints.

THE LIGHT OF THE CITY (21:23–24)

21:23-24 And the city had no need of the sun, neither of the moon, to shine in it: for the glory of God did lighten it, and the Lamb is the light thereof. And the nations of them which are saved shall walk in the light of it: and the kings of the earth do bring their glory and honour into it.

In contrast to the millennial earth and all preceding history of man, the new Jerusalem does not need the light of the sun nor the moon, for the Scriptures indicate that God Himself is the source of light in the city. Tucker points out that the new Jerusalem is distinguished by the things that are missing. There will be no temple, no sacrifice, no sun, no moon, no darkness, no gates to shut, no abomination.[21] This is another indication that this is the eternal state rather than the millennial situation, because if the sun or the moon were in existence, it would shine upon the city. The form of expression would not make impossible the existence of the sun and the moon, as this scripture merely says there is no need of them. But the position of the city on the new earth in the dimensions indicated

---

[21]W. L. Tucker, *Studies in Revelation*, p. 378.

is impossible to accommodate with the millennial scene; and as pictured here, the city is portrayed in its eternal character rather than in its existence in time. That God Himself should be the light of the city is of course entirely in keeping with many passages in the Old Testament comparing God to light; and this new situation correlates with Jesus Christ Himself being the light of the world (cf. John 1:7–9; 3:19; 8:12; 12:35). Because God is light and there is no darkness in Him, believers are exhorted to walk in the light in their present existence on this earth in keeping with their future in heaven (I John 1:5–7). The whole of the city of the new Jerusalem is designed to transmit the light in all the beauty and color previously described.

In verse 24 the nations of the saved as well as the kings of the earth are declared to walk in the light of it and bring their glory and honor into it. Some have arbitrarily assumed that because the nations are mentioned this must be a millennial situation and not the eternal state. This is an unwarranted assumption, however, for the text specifies the nations of them which are saved. The word *nations* (Gr., *ethnē*) is the word for Gentiles. The meaning is not that political entities will enter into the new Jerusalem but rather that those who are saved Gentiles, who belong to the non-Jewish races, will be in the new city.

In the eternal state, therefore, not only saved Israelites and the church will be present but also saved Gentiles who are not numbered among either Israel or the church. That the kings of the earth bring their glory and honor into the city means that those among the saved who have honored positions on earth will ascribe the glory and honor that once were theirs to their Lord and God. There is no need to strain at the preposition "into" (Gr., *eis*) as if the kings of the earth will not actually enter into the city as J. B. Smith holds.[22] This preposition is the normal one to indicate ingress, though it may not actually mean this in every instance. The text does say, however, that they bring their honor and glory not "to" the city but "into" it. The implication is that the honor and glory are brought inside and not left outside the gates. As a matter of fact, these kings are saved and have access to the city even as others.

Larkin introduces the startling point of view that children will be born in the eternal state who unlike the posterity of Adam and Eve will be sinless.[23] There is no indication whatever in Scripture that resurrected and translated beings have the quality of human sex, much less the capacity to produce offspring.

ACCESS TO THE CITY (21:25-27)

21:25-27 And the gates of it shall not be shut at all by day: for

22Smith, p. 292.
23Clarence Larkin, *Book of Revelation*, p. 207.

> there shall be no night there. And they shall bring the glory and
> honour of the nations into it. And there shall in no wise enter into it
> any thing that defileth, neither whatsoever worketh abomination, or
> maketh a lie: but they which are written in the Lamb's book of life.

A further word is given concerning the fact that the gates of the city
are never shut, because in the city there is continuous day, hence no night.
Here again is a contrast to the millennial situation in which day and night
continue as the norm for the entire earth. The brilliant light of the city,
however, dispels any possible darkness. Believers in their glorified bodies
do not need rest, and their lives are full of continuous activity even like
the holy angels.

As if in repetition of the thought of verse 24, that the kings of the
earth bring their glory and honor into the holy city, verse 26 indicates
that the glory and honor of the nations themselves come into it. Here
again the word *nations* should be translated "Gentiles," referring to the
Gentile glory in contrast to the glory of Israel or of the church. Expositors
too often have forgotten that God has a purpose for the Gentiles as well
as for Israel, and He glorifies Himself through them also. Whatever
among the Gentiles can be used to bring honor and glory to the Lord
is here also brought into the eternal state.

Verse 27, however, indicates plainly that nothing will ever enter the
city which is in any sense evil, as only those whose names are written in
the Lamb's book of life are eligible for entrance. There does not seem
to be any attempt made to keep them out. This fact is another reminder
that all who are there have entered the city as the objects of God's grace,
otherwise they too would be excluded. This will be a perfect environment
in contrast to the centuries of human sin, and the saints will enjoy this
perfect situation through all eternity to come. The inhabitants of the city
will be characterized by eternal life and absolute moral purity.

22

CONCLUDING REVELATIONS AND EXHORTATIONS

THE RIVER OF THE WATER OF LIFE (22:1)

22:1 And he shewed me a pure river of water of life, clear as crystal, proceeding out of the throne of God and of the Lamb.

As Alford notes, "The whole of the things described in the remaining portion of the book are subsequent to the general judgment, and descriptive of the consummation of the triumph and bliss of Christ's people with Him in the eternal kingdom of God."[1] As a provision for the saints and in keeping with the complete holiness and purity of the heavenly city, John sees a pure river of the water of life, clear as crystal, coming out of the throne of God and of the Lamb. This is not to be confused with the river issuing from the millennial sanctuary (Ezek. 47:1, 12) nor with that of the living waters going forth from Jerusalem (Zech. 14:8) also in the millennial scene. These millennial streams anticipate, however, this future river which is in the new Jerusalem, which speaks of the power, purity, and eternal life manifest in the heavenly city. This river corresponds to the present believer's experience of the outflow of the Spirit and eternal life. The throne is indicated as that of both God and the Lamb; this confirms that Christ is still on the throne in the eternal state, though the throne has a different character than during His mediatorial rule over the earth.

THE TREE OF LIFE (22:2)

22:2 In the midst of the street of it, and on either side of the river, was there the tree of life, which bare twelve manner of fruits, and yielded her fruit every month: and the leaves of the tree were for the healing of the nations.

Verse 2, because of its somewhat obscure presentation, has caused some difficulty to expositors. The verse declares that the tree of life is in the midst of the street and at the same time on either side of the river. The street mentioned is clearly the street of the city, as "it" is feminine (Gr., *autēs*), referring back to the city in 21:23. The visual picture presented

---

[1]Henry Alford, *The Greek New Testament*, IV, 736.

is that the river of life flows down through the middle of the city, and the tree is large enough to span the river, so that the river is in the midst of the street, and the tree is on both sides of the river. It would appear that the pure river of the water of life is not a broad body but a clear stream sufficiently narrow to allow for this arrangement. Swete offers a possible solution to the problem of this description by saying, "The picture presented is that of a river flowing through the broad street which intersects the city, a row of trees being on either side."[2] Swete interprets the word *tree* as a collective reference and finds a parallel situation in Ezekiel 47:12.[3]

The tree of life seems to have reference to a similar tree in the Garden of Eden (Gen. 3:22, 24). Its character is revealed in Genesis 3:22 as being such that if Adam and Eve had eaten of the tree of life, physical death would have been an impossibility. The tree in the new Jerusalem seems to have a similar quality and a similar intent, and though it is difficult to determine where the literal and the symbolic should be distinguished, the tree is represented as bearing fruit every month which apparently can be eaten, though the text does not say so, and also to provide leaves described as "for the healing of the nations." Those who believe that this is a millennial scene rather than the eternal state put much weight upon this statement as they ask the natural question, "Why should healing be necessary in eternity to come?"

The word for "healing" is *therapeian*, from which the English word *therapeutic* is derived, almost directly transliterated from the Greek. Rather than specifically meaning "healing," it should be understood as "health-giving," as the word in its root meaning has the idea of serving or ministering. In other words, the leaves of the tree promote the enjoyment of life in the new Jerusalem, and are not for correcting ills which do not exist. This, of course, is confirmed by the fact that there is no more curse as indicated in verse 3.

Erich Sauer interprets the healing of the nations as referring to full deliverance from the ills of life which characterized their state before eternity began and not to illness still present. He holds, however, that this should not be pressed to the point of universalism, that is, that all will be saved. He cites Duesterdieck:

> "The expression is just as little to be pressed to mean that a *then still* present sickness of the nations is supposed, as we are permitted to draw the inference from Rev. 21:4 that the tears which God will wipe away from the blessed are signs of *then still* present pain. It much rather means that just as the tears which they had shed on account of *earthly* suffering will be wiped away in the eternal life, so the heal-

[2]Henry B. Swete, *The Apocalypse of St. John*, p. 299.
[3]*Ibid.*

ing leaves of the tree of life serve for the healing of the sickness from which the nations *had* suffered during their *earthly* life, but shall never suffer again in the new earth."[4]

The word *nations* is to be translated "Gentiles" as in 21:24 and 21:26, or possibly "peoples," more general. The intimation of this passage is that while it is not necessary for believers in the eternal state to sustain life in any way by physical means, they can enjoy that which the tree provides.

THE THRONE OF GOD (22:3)

22:3 And there shall be no more curse: but the throne of God and of the Lamb shall be in it and his servants shall serve him:

To emphasize the blessedness of the new situation, verse 3 states that there is no more curse. In the millennial scene, there is a lifting of the curse upon the earth, but not a total deliverance from the world's travail brought in by sin, for in the millennium, it is still possible for a "sinner" to be "accursed" (Isa. 65:20) with resulting physical death. In the new heaven and the new earth, there will be no curse at all and no possibility or need of such divine punishment. This broad statement is justified by the fact that the throne of God and of the Lamb shall be in the new Jerusalem, and His servants will give themselves to serve Him unceasingly. To argue as Smith does that the saints will not be servants but sons in eternity is ignoring the natural explanation that they will be both.[5] What greater privilege can saints have in the eternal state than being servants of the Lord? Who would want to be perpetuated in eternal idleness and uselessness? Even if the new Jerusalem were viewed here in its millennial state, those who are in the new Jerusalem are either resurrected or translated saints; and if it is fitting for them to be servants in such a situation in time, it is also fitting that they can be servants in eternity. This is a picture of blessedness in service rather than of arduous toil.

THE BLESSEDNESS OF FELLOWSHIP (22:4-5)

22:4-5 And they shall see his face; and his name shall be in their foreheads. And there shall be no night there; and they need no candle, neither light of the sun; for the Lord God giveth them light: and they shall reign for ever and ever.

The blessedness of the servants' state is further declared in verse 4 in the fact that "they shall see his face." Immediate access to the glory of God will characterize the saints in the eternal state. Further, His name is declared to be in their foreheads indicating that they belong to Him (cf. 7:3; 14:1; also 2:17; 3:12). The fact that they shall see His face

[4]*The Triumph of the Crucified,* p. 199, quoting Friedrich Duesterdieck.
[5]J. B. Smith, *A Revelation of Jesus Christ,* p. 295.

demonstrates beyond question that these are glorified saints (I John 3:2).

Once again in verse 5, John repeats the fact that there will be no night there and no need of a candle, that is, a lamp, nor the light of the sun, for God is the light of the city. Those who are His servants have the blessed privilege of reigning forever. The eternal character of the reign of these who are described as servants is another indication that this is the eternal state. The concept that the reign of Christ must cease at the millennium, based on I Corinthians 15:24–25, is a misunderstanding. It is the character of His reign that changes. Christ continues for all eternity as King of kings and Lord of lords even though the scene of His mediatorial and millennial rule over the earth is changed to the new heaven and the new earth. There is no contradiction, therefore, in calling these saints servants and at the same time recognizing them as those who will reign with Christ.

THE CERTAINTY OF THE BLESSED HOPE (22:6–7)

22:6-7 And he said unto me, These sayings are faithful and true: and the Lord God of the holy prophets sent his angel to shew unto his servants the things which must shortly be done. Behold, I come quickly: blessed is he that keepeth the sayings of the prophecy of this book.

In reinforcement of the wonderful revelation given, the angel now states to John, "These sayings are faithful and true." The comment of A. T. Pierson as cited with variations by Smith, in summary of the wonderful blessing of verses 3–5, brings out clearly the marvelous and comprehensive character of the gracious divine provision of the saints:

And there shall be no more curse—perfect restoration. But the throne of God and of the Lamb shall be in it—perfect administration. His servants shall serve him—perfect subordination. And they shall see his face—perfect transformation. And his name shall be in their foreheads—perfect identification. And there shall be no night there; and they need no candle, neither light of the sun; for the Lord giveth them light—perfect illumination. And they shall reign forever and ever—perfect exultation.[6]

Wilbur M. Smith summarizes the state of blessedness in the holy city in these words:

All the glorious purposes of God, ordained from the foundation of the world, have now been attained. The rebellion of angels and mankind is all and finally subdued, as the King of kings assumes his rightful sovereignty. Absolute and unchangeable holiness characterizes all within the universal Kingdom of God. The redeemed, made so by

[6]*Ibid.*, pp. 295–96.

the blood of the Lamb, are in resurrection and eternal glory. Life is everywhere—and death will never intrude again. The earth and the heavens both are renewed. Light, beauty, holiness, joy, the presence of God, the worship of God, service to Christ, likeness to Christ—all are now abiding realities. The vocabulary of man, made for life here, is incapable of truly and adequately depicting what God has prepared for those that love him.[7]

The angel goes on to remind John, in words similar to Revelation 1:1, that the God of the holy prophets has sent His angel to show His servants through the Apostle John the events which will shortly occur. The descriptive phrase "shortly be done" literally translated is "what it is necessary to do quickly." Here the noun is used. In verse 7, the adverb of the same root is translated "quickly." The thought seems to be that when the action comes, it will be sudden. Also it is to be regarded as impending as if it is meant to be fulfilled at any time. In either case, it constitutes a message of warning that those who believe should be alert. From the standpoint of the agelong divine program, the events of the age were impending even at the time John wrote this message though some of them were thousands of years future.

In verse 7 the wonderful hope of the coming of Christ, especially as it relates to the believer in the present age, is stated: "Behold, I come quickly." Here John seems to be referring to Christ's coming for the church rather than His second coming to the earth, though both are in the larger context. The blessing of God is especially pronounced on the one who keeps the sayings of the prophecies of this book, a special promise repeated from Revelation 1:3, where also the note of imminency is emphasized in the expression "for the time is at hand." This verse contains the sixth of the seven beatitudes found in the book of Revelation. How ironical it is that this final book of the Bible, more neglected and misinterpreted than any other book, should carry these special notes of promised blessing to those who properly regard its promises and divine revelation. Basically, the reason is not that this book contains more or varied revelations but rather that this book above all others honors and exalts the Lord Jesus Christ.

JOHN WORSHIPS BEFORE THE ANGEL (22:8-9)

22:8-9 And I John saw these things, and heard them. And when I had heard and seen, I fell down to worship before the feet of the angel which shewed me these things. Then saith he unto me, See thou do it not: for I am thy fellowservant, and of thy brethren the prophets, and of them which keep the sayings of this book: worship God.

[7]"Revelation," *Wycliffe Bible Commentary*, p. 1524.

The tremendous impression given to John by these transcending revelations finally overwhelms him, and he records, "And I John saw these things, and heard them. And when I had heard and seen, I fell down to worship before the feet of the angel which shewed me these things." John's response is natural, but he is rebuked by the angel who informs him, as he did on previous occasions, that he is John's fellow servant who should be classified with the prophets, John's brethren, and with others who keep the sayings of the book (cf. 19:10). It should be noted here as in 19:10 that the one speaking, though an angel, is declared to be a fellow servant and related to human servants of the Lord. The angel's command is direct and to the point: "Worship God" (aorist imperative); in all acts of worship, worship God only.

COMMAND TO PROCLAIM THE PROPHECY (22:10–11)

22:10-11 And he saith unto me, Seal not the sayings of the prophecy of this book: for the time is at hand. He that is unjust, let him be unjust still: and he which is filthy, let him be filthy still: and he that is righteous, let him be righteous still: and he that is holy, let him be holy still.

Since there is blessing for the one who keeps the sayings of the prophecies given (22:7), John is commanded not to seal the sayings of the prophecies but rather to proclaim them. The justification for this urgent command is that the time is at hand. The word for "seal" (Gr., *sphragisēs*) is in the aorist subjunctive with *mē*, the negative, meaning "do not seal" or "do not begin to seal" the prophecy. As the prophecy of the book of Revelation was unfolded, it was intended to be revealed; now at its end John is especially commanded not to seal the sayings of the prophecy because the time (Gr., *kairos*), or proper season, is at hand (Gr., *eggys*), or near. The time period in which the tremendous consummation of the ages is to take place, according to John's instruction, is near. The indeterminate period assigned to the church is the last dispensation before end-time events and, in John's day as in ours, the end is always impending because of the imminent return of Christ at the rapture with the ordered sequence of events to follow.

In view of this, in verse 11 a seemingly strange command is given which has proved to be an enigma to some, namely, that John states, "He that is unjust, let him be unjust still." In effect, he advocates status quo for both the wicked and the righteous. By this he does not mean that men should remain unmoved by the prophecies of this book, but rather that if the prophecies are rejected, there is no other message that will work. If the warnings of the book are not sufficient, there is no more that God has to say. The wicked must continue in their wicked way and be judged by the Lord when He comes. The same rule, however, applies to the righteous. Their reaction to the prophecy, of course, will be different, but the exhortation in their case is to continue in righteousness and holiness. It is an either/or proposition with no neutrality possible. There is a sense also in which present choices fix character; a time is coming when change will be impossible. Present choices will become permanent in character.

The Blessed Hope and Assurance of Reward (22:12)

22:12 And, behold, I come quickly; and my reward is with me, to give every man according as his work shall be.

The second announcement alerting the reader concerning the coming of the Lord is found in verse 12 (cf. 22:7) again introduced by the word *behold* and the same expression, "I come quickly," with the verb in the present tense connoting futuristic but impending action. Added here, but not in verse 7, is the promise that the Lord is bringing His reward when He comes, that is, that believers will be rewarded at that time. This verse has in view the judgment seat of Christ as it relates to the Christian (II Cor. 5:10–11). The same standard is established for reward here as in II Corinthians 5:11, namely, that of works. It is noteworthy, however, that all final judgments relate to works whether they are in connection with Christians who are being rewarded or unsaved who are being punished. God, the righteous judge, will deal with all men's works in the proper time and order.

The Majesty of the Eternal Christ (22:13–16)

22:13-16 I am Alpha and Omega, the beginning and the end, the first and the last. Blessed are they that do his commandments, that they may have right to the tree of life, and may enter in through the gates into the city. For without are dogs, and sorcerers, and whoremongers, and murderers, and idolaters, and whosoever loveth and maketh a lie. I Jesus have sent mine angel to testify unto you these things in the churches. I am the root and the offspring of David, and the bright and morning star.

Though the means of communication seems to be the angel, it is Christ who is speaking, and here as in 22:7 and 12, the first person pronoun is used. Christ again repeats that He is the Alpha and Omega (the first and last letters of the Greek alphabet) which is interpreted as meaning the beginning and the end, the first and the last. For various combinations of these phrases, see 1:8, 11, 17; 2:8; 21:6. When the One who exists from all eternity states, "Behold, I come quickly," it means that from the divine point of view, end-time events are impending. The three pairs of titles given in verse 13 all connote the same truth, that Christ is the beginning and source of all things as well as the goal and consummation of all, in a word, the eternal God.

Here is the seventh and last beatitude of the book of Revelation. (For previous beatitudes cf. 1:3; 14:13; 16:15; 19:9; 20:6; 22:7.) The final beatitude is obscured by a debate on text, some of the best manuscripts differing from the Authorized Version which has the phrase "that do his commandments" in place of "that wash their robes." Good authorities can be cited for both readings. Walter Scott much prefers the reading for verse 14 "Blessed are they that wash their robes," rather than "Blessed are they that do his commandments." Scott observes, "Every critical scholar of note rejects the reading in our English Bibles. Obedience to commandments is *not* the ground on which eternal life is bestowed. It is God's gift to all who believe (John 5:24)."[8]

In either reading, the reference is to those who qualify for entrance, and the resultant meaning is much the same. In one case, attention is being directed to the keeping of the commandments, which is characteristic of believers, and in the other case to their cleansing by the blood of Christ with its emphasis upon the grace of God. On the basis of both facts, believers have access to the tree of life and the right to enter through the gates of the city. J. B. Smith, because of his assumption that only the church has the right to enter the city, argues against the revised reading on the ground that it would put tribulation saints in the city.[9] This is hardly sufficient, however, to determine the textual reading, and scholars will continue to differ. The right to the tree of life and the right to enter through the gates of the city are one and the same as the right to eternal salvation.

By contrast, unbelievers are characterized as being excluded and are described as "dogs, and sorcerers, and whoremongers, and murderers, and idolaters, and whosoever loveth and maketh a lie." This is the third description of unsaved people in this general passage (cf. 21:8, 27). The main emphasis in each of them is on the deceitfulness and lying of those who are unsaved. The reference to dogs refers not to the animal but to men of low character (cf. Phil. 3:2). As in the former description of the unsaved, the issue is not that they have at some time committed sins of this character but rather that these are the settled characteristics of their lives from which they were never delivered although the grace of God made possible that deliverance.

In verse sixteen the unusual term "I Jesus" is used to indicate that the Lord Jesus Christ had sent His angel to testify the truth of this book to

[8]Walter Scott, *Exposition of the Revelation of Jesus Christ*, p. 446.
[9]J. B. Smith, p. 303.

John and to deliver the book to the churches. Seiss comments on the phrase "I Jesus":

> Thus the very God of all inspiration, and of all inspired men, reiterates and affirms the highest authority for all that is herein written. Either, then, this Book is nothing but a base and blasphemous forgery, unworthy of the slightest respect of men, and specially unworthy of a place in the Sacred Canon; or it is one of the most directly inspired and authoritative writings ever given.[10]

Additional titles ascribed to Christ are "the root and offspring of David" (cf. Isa. 11:1) and "the bright and morning star" (cf. Num. 24:17; Rev. 2:28). Christ, as the morning star, heralds the coming day in His role of the One who comes for the church in the rapture. It is, of course, also true that His coming precedes the millennial kingdom. The reference to the churches of Asia is also significant. Wilbur Smith points out, "This is the first time the word church (*ekklēsia*) has occurred since the letters to the seven churches."[11]

Seiss observes how similar the conclusion of the book is to the beginning:

> Its derivation from God, the signifying of it by the angel, the seeing, hearing, and writing of it by John, the blessing upon those who give due attention to it, the nearness of the time for fulfillment of what is described, the solemn authentication from Christ, the titles by which he describes himself, and even the personal expressions of John, recur in the Epilogue, almost the same as in the Prologue.[12]

THE INVITATION OF THE SPIRIT AND THE BRIDE (22:17)

22:17 And the Spirit and the bride say, Come. And let him that heareth say, Come. And let him that is athirst come. And whosoever will, let him take the water of life freely.

As the book of Revelation comes toward its close, a special invitation is given by the Spirit and the bride. This refers to the Holy Spirit and the church. John is now reverting to the relevance and practical meaning of his prophecy for the age of which he is a part. In the light of the prophetic word, the invitation to all is given: "Come." The threefold invitation is then enforced, addressed first to the one that hears, then to the one who is thirsty, then to anyone who will. For all willing to accept the invitation, there is a proffer of the water of life without cost. A similar invitation is extended in Isaiah 55:1. The invitation to come is an urgent command, for the day will arrive when it is too late to come. Now is the day of grace. The hour of judgment is impending.

---

[10]Joesph A. Seiss, *The Apocalypse*, p. 513.
[11]W. Smith, p. 1525.
[12]Seiss, p. 521.

THE FINAL TESTIMONY OF CHRIST (22:18–20)

22:18-20 For I testify unto every man that heareth the words of the prophecy of this book, If any man shall add unto these things, God shall add unto him the plagues that are written in this book: And if any man shall take away from the words of the book of this prophecy, God shall take away his part out of the book of life, and out of the holy city, and from the things which are written in this book. He which testifieth these things saith, Surely I come quickly. Amen. Even so, come, Lord Jesus.

The urgency of the final command is supported by the solemn testimony of Christ Himself in verse 18 concerning the sacred character of the prophecy which has been given. Warning is extended that if any man add to these things, God will inflict upon him the plagues written in the book, and if any man take away from the prophecy of the book, God will take away his part out of the book of life and from the things written in the book including the holy city. Though frequently in the Bible there are other warnings against tampering with the Word of God, this is among the most solemn (cf. Deut. 4:2; 12:32; Prov. 30:6; Rev. 1:3). No one can dare add to the Word of God except in blatant unbelief and denial that the Word is indeed God's own message to man. Likewise, no one should dare take away from the words of the Book, since to do so is to do despite to the inspired Word of God. What a solemn warning this is to critics who have tampered with this book and other portions of Scripture in arrogant self-confidence that they are equipped intellectually and spiritually to determine what is true and what is not true in the Word of God. Though not stated in detail, the point of these two verses is that a child of God who reveres Him will recognize at once that this is the Word of God.

To use these verses, however, as a proof that a child of God once saved and born into the family of God can lose his salvation is, of course, applying this passage out of context. This passage assumes that a child of God will not tamper with these scriptures. It is the contrast of unbelief with faith, the blinded, fallen intellect of man in contrast to the enlightened Spirit-taught believer. Although the true child of God may not comprehend the meaning of the entire book of Revelation, he will recognize in it a declaration of his hope and that which has been assured to him in grace by his salvation in Christ.

The final testimony of the book is yet another repetition of the promise of Christ's soon return: "Surely I come quickly." In contrast to the other announcement in this chapter (vv. 7, 12) this announcement adds the word *surely* (Gr., *nai*) a particle used to enforce an affirmation. It is followed by the word *amen* (Gr., *amēn*) often translated "verily." The announcement "I come quickly" is therefore buttressed before and after by words used to emphasize the certainty of it. With the word *amen,* however, John begins his own prayer of response to this announcement: "Even so, come, Lord Jesus." Though the book of Revelation concerns itself with a broad expanse of divine dealing with men including the time of tribulation, the millennium, and the eternal state, for John the important event is the coming of the Lord for him at the rapture of the church. For this his heart longs, not only because he is on the bleak Island of Patmos in suffering and exile but because of the glorious prospect which his eyes have beheld and his ears have heard.

Seiss pictures the church as a young lady waiting for her lover to return:

> Fiction has painted the picture of a maiden whose lover left her for a voyage to the Holy Land, promising on his return to make her his beloved bride. Many told her that she would never see him again. But she believed his word, and evening by evening she went down to the lonely shore, and kindled there a beacon-light in sight of the roaring waves, to hail and welcome the returning ship which was to bring again her betrothed. And by that watchfire she took her stand each night, praying to the winds to hasten on the sluggish sails, that he who was everything to her might come. Even so that blessed Lord, who has loved us unto death, has gone away to the mysterious Holy Land of heaven, promising on his return to make us his happy and eternal Bride. Some say that he has gone forever, and that here we shall never see him more. But his last word was, *"Yea, I come quickly."* And on the dark and misty beach sloping out into the eternal sea, each true believer stands by the love-lit fire, looking, and waiting, and praying and hoping for the fulfillment of his work, in nothing gladder than in his pledge and promise, and calling ever from the soul of sacred love, "EVEN SO, COME, LORD JESUS." And some of these nights, while the world is busy with its gay frivolities, and laughing at the maiden on the shore, a form shall rise over the surging waves, as once on Galilee, to vindicate forever all this watching and devotion, and bring to the faithful and constant heart a joy, and glory, and triumph which nevermore shall end.[13]

BENEDICTION (22:21)

22:21 The grace of our Lord Jesus Christ be with you all. Amen.

As John closes this remarkable book of which he is the human author, he uses the phrase so familiar in Paul's epistles, a benediction that the grace of the Lord will be upon his readers. The expression "The grace of our Lord Jesus Christ be with you all" is probably rendered more accurately, according to the best manuscripts, "The grace of the Lord Jesus Christ be with all the saints." Nothing is clearer in the book of

[13]*Ibid.,* pp. 528-29.

Revelation than that God's blessing is on the saints but not on the wicked. Some manuscripts also omit the "Amen."

This final book of the Scriptures which began with the revelation of Jesus Christ ends with a prayer that His grace might be with those who have witnessed the scene through John's pen. Probably no book in the Bible presents in more stark contrast the grace of God as seen in the lives and destinies of the saints as compared to the righteous judgment of God on the wicked. In no other book are the issues made more specific. The book of Revelation is the presentation in the Word of God of what the saints will witness and experience in the glorious consummation of the ages. With John we can pray, "Even so, come, Lord Jesus."

Moody Press, a ministry of the Moody Bible Institute, is designed for education, evangelization, and edification. If we may assist you in knowing more about Christ and the Christian life, please write us without obligation: Moody Press, c/o MLM, Chicago, Illinois 60610.

BIBLIOGRAPHY

AINSLIE, EDGAR. *The Dawn of the Scarlet Age*. Philadelphia: The Sunday School Times Co., 1954. 150 pp.

ALFORD, HENRY. *The Greek New Testament*. Revised by EVERETT F. HARRISON. 2 double vols. Chicago: Moody Press, 1958.

ALLEN, CADY H. *The Message of the Book of Revelation*. Nashville: Cokesbury, 1939. 180 pp.

AMES, A. H. *The Revelation of St. John the Divine*. New York: Eaton & Mains, 1897. 280 pp.

ARNDT, WILLIAM F., and GINGRICH, F. WILBUR. *A Greek-English Lexicon of the New Testament*. Chicago: The University of Chicago Press, 1957. 909 pp.

ATKINSON, BENJAMIN F. *The Revelation of Jesus Christ*. Louisville: Herald Press, 1939. 212 pp.

ATKINSON, TACY W. *A Guide to the Study of Revelation*. Burlington, Iowa: Lutheran Literary Board, 1937. 86 pp. plus chart.

AUGUSTINE. *The City of God. The Fathers of The Church*. Translated by GERALD G. WALSH and GRACE MONAHAN. New York: Fathers of the Church Inc., 1952.

BAINES, T. B. *The Revelation of. Jesus Christ* (5th ed.). London: G. Morrish, 1911. 325 pp.

BALDINGER, ALBERT H. *Sermons on Revelation*. New York: George H. Doran Co., 1924. 267 pp.

BARCLAY, WILLIAM. *Letters to the Seven Churches*. London: S.C.M. Press Limited, 1957. 128 pp.

BARNES, ALBERT. *Notes, Explanatory and Practical, on the Book of Revelation*. New York: Harper & Brothers, Publishers, 1851. 506 pp.

BECKWITH, ISBON T. *The Apocalypse of John*. New York: The Macmillan Co., 1919. 794 pp.

BENNETT, EDWARD. *The Visions of John in Patmos*. London: A. S. Rouse, 1892. 320 pp.

BLANCHARD, C. A. *Light on the Last Days*. Chicago: The Bible Institute Colportage Ass'n., 1913. 149 pp.

BLEEK, FRIEDRICH. *Lectures on the Apocalypse*. Edited by LIC. TH. HOSSBACH and SAMUEL DAVIDSON and translated from the German. London: Williams & Norgate, 1875. 356 pp.

BLOOMFIELD, ARTHUR E. *All Things New*. Minneapolis: Bethany Fellowship, 1959. 272 pp.

BLUNT, HENRY. *A Practical Exposition of the Epistles to the Seven Churches of Asia*. Philadelphia: Hooker and Claxton, 1839. 249 pp.

BOETTNER, LORAINE. *The Millennium*. Philadelphia: The Presbyterian and Reformed Publishing Co., 1958. 380 pp.

BROWN, DAVID. *The Apocalypse: Its Structure and Primary Prediction*. New York: The Christian Literature Co., 1891. 224 pp.

BRUCE, WILLIAM. *Commentary on the Revelation of St. John*. London: James Speirs, 1877. 458 pp.

BUIS, HARRY. *The Book of Revelation*. Philadelphia: Presbyterian and Reformed Publishing Co., 1960. 124 pp.

BULLINGER, E. W. *The Apocalypse*. London: Eyre & Spottiswoode, 1902. 727 pp.

CHAFER, L. S. *Systematic Theology*. 8 vols. Dallas: Dallas Seminary Press, 1947.

CHARLES, R. H. *The Apocrypha and Pseudepigrapha of the Old Testament*. 2 vols. New York: Oxford University Press, 1913.

———. *A Critical and Exegetical Commentary on The Revelation of St. John*. 2 vols. New York: Charles Scribner's Sons, 1920.

CLEMENT. "Who Is the Rich Man?" Vol. II: *Ante-Nicene Fathers*. New York: The Christian Literature Co., 1893. pp. 591-604.

COATES, C. A. *An Outline of the Revelation*. London: Stow Hill Bible & Tract Depot, n.d. 250 pp.

COOK, AUGUSTA. *Light from Patmos*. London: Protestant British-Israel League, 1934. 272 pp.

COX, CLYDE C. *Apocalyptic Commentary*. Cleveland, Tenn.: Pathway Press, 1959. 352 pp.

CRISWELL, W. A. *Expository Sermons on Revelation*. Grand Rapids: Zondervan Publishing House, 1962. 184 pp.

CULLMANN, OSCAR. *Christ and Time*. Philadelphia: Westminster Press, 1950. 253 pp.

CULVER, ROBERT. *Daniel and the Latter Days*. Westwood, N. J.: Fleming H. Revell Co., 1954. 221 pp.

CUMMING, JOHN. *Lectures on the Book of Revelation, First Series*. Philadelphia: Lindsay & Blakiston, 1854. 512 pp.

DARBY, J. N. *Notes on the Apocalypse*. London: G. Morrish, 1842. 165 pp.

———. *Seven Lectures on the Prophetical Addresses to the Seven Churches*, 3rd ed., revised and corrected. London: G. Morrish, 1852. 194 pp.

DAVIS, G. W. *The Patmos Vision*. Los Angeles: McBride Printing Co., 1915. 318 pp.

DIONYSIUS. "Works of Dionysius," Vol. VI: *Ante-Nicene Fathers*. New York: The Christian Literature Co., 1893.

DOUGLAS, J. D. *The New Bible Dictionary*. Grand Rapids: Wm. B. Eerdmans Publishing Co., 1962. 1375 pp. plus plates and maps.

EASTON, WILLIAM. *Gleanings in the Book of Revelation*. London: W. H. G. Blatchley, n.d. 177 pp.

ELLIOTT, E. B. *Horae Apocalypticae*. 4 vols. London: Seeley, Burnside, and Seeley, 1846.

ENCELL, J. G. *The Exiled Prophet*. St. Louis: Christian Publishing Co., 1898. 245 pp.

EUSEBIUS. "Ecclesiastical History," Vol. IX: *The Fathers of the Church*. New York: Fathers of the Church Inc., 1953.

GAEBELEIN, ARNO C. *The Revelation*. New York: *Our Hope* Publication Office, 1915. 208 pp.

GEHMAN, W. T. "A Critique of the Historical Interpretation of Revelation." *Unpublished Master's thesis*, Dallas Theological Seminary, 1947. 62 pp.

GLOAG, PATON J. *Introduction to the Johannine Writings*. London: James Nisbet and Co., 1891. 440 pp.

GOVETT, ROBERT. *The Apocalypse Expounded by Scripture*. London: Chas. J. Thynne, 1920. 629 pp.

GRANT, F. W. *The Revelation of Jesus Christ*. New York: Loizeaux Brothers, n.d. 245 pp.

HADJIANTONIOU, G. A. *The Postman of Patmos*. Grand Rapids: Zondervan Publishing House, 1961. 149 pp.

HALDEMAN, I. M. *A Synopsis of the Book of Revelation*. Published in a pamphlet series by the author, n.d. 24 pp.

HARDIE, ALEXANDER. *A Study of the Book of Revelation*. Los Angeles: Times-Mirror Press, 1926. 369 pp.

HARRISON, NORMAN B. *The End*. Minneapolis: The Harrison Service, 1941. 239 pp.

HENDRIKSEN, WILLIAM. *And So All Israel Shall Be Saved*. Grand Rapids: Baker Book House, 1945.

———. *More Than Conquerors*. Grand Rapids: Baker Book House, 1939. 281 pp.

HENGSTENBERG, E. W. *The Revelation of St. John: Expounded for Those Who Search the Scripture*. Translated by PATRICK FAIRBAIRN. New York: Robert Carter & Bros., 1852, Volume I; Volume II, Edinburgh: T. & T. Clark, 1852.

HIPPOLYTUS. "Treatise on Christ and Antichrist," Vol. V: *Ante-Nicene Fathers*. New York: The Christian Literature Co., 1896. pp. 251-53.

HISLOP, ALEXANDER. *The Two Babylons*. 3rd ed. New York: Loizeaux Brothers, 1943. 330 pp.

HODGE, CHARLES. *Commentary on the Epistle to the Romans*. Philadelphia: James Claxton, 1864. 716 pp.

HORNE, EDWARD H. *The Meaning of the Apocalypse*. London: S. W. Partridge & Co., 1916. 301 pp.

HOSTE, WILLIAM. *The Vision of John the Divine*. Kilmarnock, Scotland: John Ritchie Limited, n.d. 192 pp.

IRENAEUS. "Against Heresies," Vol. I: *Ante-Nicene Fathers*. Edited by ALEXANDER ROBERTS and JAMES DONALDSON. New York: Charles Scribner's Sons, 1899. pp. 309-567.

IRONSIDE, H. A. *Lectures on the Book of Revelation*. New York: Loizeaux Brothers, 1930. 366 pp.

JAMIESON, ROBERT, FAUSSETT, A. R., and BROWN, DAVID. *A Commentary Critical, Experimental, and Practical on the Old and New Testaments*. Grand Rapids: Wm. B. Eerdmans Publishing Co., 1945. Six vols.

JENNINGS, F. C. *Studies in Revelation*. New York: Loizeaux Brothers, 1937. 632 pp.

KELLY, WILLIAM. *Lectures on the Book of Revelation*. London: W. H. Broom, 1874. 502 pp.

———. *The Revelation*. London: Thomas Weston, 1904. 264 pp.

KIK, J. MARCELLUS. *Revelation Twenty*. Philadelphia: Presbyterian and Reformed Publishing Co., 1955. 92 pp.

KUYPER, ABRAHAM. *The Revelation of St. John*. Translated from the Dutch by JOHN HENDRIK DE VRIES. Grand Rapids: Wm. B. Eerdmans Publishing Co., 1935. 359 pp.

LADD, GEORGE E. *Jesus and the Kingdom*. New York: Harper and Row, Publishers, 1964. 367 pp.

LANGE, JOHN PETER. *Commentary on the Holy Scriptures*. (Revelation, Vol. XXIV.) Unabridged. Translated from the German and edited by PHILIP SCHAFF. E. R. CRAVEN, American editor. Grand Rapids: Zondervan Publishing House, 1956. 446 pp.

LARKIN, CLARENCE. *Book of Revelation*. Philadelphia: Published by the author, 1919. 210 pp.

LAYMON, CHARLES M. *The Book of Revelation*. Nashville: Abingdon Press, 1960. 176 pp.

LENSKI, R. C. H. *The Interpretation of St. John's Revelation*. Columbus, O.: Lutheran Book Concern, 1935. 686 pp.

LILJE, HANNS. *The Last Book of the Bible*. Translated by OLIVE WYON. Philadelphia: Muhlenberg Press, 1957. 286 pp.

LOENERTZ, R. J. *The Apocalypse of Saint John*. Translated by HILLARY J. CARPENTER. London: Sheed & Ward, 1947. 151 pp.

LORD, DAVID N. *An Exposition of the Apocalypse.* New York: Harper & Brothers, Publishers, 1847. 542 pp.

McCARRELL, WILLIAM. *Christ's Seven Letters to His Church.* Findlay, O.: Dunham Publishing Co., 1936. 79 pp.

McDOWELL, EDWARD A. *The Meaning and Message of the Book of Revelation.* Nashville: Broadman Press, 1951. 224 pp.

McGEE, J. VERNON. *Reveling Through Revelation.* 2 vols. Los Angeles: Church of the Open Door, n.d.

McILVAINE, J. H. *The Wisdom of the Apocalypse.* New York: Anson D. F. Randolph & Co., 1886. 420 pp.

MARTIN, J. L. *The Voice of the Seven Thunders.* Bedford, Ind.: James W. Mathes, Publisher, 1870. 330 pp.

MARTYR, JUSTIN. "Dialogue with Trypho," Vol. I: *Ante-Nicene Fathers.* New York: Charles Scribner's Sons, 1899.

MILLIGAN, WILLIAM. *The Book of Revelation.* New York: George H. Doran Co., 1889. 392 pp.

———. *Discussions on the Apocalypse.* London: Macmillan and Co., 1893. 290 pp.

———. *Lectures on the Apocalypse.* London: Macmillan and Co., 1892. 239 pp.

MORGAN, G. CAMPBELL. *The Letters of Our Lord.* Westwood, N. J.: Fleming H. Revell Co., n.d. 109 pp.

MOULTON, JAMES H., and MILLIGAN, GEORGE. *The Vocabulary of the Greek Testament.* London: Hodder and Stoughton, Limited, 1930. 705 pp.

NEWELL, WILLIAM R. *The Book of the Revelation.* Chicago: Moody Press, 1935. 405 pp.

NEWTON, B. W. *Babylon and Egypt: Their Future History and Doom.* 3rd ed. London: Houlston and Sons, 1890. 642 pp.

NICOLL, W. ROBERTSON. (ed.). Vol. V: *The Expositor's Greek Testament.* Grand Rapids: Wm. B. Eerdmans Publishing Co., n.d. 494 pp.

NILES, D. T. *As Seeing the Invisible.* New York: Harper & Brothers, 1961. 192 pp.

OTTMAN, FORD C. *The Unfolding of the Ages.* New York: The Baker and Taylor Co., 1905. 511 pp.

PEAKE, ARTHUR S. *The Revelation of John.* London: Primitive Methodist Publishing House, 1919. 390 pp.

PENTECOST, J. DWIGHT. *Things to Come.* Findlay, O.: Dunham Publishing Co., 1958. 633 pp.

PETTINGILL, WILLIAM L. *The Unveiling of Jesus Christ.* Findlay, O.: Fundamental Truth Publishers, 1939. 132 pp.

POELLOT, LUTHER. *Revelation.* St. Louis: Concordia Publishing House, 1962. 314 pp.

RAMSAY, W. M. *The Letters to the Seven Churches of Asia.* London: Hodder and Stoughton, 1904. 446 pp.

ROADHOUSE, W. F. *Seeing the "Revelation."* Toronto: The Overcomer Publishers, 1932. 232 pp.

ROBERTSON, ARCHIBALD T. *Word Pictures in the New Testament.* Vol. VI. New York: Harper & Brothers, Publishers, 1933. 488 pp.

ROWLEY, H. H. *The Relevance of the Apocalyptic.* New York: Harper & Brothers, Publishers, 1946. 205 pp.

SAUER, ERICH. *The Triumph of the Crucified.* London: The Paternoster Press, 1951. 207 pp.

SCOTT, C. ANDERSON. *The Book of the Revelation.* London: Hodder and Stoughton, 1905. 337 pp.

SCOTT, WALTER. *Exposition of the Revelation of Jesus Christ.* London: Pickering and Inglis Ltd., n.d. 456 pp.

SCROGGIE, W. G. *The Book of the Revelation.* Edinburgh: The Book Stall, 1920. 214 pp.

SEISS, JOSEPH A. *The Apocalypse.* Grand Rapids: Zondervan Publishing House, 1957. 536 pp.

———. *Letters to the Seven Churches.* Grand Rapids: Baker Book House, 1956. 341 pp.

SIMCOX, WILLIAM H. *The Revelation of St. John the Divine.* Cambridge: Cambridge University Press, 1893. 248 pp.

SMITH, J. B. *A Revelation of Jesus Christ.* Scottdale, Pa.: Herald Press, 1961. 369 pp. with chart.

SMITH, WILBUR. "Revelation," *The Wycliffe Bible Commentary.* Edited by CHARLES F. PFEIFFER and EVERETT F. HARRISON. Chicago: Moody Press, 1962. 1525 pp.

SMITH, WILLIAM. (ed.). *Dictionary of Greek and Roman Geography.* 2 vols. Boston: Little, Brown, and Co., 1870.

SNELL, H. H. *Notes on the Revelation.* London: W. H. Broom, 1878. 264 pp.

SNOWDEN, JAMES H. *The Coming of the Lord.* New York: The Macmillan Co., 1919.

SPURGEON, W. A. *The Conquering Christ.* Muncie, Ind.: Published by the author, 1936. 303 pp.

STAUFFER, ETHELBERT. *Christ and the Caesars.* Translated from the German. London: S.C.M. Press Limited, 1955. 293 pp.

STEVENS, W. C. *Revelation, The Crown-Jewel of Biblical Prophecy.* 2 vols. Harrisburg, Pa.: Christian Alliance Publishing Co., 1928.

STONEHOUSE, N. B. *Paul Before the Areopagus.* Grand Rapids: Wm. B. Eerdmans Publishing Co., 1957. 197 pp.

STUART, MOSES. *A Commentary on the Apocalypse.* Edinburgh: Maclachlan, Stewart and Co., 1847. 839 pp.

SUMMERS, RAY. *Worthy Is the Lamb.* Nashville: Broadman Press, 1951. 224 pp.

SWETE, HENRY B. *The Apocalypse of St. John.* Grand Rapids: Wm. B. Eerdmans Publishing Co., n.d. 339 pp.

TAIT, ANDREW. *The Messages to the Seven Churches of Asia Minor.* London: Hodder and Stoughton, 1884. 482 pp.

TATFORD, F. A. *Prophecy's Last Word.* London: Pickering & Inglis Limited, 1947. 270 pp.

TENNEY, MERRILL C. *The Book of Revelation.* Grand Rapids: Baker Book House, 1963. 116 pp.

———. *Interpreting Revelation.* Grand Rapids: Wm. B. Eerdmans Publishing Co., 1957. 220 pp.

THIESSEN, HENRY C. *Introduction to the New Testament.* Grand Rapids: Wm. B. Eerdmans Publishing Co., 1943. 347 pp.

THOMAS, ROBERT L. "The Argument of the Book of Revelation." Unpublished Master's thesis, Dallas Theological Seminary, 1959. 331 pp.

TORRANCE, THOMAS F. *The Apocalypse Today.* Grand Rapids: Wm. B. Eerdmans Publishing Co., 1959. 155 pp.

TRENCH, RICHARD CHENEVIX. *Commentary on the Epistles to the Seven Churches in Asia.* New York: Charles Scribner & Co., 1872. 312 pp.

TUCKER, W. LEON. *Studies in Revelation.* Binghamton, N. Y.: John Young Publisher, 1935. 390 pp.

UNGER, MERRILL F. *Unger's Bible Dictionary.* Chicago: Moody Press, 1957. 1192 pp.

VAN RYN, AUGUST. *Notes on the Book of Revelation.* Kansas City, Kan.: Walterick Publishers, c. 1960. 228 pp.

VAUGHAN, C. J. *Lectures on the Revelation of John.* London: Macmillan and Co., 1870.

VEGETIUS, FLAVIUS RENATUS. *The Military Institutions of the Romans.* Translated from the Latin by LIEUTENANT JOHN CLARK, and edited by BRIG. GEN. THOMAS R. PHILLIPS. Harrisburg, Pa.: The Stackpole Co., 1944. 114 pp.

WARFIELD, B. B. *Biblical Doctrines.* New York: Oxford University Press, 1929. 665 pp.

WHITTEMORE, THOMAS. *A Commentary on the Revelation of St. John.* Boston: Universalist Publishing House, 1848. 388 pp.

WUEST, KENNETH. *Prophetic Light in Present Darkness.* Grand Rapids: Wm. B. Eerdmans Publishing Co., 1935. 135 pp.

INDEX